Beyond Ending Poverty

DIRECTIONS IN DEVELOPMENT
Poverty

Beyond Ending Poverty

The Dynamics of Microfinance in Bangladesh

Shahidur R. Khandker, M. A. Baqui Khalily, and Hussain A. Samad

WORLD BANK GROUP

ISBN (paper): 978-1-4648-0894-4
ISBN (electronic): 978-1-4648-0895-1
DOI: 10.1596/978-1-4648-0894-4

Cover photo: © Jabeer Sherazy/Institute of Microfinance. Used with the permission of Jabeer Sherazy/Institute of Microfinance. Further permission required for reuse.
Cover design: Debra Naylor, Naylor Design, Inc.

Library of Congress Cataloging-in-Publication Data
Names: Khandker, Shahidur R., author. | Khalily, M. A. Baqui, author. |
    Samad, Hussain A., 1963- author.
Title: Beyond ending poverty: the dynamics of microfinance in
    Bangladesh / Shahidur R. Khandker, M. A. Baqui Khalily, Hussain A. Samad.
Description: Washington, D.C.: World Bank, 2016. | Series: Directions in
    development | "March 2016." | Includes bibliographical references.
Identifiers: LCCN 2016015272 (print) | LCCN 2016016935 (ebook) | ISBN
    9781464808944 (pdf) | ISBN 9781464808951 | ISBN 9781464808951
Subjects: LCSH: Microfinance—Bangladesh. | Debt—Bangladesh. | Consumption
    (Economics)—Bangladesh. | Poor—Bangladesh—Social conditions.
Classification: LCC HG178.33.B3 K43 2016 (print) | LCC HG178.33.B3 (ebook) |
    DDC 332.7/42—dc23
LC record available at https://lccn.loc.gov/2016015272

Contents

Tables

Preface

Since 1983, when Grameen Bank was established in Bangladesh as a model of microfinance banking, microfinance has grown at an exponential rate worldwide; today, more than 200 million people are direct or indirect beneficiaries. Microfinance resolves the market failure of formal financial institutions by reaching out to the poor, women, and other disadvantaged groups of society not covered by the commercial banks. By easing liquidity constraints, microfinance helps to generate employment, income, and assets, as well as improve children's schooling.

Since the advent of microfinance, the premise of its improving access by the poor to financial services for consumption smoothing has never been a subject of controversy. What has been controversial is whether microfinance can alleviate poverty, in part, because of the high interest rates charged by microfinance institutions (MFIs), which offer borrowers little scope for accumulating assets. Controversy also abounds over the methods and alternative statistical assumptions used to measure benefits. That the poor lack an effective and affordable alternative financing mechanism to support income and employment generation does not necessarily mean that microfinance is a panacea—it involves the entrepreneurial skills of borrowers, which many of the poor may lack.

It is little wonder that studies evaluating the benefits of microfinance have produced conflicting results. Some studies have found substantial positive effects, while others have found none or even negative ones. The most substantive evaluation of microfinance, carried out by Shahid Khandker and others at the World Bank over the past decade, unequivocally demonstrated the positive role of microfinance. Of course, study findings are contextual: They are positive in conducive environments and less so in unfavorable ones. Microfinance must be distinguished from antipoverty schemes (e.g., conditional cash transfers) because benefits from microfinance-supported activities, which involve participants' entrepreneurial skills and ability, take time to be realized. The World Bank's 1991/92 cross-sectional study interviewed households in villages where the program had been in place for at least three years prior to the survey, and the inherent ability bias was resolved by sorting out self-selection in program participation in an innovative way.

Notwithstanding the limitations of study approaches and controversies over measuring benefits, the recent past has witnessed phenomenal growth in MFIs around the world. Bangladesh alone has more than 750 registered MFIs today, compared to only a few in the early 1990s. With rising competition among the

MFIs with limited diversification of product design and marketing, it is possible that continued borrowing could create conditions for overindebtedness, resulting in the poor's being trapped in poverty. Like other well-intentioned missions, the MFIs may have drifted off course.

This book addresses two major issues concerning microfinance growth and its development impact. First, it evaluates the dynamics of microfinance coverage. Second, it estimates microfinance's causal impact on arresting poverty and promoting other forms of household welfare. To facilitate the book's undertaking, the World Bank and the Institute of Microfinance in Bangladesh together provided financial support to revisit in 2010/11 the same households and communities that were first visited in 1991/92 and again in 1998/99. The resulting long panel survey of 1991/92–2010/11 provided a unique opportunity to examine the dynamics of policy quagmires now facing MFIs around the world.

The book confirms the positive effects of continued borrowing from a microfinance program. Despite a manifold increase in microfinance borrowing, loan recovery has not declined and long-term borrowers are not trapped in poverty or debt. The book also confirms that interest rates are not too high for realizing returns on investment, although the MFIs have scope for lowering them. In addition, the book highlights some of the challenges faced by the microfinance industry and its beneficiaries for sustaining benefits and coverage of services.

Given the worldwide attention that microfinance has received in recent years, it is not surprising that it has also attracted serious criticism, including the argument that it is a fad with less-than-expected benefits for the poor. Surely, microfinance is not without any pitfalls. The book addresses some of the criticisms—including whether pushing microfinance has made it redundant as a tool for poverty reduction—while investigating whether it still matters for the poor after two decades of extensive growth.

The book's findings confirm that improved access to financial services from institutions, even if nongovernmental, has provided many poor people with an opportunity to borrow at interest rates much lower than those charged by local moneylenders, the only other source of borrowing for many. The inclusive microfinance movement would not have been possible without experiments in inclusive financial instruments. Bangladesh has cleared pathways to such inclusive finance, led in part by Grameen Bank, along with the concessionary financing support provided by the Government of Bangladesh and the World Bank to a host of nongovernmental organizations (NGOs) through the establishment of a wholesale microfinance agency, known as PKSF (*Palli Karma-Sahayak Foundation*).

Bangladesh's pioneering experience with microfinance over the past two decades will be illuminating to policy makers and practitioners in Bangladesh and other countries facing similar issues. The lessons learned cover benefits and costs, pitfalls and strengths of group-based microlending, and the policy conundrum that has recently emerged. The book is expected to contribute to the ongoing debate on the cost-effectiveness of microfinance as a tool for inclusive growth and development. It is also expected to fill knowledge gaps in understanding the various virtues of microfinance against its portrayal as having drifted from its original poverty-reduction mission.

Acknowledgments

The book's undertaking would not have been possible without the ongoing collaboration and generous support provided by the World Bank's Research Committee, Bangladesh's Institute of Microfinance (InM), and the International Food Policy Research Institute (IFPRI). The book's initial research was funded by the World Bank, while the World Bank's Research Committee provided additional funding to complete the research and initial drafting of the book chapters. The InM provided financial support for both data collection and processing, as well as processing of the book. IFPRI provided an excellent research environment for the book's lead author, Shahidur R. Khandker, who is currently a visiting senior research fellow at IFPRI since his retirement from the World Bank in September 2014.

We are indebted to Indermit Gill and Shiva Makki of the World Bank's Research Committee, without whose active support the original manuscript would not have come to fruition. We are grateful to Will Martin, Francisco Ferriera, and Asli Demirgüç-Kunt of the World Bank for their kind support in undertaking research that later helped to produce this book. We are indebted to Martin Rama, Zahid Hussain, Mustafa Mujeri, Siddiq Osmani, and Salman Zaidi for their helpful comments on an earlier draft of the manuscript. We are deeply indebted to Wahiduddin Mahmud and Qazi Kholiquzzaman of the Institute of Microfinance for their encouragement to undertake and complete the research study. We express our deep gratitude to Maximo Torero and Shahid Rashid at IFPRI for providing an excellent research facility in which to complete the book's undertaking.

In addition to financial support, the InM kindly provided support for conducting data cleaning and analysis in preparation for drafting the book's manuscript. We are deeply grateful for the excellent research assistance offered by many research staff members from the InM, especially Syed Badruddoza, Bashir Ahmed, Kazi Zahidul Huq, Shahadat Hussain, Syed Rafiquzzaman, and Ferdous Ara Khandker. Administrative staff of the World Bank, InM, and IFPRI jointly provided excellent logistic support to carry out the survey, data analysis, and book preparation. We extend our special thanks to Estella Malayika of the World Bank, Ifrat Jahan of InM, and Juvy Villaroman and Evelyn Go of IFPRI for administrative support provided during the book's production. We are also indebted to

Norma Adams, consultant editor for the World Bank, for kindly providing excellent editorial support to produce the book's chapter contents and final manuscript for publication, and Steve Pazdan and Jewel McFadden in the Publishing and Knowledge Division, for skillfully shepherding the manuscript through production.

We extend special thanks to our colleagues, without whose support the book's contents would not have been realized. The book draws extensively on the findings of jointly published or unpublished works by many distinguished researchers who have worked on microfinance-related research issues. We are deeply indebted to Rashid Faruqee, Gayatri Koolwal, Jonathan Haughton, Siddiq Osmani, and Syed Badruddoza for their kind contributions in the area of microfinance and development through our collaborative research work.

Finally, we, the coauthors of this book, not our research collaborators, are responsible for any errors or omissions remaining in our analysis and the findings presented herein. We are also accountable for the book's policy discussions. The views expressed in the book are thus entirely our own and should in no way be attributed to those of the World Bank, InM, or IFPRI, which supported the book's research and publication.

About the Authors

Shahidur R. Khandker (PhD, McMaster University, Canada, 1983) is currently a visiting senior research fellow at the International Food Policy Research Institute (IFPRI) and a former lead economist in the Development Research Group of the World Bank. He has authored more than 50 articles in peer-reviewed journals, including the *Journal of Political Economy*, *Review of Economic Studies*, *World Bank Economic Review*, and *Journal of Development Economics*. He has also written various books, including the *Handbook on Impact Evaluation: Quantitative Methods and Practices*, coauthored with Gayatri Koolwal and Hussain Samad and published by the World Bank; *Seasonal Hunger and Public Policies: Evidence from Northwest Bangladesh*, coauthored with Wahiduddin Mahmud and published by the World Bank; *Fighting Poverty with Microcredit: Experience in Bangladesh*, published by Oxford University Press; and *Handbook on Poverty and Inequality*, coauthored with Jonathan Haughton and published by the World Bank. He has written several book chapters and more than three dozen discussion papers at the World Bank on poverty, rural finance and microfinance, agriculture, and infrastructure. His work spans some 30 countries and covers a wide range of development issues, from microfinance and rural finance, agriculture, and infrastructure to poverty, seasonality, and energy.

M. A. Baqui Khalily (PhD, Ohio State University, 1991) is the founding executive director of the Institute of Microfinance (InM), a center of excellence in research on global microfinance and development. He served in this capacity for six years before retiring in early 2016. He is also a retired professor from the Department of Finance, University of Dhaka. His extensive research, encompassing more than 20 countries, focuses on rural finance, microfinance, enterprise development, climate change, and capital markets. He has authored and coauthored a variety of papers published in national and international journals, and has coauthored several books on microfinance and insurance. His recent areas of interest include climate change; inclusive finance for inclusive growth; poverty analysis; impact assessment; and the governance, financial structure, and performance of microfinance institutions (MFIs).

Hussain A. Samad (MS, Northeastern University, 1992) is a consultant at the World Bank with more than 19 years of experience in impact evaluation, monitoring and evaluation, data analysis, research, and training on development issues. He has been involved in many World Bank research studies covering such areas as rural electrification, energy poverty, microfinance, poverty, seasonality, migration, and household air pollution. Throughout his long career, he has co-authored books, articles in peer-reviewed journals, and reports; provided technical support to regions, field offices, and consulting firms; presented in seminars; designed course materials for training; and conducted hands-on training in workshop settings.

Abbreviations

AR	autoregressive
ASA	Association for Social Advancement
BBS	Bangladesh Bureau of Statistics
BIDS	Bangladesh Institute of Development Studies
BKB	Bangladesh Krishi Bank
BRAC	Bangladesh Rural Advancement Committee
BRDB	Bangladesh Rural Development Board
CDF	Credit and Development Forum
CGAP	Consultative Group to Assist the Poor
DDD	difference-in-difference-in-difference
FE	fixed-effects (method)
FE-IV	fixed-effects–instrumental variables
GDP	gross domestic product
GMM	generalized method of moments
HIES	Household Income and Expenditure Survey
IDA	International Development Association
IFPRI	International Food Policy Research Institute
InM	Institute of Microfinance
IV	instrumental variables (method)
kcal	kilocalorie
LDV	lagged dependent variable
LSMS	Living Standards Measurement Study
MFI	microfinance institution
MIX	Microfinance Information eXchange
MRA	Microcredit Regulatory Authority
NCB	nationalized commercial bank
NGO	nongovernmental organization
OLM	ordered logit model
OLR	ordered logit regression

OLS	ordinary least squares
PKSF	Palli Karma-Sahayak Foundation (Rural Employment Support Foundation)
PO	partner organization
PRIME	Programme Initiative for Monga Eradication
PSID	Panel Study of Income Dynamics
PSM	propensity-score matching
PSU	primary sampling unit
RAKUB	Rajshahi Krishi Unnayan Bank
RCT	randomized control trial
RNF	rural nonfarm
ROA	return on assets
SMEs	small and medium-size enterprises
VBSP	Vietnam Bank for Social Policy
WHO	World Health Organization

CHAPTER 1

Introduction

Overview

Microfinance has been viewed as an antipoverty, inclusive financial program because it targets and reaches the poor, especially women, as well as small producers and entrepreneurs, who often have limited access to formal financial institutions. Despite microfinance's overwhelming success in reaching the poor and other disadvantaged groups through its innovative program design, its induced benefits—measured in terms of income, consumption, and other dimensions of household welfare—are still debated. Some studies have found substantial positive effects, while others have found none or even negative ones. The most substantive evaluation of microfinance to date, carried out two decades ago by researchers at the World Bank, examined three well-known credit programs in Bangladesh using 1991/92 cross-sectional survey data (Khandker 1998; Pitt and Khandker 1998). That research found that microfinance helped to promote household welfare, including reduction of poverty, and that the impacts of credit were higher for women than for men.

Since then, these findings have been debated by those arguing that the statistical assumptions used in earlier studies to identify program benefits were too restrictive.[1] Various studies using methods with less restrictive assumptions, such as randomized control trials (RCTs), have found limited or no benefits from microfinance. RCT assessments are often based on short-term program effects (e.g., 18 months of intervention). However, since microfinance is not a cash transfer and its benefits from self-employed activities occur over time, measuring its effects requires a certain minimum length of program membership.[2] The 1991/92 cross-sectional survey data used in the earlier studies of World Bank researchers interviewed households in villages where the program had been in place for at least three years prior to the survey (Pitt and Khandker 1998). A follow-up study, using panel data over a seven-year period (1991/92–1998/99), confirmed the earlier 1991/92 results on the positive, although somewhat muted, benefits of microfinance (Khandker 2005).

Can Microfinance Uplift the Poor?

Bangladesh has witnessed phenomenal growth in microfinance over the past two decades. By 2013, some 32 million members of microfinance institutions (MFIs) had received a total of more than US$7.2 billion in annual disbursements, with an outstanding balance of $4.5 billion (CDF 2013), equivalent to 3 percent of the country's gross domestic product (GDP). Today, Bangladesh has more than 750 registered MFIs with a network of over 17,000 branches, compared to only a handful in 1991/92. With rising competition among the MFIs in a market with limited diversification of product design and marketing, continued borrowing by poor households could create the conditions for market saturation, resulting in village diseconomies. In addition, microfinance growth could create microdebt dependencies, whereby participants with the possibility of borrowing from multiple sources could become overindebted or trapped in poverty. It is therefore alleged that too much credit or too many MFIs are not good for borrowers or the economy. It is further alleged that the MFIs, like other well-intentioned missions that drifted off course, are charging interest rates that are too high, which are not conducive to lifting the poor out of poverty. Other critics contend that microfinance alone is not enough to uplift the poor; training, marketing, and other inputs not often provided by microfinance agencies are also required. Following this line of argument, pushing microfinance further would only make it redundant as an instrument for poverty reduction and economic development. Is this a reality in Bangladesh after 20 years of its microfinance?

Inclusive Microfinance

Microfinance has been viewed as an inclusive finance program because of its role in extending financial services to the poor and other disadvantaged groups not covered by traditional financial services. Beyond creating self-employment for the unemployed, especially among rural women, microfinance helps the rural population in various other ways that are emerging over time. Even if microfinance cannot assault poverty directly (if indeed this is the case), this does not diminish its vital role in a socioeconomic setting such as Bangladesh where, for various reasons, many economic agents lack access to institutional finance needed for working capital and other purposes of finance. Microfinance can play an important role even amid severe competition among the MFIs for the same clientele, where the rural poor may have easy financial access to more than one MFI. One emerging role of microfinance is cash transfer. Because of their outreach, Bangladesh's MFIs are increasingly engaged in remittance or cash transfer in rural areas. For example, the Bangladesh Rural Advancement Committee (BRAC), the country's largest nongovernmental organization (NGO), has a famous cash transfer program called bKash (*b* refers to BRAC and *Kash* stands for cash), whereby cash can easily be transferred to remote areas within minutes. Precisely because of such emerging roles, it is time to revisit the issues of increased indebtedness among microfinance borrowers and the relevance of borrowing from multiple MFI sources in poverty reduction and social emancipation.

In today's Bangladesh, microfinance plays a much more important role than it did in the 1990s, when its main purpose was limited to savings mobilization and credit disbursement. Nowadays, microfinance's role as an instrument for initiating productive employment is appreciated as much as its traditional roles of supporting the working capital needs of entrepreneurs without easy access to institutional finance, facilitating savings mobilization among the poor, and smoothing consumption in rural settings characterized by covariate risk in production and income generation. As its roles have become more diversified over time, microfinance has become more appealing to policy makers as an instrument for promoting universal access to finance rather than simply microcredit for employment generation and poverty reduction.

The sheer number of MFI members—more than 30 million people, even after accounting for multiple program memberships—represents an outstanding success for improving Bangladesh's access to institutional financial services. For the relatively poorer population, MFIs are more inclusive. In today's Bangladesh, this means that 65 percent of the total rural population of 110 million can be linked with institutional financial services, such as opening an account with a financial network.

Providing increased and diversified levels of financial services in a competitive environment may also mean higher transaction costs for the MFIs; for example, they may experience a high loan default rate despite close monitoring among group members through enforced group liability. Because MFI performance, both outreach and financial viability,[3] is interlinked with the performance of program borrowers, evaluating members' benefit structures also means evaluating MFI cost structures to determine whether the services they provide are cost-effective for both MFI delivery and MFI members (i.e., for borrowing, savings, and accessing other offered services).

Assessing the Dynamics of Program Benefits

Evaluating the dynamics of benefits accrued to households amid increasing levels of indebtedness and multiple program membership obviously requires long household panel data. Long program-level panel data are also required to evaluate the dynamics of MFIs in terms of their outreach, cost efficiency, and other performance indicators. The analysis of program-level dynamics using longer period data can help study such dynamic issues as MFI competitiveness and cost efficiency. A logical framework of program evaluation in terms of inputs, outputs, outcomes, and impacts is therefore an appropriate way to evaluate the dynamics of the program benefits accrued to and costs incurred by households (i.e., the MFI impacts). Program-level data analysis offers insights into other aspects of the logical framework in terms of the dynamics of program outreach, product diversification, loan recovery, and cost efficiency of the MFIs across programs and over time. Earlier research conducted by Khandker (1998) followed this approach;

however, that study used cross-sectional household survey data jointly collected in 1991/92 by the Bangladesh Institute of Development Studies (BIDS) and the World Bank. It also used program-level data of three major programs active in Bangladesh at that time to evaluate their outreach and cost efficiency. At the time of the survey, microfinance programs had just started and were involved in targeting the poor (defined by landholdings of less than half an acre), especially women, in an effort to promote self-employment and generate income in a bid to reduce poverty. The effort was also geared toward making Grameen Bank and other microfinance programs self-sustaining as they were heavily subsidized by donors, including the government, at that time.

Evolution of the Microfinance Industry

Bangladesh's microfinance industry has undergone a dramatic evolution over the last 20 years. In the early stages, it was funded largely by the Government of Bangladesh and several bilateral donors. An International Development Association (IDA) project of the World Bank provided a large amount of aid to smaller and local NGOs that, unlike Grameen Bank and BRAC, were not receiving bilateral donor funds from abroad. In 1996, the Bangladesh government, with IDA funding, established the Rural Employment Support Foundation (*Palli Karma-Sahayak Foundation*), hereafter referred to by its Bangla acronym, PKSF. A wholesale agency for retailing the microfinance operations of many highly competitive NGO-MFIs, which were dynamic in promoting the cause of microfinance in Bangladesh, PKSF has become an instrument for promoting the coverage and scope of microfinance in Bangladesh. It has also played a catalytic role in creating similar apex organizations outside Bangladesh with World Bank funding support.

With an appropriate incentive mechanism in place through PKSF, the microfinance program that emerged after 1996 no longer used large donor funds to support operations. It was no longer limited to providing credit and other services to the poor as defined by landholdings, and many borrowers had moved beyond the landholding threshold. Rather, it was evolving into a program that witnessed many of its MFI members attaining complete self-sufficiency and thus graduating from subsidy dependence. The program was becoming a highly competitive, thriving microfinance industry that increasingly supported agriculture and related services, along with nonagricultural activities. Over time, the program began introducing a variety of financial services to its members, including cash transfer and crop and health insurance. Thus, evaluating today's microfinance is a more encompassing and demanding task than it was 25 years ago. Indeed, the recent phenomena of borrowers' indebtedness and multiple program membership are dynamic issues that have evolved over time.

Revisiting the Policy Quagmires

In 2010/11, the World Bank and Bangladesh's Institute of Microfinance (InM) together provided financial support to re-survey the same households and communities that had first been visited in 1991/92 and again in 1998/99. The resulting long panel survey of 1991/92–2010/11 provides a unique opportunity to revisit the policy quagmires now confronting MFIs around the world. More specifically, the long panel survey data help in examining the following dynamic issues: (a) whether the effects of short- and long-term loans have varied, (b) whether the changing effects of market conditions have contributed to market saturation and village-level diseconomies, (c) whether market saturation and multiple program membership have been adversely affecting household welfare, and (d) whether the benefits of microfinance are lacking due to the absence of noncredit inputs. These data also provide an avenue for determining whether the benefits accrued to participants are meeting the cost of borrowing, if interest rates are too high, whether program design (e.g., credit or credit plus) matters, who benefits most from microfinance interventions, and how the spillover effects of microfinance growth might benefit or harm nonparticipants and the overall village economy.

The long panel survey can also be used to verify earlier research findings that used cross-sectional or short-term panel surveys in order to reconfirm or refute the earlier witnessed positive effects of microfinance on the household welfare of borrowers, as well as nonborrower program beneficiaries. Data analysis using the long panel survey can be expected to highlight whether multiple program membership has increased over time as a result of competition among the MFIs. Indeed, data analysis shows that multiple program membership, which was nonexistent in 1991/92, accounted for 8.9 percent of borrowers in 1998/99 and 31.9 percent in 2010/11. Yet such growth has not caused a decline in MFI loan recovery. One can infer from such observations that long-term borrowers of MFIs may not be trapped in poverty or debt as many have contended in recent years. This hypothesis, however, requires a thorough examination. Furthermore, returns to projects supported under microfinance must be evaluated against the interest rates charged by the MFIs to determine whether they are too high for realizing sufficient returns from investment undertaken by borrowers and supported by the microfinance industry. Moreover, the industry and its beneficiaries may be facing other types of challenges and constraints to sustaining the benefits and coverage of microfinance services. Only an in-depth analysis of long panel data can reveal the dynamics of what has become a highly competitive industry with a variety of actors.

Since microfinance's inception in Bangladesh during the 1980s, its growth has attracted worldwide attention; in many countries, microfinance services have expanded many times over to reach the poor, especially women and small producers. Given such tremendous growth, it is not surprising that microfinance has also attracted serious criticism, including the argument that the program could be a fad with less-than-expected benefits for the poor. Microfinance is not without its pitfalls; thus, it is an empirical challenge to demonstrate that it ultimately matters for the poor. Critics have often failed to realize that improved access to financial services from institutions, even if nongovernmental, has provided many poor people an opportunity to borrow at much lower interest rates than those charged by local moneylenders, the only other borrowing source for many. Thus, the inclusive-finance-through-microfinance movement is itself a milestone in development that, without the inclusive finance experiments led by Grameen Bank and others in Bangladesh, would not have been possible.

Purpose and Organization of the Book

Led in part by Grameen Bank, along with the concessionary financing support provided by the Government of Bangladesh and the World Bank, Bangladesh has cleared pathways to inclusive finance for a host of NGOs through establishment of the PKSF wholesale microfinance agency. This book attempts to unearth some of the key challenges that policy makers and practitioners in Bangladesh and elsewhere now face in sustaining microfinance growth. The book provides a snapshot of Bangladesh's pioneering experience with microfinance, covering key topics supported by both program and household data over a 20-year period. It discusses the lessons learned in terms of benefits and costs, the pitfalls and strengths of group-based microlending, and the policy conundrum that has recently emerged.

The book is organized into 11 chapters. Chapter 2 examines sources of rural nonfarm (RNF) growth in Bangladesh and how the dynamics of that sector have influenced overall income growth and poverty reduction. This analysis sets the stage for learning how microfinance growth has accommodated RNF growth, and hence overall growth and development. Chapter 3 reviews the success of MFIs in Bangladesh, examines their funding sources, and investigates the timing of their entry into the microfinance market on subsequent performance. Chapter 4 compares alternative estimates of the socioeconomic benefits accrued by MFI program participants to explore whether the benefits vary by estimation method and timing of program participation, how the changing effects of market conditions contribute to market saturation and village diseconomies, and whether market saturation and multiple program membership are adversely affecting household welfare. Chapter 5 examines the recent phenomenon of overindebtedness among microfinance borrowers in Bangladesh, including the role of overlapping MFI memberships and other influencing supply-and-demand factors. Chapter 6 revisits the controversies surrounding the role of microfinance in poverty reduction in order to determine whether earlier findings on its benefits can be substantiated and whether program participants are trapped in poverty. Chapter 7 investigates the direct and indirect impacts of microfinance expansion in Bangladesh on poor farmers, including linkages between farm and nonfarm production and employment. It also examines the overall effect of microfinance growth on agricultural employment and wages. Chapter 8 considers the distributional or heterogeneous effects of microfinance across households and areas over time to resolve the dilemma of an average program effect. Chapter 9 differentiates the noncredit impacts of several types of MFI programs, exploring the potential benefits from credit and noncredit inputs and program design. Chapter 10 examines the growth and rate of return on MFI-supported RNF microenterprises over the past decade, major sector constraints, and opportunities for growth. Backward linkages with agriculture and diversification of income-earning activities within the sector are also addressed. Finally, chapter 11 summarizes what has been learned and—within the context of microfinance's changing role beyond ending poverty—offers recommendations to address the current challenges faced by the microfinance sector and MFI borrowers.

Notes

1. These claims were later invalidated (Pitt 2014a, 2014b; Pitt and Khandker 2012). In fact, Pitt and Khandker (2012) found that many of the claims by Roodman and Morduch (2014) regarding the study by Pitt and Khandker (1998) were based on a flawed econometric understanding and a lack of due diligence in formulating and interpreting statistical models employed in Pitt and Khandker (1998).
2. RCT models are not appropriate over a longer term as the basic tenets of RCT are violated over a longer period of program exposure. Such violations are not necessarily valid with quasi-experimental models applied in the seminal study of Pitt and Khandker (1998).
3. The financial viability of MFIs refers not only to loan recovery rates, but also to the cost efficiency of their operations, the interest rates they charge against, and other services offered to clientele.

Bibliography

CDF (Credit Development Forum). 2013. *Bangladesh Micro Finance Statistics*. Dhaka: CDF.

Khandker, Shahidur R. 1998. *Fighting Poverty with Microcredit: Experience in Bangladesh*. New York: Oxford University Press.

———. 2005. "Microfinance and Poverty: Evidence Using Panel Data from Bangladesh." *World Bank Economic Review* 19 (2): 263–86.

Pitt, Mark. 2014a. "Response to 'The Impact of Microcredit on the Poor in Bangladesh: Revisiting the Evidence.'" *Journal of Development Studies* 50 (4): 605–10.

———. 2014b. "Re-Re-Reply to 'The Impact of Microcredit on the Poor in Bangladesh: Revisiting the Evidence.'" Working Paper 6801, World Bank, Washington, DC.

Pitt, Mark, and Shahidur Khandker. 1998. "The Impact of Group-Based Credit Programs on Poor Households in Bangladesh: Does Gender of the Participant Matter?" *Journal of Political Economy* 106: 958–96.

———. 2012. "Replicating Replication: Due Diligence in Roodman and Morduch's Replication of Pitt and Khandker (1998)." Working Paper 6273, World Bank, Washington, DC.

Roodman, David, and Jonathan Morduch. 2014. "The Impact of Microcredit on the Poor in Bangladesh: Revisiting the Evidence." *Journal of Development Studies* 50 (4): 583–604.

CHAPTER 2

Rural Nonfarm Growth and Poverty Reduction

Introduction

Poverty reduction in Bangladesh has progressed remarkably over the past several decades. Overall poverty, which was 57 percent in 1991, had fallen to 32 percent by 2010, with an average annual reduction rate of 1.25 percentage points. Over the same period, extreme poverty was reduced from 41 percent to 18 percent. In rural areas, where more than 70 percent of the country's 160 million people live, overall poverty fell from 59 percent in 1991/92 to 35 percent in 2010.[1] Part of this decline can be attributed to an economic growth rate of more than 6 percent a year over the last decade (World Bank 2012). Microfinance growth in rural areas was another major factor contributing to overall poverty reduction over that period.

While chapter 3 covers microfinance growth over time and chapter 6 addresses the role of microfinance in poverty reduction, the focus of this chapter's analysis is the extent of overall poverty reduction in Bangladesh over the past decade, including the urban/rural divide. The chapter examines sources of rural income growth and their role in poverty reduction. Special emphasis is given to rural nonfarm (RNF) growth and how the dynamics of that sector have influenced overall income growth and poverty reduction. As chapter 3 will demonstrate, microfinance institutions (MFIs) in Bangladesh mainly support RNF activities, although, in recent years, they have started supporting agriculture and activities in urban areas. This chapter's analysis sets the stage for determining why and how microfinance expansion over the last decade has helped reduce poverty through income and employment generation in the RNF sector and the induced effect on farm income growth.

This chapter's analysis is based on two data sets. The first one is derived from the Household Income and Expenditure Survey (HIES) for years 2000, 2005, and 2010. The HIES, conducted by the Bangladesh Bureau of Statistics (BBS), collects household-level data on progress in living standards and nutritional status that can be used to formulate appropriate policies related to poverty reduction and evaluate various policies and programs, including microfinance, on the living conditions of the population.

The second data set—drawn from three-period panel surveys spanning more than 20 years (from 1991/92 to 2010/11)—is useful for tracing the poverty-reduction contribution of microcredit programs over time. Notable studies that have used earlier rounds of this survey include Pitt and Khandker (1998), based on the 1991/92 data, and Khandker (2005), which used the panel data covering the 1991/92 and 1998/99 survey rounds. The present study is drawn primarily from this long panel data set.

Poverty Trends

The poverty figures reported in table 2.1 are derived from the HIES data, using poverty lines based on the cost-of-basic-needs method, including the cost of a minimum food basket (food poverty line) and an allowance for nonfood expenditures.[2] Using the HIES data, table 2.1 shows that moderate poverty in rural areas fell from 58.7 percent in 2000 to 35.2 percent in 2010, with an average annual reduction of 2.6 percentage points over the decade. Over the same period, extreme poverty declined by about the same rate (i.e., 2.6 percentage points per year). However, as table 2.1 shows, despite significant progress in poverty reduction, urban/rural disparity remains a concern.

In addition to the cost of a minimum food basket, actual food intake in terms of daily kilocalories (kcal) per person can be used to directly measure food poverty. Using the direct calorie-intake method of poverty estimation, two cutoff points of daily per capita intake can be considered. The higher one (2,122 kcal), used by the cost-of-basic-needs method to estimate the food poverty line, refers to what is called moderate calorie-intake deficiency. The lower one (1,805 kcal) may be considered to represent severe deficiency. In line with the overall poverty estimates shown in table 2.1, the proportions of people deficient in calorie intake, both moderate and severe, can be seen to have declined steadily since the early 1990s (table 2.2).[3]

Unlike the findings in table 2.1, however, the urban population in 2005 appears to have had higher levels of both moderate and severe food deficiency, compared to the rural population. In 2005, moderate poverty in urban areas was slightly more than 28 percent, while moderate food deficiency was about 43 percent. While overall estimates of moderate poverty in 2005 were about the same for rural and urban areas, estimates of extreme poverty offer a more encouraging picture when the caloric consumption method, instead of cost of basic needs, is used. Nonetheless, the improvements in calorie-intake deficiency have been far less encouraging than the poverty estimates based on the cost-of-basic-needs approach (Khandker and Mahmud 2012).

In contrast to the recent economic growth pattern of many developing countries in South Asia and other regions, where income inequality has increased (Mahmud and Chowdhury 2008), Bangladesh appears to have been relatively pro-poor. The main stimulus to its recent economic growth has come from outside

Table 2.1 Moderate and Extreme Poverty Rates in Bangladesh: 1991/92–2010

percent

Year	Moderate poverty			Extreme poverty		
	Rural	Urban	National	Rural	Urban	National
1991/92	58.7	42.7	56.6	43.7	23.6	41.0
1995/96	54.5	27.8	50.1	39.4	13.7	35.1
2000	52.3	35.2	48.9	37.9	20.0	34.3
2005	43.8	28.4	40.0	28.6	14.6	25.1
2010	35.2	21.3	31.5	21.1	7.7	17.6

Source: HIES, various years.
Note: Method is based on the cost of basic needs.

Table 2.2 Percentage of Population with Moderate and Severe Food Intake Deficiency: 1991/92–2005

Year	Moderate deficiency (<2,122 kcal/person/day)			Severe deficiency (<1,805 kcal/person/day)		
	Rural	Urban	National	Rural	Urban	National
1991/92	47.6	46.7	47.5	28.3	26.3	28.0
1995/96	47.1	49.7	47.5	24.6	27.3	25.1
2000	42.3	52.5	44.3	18.7	25.0	20.0
2005	39.5	43.2	40.4	17.9	24.4	19.5

Source: HIES, various years.
Note: kcal = kilocalorie.

agriculture, particularly labor-intensive garment exports, micro- and small-scale enterprises in the manufacturing sector and services, and remittances from migrants working abroad. In the 1990s, income inequality increased because, even within a generally employment-intensive growth pattern, the major share of benefits was reaped by those who were initially wealthy. Also, growth was not strong enough to increase wages in the vast agricultural and informal labor markets. Since the late 1990s, however, real wages in the agricultural and other informal labor markets have shown strong upward trends. The HIES data from 2000 and later years shows that income inequality in urban and rural areas, if not improved, at least has not worsened; as a result, poverty has declined at a faster rate.

Despite widespread poverty, low per capita public social spending, and poor governance of service delivery systems, Bangladesh has also achieved rapid improvements in many human development indicators in recent years (e.g., girls' school enrollment, child mortality, and rates of modern contraceptive usage). Much of this progress has resulted from the adoption of low-cost solutions. In the health sector, for example, use of oral rehydration saline for diarrhea treatment has led to a significant decrease in child mortality. Progress has also resulted from increased public awareness created by effective social mobilization campaigns.[4] Despite these cited achievements, child malnutrition rates remain among the highest in the world; an estimated 46 percent of children under five are malnourished in Bangladesh, compared to 27 percent in Sub-Saharan Africa (UNICEF 2011).[5]

Thus, beyond low-cost solutions, further progress in Bangladesh will depend on the amount of public social spending, quality of services, inclusive economic growth, and synergies in poverty reduction. A key challenge for this study is to determine whether and to what extent microfinance growth has contributed to the continued reduction in poverty over the years, especially in rural areas, where the MFIs have been the most active.

Income Growth Trends

To answer these questions, this section examines the (a) trend in overall rural income in 1991–2011, (b) growth in shares of farm and nonfarm income over time, (c) major components of farm and nonfarm income and their growth over time, and (d) variations in shares of each sector over time. Given the growth in RNF income over the 20-year period, the study also examines income and occupational mobility across sectors over time.

Farm and Nonfarm Income

Using data sets from the respective three rounds of the HIES and long panel survey, the study examined growth in farm and nonfarm income and their respective shares in total income over time as a way to better understand the scope of RNF growth in overall rural income growth (table 2.3). Table 2.3a shows that overall income grew by 1.8 percent per year in real terms during 2000–05 and by 6.9 percent per year during 2005–10, with an overall growth rate of 4.7 percent a year. Table 2.3b shows that income grew by only 0.4 percent a year in real terms during 1991/92–1998/99 and by 9.2 percent a year during 1998/99–2010/11, with an overall average growth rate of 6.1 percent a year over the 20-year period.

Figure 2.1 shows how overall income growth by four major sources (agriculture, commerce and business, labor wages, and other) changed over time. As shown, agriculture dominated in the mid-1990s, but its role declined over time. In 1995/96, for example, it accounted for 35 percent of total rural income, falling to 30 percent in 2010. Conversely, labor wages contributed some 27 percent of total rural income in the mid-1990s, increasing to nearly 30 percent by 2010.

Both the HIES and long panel survey show that the share of RNF income has been consistently higher than that of the farm sector. Using the HIES data, RNF income averaged about 55 percent over the 2000–10 period, spiking to 62 percent in 2005. Using the long panel survey data, its share increased by nearly 19 percent (from 56.4 percent to 75.2 percent) from 1991/92 to 2010/11. The HIES data indicate that some 70 percent of rural households drew income from both farm and nonfarm sources over the 2000–10 period. The long panel survey data shows that some 70 percent of rural households drew income from both sources in 1991/92, and this percentage increased to 93 percent by 2010/11. Thus, it is not surprising that an increasing percentage of rural households draw income from both farm and nonfarm sources.

Table 2.3 Household Welfare in Rural Bangladesh

a. Using HIES data

Welfare indicator	2000 (N = 2,758)	2005 (N = 2,917)	2010 (N = 3,459)
Per capita total income (Tk./month)	855.3	932.5	1,254.7
Farm income (%)	45.2	38.4	46.5
Nonfarm income (%)	54.7	61.6	53.5
Share of households drawing income from both farm and nonfarm sources (%)	71.4	77.2	71.6
Per capita farm income (Tk./month)	323.1	296.8	588.8
Agricultural crop production (%)[a]	46.8	50.9	44.1
Livestock and fisheries (%)	21.9	26.3	35.3
Wage income (%)	31.3	22.8	20.6
Per capita nonfarm income (Tk./month)	532.2	635.7	666.0
Microenterprise self-employment (%)	21.3	18.1	21.8
Wage and salaried employment (%)	27.8	30.7	36.1
Miscellaneous nonfarm self-employment (%)[b]	39.0	39.6	28.9
Remittances (%)	11.9	11.6	13.2

b. Using long panel survey data

Welfare indicator	1991/92 (N = 1,509)	1998/99 (N = 1,758)	2010/11 (N = 2,322)
Per capita total income (Tk./month)	561.8	576.3	1,212.8
Farm income (%)	43.6	39.7	24.8
Nonfarm income (%)	56.4	60.3	75.2
Share of households drawing income from both farm and nonfarm sources (%)	70.2	90.0	92.7
Per capita farm income (Tk./month)	164.3	178.9	153.1
Agricultural crop production (%)[a]	45.6	52.6	33.8
Livestock and fisheries (%)	20.2	22.5	46.9
Wage income (%)	34.1	24.9	19.4
Per capita nonfarm income (Tk./month)	397.5	397.5	1,059.8
Microenterprise self-employment (%)	38.2	36.1	30.4
Wage and salaried employment (%)	44.5	25.2	24.1
Miscellaneous nonfarm self-employment (%)[b]	12.9	28.5	30.4
Remittances (%)	4.3	10.2	15.1

Sources: HIES 2000, 2005, 2010; World Bank/BIDS survey 1991/92 and 1998/99; World Bank/InM survey 2010/11.
Note: Figures are consumer price index–adjusted: 2000 = 100 (table 2.3a); 1991/92 = 100 (table 2.3b).
a. Receipts from crop, vegetable, and fruit production, as well as other horticultural activities.
b. Receipts from self-employed professionals (e.g., lawyers, doctors, and tutors); rental income from properties and assets; interest and profits from savings and investments, and safety-net programs and charities.

Farm Income: Sector Composition

Table 2.3 also shows trends in various components of farm income (agricultural crop production, livestock and fisheries, and wage income) and RNF income growth over the survey periods. Data from both surveys show that income shares from agricultural crop production and farm wages declined over

Figure 2.1 Income Sources for Rural Households

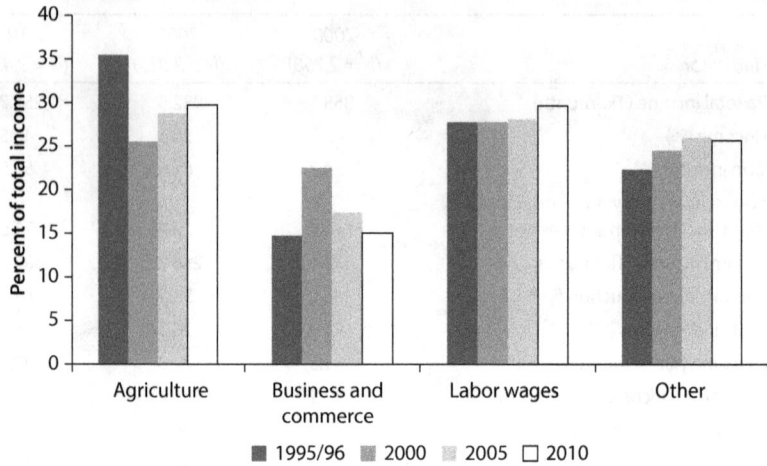

Source: HIES, various years.

time, while shares of livestock and fisheries increased. Using the HIES data, agricultural crop production accounted for 44.1 percent of farm income in 2010, followed by livestock and fisheries at 35.3 percent and wage income at 20.6 percent. Using data from the long panel survey, livestock and fisheries accounted for 46.9 percent of farm income in 2010/11; agricultural crop production and wage income followed at 33.8 percent and 19.4 percent, respectively. It is noteworthy that both surveys show an increasing share of the livestock and fisheries component.

Which Households Engage in RNF Activities?

Figure 2.2 shows how the share of RNF income varies with household income growth over time. For both data sets and all survey years, a similar pattern is observed. For low-income households, the share of RNF income is quite low. The RNF share reaches its highest point for middle-income households before decreasing for high-income households. This trend is captured by an inverted U-shaped curve (figure 2.2a and 2.2b).

This trend is not surprising. Low-income households depend mainly on wage labor in the farm sector. Most nonfarm income is derived from activities requiring entrepreneurial skills that most low-income households lack, explaining why microcredit lenders tend not to extend microloans to such households. Middle-income households are those mainly engaged in RNF activities; thus, the share of nonfarm income in total income is highest for this group. Better-off households in rural Bangladesh engage mainly in farm-based, self-employment activities; as a result, their share of nonfarm income is low, similar to what is observed for low-income households.

Figure 2.2 Trend in Share of Nonfarm Income with Increasing Household Income

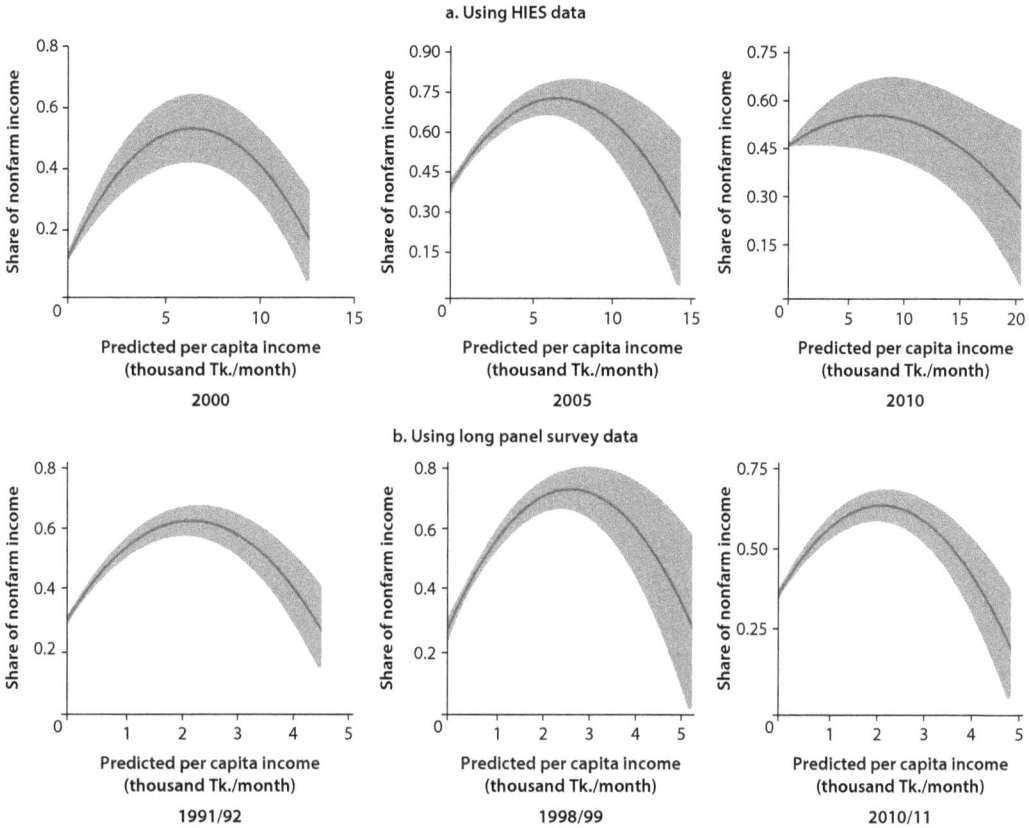

a. Using HIES data

Predicted per capita income (thousand Tk./month)	Predicted per capita income (thousand Tk./month)	Predicted per capita income (thousand Tk./month)
2000	2005	2010

b. Using long panel survey data

Predicted per capita income (thousand Tk./month)	Predicted per capita income (thousand Tk./month)	Predicted per capita income (thousand Tk./month)
1991/92	1998/99	2010/11

Sources: HIES 2000, 2005, 2010; World Bank/BIDS survey 1991/92 and 1998/99; World Bank/InM survey 2010/11.
Note: Shaded areas represent bandwidth for 95 percent confidence interval.

Nonfarm Income: Sector Composition

For the nonfarm sector (microenterprise self-employment, wage and salaried employment, miscellaneous nonfarm self-employment, and remittances), an interesting development in RNF income growth is observed. Using the HIES data, microenterprise income accounted for 21.8 percent of overall RNF income in 2010 (table 2.3a); using the long panel survey data, it accounted for 30.4 percent in 2010/11 (table 2.3b).[6] The 21.8 percent figure using the HIES data means that microenterprise activities as a share of overall household income was only about 12 percent in 2010 (53.5 x 0.218) (table 2.3a). The corresponding figure for 2010/11 using the long panel survey data was consistently about 22 percent (table 2.3b). According to the HIES data, the share of nonfarm wage and salaried employment increased from 27.8 percent in 2000 to 36.1 percent in 2010; over the same period, the share of miscellaneous nonfarm self-employment declined from 39.0 percent to 28.9 percent. Using the long panel survey data, the share of remittances increased from just 4.3 percent in 1991/92 to 15.1 percent by 2010/11, while it hovered at about 12 percent over the 2000–10 period, using the HIES data.

Table 2.4 Transition Matrix of Major Household Income Sources

Income source, 1991/92 status (% households)	Income source, 2010/11 status (% households)						
	Agricultural crop production	Livestock and fisheries	Farm-sector wages	Nonfarm micro-enterprises	Nonfarm wages and salaried employment	Remittances	Other
Agricultural crop production (20.9%)	6.0	10.4	6.2	25.6	23.5	16.0	12.4
Livestock and fisheries(1.8%)	1.0	2.3	0.0	58.7	12.4	18.9	6.2
Farm-sector wages (17.4%)	2.2	6.9	19.4	32.7	20.1	11.8	6.9
Nonfarm micro-enterprises (25.7%)	2.1	3.3	2.5	55.9	16.2	10.6	9.3
Nonfarm wages and salaried employment (29.4%)	1.2	2.8	6.6	30.1	34.2	16.8	8.4
Remittances (0.8%)	3.7	0.0	0.0	59.2	23.6	11.7	1.9
Other (3.9%)	4.2	17.0	3.7	30.2	6.8	27.6	10.5

Sources: World Bank/BIDS survey 1991/92 and 1998/99; World Bank/InM survey 2010/11.
Note: Households may draw income from multiple sources; the distribution reported here is based on those sources that bring in the highest income.

RNF Share in Income Mobility

Using the long panel survey data, table 2.4 presents the distribution of households by their major income sources in 2010/11, grouped by their major income sources in 1991/92.[7] As shown, the majority of rural households have increasingly drawn income from RNF activities over time.

Table 2.4 illustrates how a majority of households have increasingly diversified their income over time to mitigate risk. Interestingly, among the 20.9 percent of households that drew income from agricultural crop production in 1991/92, 25.6 percent received income from nonfarm microenterprises in 2010/11. Among the 25.7 percent of households that drew income from nonfarm micro-enterprises in 1991/92, 55.9 percent retained such nonfarm activities as their major income source in 2010/11.

Poverty Reduction and Growth of the Rural Nonfarm Sector

To evaluate the importance of the RNF sector in Bangladesh's rural economy, this section assesses the contribution of each component sector in the country's total income growth. Table 2.5a presents the role of the various components of farm and nonfarm income growth in total income growth using the HIES data, while table 2.5b provides a similar analysis using the long panel survey data.[8] Both data sets confirm that the nonfarm sector plays a larger role than the farm sector in Bangladesh's total income growth. According to the long panel survey data, a 10 percent increase in RNF income raises total income by as much as 4.43 percent, compared to only 1.32 percent for a similar growth in farm income. The corresponding figures using the HIES data are 0.50 percent and 0.32 percent, respectively.

And the difference in the contributions of the farm and nonfarm components is statistically significant for both data sets.

Table 2.5 also shows the respective roles of various components of farm and nonfarm income in total income. Test of equality examines whether farm and nonfarm income components are separable in their distinct effects on

Table 2.5 Estimates of Sectoral Composition and Its Effect on Income Growth
a. Using HIES data
Upazila-level fixed effects, N = 9,134

Explanatory variable	Log per capita			
	Total income, model 1 (Tk./month)	Total income, model 2 (Tk./month)	Farm income (Tk./month)	Nonfarm income (Tk./month)
Log per capita farm income (Tk./month)	0.032** (13.59)	n.a.	n.a.	n.a.
Log per capita nonfarm income (Tk./month)	0.050** (17.48)	n.a.	n.a.	n.a.
Log per capita income from agricultural crop production (Tk./month)	n.a.	0.018** (11.60)	0.342** (27.89)	n.a.
Log per capita income from livestock and fisheries (Tk./month)	n.a.	0.013** (8.06)	0.347** (25.36)	n.a.
Log per capita income from farm-sector wages (Tk./month)	n.a.	0.003* (1.81)	0.201** (16.32)	n.a.
Log per capita income from nonfarm microenterprises (Tk./month)	n.a.	0.034** (13.04)	n.a.	0.199** (16.48)
Log per capita income from nonfarm wages and salaried employment (Tk./month)	n.a.	0.029** (14.00)	n.a.	0.208** (19.12)
Log per capita income from miscellaneous sources (Tk./month)	n.a.	0.018** (12.91)	n.a.	0.316** (22.36)
Log per capita income from remittances (Tk./month)	n.a.	0.020** (11.08)	n.a.	0.164** (18.45)
R^2	0.308	0.236	0.644	0.574
Test statistics for equality of farm and nonfarm income	$F(1, 136) = 19.79$, $p > F = 0.000$	n.a.	n.a.	n.a.
Test statistics for equality among farm income components (crops, livestock, and wages)	n.a.	$F(2, 136) = 32.27$, $p > F = 0.000$	$F(2, 136) = 66.35$, $p > F = 0.000$	n.a.
Test statistics for equality between nonfarm income components (microenterprises, wages, salary, miscellaneous sources, and remittances)	n.a.	$F(2, 136) = 10.86$, $p > F = 0.000$	n.a.	$F(2, 136) = 63.12$, $p > F = 0.000$

table continues next page

Table 2.5 Estimates of Sectoral Composition and Its Effect on Income Growth (continued)

b. Using long panel survey data
Household-level fixed effects, N = 1,509

Explanatory variable	Log per capita			
	Total income, model 1 (Tk./month)	Total income, model 2 (Tk./month)	Farm income (Tk./month)	Nonfarm income (Tk./month)
Log per capita farm income (Tk./month)	0.132** (13.81)	n.a.	n.a.	n.a.
Log per capita nonfarm income (Tk./month)	0.443** (19.25)	n.a.	n.a.	n.a.
Log per capita income from agricultural crop production (Tk./month)	n.a.	0.080** (11.72)	0.412** (21.06)	n.a.
Log per capita income from livestock and fisheries (Tk./month)	n.a.	0.062** (8.36)	0.391** (27.05)	n.a.
Log per capita income from farm-sector wages (Tk./month)	n.a.	0.035** (5.58)	0.362** (30.30)	n.a.
Log per capita income from nonfarm microenterprises (Tk./month)	n.a.	0.178** (16.08)	n.a.	0.327** (22.49)
Log per capita income from nonfarm wages and salaried employment (Tk./month)	n.a.	0.098** (12.63)	n.a.	0.241** (18.44)
Log per capita income from miscellaneous sources (Tk./month)	n.a.	0.118** (11.99)	n.a.	0.266** (13.71)
Log per capita income from remittances (Tk./month)	n.a.	0.121** (12.48)	n.a.	0.196** (12.96)
R^2	0.663	0.494	0.714	0.709
Test statistics for equality of farm and nonfarm income	$F(1, 86) = 114.55$, $p > F = 0.000$	n.a.	n.a.	n.a.
Test statistics for equality among farm income components (crops, livestock, and wages)	n.a.	$F(2, 86) = 12.95$, $p > F = 0.000$	$F(2, 86) = 3.86$, $p > F = 0.025$	n.a.
Test statistics for equality between nonfarm income components (microenterprises, wages, salary, miscellaneous sources, and remittances)	n.a.	$F(2, 86) = 2.77$, $p > F = 0.068$	n.a.	$F(2, 86) = 7.86$, $p > F = 0.000$

Sources: HIES 2000, 2005, and 2010; World Bank/BIDS survey 1991/92 and 1998/99; World Bank/InM survey 2010/11.
Note: Figures in parentheses are t-statistics. In table 2.5a, regressions are restricted to common upazilas across three years. Regressions control for characteristics of households (e.g., age, sex, and education of head and log land and nonland assets) and villages (e.g., availability of paved roads, electricity, and other infrastructure; presence of banks and MFIs; price of consumer goods; and male and female wages), as well as household occupation dummies based on major income source. HIES = Household Income and Expenditure Survey; MFI = microfinance institution; n.a. = not applicable.
Significance level: * = 10 percent, ** = 5 percent.

income growth. While this is true for both farm and nonfarm components at one percent level of significance using the HIES (table 2.5a), this is not the case with farm income components using the long panel survey (table 2.5b). As shown in table 2.5a, livestock and fisheries contribute the most to growth in farm income (with a response elasticity of 0.347), followed by agricultural crop production (0.342) and income from farm wages (0.201). Table 2.5b shows a slightly larger role for agricultural crop production (with a response elasticity of 0.412), followed by livestock and fisheries (0.391) and income from farm wages (0.362).

In terms of RNF income growth using the HIES data, income from RNF miscellaneous sources has the highest response elasticity (0.316), followed by RNF wages (0.208), microenterprise income (0.199), and remittances (0.164). Using the long panel survey data, however, shows that microenterprise income growth matters most in raising RNF income growth (with a response elasticity of 0.327), followed by RNF miscellaneous sources (0.266), RNF wages (0.241), and remittances (0.196).

The larger role of rural microenterprise income in total rural income is further evidenced by the total income growth equation (Model 2) of tables 2.5a and 2.5b. Analysis of both data sets confirms that microenterprise income growth contributes the most to total income growth in terms of response elasticity. More specifically, the microenterprise income elasticity with respect to total rural income is 0.034 according to the HIES data and 0.178 using the long panel survey data. It thus follows that RNF income growth matters a lot to Bangladesh's overall income growth and, within the RNF sector, microenterprise income growth matters the most for promoting the country's overall RNF income growth.

Roles of Farm and Nonfarm Income Growth in Poverty Reduction

Given the rising trend in RNF growth vis-à-vis farm income growth, what relative roles do nonfarm and farm income growth play in poverty reduction?

It is possible that growth in both farm and nonfarm income played an important role in reducing rural poverty over the period. As previously noted, among the various sources of rural income, microenterprises are a major source of overall income growth. That being so, microenterprise income growth must be an important underlying factor in reducing both types of poverty.

Table 2.6 also presents the relationships between microenterprise participation and household welfare over time. The findings show that both moderate and extreme poverty rates are substantially lower for households with microenterprises. For example, using the HIES data, the findings show that moderate poverty in 2010 was 10.1 percentage points lower for households that engaged in microenterprises (26.8 percent versus 36.9 percent). Similarly, the long panel survey data show that moderate poverty in 2010/11 was 25.4 percent for those with microenterprises, compared to 32.9 percent for those without such nonfarm activities. For both data sets, the difference in the moderate poverty rate is statistically significant. Extreme poverty follows the same trend for both surveys. Thus, it is probably fair to say that microenterprise income growth might have

Table 2.6 Household Poverty Trend by Adoption of Nonfarm Microenterprise Activity

	HIES data			Long panel survey data		
Poverty indicator (%)	Households with nonfarm enterprise	Households without nonfarm enterprise	All households	Households with nonfarm enterprise	Households without nonfarm enterprise	All households
	2000 *(N = 2,758)*			**1991/92** *(N = 1,509)*		
Moderate	54.1	61.5 (−5.29)	59.7	77.3	80.3 (−1.26)	78.2
Extreme	39.6	48.6 (−6.57)	46.4	62.5	70.2 (−2.90)	64.8
	2005 *(N = 2,917)*			**1998/99** *(N = 1,758)*		
Moderate	36.3	44.1 (−5.85)	42.2	51.4	56.8 (−2.04)	52.9
Extreme	23.2	29.6 (−5.50)	28.1	36.0	43.5 (−2.88)	38.1
	2010 *(N = 3,459)*			**2010/11** *(N = 23,22)*		
Moderate	26.8	36.9 (−6.14)	34.6	25.4	32.9 (−3.65)	27.5
Extreme	15.9	22.2 (−5.04)	20.7	11.9	19.5 (−4.76)	14.0

Sources: HIES 2000, 2005, and 2010; World Bank/BIDS survey 1991/92 and 1998/99; World Bank/InM survey 2010/11.
Note: Figures in parentheses are t-statistics of the differences between households with and without enterprises. HIES = Household Income and Expenditure Survey.

played a critical role not only in raising overall rural income but also in reducing both moderate and extreme poverty.

Effects of RNF Enterprise Income on Income and Expenditure Growth

This leads one to ask whether participation in a microenterprise activity indeed causes income and expenditure to rise and poverty to fall. The relationships between poverty and enterprise adoption reported in table 2.6 are not causal, meaning that it is not known whether the households that adopted microenterprises were better off initially or whether adopting microenterprise activities led to income and expenditure growth and poverty reduction.

To investigate this causality, the study estimated the net effect of microenterprise participation on these household outcomes after controlling for other factors, including the decision to participate in a microenterprise activity and the initial conditions for growth potential already in place. We considered the standard welfare-outcome variable Y_{ijt} (per capita income, per capita consumption, and whether a household is moderately or extremely poor) measuring the outcome of household i in upazila or village j in year t conditional on its participation in a microenterprise activity (M_{ijt}), expressed as follows:

$$Y_{ijt} = \beta^y X_{ijt} + \lambda^y V_{jt} + \delta M_{ijt} + \mu_{ij} + \eta_j + \varepsilon_{ijt}^y,\qquad(2.1)$$

where X and V are the respective household- and village-level exogenous characteristics, μ and η are the respective household- and village-level unobserved determinants of the outcome, δ measures the estimates of RNF enterprise adoption, and ε is the random error term.

The fixed-effects (FE) results are shown in table 2.7. In equation (2.1), participation in RNF enterprises (proxied by M) and household-level outcomes (Y),

Table 2.7 Effects of Adopting RNF Enterprises on Income, Expenditure, and Poverty

Data source and estimation techniques	Log per capita total income (Tk./month)	Log per capita total expenditure (Tk./month)	Moderate poverty	Extreme poverty
HIES data, upazila-level fixed effects (N = 9,134)	0.295**	0.098**	−0.081**	−0.067**
	(13.38)	(7.22)	(−6.50)	(−5.51)
	$R^2 = 0.058$	$R^2 = 0.191$	$R^2 = 0.082$	$R^2 = 0.092$
Long panel survey data, household-level fixed effects (N = 1,509)	0.543**	0.029**	−0.026*	−0.044**
	(13.07)	(2.06)	(−1.74)	(−3.16)
	$R^2 = 0.223$	$R^2 = 0.415$	$R^2 = 0.324$	$R^2 = 0.350$

Sources: HIES 2000, 2005, and 2010; World Bank/BIDS survey 1991/92 and 1998/99; World Bank/InM survey 2010/11.
Note: Figures in parentheses are t-statistics. Regressions control for all household and village characteristics included in models reported in table 2.5, as well as exogenous characteristics of the initial year. RNF = rural nonfarm; HIES = Household Income and Expenditure Survey.
Significance level: * = 10 percent, ** = 5 percent.

such as poverty status, may be defined by the same characteristics. As adoption of RNF enterprises depends critically on access to credit, we may consider the village-level variable, such as access to microcredit, as the instrument. The endogeneity test statistics show that adoption of a microenterprise activity as an additional activity is endogenously determined by the same characteristics that also affect the outcomes. Thus, household adoption of a microenterprise activity *causally* increases both income and expenditure, thus reducing poverty.

For example, adoption of microenterprise activities increases household per capita income by more than 30 percent. If one assumes that growth in income or expenditure has been accumulated over the duration of a microenterprise's operation (about 10 years on average), then one can infer that a household's adoption of an enterprise activity increases per capita income by 3 percent a year and per capita consumption by 1 percent a year. Moreover, using the HIES data, microenterprise adoption has resulted in reductions of moderate and extreme poverty amounting to 8.1 percentage points and 6.7 percentage points, respectively. Using the long panel survey data, the corresponding reduction rates are 2.6 percentage points for moderate poverty and 4.4 percentage points for extreme poverty. These findings bolster our hypothesis that expansion of RNF enterprises is an effective way to accelerate poverty reduction in rural Bangladesh.

Linkages between Farm Income Growth and RNF Enterprise Expansion

It is argued that rural farm and RNF sectors comprise a virtuous cycle, whereby one drives the other. Although it is difficult to isolate what drives which growth, it is plausible that there are both backward and forward linkages between farm and nonfarm growth in any developing economy. Thus, as many rural households draw income from farm and nonfarm sources, especially RNF enterprise activities, it is highly relevant to examine the extent of backward and forward linkages between farm income growth and the expansion of RNF enterprises.

Theory and Evidence

A large body of literature discusses possible linkages between farm and nonfarm sectors in raising income and productivity. The ability of farm/nonfarm linkages to affect growth and poverty can depend heavily on an area's initial conditions related to agriculture. Many studies have shown that RNF growth, at least at the outset, depends on growth in agricultural productivity (Deichmann, Shilpi, and Vakis 2009; Haggblade, Hazell, and Reardon 2010; Johnson 2000; Johnston and Mellor 1961; Mellor 1976; Ranis and Stewart 1973).

In this context, however, the heterogeneity of the RNF sector also needs to be taken into account (Haggblade, Hazell, and Reardon 2010; Lanjouw and Feder 2001; Lanjouw and Lanjouw 2001). Foster and Rosenzweig (2004), for example, distinguish between nonfarm goods that are traded (financed by spatially mobile, nonlocal capital) and nontraded (locally financed). Using rural household panel data from India spanning 1970–2000, they find that only such nontradable non-farm activities as services are positively influenced by agricultural productivity growth. By contrast, tradable nonfarm activities, such as small manufacturing, move into areas with lower wages, implying a negative relationship with agricul-tural productivity growth.

Using individual employment data from the 2000 HIES, Deichmann, Shilpi, and Vakis (2009) also examine the effects of rural farm/nonfarm linkages by dividing nonfarm activities into low-return wage work (paying equal to or less than the median agricultural wage of a village), high-return wage work, and self-employment. With the dependent variable as occupational choice, they use multinomial logit regressions to find that proximity to urban centers—their measure for the extent of farm/urban linkages—is a necessary condition for growth in high-return nonfarm wage work and self-employment. That means that greater agricultural potential alone is not enough[9]; in fact, more isolated regions with greater agricultural potential are much less likely to engage in these activities.[10]

What Is the Net Effect of Farm Income Growth on RNF Income Growth?

Given that farm and nonfarm income are jointly determined by the interactions among various linkage factors, the challenge is to identify the net effect of farm income growth on RNF income growth. Our a priori assumption is that RNF growth initially responds to farm income growth and later feeds into rural farm income through enhanced demand for nonfarm goods and services as progress and linkages continue. However, it is still possible to discern the net effect of farm income growth on nonfarm growth by assuming agroclimate factors that affect farm income growth directly and only indirectly affect nonfarm income through the induced effects of farm income. In this way, we can argue that the directional change is from farm income to nonfarm income only.

This identification issue requires that we test for whether farm income growth is identified from nonfarm income growth. Table 2.8 shows two sets of estimates for each data set. The first set of results consists of a panel FE model that regresses nonfarm income growth on farm income growth, after controlling for a

Table 2.8 Role of Farm Income Growth in Nonfarm Income Growth

Dependent variable log nonfarm income (Tk./year)

	Model 1				Model 2			
	HIES data (N = 9,134)		Panel data (N = 1,590)		HIES data (N = 9,134)		Panel data (N = 1,590)	
Explanatory variable	Upazila FE	Upazila FE with IV	House-hold FE	Household FE with IV	Upazila FE	Upazila FE with IV	House-hold FE	Household FE with IV
Year is 2005 (1 = yes; 0 = no)	−0.934 (−0.51)	2.792 (0.37)			−0.637 (−0.45)	3.390 (0.44)		
Year is 2010 (1 = yes; 0 = no)	−0.813 (−0.49)	2.544 (0.34)			−0.526 (−0.43)	3.129 (0.41)		
Year is 1998/99 (1 = yes; 0 = no)			1.150 (1.47)	0.837 (0.93)			0.914 (1.14)	0.799 (0.89)
Year is 2010/11 (1 = yes; 0 = no)			3.591** (2.05)	1.847 (0.76)			5.020** (3.28)	2.760 (1.30)
Log farm income (Tk./year)	−0.020** (−2.75)	0.573** (2.23)	0.0002 (0.02)	0.525* (1.82)	−0.020** (−2.74)	0.582** (2.24)	−0.001 (−0.09)	0.462* (1.78)
Village has microcredit programs					0.004 (0.01)	−0.305 (−0.65)		
Proportion of village population participating in microcredit programs							0.546 (1.11)	0.062** (2.11)
R^2	0.359	0.111	0.407	0.158	0.359	0.104	0.407	0.214
Endogeneity test		$\chi^2(1) = 7.48$, $p = 0.006$		$\chi^2(1) = 3.92$, $p = 0.048$		$\chi^2(1) = 7.57$, $p = 0.006$		$\chi^2(1) = 4.03$, $p = 0.045$
Over-identification test		$\chi^2(5) = 0.91$, $p = 0.969$		$\chi^2(3) = 3.37$, $p = 0.339$		$\chi^2(5) = 0.97$, $p = 0.965$		$\chi^2(3) = 2.95$, $p = 0.399$
Under-identification test		$\chi^2(6) = 11.59$, $p = 0.072$		$\chi^2(4) = 9.95$, $p = 0.041$		$\chi^2(6) = 11.45$, $p = 0.075$		$\chi^2(4) = 10.34$, $p = 0.035$

Sources: HIES 2000, 2005, and 2010; World Bank/BIDS survey 1991/92 and 1998/99; World Bank/InM survey 2010/11.
Note: Figures in parentheses are t-statistics. For IV implementation, agricultural potentials and their interactions with household education and landholding are used as the excluded instruments for farm income in the first stage. Regression also controls for household and community characteristics, as noted in table 2.5a. HIES = Household Income and Expenditure Survey; FE = fixed effects; IV = instrumental variables.
Significance level: * = 10 percent, ** = 5 percent.

set of household and community characteristics influencing both types of growth, including initial characteristics. The second set of results applies a fixed-effects–instrumental variables (FE-IV) method that uses a two-stage procedure to run nonfarm income growth against farm income growth. The first-stage regression involves running farm income growth as a function of all exogenous factors and a set of instruments to separate farm income growth from nonfarm income growth. The second-stage regression involves running a nonfarm growth model based on the predicted values of farm income instead of actual farm income growth. The first-stage instruments in the farm income model are agroclimate factors (e.g., number of rainy months per year, irrigation, and elevated land) and their interaction with household characteristics (e.g., age, education, and landholding). A number of tests are used for identifying such restrictions to justify whether FE-IV is more appropriate than a simple FE model.

The simple FE model for both data sets indicates that the effect of farm income growth on RNF income growth is either zero or negative (table 2.8). Thus, the farm/nonfarm income growth elasticity is –0.020 in the case of HIES data, meaning that higher growth in farm income reduces growth in overall RNF income. That is, higher income growth in the farm sector does not necessarily promote RNF growth.

However, the results differ when we used the FE-IV model. In this case, the findings show that farm income growth increases RNF growth significantly. For both sets of results, a 10 percent increase in farm income growth increases RNF income growth by 5–6 percent. This is indeed a high elasticity of growth in the farm/nonfarm linkage models. All three tests of identification restrictions show that farm income growth can be a good predictor of nonfarm income growth. This is not to say that farm income growth will automatically lead to nonfarm income growth and vice versa. What is needed is a deeper understanding of the major features of the nonfarm sector and constraints impeding its growth.

Does Microfinance Placement Matter?

To investigate whether placement of microcredit programs makes a difference in RNF growth, we included "microcredit program placement variable at village level" as an additional regressor in the model using the HIES data and "proportion of microcredit participants in the village" as an additional regressor in the model using the long panel survey data. For the HIES data, Model 2 does not show any change in the farm-income impact from that in Model 1, and microcredit program placement apparently plays no role in nonfarm income growth. However, the findings from the long panel survey data show that the elasticity of farm income has decreased from 0.53 to 0.46, suggesting that the presence of microcredit programs may have an independent effect on nonfarm income growth. That is indeed the case. A 10 percentage point increase in microcredit participation in the village increases nonfarm income growth by 0.6 percent.

RNF Enterprise Growth: A Closer Look

The research findings show that expansion of RNF enterprises is a critical factor in overall income growth and poverty reduction in rural Bangladesh. Moreover, farm income growth has an important linkage with RNF income growth, especially that of RNF enterprises. Having established that nonfarm growth matters a lot for overall income growth and poverty reduction, the next task is to examine the characteristics that influence the expansion and growth of the RNF enterprise sector.

According to the HIES data, 1,427 RNF enterprises were owned by 5,027 households in 2000, while 1,426 were owned by 6,027 households in 2005, and 1,909 units by 7,830 households in 2010 (table 2.9a). This means that

Table 2.9 Distribution of RNF Enterprises in Bangladesh by Activity Type

a. Using HIES data

Sector	2000 (N = 1,427)	2005 (N = 1,426)	2010 (N = 1,909)
Manufacturing and processing[a]	11.9	10.3	13.9
Transport[b]	9.3	6.3	13.1
Trade[c]	2.4	2.5	2.3
Services[d]	65.3	75.8	61.5
Miscellaneous activities[e]	11.1	5.1	9.2

b. Using long panel survey data

Sector	1991/92 (N = 775)	1998/99 (N = 1,031)	2010/11 (N = 1,089)
Manufacturing and processing[a]	19.7	12.0	7.9
Transport[b]	14.2	30.0	32.7
Agricultural trade[c]	19.0	14.0	16.7
Nonagricultural trade[c]	38.9	39.6	38.2
Services[d]	8.2	4.4	4.5

Sources: HIES 2000, 2005, 2010; World Bank/BIDS survey 1991/92 and 1998/99; World Bank/InM survey 2010/11.

Note: RNF = rural nonfarm; HIES = Household Income and Expenditure Survey.

a. Manufacturing and processing covers food and beverages, tobacco, textiles, wood and furniture, rubber/plastic, and basic metal and nonmetal products.

b. Transport includes operation and rental of various transport vehicles.

c. Trade includes wholesale and retail trading of various agricultural and nonagricultural products; agricultural trade includes livestock, poultry, vegetables, fruits, and rice, while nonagricultural trade includes furniture, utensils, shoes, clothing, operating stores, and shops.

d. Services include skills-based or specialized activities, such as those provided by carpenters, masons, blacksmiths, electricians, barbers, tailors, real estate agents, social workers, counselors, bankers, doctors, and restaurant and hotel owners.

e. Miscellaneous activities include other small activities.

28.4 percent of households were involved in RNF enterprise activities in 2000, compared to 23.7 percent in both 2005 and 2010. However, using the long panel survey data, 51.4 percent of households (775 out of 1,509 households) owned RNF enterprises in 1991/92, compared to 68.3 percent in 1998/99 (1,031 households) and 72 percent (1,089 households) in 2010/11. The much higher percentage of households shown using the long panel survey data is probably because the 1991/92 survey selected households from areas with higher concentrations of microcredit programs. Indeed, in the early 1990s, pro-poor programs of MFIs, including Grameen Bank and BRAC, targeted poorer regions from the outset.

Microenterprise Types

RNF enterprise activities include manufacturing and processing, transport, trade, services, and miscellaneous activities. According to the HIES data, the services sector is the most dominant activity for all three survey years, accounting for 65.3 percent of all RNF enterprise activities in 2000, 75.8 percent in 2005, and 61.5 percent in 2010 (table 2.9a). Manufacturing and processing follows at a distant second, accounting for only 13.9 percent in 2010, followed by the transport sector at 13.1 percent. But using the long panel survey data, trade (agricultural and non-agricultural) is the most dominant RNF enterprise activity over the survey periods (table 2.9b). And trade of nonagricultural goods takes precedence over agricultural trading. In 2010/11, nonagricultural trade accounted for 38.2 percent of RNF enterprise activities, followed by transport (32.7 percent), agricultural trade (16.7 percent), manufacturing and processing (7.9 percent), and services (4.5 percent).

Salient Features

Certain characteristics of the RNF enterprises have changed little over time, while others have changed substantially (table 2.10). According to the HIES data, the share of registered enterprises increased from 9.9 percent in 2000 to 18.2 percent in 2010 (table 2.10a). In 2010, only 16.7 percent of enterprises were home based using the HIES data. However, according to the long panel survey data, the majority of enterprises in 2010/11 (68.1 percent) were home based (table 2.10b).

Table 2.10 Salient Features of RNF Enterprises in Bangladesh
a. Using HIES data

Enterprise characteristic	2000 (N = 1,427)	2005 (N = 1,426)	2010 (N = 1,909)
Years in business	7.2	9.2	10.0
		(−1.33)	(−2.12)
Share of registered enterprises (%)	9.9	14.7	18.2
		(−3.85)	(−2.61)
Share of home-based enterprises (%)	11.9	14.2	16.7
		(−1.80)	(−1.94)
Months operated per year	10.3	10.7	10.9
		(−3.79)	(−3.00)
Number of workers	1.6	1.7	1.4
		(−0.75)	(2.52)
Share of hired labor in total workforce (%)	11.0	10.0	8.7
		(0.88)	(1.69)
Owner's sex (1 = male, 0 = female)	0.964	0.948	0.955
Owner's age (years)	44.5	46.1	46.7
Owner's education (years)	3.2	3.5	3.5

b. Using long panel survey data

Enterprise characteristic	1991/92 (N = 775)	1998/99 (N = 1,031)	2010/11 (N = 1,089)
Years in business	8.5	9.0	9.5
Share of home-based enterprises (%)	22.3	15.2	68.1
Months operated per year	9.3	9.2	10.1
Owner's sex (1 = male, 0 = female)	0.964	0.917	0.948
Owner's age (years)	41.6	44.3	45.7
Owner's education (years)	2.6	2.3	3.2

Sources: HIES 2000, 2005, and 2010; World Bank/BIDS survey 1991/92 and 1998/99; World Bank/InM survey 2010/11.
Note: Owner's characteristics covered are for head of household that owns the enterprise. Figures in parentheses are t-statistics of the differences with the value from previous year. RNF = rural nonfarm; HIES = Household Income and Expenditure Survey.

Most RNF enterprises rely on family labor. For example, according to the HIES data, hired workers comprised less than 9 percent of the workforce in 2010. The RNF enterprises operate about 10 months out of the year on average, indicating that many work year-round. A similar pattern emerges for RNF enterprises covered in the long panel survey. Though not necessarily home based, the enterprises operate year-round. Males dominate the enterprise sector, with owners averaging less than four years of formal schooling.

Dynamics of RNF Enterprise Activities

To better understand the trends of various elements within RNF enterprise activities over time, we examined their transition, using the long panel survey data.[11] Table 2.11 shows that, in 1998/99, more than half of the surveyed households (about 52 percent) had no nonfarm activities; of those, nearly three-fourths remained without such activities in 2010/11. However, the 2010/11 survey also shows that about 11 percent of those households had adopted nonagriculture-based trade. Of the 6 percent of households engaged in manufacturing and processing in 1998/99, only about 33 percent remained in that sector by 2010/11, with another 40 percent having left RNF enterprise activities altogether. Of the 14 percent of households engaged in transport-related activities (operating or renting out transport vehicles) in 1998/99, about 53 percent of those households were still engaged in this occupation in 2010/11, while 35 percent had left RNF enterprise activities. Nonagriculture-based trade constituted the highest share among RNF enterprise activities in 1998/99—more than 19 percent of the sample. Among those households, about 36 percent did not change their occupation, while nearly 40 percent left RNF enterprise activities. Overall, a significant share of households in 2010/11 was engaged in the same activities as in 1998/99, while about one-third had simply left RNF enterprise activities.

Table 2.11 Transition among RNF Enterprise Activities, 1998/99–2010/11
N = 3,264

	2010/11 (%)→					
1998/99 (% households) ↓	No RNF enterprise activity	Manufacturing and processing	Transport	Agriculture-based trading	Non-agriculture-based trading	Services
No RNF enterprise activity (51.6)	73.7	2.0	7.7	4.5	10.8	1.3
Manufacturing and processing (6.2)	40.2	33.3	7.0	2.6	14.5	2.4
Transport (14.1)	35.2	1.1	53.3	2.7	7.4	0.3
Agriculture-based trade (6.8)	39.3	2.3	10.7	32.2	15.4	0.1
Nonagriculture-based trade (19.3)	39.9	3.8	9.9	7.5	35.6	3.3
Services (2.0)	49.1	4.4	8.6	8.8	25.7	3.4

Sources: World Bank/BIDS survey 1998/99; World Bank-InM survey 2010/11.
Note: RNF = rural nonfarm.

Farm-Sector Linkages

RNF enterprise activities also vary among themselves in ways that are unique compared to other types of activities. One way to capture this variation is to examine the extent to which these activities are linked to the farm sector. Households may engage in several major types of RNF activities linked to the farm sector: (a) agricultural processing, such as oil milling, paddy husking, rice parsing, and flour milling; (b) agricultural equipment-making and repair; and (c) trading of agricultural produce (e.g., rice, fruits, and vegetables). The remaining households are engaged in RNF enterprises that are not linked to the farm sector or have no RNF enterprise activities (table 2.12).

Table 2.12 shows that, among households that had adopted RNF enterprise activities, only about 8 percent were engaged in activities linked to the farm sector, compared to 34–39 percent that had adopted activities not dependent on the farm sector. Obviously, households engaged in RNF enterprise activities linked to the farm sector are subject to the same volatility and seasonality that farm-sector activities face. Conversely, households engaged in RNF enterprise activities not linked to the farm sector (e.g., nonagriculture-based trade, transport, craftworks, furniture-making, and services) can be said to have overcome their dependency on the farm sector, which may indicate a certain progress toward industrialization.

Table 2.13 shows the transition of these households from 1998/99 to 2010/11. Nearly 40 percent of the households involved in farm-based RNF enterprise activities in 1998/99 left these activities by 2010/11, while about 35 percent continued on with them. This means that about 26 percent of households switched from farm-based to purely nonfarm-based activities during the 12-year period between the two surveys. However, a majority (54 percent) of households that were engaged in nonfarm-based enterprise activities in 1998/99 remained in these activities in 2010/11, while 39 percent left RNF enterprise activities. Finally, while the vast majority of nonadopters of RNF activities in 1998/99 remained so in 2010/11, about 21 percent of them had adopted nonfarm-based enterprise activities in 2010/11. Thus, the transition toward purely nonfarm activities appears to have more than compensated for any transition in the opposite direction.

Another way to classify RNF enterprise activities is by their level of complexity, sophistication, and scale. In this exercise, we distinguish between basic activities (including all activities linked to the farm sector and those that are simple in nature and scale) and more advanced ones. For example, making molasses or

Table 2.12 Household Distribution by RNF Enterprise Activity, Based on Farm-Sector Linkage

Household type	1998/99 (%) N = 2,558	2010/11 (%) N = 3,264
With RNF enterprise activities linked to the farm sector	7.9	7.5
With RNF enterprise activities not linked to the farm sector	38.9	34.3
Without RNF enterprise activities	53.2	58.2

Sources: World Bank/BIDS survey 1998/99; World Bank/InM survey 2010/11.
Note: RNF = rural nonfarm.

Table 2.13 Household Transition in RNF Enterprises Based on Farm-Sector Linkage of Activities, 1998/99–2010/11

1998/99 household type	2010/11 household transition		
	With RNF enterprise activities linked to farm sector (%)	With RNF enterprise activities not linked to farm sector (%)	Without RNF enterprise activities (%)
With RNF enterprise activities linked to farm sector	34.8	25.7	39.5
With RNF enterprise activities not linked to farm sector	6.9	54.1	39.0
Without RNF enterprise activities	5.1	21.2	73.8

Sources: World Bank/BIDS survey 1998/99; World Bank/InM survey 2010/11.
Note: RNF = rural nonfarm.

Table 2.14 Distribution of Households by RNF Enterprise, Based on Sophistication Level of Activities

Household type	1998/99 (%) N = 2,558	2010/11 (%) N = 3,264
With basic RNF enterprise activities	28.8	24.7
With advanced RNF enterprise activities	17.9	17.1
Without RNF enterprise activities	53.3	58.2

Sources: World Bank/BIDS survey 1998/99; World Bank/InM survey 2010/11.
Note: RNF = rural nonfarm.

Table 2.15 Household Transition in RNF Enterprises from Basic to Advanced Activities, 1998/99–2010/11

1998/99 household type	2010/11 household transition		
	With basic RNF enterprise activities	With advanced RNF enterprise activities	Without RNF enterprise activities
With basic RNF enterprise activities	47.3	15.0	37.7
With advanced RNF enterprise activities	22.4	36.8	40.8
Without RNF enterprise activities	15.0	11.2	73.8

Sources: World Bank/BIDS survey 1998/99; World Bank/InM survey 2010/11.
Note: RNF = rural nonfarm.

brown sugar (*gur*) is a basic activity, compared to running a bakery, which is a more advanced activity. Other examples are cane or bamboo works (basic activity) and furniture-making (advanced activity) and rickshaw/bicycle repair (basic activity) and automobile repair (advanced activity).

Table 2.14 shows that, among the households engaged in RNF enterprise activities, the majority of those sampled were involved in basic activities for both 1998/99 and 2010/11, at about 29 percent and 25 percent, respectively. Over time, the extent of basic activities dropped somewhat, but this did not lead to an increase in advanced activities, which remained at about 17–18 percent.

Next, we examined the transition within these activities over time. Table 2.15 shows that only 15 percent of households involved in basic RNF enterprise activities in 1998/99 switched to more advanced activities by 2010/11, while about 38 percent left RNF enterprise activities. Among those involved in advanced activities in 1998/99, only about 37 percent remained in such activities, while 22 percent moved backward to basic activities. Among nonadopters in 1998/99, only about 11 percent moved to advanced activities, while 15 percent moved to basic activities.

Thus, we can conclude that the progression from basic activities toward more advanced ones over time did not occur to the extent that one would have hoped. This is probably because demand for advanced activities in rural Bangladesh is still limited. For example, switching from rickshaw/bicycle repair to automobile repair cannot progress steadily without enough automobiles in rural areas. In short, the market for more advanced activities depends on broad-based growth of the rural economy, which has either not yet occurred or is happening at a slow pace.

Determinants of RNF Enterprise Adoption: Does Microfinance Play a Role?

The increasing reliance of Bangladeshi households on the RNF sector, particularly enterprise activities, as a major source of income has perhaps been motivated by the availability of credit through MFIs, especially for the poor. To investigate this assumption, we estimated the determinants of household participation in the RNF sector as a major income source. Given that one-quarter of households operate microenterprise activities and more than one-third of nonfarm income is generated from these activities, a key question is why certain households participate in nonfarm activities while others do not. More specifically, we need to distinguish the precise roles of the underlying factors determining microenterprise participation and determine whether financial institutions play any role in such participation.

To answer these questions, we considered the probability function of RNF enterprise participation (M), expressed by the following equation:

$$M_{ijt} = \alpha^m \tau_t + \beta^m X_{ijt} + \gamma^m V_{jt} + \mu_{ij} + \eta_j + \varepsilon_{ijt}^m, \qquad (2.2)$$

where X_{ijt} is a vector of household (i) characteristics influencing the participation in any RNF enterprise activity in j-th village; V_{jt} is a vector of village-level characteristics, including village electrification, share of irrigated land, prices of consumer goods, program placement of microcredit and other financial institutions, and village-level prices and wages; τ_t represents the dummy variables for the year; α, β, and γ are unknown parameters to be estimated; and ε_{ijt} is a zero-mean disturbance term representing the unmeasured determinants of M_{ijt} that vary across households. It should be noted that household participation is also affected by unobserved household heterogeneity and upazila- or village-level heterogeneity represented by the error terms μ_{ij} and η_j, respectively.

Table 2.16 provides estimates for some of the household and community characteristics determining the adoption of an RNF enterprise activity. Using the HIES data, the regression is a linear probability model of the

Table 2.16 Determinants of RNF Enterprise Growth: Role of MFI Program Placement
Dependent variable is household adoption of RNF activities

Explanatory variable	HIES data (upazila FE) (N = 9,134)		Long panel survey data (household FE) (N = 1,509)	
	Estimates	Mean and standard deviation of explanatory variables	Estimates	Mean and standard deviation of explanatory variables
Year is 2005 (1 = yes, 0 = no)	−0.834*	0.314		
	(−1.87)	(0.464)		
Year is 2010 (1 = yes, 0 = no)	−0.956**	0.345		
	(−2.24)	(0.475)		
Year is 1998/99 (1 = yes, 0 = no)			0.697	0.319
			(1.55)	(0.466)
Year is 2010/11 (1 = yes, 0 = no)			0.507	0.417
			(1.08)	(0.493)
Head's sex (1 = male, 0 = female)	0.080**	0.900	0.220**	0.894
	(4.89)	(0.300)	(6.60)	(0.308)
Head's age (years)	−0.001**	45.4	−0.001*	45.1
	(−2.51)	(13.9)	(−1.88)	(13.7)
Head's education (years)	0.001	2.74	−0.012**	2.92
	(0.49)	(4.08)	(−3.32)	(3.69)
Adult males in household (age > 18)	0.031**	1.32	0.009	1.75
	(4.11)	(0.81)	(1.19)	(1.13)
Adult females in household (age > 18)	0.007	1.37	0.006	1.72
	(1.01)	(0.66)	(0.70)	(1.06)
Log of household land asset (decimal)	−0.042**	111.4	−0.014*	96.2
	(−12.51)	(0.335)	(−1.78)	(244.9)
Log of household nonland asset (Tk.)	0.088**	95,882.4	0.051**	45397.5
	(15.35)	(287365.1)	(4.93)	(90265.8)
Village price of rice (Tk./kg)	0.004	11.1	0.002	9.43
	(0.74)	(2.27)	(0.20)	(2.03)
Village male wage (Tk./day)	−0.0003	100.7	0.002	49.9
	(−1.46)	(52.4)	(1.17)	(23.4)
Village female wage (Tk./day)	0.0002	68.5	0.0004	23.6
	(0.71)	(36.9)	(0.29)	(12.6)
Village has electricity	−0.018	0.673	0.013	0.710
	(−0.73)	(0.459)	(0.36)	(0.454)
Village has paved road (1 = yes, 0 = no)	0.014	0.436		
	(0.84)	(0.495)		
Village road accessible year-round (1= yes, 0 = no)			−0.039	0.853
			(−1.20)	(0.354)
Proportion of irrigated land in village	−0.011	0.672	−0.056	0.648
	(−0.30)	(0.283)	(−1.24)	(0.344)

table continues next page

Table 2.16 Determinants of RNF Enterprise Growth: Role of MFI Program Placement *(continued)*
Dependent variable is household adoption of RNF activities

Explanatory variable	HIES data (upazila FE) (N = 9,134)		Long panel survey data (household FE) (N = 1,509)	
	Estimates	Mean and standard deviation of explanatory variables	Estimates	Mean and standard deviation of explanatory variables
Village has commercial banks (1= yes, 0 = no)	−0.007 (−0.34)	0.234 (0.426)	0.044 (1.16)	0.129 (0.335)
Village has microcredit programs (1= yes, 0 = no)	−0.047 (−1.15)	0.943 (0.232)		
Proportion of village population participating in microcredit programs			0.241** (2.92)	0.517 (0.245)
R^2		0.098		0.065
Mean of the dependent variable		0.239		0.444

Sources: HIES 2000, 2005, and 2010; World Bank/BIDS survey 1991/92 and 1998/99; World Bank/InM survey 2010/11.
Note: Figures in parentheses are t-statistics in Estimates columns and standard deviations in Mean and standard deviation columns. Estimation regressions also control for exogenous characteristics of the initial year and household occupation dummies based on major source of income. RNF = rural nonfarm; MFI = microfinance institution; FE = fixed effects; HIES = Household Income and Expenditure Survey.
Significance level: * = 10 percent, ** = 5 percent.

participation rate among rural households over the three survey periods. Because the upazila was the lowest common unit for which households were interviewed over the three survey periods, an upazila-level FE method can be operationalized (column 1). For the long panel survey data, a household FE method is used (column 2).[12]

Because most RNF activities are family operated, household characteristics play a significant role in their adoption. For example, households with greater land assets are more likely to be engaged in farming than RNF activities. Conversely, those with larger nonland assets are more likely to be involved in RNF activities. Also, since family labor is preferable to (and cheaper than) hired labor, households with more adult male members are more likely to be engaged in RNF activities than those with fewer adult male members, according to the HIES data. With the increase of one adult male member, the probability of a household adopting an RNF enterprise activity rises by nearly 3 percentage points, according to the HIES data. Households headed by individuals with higher levels of education are less likely to be involved in RNF enterprise activities, according to the long panel survey data. Also, male-headed households are more likely to be engaged in RNF enterprise activities.

The placement of microcredit programs in villages can result in higher household participation in RNF enterprise activities, as well as microcredit programs. Thus, these two types of participation are likely to be correlated. For example, a 10 percent increase in microcredit participation by the village population is likely to increase the household participation rate in RNF enterprise activities by 2.4 percentage points.

Summary

Findings from this chapter of a three-period household panel survey suggest that household income generally grew over the 20-year period, as did household share of nonfarm income. Increasingly, rural households have drawn a large percentage of their income (as much as 75 percent in some cases) from nonfarm sources. It is also observed that the majority of rural households—some 70 percent using the HIES data and 90 percent using the long panel survey data—draw their income from both farm and nonfarm sources, indicating that the percentage of farm-only or nonfarm-only households is declining in rural Bangladesh. Whether this finding is an indication of opportunities and diversification of the rural economy or the sheer need to diversify income is not quite obvious. Also, data analysis shows that, in the farming sector, income from agricultural crop production and wages has declined over time, while income from livestock and fisheries has increased. Income from self-employed enterprises comprises about 30 percent of total nonfarm income, and this share is increasing over time. Middle-income households are largely involved in rural enterprise activities; wealthier households engage primarily in farm activities, while low-income households are involved mainly in the agricultural-wage sector.

Over the past 20 years, poverty in Bangladesh has declined substantially. Moderate poverty decreased from a high of 78.0 percent to only 27.5 percent, while extreme poverty declined from 64.8 percent to only 14.0 percent. More interestingly, income growth over the period was nearly 29 percent higher for those households that adopted RNF enterprise activities, compared to nonadopters. Likewise, poverty reduction—both moderate and extreme—was nearly 8 percentage points higher for households with RNF enterprise activities than for their nonadopter counterparts.

Although farm and nonfarm activities are complementary in overall income growth, the direction of change in RNF growth is primarily driven by farm income growth. Estimates show that a 10 percent increase in farm income growth increases nonfarm growth by 6 percent. Thus, farm income growth is a good predictor of RNF growth. At the same time, RNF income growth matters significantly in overall income growth; within the RNF sector, enterprise income growth matters most, promoting both income growth and poverty reduction.

In terms of sector-wise composition, commerce and business account for the majority of RNF enterprise activities, at about 50 percent. In terms of sector dynamics, more than two-thirds of households who were engaged in RNF enterprises in 1998/99 remained active in the sector over time. The remaining one-third left the sector owing to poor performance, becoming comparatively worse off in terms of income and expenditure. However, a small percentage graduated, gradually switching from backward-linkage activities to more advanced ones.

These findings confirm that structural transformation of the RNF enterprise sector has not occurred as rapidly as expected over the last decade (1998/99–2010/11). The findings also show that households with active RNF enterprises located close to growth centers have enjoyed higher rates of return than those with enterprises located far from such centers, highlighting the important role of market demand in RNF enterprise growth.

What causes microenterprise activity to grow over time? Our econometric analysis confirms that, while household assets, education, and other factors mattered, placement of microcredit programs, such as Grameen Bank, also helped rural households to adopt enterprise activities. Moreover, village population density in terms of program participation influenced household participation in rural enterprise activities. As mentioned, the research findings showed that a 10 percent increase in a village population's microcredit participation increased household participation in RNF enterprise activities by 2.4 percentage points, showing a demonstration effect.

Notes

1. The corresponding extreme poverty rates were 44 percent and 21 percent, respectively (table 2.1).

2. While estimation of moderate poverty compares household per capita total expenditure with the aggregate poverty line (allowing for the costs of both food and nonfood items), extreme poverty compares household per capita total expenditure with the food poverty line. More specifically, the calculation of moderate poverty is based on the official poverty line, which includes the food poverty line and an allowance for nonfood expenditures. The food poverty line is calculated by estimating the cost of a food basket needed to maintain the per capita daily caloric requirement (2,120 calories) recommended by the Food and Agriculture Organization (FAO) and the World Health Organization (WHO) (FAO/WHO 1973). For Bangladesh, the food basket contains mostly rice, as well as such other food items as pulses, milk, meat, fish, fruits, and vegetables in specific quantities. The cost of the food basket is calculated using local prices. Extreme poverty, by contrast, is defined by a household's total consumption expenditure on food and nonfood falling short of the food poverty line.

3. The estimates for 2010 are not yet available from the published results.

4. In Bangladesh, the scaling up of programs through the spread of new ideas has been helped by the strong presence of nongovernmental organizations and the density of settlements (Ahluwalia and Mahmud 2004; Mahmud 2008).

5. Malnourishment is measured by the proportion of underweight children for a given age.

6. In many cases, households do not adopt microenterprise activities as their only source of income; rather, they also engage in some farm activities. But those households without farm income that adopt microenterprises often draw income from other nonfarm sources, such as nonfarm wages and salaries, remittances, and interest income. The higher share of microenterprise income observed using the long panel survey can perhaps be explained by the many surveyed households that were members of microcredit programs and who thus adopted RNF activities.

7. Such a transition matrix cannot be prepared for HIES as the data are not observed for the same households over time.

8. The HIES data uses upazila-level, simple fixed effects (FE), and the long panel survey data uses household-level, simple FE. An upazila is the lowest geographical administrative unit in rural Bangladesh, consisting of a number of villages.

9. Their measure of agricultural potential is a crop suitability index reflecting the suitability of a region to grow various cash crops. This index comes from a spatial database of crop suitability constructed by the FAO and the Bangladesh Agricultural Research Council as part of a project to develop a database of agroecological zones in Bangladesh. The index takes into account individual crop characteristics, input/management levels, soil characteristics, hydrologic and climate conditions, and seasonal variability. They argue that since this index is determined by inherent land and water quality, as well as the climate conditions of a location, it helps to avoid the potential endogeneity problems that arise when farm income, productivity, or employment is used as a regressor.

10. They also find that low-return nonfarm jobs are driven by local demand and are distributed much more evenly across areas. Access to smaller rural towns (i.e., a population of about 5,000), as opposed urban-center access, has little effect on nonfarm activities except for nontradable service works.

11. The 1991/92 data are not used for this exercise because the activities categorized under RNF enterprises in 1991/92 are not very compatible with those in 1998/99 or 2010/11. On the other hand, individual activities under RNF enterprises are defined in the same way for both 1998/99 and 2010/11.

12. An alternative to using upazila-level fixed effects (FE) is using upazila-level FE interacted with year times upazila, which controls for upazila-level, time-varying heterogeneity. The results of the alternative model are quite similar to the ones presented in column 1. Similarly, using the long panel survey data, household-level FE does not control for household time-varying heterogeneity. Thus, we used household-level FE, controlling for the initial conditions of households and communities. The results using this second method are quite similar to the household FE results and are therefore not reported here.

Bibliography

Ahluwalia, Isher J., and Wahiduddin Mahmud. 2004. "Economic Transformation and Social Development in Bangladesh." *Economic and Political Weekly* 39 (36): 4009–11.

Deichmann, Uwe, Forhad Shilpi, and Renos Vakis. 2009. "Urban Proximity, Agricultural Potential and Rural Non-farm Employment: Evidence from Bangladesh." *World Development* 37 (3): 645–60.

FAO/WHO (Food and Agriculture Organization/World Health Organization).1973. *Energy and Protein Requirements*. FAO Nutrition Meetings Report Series 52 and WHO Technical Report Series 522, report of a Joint FAO/WHO ad hoc Expert Committee. Geneva: Food and Agriculture Organization and World Health Organization.

Foster, Andrew D., and Mark R. Rosenzweig. 2004. "Agricultural Productivity Growth, Rural Economic Diversity, and Economic Reforms: India, 1970–2000." *Economic Development and Cultural Change* 52 (3): 509–42.

Haggblade, S., P. Hazell, and T. Reardon. 2010. "The Rural Non-Farm Economy: Prospects for Growth and Poverty Reduction." *World Development* 38 (10): 1429–41.

Johnson, D. Gale. 2000. "Population, Food and Knowledge." *American Economic Review* 90 (1): 1–14.

Johnston, Bruce, and John Mellor. 1961. "The Role of Agriculture in Economic Development." *American Economic Review* 4: 566–93.

Khandker, Shahidur R. 2005. "Microfinance and Poverty: Evidence Using Panel Data from Bangladesh." *World Bank Economic Review* 19 (2): 263–86.

Khandker, Shahidur R., and Wahiduddin Mahmud. 2012. *Seasonal Hunger and Public Policies: Evidence from Northwest Bangladesh.* Washington, DC: World Bank.

Lanjouw, Peter, and Gershon Feder. 2001. "Rural Non-Farm Activities and Rural Development: From Experience towards Strategy." Rural Development Strategy Background Paper, World Bank, Washington, DC.

Lanjouw, J. O., and P. Lanjouw. 2001. "The Rural Non-Farm Sector: Issues and Evidence from Developing Countries." *Agricultural Economics* 26 (1): 1–23.

Mahmud, Wahiduddin. 2008. "Social Development: Pathways, Surprises, and Challenges." *Indian Journal of Human Development* 2 (1): 79–92.

Mahmud, Wahiduddin, and Anis Chowdhury. 2008. "South Asian Economic Development: Impressive Achievements but Continuing Challenges." In *Handbook on the South Asian Economies*, edited by Wahiduddin Mahmud and Anis Chowdhury, 1–24. Cheltenham, UK: Edward Elgar.

Mellor, J. W. 1976. *The New Economic Growth: A Strategy for India and the Developing World.* Ithaca, NY: Cornell University.

Pitt, M., and S. Khandker. 1998. "The Impact of Group-Based Credit Programs on Poor Households in Bangladesh: Does Gender of the Participant Matter?" *Journal of Political Economy* 106: 958–96.

Ranis, G., and F. Stewart. 1973. "Rural Nonagricultural Activities in Development: Theory Application." *Journal of Development Economics* 40: 75–101.

UNICEF (United Nations Children's Fund). 2011. *The State of the World's Children 2010/11.* New York: UNICEF.

World Bank. 2012. *Bangladesh: Towards Accelerated, Inclusive, and Sustainable Growth—Opportunities and Challenges.* Washington, DC: World Bank.

CHAPTER 3

Institutional Growth and MFI Performance

Introduction

As documented in chapter 2, microfinance growth has helped expand rural nonfarm (RNF) enterprises, the major source of rural income growth and poverty reduction. However, it is important to examine the performances of microfinance institution (MFIs) in terms of their cost-efficiencies in providing financial and other services to the poor before we assess their impacts on a variety of household welfare indicators. Microfinance programs in Bangladesh have been running for more than two decades, primarily with the social goal of outreach to the rural poor to enhance nonfarm employment and income generation in order to lift the poor out of poverty.[1] More than 90 percent of microcredit borrowers in Bangladesh are women. By 2012, Grameen Bank, Bangladesh Rural Advancement Committee (BRAC), and other MFIs had reached more than 10 million rural households in Bangladesh, representing nearly 60 percent of the rural population; by that year, annual disbursement of microfinance programs was nearly US$1.8 billion, with an outstanding balance of US$1.5 billion. Palli Karma-Sahayak Foundation (PKSF), the country's wholesale microfinance lending facility, has orchestrated microfinance penetration through a wide network of small but highly competitive partner organizations (POs).[2]

This chapter reviews the outstanding success of MFIs in Bangladesh in terms of membership growth, lending volume, loan recovery, savings mobilization, and other MFI growth indicators. Using aggregate program-level data, it investigates MFI funding sources, including savings mobilization from members and donors. It also examines the effect of timing of the entry into the Bangladesh microfinance market on subsequent performance in a competitive environment. Understanding MFI institutional growth and performance is a prerequisite for a better understanding of the context in which microfinance-induced benefits are accrued to households, individuals, and rural economic activities (including the nonfarm and farm sectors). With this objective in mind, we present this limited institutional analysis of microfinance as it emerged over the years in Bangladesh.

Trends in MFI Growth Indicators

The MFIs, which started in the 1970s, predominantly with Grameen Bank and BRAC, grew considerably in both scale and scope over the next few decades, particularly during the 1990s. That decade witnessed the entry of the Association for Social Advancement (ASA) and other major nongovernmental organization (NGO)–MFIs, the increased availability of donor funding, and the formation of PKSF in 1994. With the rapid establishment of new branches throughout rural Bangladesh, intensified disbursements, and expansion of service portfolios, microfinance operations grew at a phenomenal rate (box 3.1).

Clientele Outreach and Loan Disbursement

MFI membership grew from about 8 million in 1996 to more than 34 million by 2010. Figure 3.1 shows that membership grew steadily in 1996–2008, after which it started to decline, albeit slowly.

MFI membership grew by well over 10 percent annually during 2003–08, after which growth turned negative due to the decline in non-Grameen MFI membership (table 3.1).

Table 3.1 also shows the annual growth in outstanding borrowers of the MFIs. Like membership growth, the increase in outstanding borrowers grew at a rapid pace before becoming negative in 2008, perhaps indicating a certain degree of market saturation.

With steady membership growth, MFI loan disbursement also increased steadily (figure 3.2). The amount disbursed was slightly more than Tk. 32 billion

---

Box 3.1 Snapshot of Microfinance Expansion in Bangladesh

Microfinance expansion in Bangladesh can be divided into three phases:

1. Pre-1994. This phase of limited expansion focused mainly on rural nonfarm activities via mobilization of group-based savings and lending (Khandker 1998).
2. 1995–2004. This phase featured rapid expansion; Palli Karma-Sahayak Foundation emerged as the wholesale funding agency, and many small nongovernmental organizations entered the market with access to institutional funds for their own lending (versus relying on the savings of borrowers).
3. Post-2004. This phase has witnessed fierce competition among the microfinance institutions (MFIs). A variety of microfinance and other noncredit products, including skills-based training and marketing assistance, have been developed to meet the specific needs of clientele, including programs for the ultra-poor.

Increasingly, urban areas have been targeted, and the newer emerging MFIs have placed greater emphasis on profitability. To temper risky borrowing and lending during this expansion, the Bangladesh government passed legislation in 2006 requiring all MFIs to be licensed and establishing the Microcredit Regulatory Authority (MRA) to monitor MFI activities and targeting. In 2011, the MRA also set a 27 percent ceiling on interest rates for loans.

Figure 3.1 Growth Trend in Microfinance Membership, 1996–2010

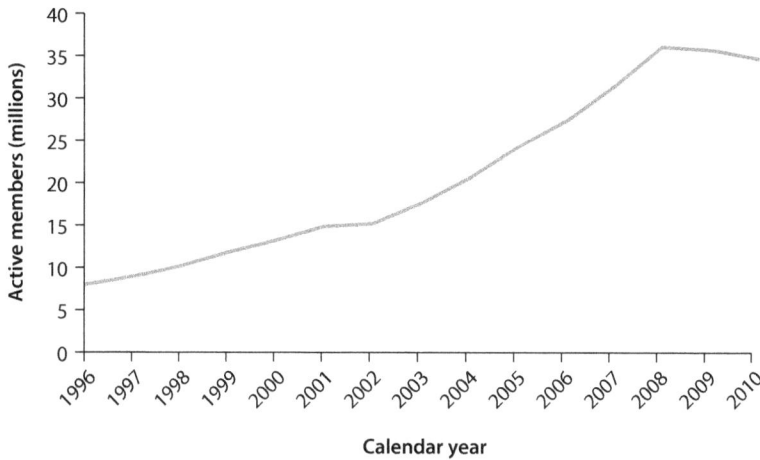

Sources: CDF 1996–2007; Grameen Bank 2010; InM and CDF 2008–10.
Note: The findings reported in this figure are provisional.

Table 3.1 Yearly Growth in Microfinance Clientele in Bangladesh, 2003–10
percent

Calendar year	Active members	Outstanding borrowers
2003	15.71	17.12
2004	16.49	15.88
2005	17.85	21.25
2006	12.50	16.14
2007	14.39	16.11
2008	14.47	16.35
2009	−0.55	−9.21
2010	−3.04	0.54

Sources: CDF 1996–2007; Grameen Bank 2010; InM and CDF 2008–10.

in 1997, growing to about Tk. 372 billion by 2010. Like membership growth, loan disbursement also fell between 2009 and 2010.

How Much Savings Was Mobilized?

Savings for the MFIs was about Tk. 8 billion in 1996, increasing steadily to Tk. 161 billion by 2010 (figure 3.3). Net savings growth appears to have been little affected by the drop in membership in 2009/10. By itself, savings is a good measure of program outreach and benefit; however, it often makes more sense to express it as a percentage of loans outstanding.

The trend in savings as a percentage of loans outstanding fluctuated somewhat, unlike savings alone, which grew monotonically. Savings as a percentage of loans outstanding dropped from close to 50 percent in 1996 to a little over 40 percent in 1998, before jumping to about 64 percent in 2004 and then falling

Figure 3.2 MFI Loan Disbursement Trend in Bangladesh, 1997–2010

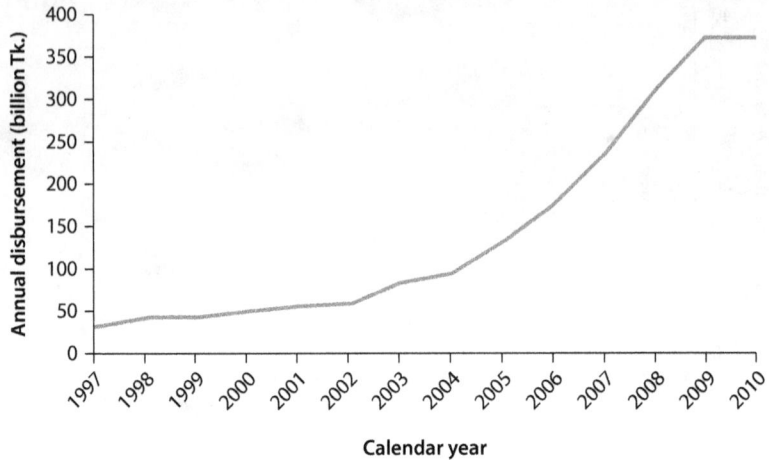

Sources: CDF 1996–2007; Grameen Bank 2010; InM and CDF 2008–10.
Note: The findings reported in this figure are provisional. MFI = microfinance institution.

Figure 3.3 Savings Mobilized by MFIs in Bangladesh, 1996–2010

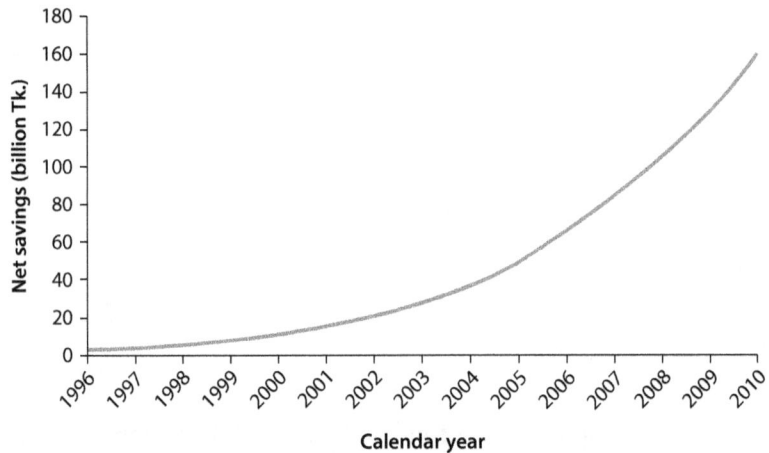

Sources: CDF 1996–2007; Grameen Bank 2010; InM and CDF 2008–10.
Note: The findings reported in this figure are provisional. MFI = microfinance institution.

to 45 percent over the next four years (figure 3.4). It eventually recovered to attain its highest value of 69 percent in 2009. Since cumulative savings increased monotonically over time, the zigzag pattern observed in figure 3.4 is due entirely to the volume of loans outstanding.

Loans outstanding can dip in a particular period in two ways: (a) low loan recovery rate and (b) high credit demand for extraneous factors. The 1998 dip in the ratio of savings to loans outstanding was due to a major flood, which resulted in slack economic activities, in turn, causing loan recovery to fall. Similarly, the

Figure 3.4 Savings as a Percentage of MFI Loans Outstanding in Bangladesh, 1996–2010

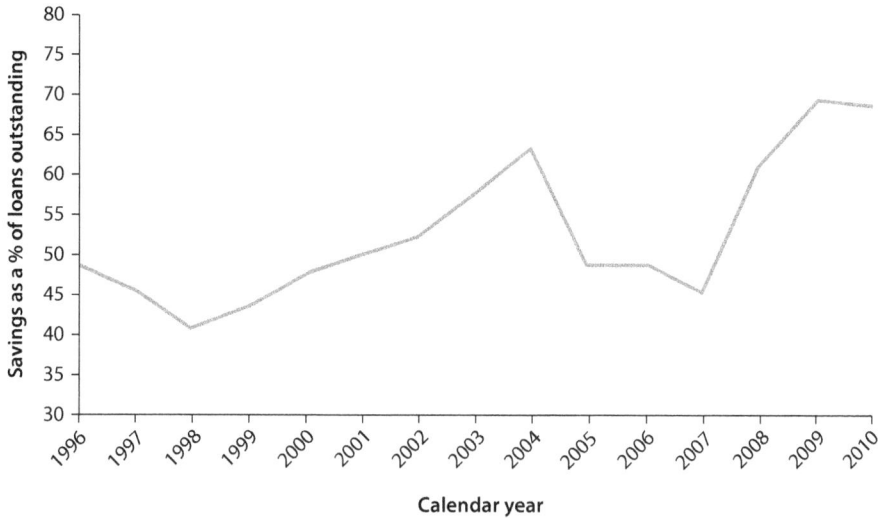

Sources: CDF 1996–2007; Grameen Bank 2010; InM and CDF 2008–10.
Note: The findings reported in this figure are provisional. MFI = microfinance institution.

2007 dip in the ratio was due to the major economic slowdown experienced worldwide, along with political turmoil witnessed inside Bangladesh. Thus, during both periods of economic stress, loans outstanding climbed too high relative to cumulative savings mobilized, compared to other periods. This finding suggests that MFI performance is not entirely insensitive to the aggregate economy or political turmoil affecting an economy. However, the low performance measured by the savings-to-loan ratio was temporary; in both cases, the MFIs bounced back within a year or two from their dip status.

Growth and Sector Composition of MFI Lending

Bangladesh's outstanding success in MFI coverage in terms of membership growth has been accompanied by a remarkable growth in loan disbursement. Figure 3.5 shows that loan disbursement in 1996 amounted to less than Tk. 50 billion, which increased to Tk. 220 billion in 2010, with an average growth rate of almost 25 percent per year; over the same period, there was a sevenfold increase in the growth of loan disbursements per borrower.

Table 3.2 compares the sector-wise distribution of loans in 2006 and 2010. The figures shown are taken from a balanced panel of 129 MFIs in Bangladesh. Small and medium-size enterprises (SMEs) dominated the industry portfolio, explaining more than two-thirds of the total MFI loan volume. Agriculture-related activities had the second highest share; however, agriculture comprises a diverse set of activities, including crop production, fisheries, livestock and poultry, and food processing. Livestock and poultry accounted for the highest single

Figure 3.5 Dynamics of MFI Loan Disbursement, 1995–2010

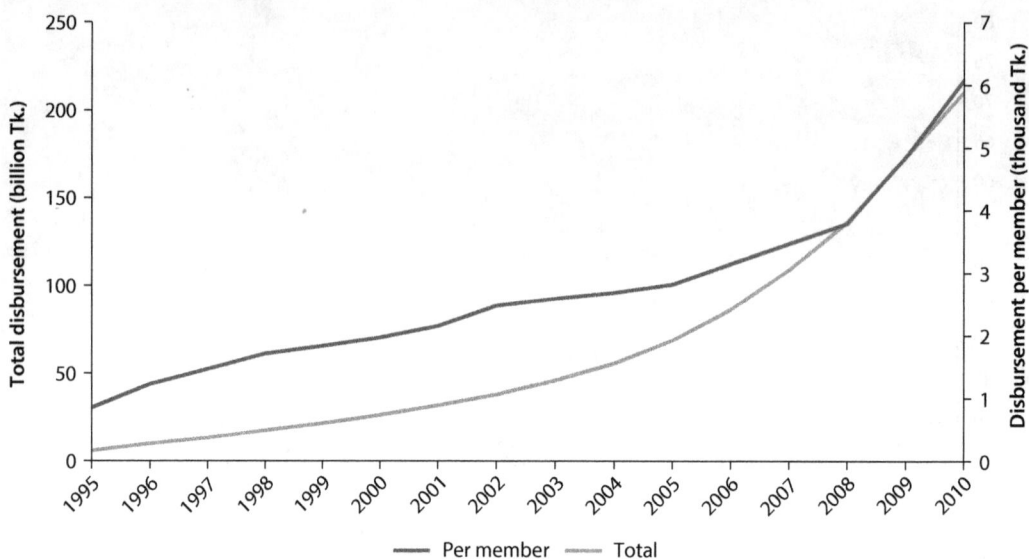

Sources: Bangladesh Microfinance Statistics 2006–11; CDF Statistics 1998.
Note: MFI = microfinance institution.

Table 3.2 Comparison of Sector-Wise Distribution of Microfinance Disbursement

	Year	
Sector	*2006*	*2010*
Crop production	11	18
Fisheries	4	3
Livestock and poultry	14	6
Cottage and food processing	6	2
Transport	3	4
Health	0	1
Education	0	1
Housing	1	1
SMEs[a]	61	64

Source: Calculations based on a balanced panel of 129 institutions among microfinance institutions
(Bangladesh Microfinance Statistics 2007, 2011).
Note: SMEs = small and medium-size enterprises.
a. SMEs generally include trade and manufacturing.

activity in agriculture-related activities, while crop production had the second largest loan recipient activity over time.

To illustrate the dynamics of microlending in Bangladesh, figure 3.6 compares the sector-wise distribution for the above-mentioned years: 2006 and 2010. As shown, in 2006, SMEs, comprising small trade and manufacturing, accounted for 61 percent of the MFI loan portfolio, and their share increased slightly to 64 percent in 2010. By contrast, agriculture-related activities accounted for 35 percent of the MFI portfolio in 2006, falling to 29 percent in 2010. One can

Figure 3.6 Sector-Wise Disbursement of Microfinance

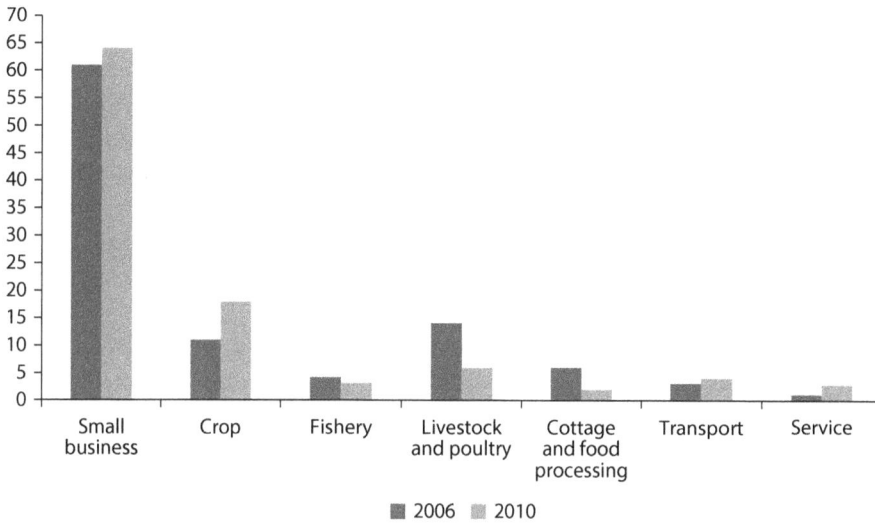

Source: Calculations based on a balanced panel of 129 institutions among microfinance institutions (Bangladesh Microfinance Statistics 2007, 2011).
Note: Small business comprises trade and manufacturing; service covers health, education, and housing.

attribute this drop to the increasing constraints to investing in the livestock, poultry, and fisheries sectors between 2006 and 2010. Such constraints might include, but not be limited to, a global crisis in the poultry sector, higher salinity in southwestern areas, and tightened export of fisheries.

Have MFIs Drifted from Their Social Objective?

MFIs have traditionally targeted poor rural women through generating self-employment in the RNF sector in order to empower them in the household decision-making process. But competition among NGO-MFIs for the same target group has become fierce over time. Given the phenomenal growth and diversification of Bangladesh's microfinance programs over the years, as well as recent policy attempts to regulate this growth, an obvious question arises: What direction is microfinance taking with respect to its original socially motivated outlook?

Recent Trends

Microfinance can have short-term effects on augmenting income for poor households and smoothing consumption amid seasonality and other shocks. At the same time, this system of lending has created such innovations as group liability contracts and dynamic incentives, showing that many of the poor, including women and other vulnerable groups, could be profitable clients for financial institutions. In that sense, microfinance has become a broad-based policy instrument in developing countries to assist the poor.[3] These advantages have also drawn profit-motivated lending institutions into microfinance markets.

But as microfinance becomes more widespread, profit-seeking behavior increases, and household borrowing rises rapidly across various groups, policy makers need to understand whether the benefits are sustainable in the long run—not only in terms of those received by borrowers, but also in terms of timely loan recovery by the MFIs amid an expanding, diversified client base.

Much scrutiny has followed the rapid expansion and broadening of the range of players in microfinance markets, with many arguing that many MFIs are increasingly generating cycles of indebtedness by charging prohibitive interest rates and targeting households that lack the means to repay.[4] As a result, many policy makers have questioned whether the MFIs can continue to sustainably serve the needs of the poor.

A handful of studies have examined recent trends in MFI strategies and performance as microfinance markets have grown more saturated. Cull, Demirgüç-Kunt, and Morduch (2009), for example, provided an interesting overview of MFI profitability and incentives over time, contrasting the early characteristics of MFIs around the world in the 1970s (government-run, with highly subsidized interest rates and relaxed loan recovery), the 1980s (increased targeting of nonfarm enterprises over farmers), and the 1990s (more emphasis on profitability, with rising interest rates). They concluded that microfinance is likely to take multiple paths going forward, as commercial investment in microfinance seeks a clientele that differs from the more socially oriented institutions currently serving poorer customers.

Multiple Mechanisms at Work

A competitive environment will likely lower transaction costs, inducing the MFIs to offer borrowers lower interest rates and penalties for nonrepayment. Easier borrowing terms can improve outreach and credit access for poor households constrained by lack of available credit. This will draw in a larger pool of borrowers, including potentially risky clients that may borrow across multiple MFIs and have high default rates. Increasingly, clientele may borrow from multiple sources, as evidenced by experience in Uganda (McIntosh, de Janvry, and Sadoulet 2005) and Bolivia (Vogelgesang 2003). Yet the policy perspective is that more entrepreneurial clients better able to repay can be found to borrow larger amounts than can the more vulnerable, supply-constrained borrowers found among women and the ultra-poor.

McIntosh and Wydick (2005) showed that MFIs tend to cross-subsidize across clients. They use higher returns on more profitable borrowers to subsidize their costs of lending to poorer ones. However, when new MFIs enter the market, they create competition for more profitable borrowers, reducing these rents. As a result, less profitable borrowers may end up being dropped. Their study also argued that competition can aggravate existing asymmetric information problems, as information on borrowers is diluted across a larger group of lenders (see also Hoff and Stiglitz 1998). This worsens the terms of loan contracts for borrowers (e.g., loan interest rates). Those borrowers with a greater demand for credit then begin to obtain multiple loans, creating overlapping debt problems that further deteriorate the terms of loan contracts for all borrowers.

Asymmetric information problems, compounded by many more lenders in the microfinance market, have led to stricter monitoring by agencies and centralized coordination across MFIs to help address the issues of overlapping debt and growing default rates.[5] But greater regulation may actually limit MFI outreach to poorer individuals. Cull, Demirgüç-Kunt, and Morduch (2011) examined the effects of financial regulation on MFI targeting and performance, using 2003/04 data from the Microfinance Information eXchange (MIX) on about 350 leading MFIs across 67 countries.[6] They found that, while regulation of MFIs might help to control the problem of adverse borrower selection, it may also lower social welfare as more profit-oriented MFIs work to sustain their profit rates while limiting access to groups that are more costly to reach, including women and the poor. Older, less profit-oriented MFIs may not limit their outreach, but may see their profit rates fall with greater regulation. Tracking the targeting strategies and performance of older versus newer MFIs is an important factor for understanding the direction that microfinance is taking, and, as a result, identifying appropriate policies for managing the growth and development of these groups.[7]

Obviously, local economic conditions matter in MFI performance. Ahlin, Lin, and Maio (2011), for example, used MIX data to show that country context is a large determinant of MFI performance. MFIs are more likely to cover costs where economic growth is stronger; and those in financially deeper economies have lower default and operating costs and charge lower interest rates. In addition, certain longstanding NGOs within countries may not necessarily change their objective function over time. Salim (2013), for example, showed that actual branch placement decisions of these institutions are inconsistent with a profit-motivated objective function. Therefore, competition does not necessarily bring changes that lead away from the social objective of microfinance targeting.

Evidence of Competitiveness in MFI Performance[8]

Bangladesh's extensive and intensive MFI coverage provides a quite interesting context for examining some of the major supply-side issues related to the performance of MFIs, including their loan recovery ability from rural borrowers, recent portfolio shifts across various lending and savings products, product pricing trends, and targeting strategies. In Bangladesh, where the number of registered MFIs has increased from about 50 to more than 750 over a 20-year period (1985–2005), more than 60 percent of rural households are microfinance members, and more than 90 percent of villages now have access to at least one registered microfinance program (CDF 2006).

How Do Restructured Programs Affect Borrower Benefits?

Over time, Bangladesh's group-based microfinance program has been variously restructured. For example, after 1998, Grameen Bank replaced its strict weekly loan repayment schedule with more flexible schemes. BRAC, ASA, PKSF, and other group-based lenders have undertaken similar restructuring.

Are program benefits changing over time because of changing structures of microcredit programs? Given the increased competition among many MFIs in rural Bangladesh, terms and conditions are being eased in ways that may allow a single borrower to secure loans from multiple sources at the same time. Is this a reflection of supply constraints on borrowers from a single source? Has it led to rising indebtedness with lower loan repayments?

To answer these key research questions, a study by Khandker, Koolwal, and Badruddoza (2013) examined NGO-MFI performance and targeting decisions in Bangladesh during 2005–10, a highly competitive period for the country's microfinance. To address rapid market entry, the Bangladesh government introduced new regulatory policies in 2006/07, the most important of which was 2006 legislation requiring the licensing of all MFIs and establishment of the Microcredit Regulatory Authority (MRA) to guide and monitor MFI strategies.[9] Thus, the study period spanned conditions before and after these regulations were introduced.

Investigating Performance and Targeting

The study used an MFI-level panel from the 2005–10 rounds of the Bangladesh Credit and Development Forum (CDF) survey to examine the role of initial local and MFI characteristics, including age, on MFI performance.[10] Also, various indicators were used to measure the extent of MFI competition on MFI performance and targeting. The study sample comprised 117 NGO-MFIs, including Bangladesh's three largest NGOs (BRAC, ASA, and Proshika). MFI banks, including Grameen Bank, were technically excluded from the sample; however, several Grameen-named NGOs were covered (e.g., Grameen Social and Economic Advancement and Grameen Prosar Society).[11] The sample NGO-MFIs were surveyed consistently over the six-year period. The CDF survey focused on supply-side information on credit-based NGOs, including their portfolios, return rates, and other decisions related to their location, targeting, and expansion. It did not contain direct indicators of competition that each MFI was facing over the period; however, it did include data on the timing of inception of each MFI, which can affect their strategies in a competitive environment.

The MFIs were grouped according to whether they began operations (a) before 1990, (b) in 1991–95, (c) in 1996–2000, or (d) after 2001. This categorization was used as a proxy for the extent of competition that the MFIs were facing at their outset, which likely affected their initial strategies. The CDF data also elicited a number of interesting indicators about how the MFIs were performing over the period. In addition to analyzing MFI scope and coverage across urban and rural areas, covering such policies as interest rates on savings and loans, the study examined various measures of borrower riskiness, share of members without loans, extent of savings products in MFI portfolios, and loan recovery rates by gender and sector (agriculture and nonagriculture).

Features of Key Indicators across Years

Table 3.3 presents summary statistics on outcomes of particular interest primarily in rural areas (e.g., whether competition among lenders caused declining interest rates or easing of loan terms over the period).[12] As shown, interest rates on savings fell slightly over the period, while interest rates on loans remained fairly flat; however, trends in these variables varied by age of MFI, as discussed below. Loan coverage appears to have expanded over the period, as reflected by trends in average share of net savings to loans disbursed, as well as a decline in the share of active members without a loan. The share of borrowers at risk or overdue, however, also increased rapidly between 2005 and 2010. In rural areas, that share rose from about 6 percent to 10 percent. Loan recovery rates

Table 3.3 Descriptive Statistics on Selected MFI Outcomes, 2005–10

Indicator	Year (%)					
	2005	2006	2007	2008	2009	2010
Interest rate on savings	5.70	5.66	5.47	5.35	5.27	5.37
	[1.70]	[1.06]	[1.03]	[0.97]	[0.94]	[0.75]
Interest rate on loans	13.45	14.08	13.41	13.21	13.43	13.87
	[3.74]	[2.03]	[2.92]	[3.15]	[2.64]	[1.89]
Share of net savings to loans disbursed, rural areas	9.00	9.00	7.00	6.00	6.00	5.00
	[0.09]	[0.07]	[0.06]	[0.04]	[0.06]	[0.03]
Share of active members without loans, rural areas	11.00	8.00	6.00	6.00	6.00	7.00
	[0.19]	[0.15]	[0.10]	[0.11]	[0.09]	[0.13]
Share of at-risk borrowers, rural areas	6.00	5.00	5.00	8.00	8.00	1.00
	[0.13]	[0.09]	[0.09]	[0.13]	[0.13]	[0.15]
Share of overdue rural borrowers	6.00	7.00	6.00	8.00	8.00	1.00
	[0.12]	[0.11]	[0.10]	[0.13]	[0.13]	[0.15]
Loan recovery rate, rural women	83.30	85.82	86.68	83.28	85.79	87.10
	[35.75]	[33.13]	[32.15]	[35.71]	[32.05]	[31.09]
Loan recovery rate, rural men	44.36	46.77	53.34	56.74	58.70	56.52
	[48.33]	[49.08]	[48.83]	[48.49]	[47.78]	[48.29]
Share of loans disbursed, agricultural crops	16.00	17.00	18.00	2.00	22.00	2.00
	[0.15]	[0.18]	[0.17]	[0.17]	[0.19]	[0.17]
Share of loans disbursed, small business	46.00	45.00	47.00	48.00	48.00	48.00
	[0.24]	[0.25]	[0.24]	[0.24]	[0.25]	[0.26]
Share of loans disbursed, housing	3.00	3.00	3.00	5.00	5.00	5.00
	[0.05]	[0.05]	[0.05]	[0.09]	[0.09]	[0.09]
Loan recovery rate, agricultural crops	52.98	58.59	73.51	68.71	73.36	78.28
	[48.88]	[48.45]	[42.81]	[45.13]	[41.75]	[39.17]
Loan recovery rate, small business	61.41	67.65	83.50	76.61	79.79	86.59
	[47.60]	[45.83]	[35.16]	[41.18]	[37.68]	[31.06]
Loan recovery rate, housing	34.51	42.04	45.64	32.96	33.24	32.66
	[46.15]	[48.35]	[48.32]	[46.54]	[46.38]	[46.42]

Source: CDF survey 2005–10.
Note: Standard deviations are shown in brackets. MFI = microfinance institution.

increased over time. Agrifinance had the highest increase over the period (compared to small business and housing loans), and recovery rates in this sector also accelerated over the period.

Trends in Outcomes

The CDF yearly data show the dynamics of changing MFI characteristics over time, revealing some interesting differences by age of MFI; the results are summarized here (for details, see Khandker, Koolwal, and Badruddoza 2013). While the newer MFIs tended to be headquartered primarily in rural areas, they tended to have a much greater share of urban members compared to the older MFIs. For most MFIs, interest rates on savings tended to decline gradually over the period, but rates remained slightly higher in 2009/10 for the newest group of MFIs. Interest rates on loans tended to be 1–2 percentage points higher for the newer MFIs. Clearly, a lower trend was exhibited in both savings and lending for all MFI clientele after 2006 when the Bangladesh Bank (the central bank) established the MRA. Whether these declines resulted from the MRA's regulations remains a question.[13]

Except for the oldest MFIs, where the trend has been fairly flat, the share of active members without loans across the newer MFIs appears to have increased over the period. Interestingly, the newer MFIs offered a much greater share of savings products in their 2005 portfolios; by 2010, however, that share had declined substantially, converging toward the older MFIs. Also, the newer MFIs did not necessarily have higher shares of risky borrowers. While those that were started in the 1996–2000 period exhibited increased overdue/default rates, the oldest ones experienced the highest surge in loan defaults. For MFIs that began after 2000, default rates either fell or rose at a more gradual pace compared to other groups. However, for all MFIs, the surge in loan defaults started in 2007.

MFI Funding Sources

At the outset of Bangladesh's microfinance movement, donor funding was substantial (Khandker 1998). Such early starters as Grameen Bank and BRAC achieved self-sufficiency and thus did not require subsidized funds. Over time, reliance on donor funds declined substantially, from 16 percent in 1997 to just 2 percent in 2010 (figure 3.7). Yet smaller and more recently established NGO-MFIs require donor and subsidized funds for their institutional development. In recent years, the PKSF wholesale agency, with government and World Bank and other donor support, has provided NGO-MFIs that lacked access to international donors a cheaper source of funding for on-lending and institutional development.

Table 3.4 highlights how MFIs have increasingly relied on their own funding sources over time. In 1997, PKSF accounted for more than 9 percent of total MFI funds and less than 11 percent in 2010, despite the rapid expansion of

Figure 3.7 Comparison of MFI Funding Distribution over Time

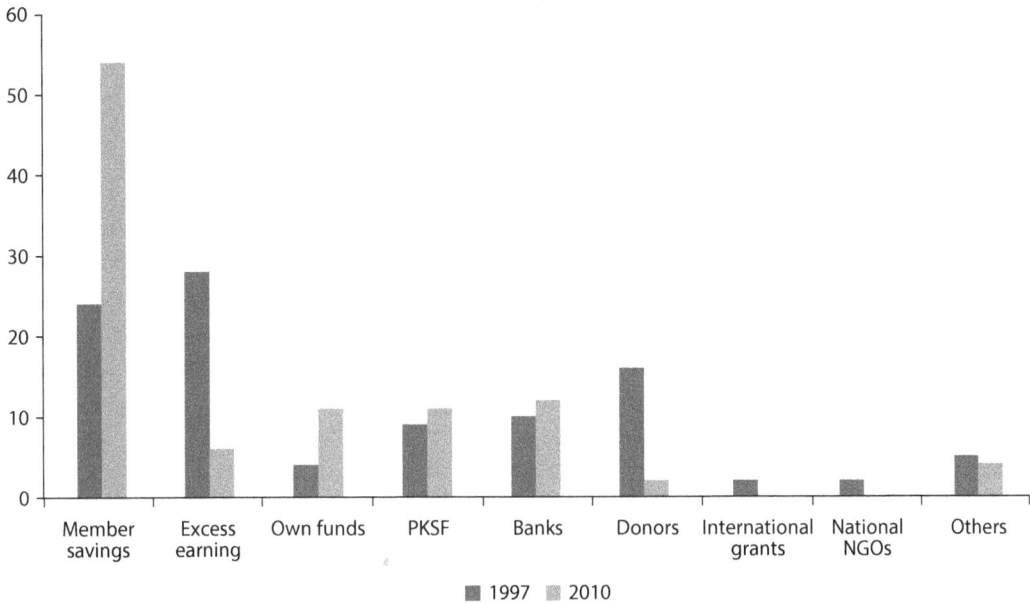

Sources: Bangladesh Microfinance Statistics 2006–11; CDF Statistics 1998.
Note: MFI = microfinance institution; PKSF = Palli Karma-Sahayak Foundation; NGO = nongovernmental organization.

Table 3.4 Percent Distribution of MFI Funding Sources, 1997, 2005–10

Year	Member savings	Excess earnings	Own funds	PKSF	Bank	Donor	International grant	National NGO[a]	Other[b]
1997	24.0	28.0	3.9	9.5	9.7	16.0	1.6	2.4	4.8
2005	29.9	25.9	4.0	13.5	17.0	7.6	0.3	0.4	1.4
2006	24.7	22.9	4.9	14.7	20.0	5.2	0.3	0.2	7.1
2007	20.9	22.9	5.6	15.6	23.9	4.6	0.3	1.1	5.2
2008	25.8	18.1	5.8	21.6	16.0	3.0	0.3	0.2	9.2
2009	47.2	5.5	13.9	11.1	12.2	2.1	0.1	0.1	7.9
2010	54.4	6.3	11.4	10.5	11.6	1.8	0.2	0.0	3.8

Source: Bangladesh Microfinance Statistics 2006–11; CDF Statistics 1998.
Note: MFI = microfinance institution; PKSF = Palli Karma-Sahayak Foundation; NGO = nongovernmental organization; ASA = Association for Social Advancement; BRAC = Bangladesh Rural Advancement Committee; CDF = Credit and Development Forum.
a. National NGOs include ASA, BRAC, CDF, and Proshika.
b. Other includes individual funding and insurance.

microfinance activities. Similarly, borrowing from commercial banks explained less than 10 percent of MFI funds in 1997 and close to 12 percent in 2010. Over the same period, member savings mobilized by the MFIs and own funds grew by about 30 percent and 8 percent, respectively, while excess earnings of the MFIs fell by about 22 percent. In 2010, member savings and excess earnings together accounted for nearly two-thirds of total funds used for on-lending and institutional development. This demonstrates an overall self-reliance of MFIs in Bangladesh from donor support.

Cost versus Operational Efficiency

The concept of cost efficiency is a measure by which to judge an organization's performance in managing its operations. Organizational efficiency can be measured in various ways, one of which is to determine whether an organization operates at the lowest cost of inputs for a given quantity of output. The Consultative Group to Assist the Poor (CGAP), a consortium of 28 development agencies that support microfinance, provides nine ratios for measuring the efficiency and productivity of MFIs (CGAP 2003). The most common measure of efficiency, operational efficiency, is defined by operating expenses as a percentage of average gross loan portfolio or total assets.

A second way to measure efficiency is to assess an organization's financial efficiency, determined by whether the cost per unit of principal lent is equal to the rate of interest borrowers are charged. This means that, to meet the financial efficiency criterion, a program should charge an interest rate that generates revenue from its operations equal to or greater than the cost per unit of principal lent. This is called the break-even interest rate, expressed by the following equation:

$$r \geq (i + \alpha + \rho)/(1 - \rho), \tag{3.1}$$

where r equals the interest rate charged per unit of principal lent, i equals the cost of raising loanable funds per unit of principal lent, α is the expected cost of administering and supervising a loan per unit of principal lent, and ρ is the expected financial loss per unit of principal lent or simply the loan default rate.

Table 3.5 presents the break-even interest rate and other relevant indicators of financial efficiency for alternative sets of MFIs in Bangladesh over a six-year period (2006–11). It appears that scale of operations is an important factor for determining the extent of an organization's financial efficiency. Grameen Bank, established in 1983 as a specialized bank for microfinance operations, was financially efficient over the period. In 2004, its break-even interest rate was only 8.9 percent against its lending rate of 18.48 percent; in 2007, its break-even rate was 10.3 percent against its 18.94 percent lending rate. The findings show that all of the larger MFIs were financially more efficient than the smaller NGO-MFIs. Thus, scale of operations as measured by, for example, volume of loans outstanding, is an important indicator of an MFI's financial success.

A Global Perspective

To put the performance of Bangladesh's MFIs in a global context, the study examined the most recent (2004–12) operational efficiency data and critical performance indicators for Bangladesh's leading MFIs, relative to those of India, Indonesia, Mexico, Thailand, and Vietnam (annex 3A). The analysis showed that women comprise the overwhelming majority of beneficiaries in many such

Table 3.5 Operational Efficiency of MFIs in Bangladesh by Size and Year, 2006–11

Indicator	Small	Medium	Large	Very large	Grameen Bank
2006					
Total borrowers (no.)	6,320	43,151	200,913	2,622,673	5,960,000
Total members (no.)	8,156	52,202	231,622	3,167,839	6,908,704
Loans outstanding (million Tk.)[a]	26.80	184.00	913.00	12356.85	33259.14
Lending interest rate (%)	20	18	18	26	21
Cost per Tk. loan (Tk.)[b]	0.23	0.21	0.17	0.12	0.10
Profit (million Tk.)	1.24	9.32	45.40	1302.37	1398.16
Break-even interest rate (%)[c]	28	24	22	25	21
2007					
Total borrowers (no.)	7,072	43,472	188,944	3,168,096	6,160,000
Total members (no.)	8,317	52,468	210,248	3,731,243	7,411,229
Loans outstanding (million Tk.)[a]	40.70	227.00	982.00	16424.68	36337.27
Lending interest rate (%)	24	20	18	25	19
Cost per Tk. loan (Tk.)[b]	0.21	0.20	0.15	0.15	0.12
Profit (million Tk.)	1.83	10.20	40.40	891.38	106.91
Break-even interest rate (%)[c]	30	25	20	29	24
2008					
Total borrowers (no.)	4,906	39,796	162,757	3,308,356	6,210,000
Total members (no.)	5,920	49,161	198,027	4,165,898	7,670,203
Loans outstanding (million Tk.)[a]	37.30	229.00	857.00	20863.12	44412.11
Lending interest rate (%)	20	20	21	23	18
Cost per Tk. loan (Tk.)[b]	0.16	0.16	0.18	0.13	0.10
Profit (million Tk.)	1.84	22.50	11.00	790.14	1304.67
Break-even interest rate (%)[c]	25	22	24	26	20
2009					
Total borrowers (no.)	5,653	39,173	148,915	2,826,228	6,430,000
Total members (no.)	6,726	47,245	176,109	4,124,144	7,970,000
Loans outstanding (million Tk.)[a]	40.60	259.00	966.00	20909.88	56359.03
Lending interest rate (%)	23	21	21	25	17
Cost per Tk. loan (Tk.)[b]	0.47	0.18	0.18	0.13	0.10
Profit (million Tk.)	1.39	5.65	7.13	1257.63	371.57
Break-even interest rate (%)[c]	28	24	24	25	20
2010					
Total borrowers (no.)	5,841	38,205	145,511	2,811,595	6,610,000
Total members (no.)	7,373	48,031	180,460	3,795,186	7,686,047
Loans outstanding (million Tk.)[a]	47.50	330.00	1100.00	23039.32	66349.53
Lending interest rate (%)	19	18	19	26	18
Cost per Tk. loan (Tk.)[b]	0.18	0.13	0.13	0.13	0.11
Profit (million Tk.)	1.78	8.79	27.10	1655.36	757.24
Break-even interest rate (%)[c]	24	18	20	27	22
2011					
Total borrowers (no.)	5,648	39,789	164,670	2,686,031	6,580,000
Total members (no.)	7,291	50,160	199,177	3,475,282	7,563,218

table continues next page

Table 3.5 Operational Efficiency of MFIs in Bangladesh by Size and Year, 2006–11 *(continued)*

Indicator	Small	Medium	Large	Very large	Grameen Bank
Loans outstanding (million Tk.)[a]	47.20	385.00	1360.00	28367.35	75293.69
Lending interest rate (%)	22	20	19	25	19
Cost per Tk. loan (Tk.)[b]	0.17	0.13	0.12	0.12	0.11
Profit (million Tk.)	1.28	15.30	60.70	2158.89	683.56
Break-even interest rate (%)[c]	24	17	17	23	21

Sources: Annual reports of various MFIs.
Note: We augmented the work of Quayes and Khalily (2013), but followed an alternate definition of MFI size (the same borrower cut-off points are used by Bangladesh's MRA): small = up to 25,000 members, medium = 25,000–100,000 members, large = 100,000–500,000 members, and very large = more than 500,000 members. Some 180 MFIs are classified as small, 45 as medium, 16 as large, and 4 (Bangladesh Rural Advancement Committee, Association for Social Advancement, Basic Unit for Resources and Opportunities of Bangladesh, and Thengamara Mohila Sabuj Sangha) as very large.
a. Monetary figures are in Bangladeshi Taka (Tk.).
b. Cost per loan equals operating cost as percentage of loans outstanding.
c. Break-even interest rate equals total cost as percentage of loans outstanding.

organizations, with membership as high as 100 percent. The loan amount per borrower ranged from 4 percent to 50 percent of net per capita income. For example, in 2012, Grameen Bank's loan per capita explained 20 percent of per capita national income, compared to 57 percent for the Vietnam Bank for Social Policy (VBSP).

Operational efficiency as defined by the CGAP—operational cost (financial expenses plus operating cost and provision for bad loans) as a percent of assets—varied by program, with a percentage higher than 100 indicating that a program is operationally efficient. According to the CGAP definition, Grameen Bank and BRAC are among the top few of the world's most operationally efficient MFIs.

Summary

In the early 1990s, Bangladesh had only a few MFIs with substantial government and donor support that focused primarily on poverty alleviation via microlending. In recent years, however, MFIs in Bangladesh have been extending coverage of other financial products such as remittance transfers and microinsurance and as such have been experiencing greater competition and something close to market saturation in lending. Incentives for MFIs may therefore be changing to adapt to these new circumstances. To compete with other lending groups, MFIs may have to expand more rapidly and thus lower their costs. Karlan and Zinman (2011) argued that, as microlending organizations compete and evolve into their second generation, they can often end up looking more like traditional retail or small-business lenders (i.e., for-profit lenders extending individual liability credit in increasingly urban and competitive settings).

These shifts may have significant implications for the poor and ultra-poor. If competition among MFIs centers on better-off or more profitable borrowers, then poorer borrowers may be left behind (McIntosh and Wydick 2005). If the poor are not adequately being targeted through microfinance, then its subsidization, grant funds, and institutional perquisites may be substituted with other, more efficient means of poverty alleviation.

This analysis indicates that MFIs in Bangladesh are relying increasingly on resources mobilized by the MFIs and less on donor or concessionary funds. Over the past decade, MFI competition has increased rapidly, with a surge in new MFIs and increased borrowing across multiple MFIs by poor clients. However, we find evidence somewhat counter to policy claims that newer MFIs are less risk averse in their targeting, or that increased borrowing among households due to MFI competition has led to lower recovery rates. There is also considerable competition in terms of program lending. Even though newer MFIs are likely to attract riskier clients, this is not the case for older MFIs. Loan recovery rates are also the highest among the newest MFIs for women, suggesting that there may be distinct products offered by MFIs to attract better-risk clients. The portfolios of the newer MFIs have changed in unexpected ways. Agricultural credit has increased but savings products have declined, with rising loan activity among these groups relative to older MFIs.

Important socioeconomic and agroclimate factors affect the performance of MFIs in Bangladesh. Econometric analysis carried out by Khandker, Koolwal, and Badruddoza (2013) showed that access to better infrastructure and markets leads to lower loan interest rates. For example, better initial access to infrastructure and education in the MFI's headquarters district (e.g., improved access to markets and roads and higher literacy among men) leads to higher interest rates on savings. Where there are more banks in the headquarters district, loan interest rates tend to be higher; conversely, they are lower where there is a greater presence of NGOs. One explanation could be that NGOs that provide microcredit tend to be located in areas that are not as well served by commercial banks. Traditionally, it is not expected that commercial banks and MFIs will be in direct competition since the poor rarely have the collateral to borrow from commercial institutions; rather, the main effects of competition are between the NGOs themselves. Also, the effect of agroclimate characteristics on borrower risk and overall loan recovery tends to be strongest in rural areas. A greater proportion of land below river, for example, has a strong negative impact on loan recovery rates across the board. Thus, policies, along with local socioeconomic and agroclimate conditions, matter to MFI performance in Bangladesh.

Annex 3A: Comparative Perspective of MFI Performance, 2004–12

Country, MFIs	Active borrowers (million)	Women borrowers (%)	Assets (million US$)	Gross loan portfolio (million US$)	Mean loan/borrower (US$)	Mean loan/GNI cap (%)	Deposits/loans (%)	Net return (% of assets)	Financial revenue (% of assets)	Financial expense (% of assets)	Provision for bad loans (% of assets)	Operating expense (% of assets)	Borrowers per staff member	Average salary/GNI per capita	Offices (no.)	Operational self-sufficiency (%)
2004																
Bangladesh																
Grameen Bank	3.70	96	0.52	0.34	91	22	—	0.2	15.5	7.3	1.8	6.2	284	—	—	101
BRAC	3.99	99	0.29	0.24	61	15	53	3.4	23.7	3.9	4.6	11.8	211	3.4	1,483	117
ASA	2.77	97	0.27	0.20	73	18	36	15.4	24.6	2.7	0.2	6.2	243	3.2	1,966	269
Indonesia																
BRI	2.00	50	—	2.04	637	57	162	—	—	—	—	—	—	—	—	—
Thailand																
Village Fund[a]	7.50	48	—	3.00	402	16	—	—	—	—	—	—	—	—	80,000	—
Vietnam																
VBSP	3.74	—	0.98	0.86	229	42	—	(4.3)	4.8	3.8	0.3	5.0	653	—	—	52
2008																
Bangladesh																
Grameen Bank	6.21	97	1.12	0.64	103	20	145	1.7	16.1	7.7	0.5	6.2	256	3.4	2,539	111
BRAC	6.33	96	0.67	0.65	102	20	35	2.3	24.2	8.2	3.6	10.1	237	3.7	2,700	111
ASA	5.88	80	0.51	0.46	79	15	35	5.9	22.6	1.9	1.4	13.4	262	4.4	3,304	135
India																
SKS	3.52	100	0.60	0.48	137	13	0	3.7	25.8	8.9	0.5	10.6	263	2.8	1,354	129
Spandana	2.43	100	0.36	0.37	151	14	0	6.9	27.0	9.1	1.2	6.0	382	2.6	942	166
Indonesia																
BRI	4.46	—	—	3.80	853	45	132	—	—	—	—	—	—	—	—	—
Thailand																
Village Fund[b]	6.33	48	—	2.92	461	12	15	—	—	—	—	—	—	—	80,000	—

table continues next page

Country, MFIs	Active borrowers (million)	Women borrowers (%)	Assets (million US$)	Gross loan portfolio (million US$)	Mean loan/borrower (US$)	Mean loan/GNI cap (%)	Deposits/loans (%)	Net return (% of assets)	Financial revenue (% of assets)	Financial expense (% of assets)	Provision for bad loans (% of assets)	Operating expense (% of assets)	Borrowers per staff member	Average salary/GNI per capita	Offices (no.)	Operational self-sufficiency (%)
Vietnam																
VBSP	6.79	35	3.14	3.02	444	50	2	(2.3)	6.9	1.4	0.8	7.0	870	8.8	610	75
2012																
Bangladesh																
Grameen Bank	6.71	96	1.90	1.01	150	20	163	0.9	17.0	8.3	1.6	6.2	301	3.8	2,567	106
BRAC	4.19	96	0.79	0.75	179	24	42	5.8	25.3	7.0	2.8	9.6	237	4.7	2,119	130
ASA	4.18	85	—	0.64	153	20	33	—	—	—	—	—	199	—	3,025	—
India																
SKS	4.31	100	0.41	0.44	101	7	0	(15.8)	17.8	7.8	12.1	13.7	399	1.7	1,261	53
Spandana	2.38	91	0.24	0.41	172	12	0	(46.9)	10.2	0.2	52.3	4.6	513	1.9	1,163	18
Bandhan	4.43	100	0.98	0.81	184	12	0	4.7	20.5	9.4	0.5	3.8	387	1.5	1,803	151
SKDRDP	2.31	62	0.45	0.38	166	11	0	2.6	15.0	7.8	0.1	4.6	395	1.3	88	120
SHARE	2.13	100	0.19	0.36	167	11	0	(46.4)	12.8	7.4	46.4	5.4	576	2.1	841	22
Mexico																
Compartamentos B	2.50	94	1.33	1.13	452	4	0	13.0	62.4	4.5	5.3	33.1	171	1.5	484	145
Vietnam																
VBSP	7.10	51	5.87	5.47	770	57	4	(2.0)	6.9	6.8	0.1	2.1	883	8.8	63	78

Source: Microfinance Information eXchange 2014.

Note: All MFIs with at least 2 million active borrowers are shown. BRI = Bank Rakyat Indonesia; SHARE = Science Health Allied Research Education; SKDRDP = Shree Kshetra Dharmasthala Rural Development Project; SKS = Swayam Krishi Sangam (Telegu for Self-Help Union); VBSP = Vietnam Bank for Social Policy; MFI = microfinance institution; GNI = gross national income; BRAC = Bangladesh Rural Advancement Committee; ASA = Association for Social Advancement; — = not available.

a. Village Fund central office provided 2004 data.

b. 2009 estimates.

Notes

1. In 2006, about half of annual microcredit disbursements in Bangladesh were provided through NGOs, about 30 percent through Grameen Bank, and the rest through state-owned and private banks (CDF 2006).

2. PKSF, a wholesale agency established by the Bangladesh government in the 1990s, lends government- and donor-funded money to its POs for on-lending as microcredit disbursements. As of March 2010, PKSF had lent Tk. 88.5 billion to more than 250 POs, which, in turn, had disbursed about Tk. 525 billion to some 10 million micro-credit members.

3. However, the evidence on poverty reduction is mixed. Some studies have shown significant positive impacts of microfinance on income, consumption, and schooling (Khandker 1998, 2005; Pitt and Khandker 1998). Other studies have found that microfinance did not have significant impacts on average consumption (Karlan and Zinman 2010), but did tend to enhance the incomes of households that already had their own businesses (Banerjee and others 2010) or were self-employed in agriculture (Crépon and others 2011). Chapter 6 provides more details on the poverty effects of microfinance.

4. In 2010, for example, the Indian state of Andhra Pradesh decided to rein in microlenders after a string of suicides by indebted borrowers. Bangladesh's ruling party also set up a political committee in early 2011 to critically review the interest rates that Grameen Bank was charging its loan participants, which ultimately led the Microcredit Regulatory Authority (MRA) to set an interest rate ceiling of 27 percent on loans provided by the MFIs. Similar issues have emerged in Latin America (e.g., the 2001 convergence of economic crisis and public backlash against microfinance lenders in Bolivia) and Africa (e.g., the 2003 Usury Act in South Africa, which led to the establishment of the Microfinance Regulatory Council, which was to provide for effective consumer protection amid widespread concern about high interest rates and abusive practices in the unregulated microlending market that boomed during the mid-1990s).

5. de Janvry, McIntosh, and Sadoulet (2010), for example, consider a lender in Guatemala who gradually started to use credit bureaus across its branches without informing borrowers. One year later, the authors ran an experiment by informing the borrowers about this use of credit bureau by the lender. The timing of the two experiments allowed them to identify the supply-and-demand side effect. They found an increase in the ejection rate, but that borrowers were better performing and received larger loans. Once borrowers became aware of the bureau, their performance improved modestly, but some worse-performing members were ejected, and women were more likely to lose access to credit.

6. MIX is a nonprofit, private-sector organization focused on promoting information exchange in the microfinance industry.

7. For example, using MIX data between 1999 and 2006, Gonzales (2007) found that the three main drivers of MFIs' operating expenses were age, relative loan size, and scale.

8. This section is drawn heavily from Khandker, Koolwal, and Badruddoza (2013).

9. In 2011, for example, the MRA capped the interest rate on loans that MFIs could charge at 27 percent.

10. Chapter 5 further discusses the issues of MFI competition, household indebtedness, and multiple borrowing, using long-term panel household data.

11. It should be noted that these NGOs are not subsidiaries of Grameen Bank.

12. MFIs in Bangladesh have been slowly extending their services to urban areas, although the extent of such coverage is quite limited (Khandker, Koolwal, and Badruddoza 2013).

13. In 2006, the first regulation of the MRA was to request that all NGOs get licensed to perform as MFIs under certain conditions, such as membership and equity. However, the MRA did not set an interest rate ceiling until 2011. The possible consequence of this interest ceiling is beyond the scope of our study, as the data coverage does not extend beyond 2010.

Bibliography

Ahlin, Christin, Jocelyn Lin, and Michael Maio. 2011. "Where Does Microfinance Flourish? Microfinance Institution Performance in Macroeconomic Context." *Journal of Development Economics* 95: 105–20.

Banerjee, Abhijeet, Esther Duflo, Rachel Glennerster, and Cynthia Kinnan. 2010. "The Miracle of Microfinance? Evidence from a Randomized Evaluation." Working Paper, Massachusetts Institute of Technology, Cambridge, MA. http://econ-www.mit.edu /files/4162.

CDF (Credit and Development Forum). 2006. *CDF Statistics: Microfinance Data Bank of MFI-NGOs*. Dhaka: CDF.

CGAP (Consultative Group to Assist the Poor). 2003. *Annual Report 2003*. Washington, DC: CGAP.

Crépon, Bruno, Florencia Devoto, Esther Duflo, and William Parienté. 2011. "Impact of Microcredit in Rural Areas of Morocco: Evidence from a Randomized Evaluation." Working Paper, Massachusetts Institute of Technology, Cambridge, MA.

Cull, Robert, Asli Demirgüç-Kunt, and Jonathan Morduch. 2009. "Microfinance Meets the Market." *Journal of Economic Perspectives* 23 (1): 167–92.

———. 2011. "Does Regulatory Supervision Curtail Microfinance Operation and Outreach?" *World Development* 39 (6): 949–65.

de Janvry, Alain, Craig McIntosh, and Elisabeth Sadoulet. 2010. "The Supply and Demand Side Impact of Credit Market Information." *Journal of Development Economics* 93: 173–88.

Gonzales, Adrian. 2007. "Efficiency Drivers of Microfinance Institutions (MFIs): The Case of Operating Costs." *MicroBanking Bulletin* 15, Microfinance Information eXchange, Washington, DC.

Grameen Bank. 2010. *Annual Report*. Dhaka, Bangladesh.

Hoff, Karla, and Joseph E. Stiglitz. 1998. "Moneylenders and Bankers: Price-Increasing Subsidies in a Monopolistically Competitive Market." *Journal of Development Economics* 55: 485–518.

Karlan, Dean, and Jonathan Zinman. 2010. "Expanding Credit Access: Using Randomized Supply Decisions to Estimate the Impacts." *Review of Financial Studies* 23 (1): 434–64.

———. 2011. "Microcredit in Theory and Practice: Using Randomized Credit Scoring for Impact Evaluation." *Science* 332 (6035): 1278–84.

Khandker, Shahidur R. 1998. *Fighting Poverty with Microcredit: Experience in Bangladesh.* New York: Oxford University Press.

———. 2005. "Microfinance and Poverty: Evidence Using Panel Data from Bangladesh." *World Bank Economic Review* 19 (2): 263–86.

Khandker, Shahidur R., Gayatri B. Koolwal, and Syed Badruddoza. 2013. "How Does Competition Affect the Performance of MFIs?" Policy Research Working Paper 6408, World Bank, Washington, DC.

McIntosh, Craig, Alain de Janvry, and Elisabeth Sadoulet. 2005. "How Rising Competition among Microfinance Institutions Affects Incumbent Lenders." *The Economic Journal* 115 (506): 987–1004.

McIntosh, Craig, and Bruce Wydick. 2005. "Competition and Microfinance." *Journal of Development Economics* 78 (2): 271–98.

Microfinance Information eXchange (MIX). 2014. Various factsheets, https://www.themix.org/.

Pitt, M., and S. Khandker. 1998. "The Impact of Group-Based Credit Programmes on Poor Households in Bangladesh: Does Gender of the Participant Matter?" *Journal of Political Economy* 106: 958–96.

Quayes, Shakil, and Baqui Khalily. 2013. "Efficiency of Microfinance Institutions in Bangladesh." InM Working Paper 19, Institute of Microfinance, Dhaka.

Salim, Mir M. 2013. "Revealed Objective Functions of Microfinance Institutions: Evidence from Bangladesh." *Journal of Development Economics* 104: 34–55.

Vogelgesang, Ulrike. 2003. "Microfinance in Times of Crisis: The Effects of Competition, Rising Indebtedness, and Economic Crisis on Repayment Behavior." *World Development* 31 (12): 2085–114.

CHAPTER 4

Dynamics of Microfinance Benefits

Introduction

As discussed in chapter 1, the most substantive evaluation of microcredit was carried out two decades ago by researchers at the World Bank. That evaluation found that microcredit helped promote household welfare, and that the impacts of credit were higher for women than for men (Khandker 1998; Pitt and Khandker 1996, 1998; Pitt and others 1999; Pitt, Khandker, and Cartwright 2006).[1] The evaluation's findings, resulting from the examination of three well-known credit programs in Bangladesh using the 1991/92 cross-sectional survey data, have since been debated because of restrictive statistical assumptions for model identification of program benefits (Morduch 1998; Roodman and Morduch 2009, 2014). As previously mentioned, the claims of statistical limitations were also invalidated (Pitt 1999, 2014; Pitt and Khandker 2012).

Various studies that have utilized less restrictive assumptions, using methods with randomized control trials (RCTs), have found limited or no benefits from microfinance.[2] But such studies have often been based on assessments of short-term program effects (e.g., RCT may be limited to 18 months of intervention). Since microfinance is not cash transfer, measuring its effects requires a certain minimum length of program membership. Furthermore, the benefits from self-employed activities also take time to be realized. Keeping these requirements in mind, the earlier study of Pitt and Khandker (1998) used a cross-sectional survey of households in villages where the microfinance program had been in place for at least three years prior to the survey. The follow-up study, as well as other panel data analysis from Bangladesh, confirms the earlier benefits of microfinance (e.g., Islam 2011; Khandker 2005) (annex 4A).

As RCT design was beyond the scope of the study carried out in 1991/92, the analysis of the cross-sectional survey and follow-up surveys can only be done within the framework of quasi-experimental design. Long panel household survey data provides a unique opportunity to utilize alternative quasi-experimental methods to estimate the benefits accrued to microfinance program participants. It also allows for examining certain dynamics of microfinance, such as its time-varying effects, market saturation owing to competition among the microfinance institutions (MFIs), diseconomies of scale of borrowing, and the aggregate village-level effect of program participation.

This chapter uses data from the long panel survey spanning more than 20 years to compare alternative estimates of the socioeconomic benefits accrued by microfinance program participants. More specifically, it explores whether the benefits of program participation vary by estimation method, whether the benefit estimates vary by timing of program participation, whether the changing effects of market conditions contribute to market saturation and village-level diseconomies, and whether market saturation and multiple program membership are adversely affecting household welfare.

Dynamics of Microcredit Participation

The findings of the supply-side analysis presented in chapter 3 lend support to the common perception that the MFIs have peaked in terms of membership growth, loan disbursement, and savings mobilization and that government-led programs (e.g., Palli Karma-Sahayak Foundation [PKSF]) have played a key role in MFI growth and competition over the past two decades.[3] But program-level data only show aggregate MFI behavior and not whether or how much program participants have benefited from gaining access to various types of products offered by the MFIs. Studying the behavior of MFI program participants in terms of borrowing, savings, and loan repayment requires household survey data that cover a long time period. Fortunately for our study, the long panel household data span a period of 20 years (1991/92–2010/11), roughly corresponding to the three phases of MFI growth (box 3.1). Thus, the long panel data offer three historical snapshots of household behavior over this period (appendix A).

Descriptive Statistics of Behavioral Outcomes

The first round of the cross-sectional survey, conducted in 1991/92, was studied to determine the role of microfinance in the social and economic advancement of the poor. Carried out jointly by the World Bank and the Bangladesh Institute of Development Studies (BIDS), the survey covered 1,769 households randomly selected from 87 villages (72 program and 15 control villages) in 29 *upazilas* (rural subdistricts).[4] The second survey round, conducted in 1998/99 with the help of BIDS, could not retrace 131 of the original 1,769 households from the first round (1991/92); thus, the remaining 1,638 available households were surveyed, implying an attrition rate of 7.4 percent. The second round (1998/99) also included new households from the originally surveyed villages, along with newly selected ones. A total of 2,599 households were surveyed (2,226 from the originally surveyed villages and 373 from the new ones). Among the 2,226 households, 279 were newly sampled ones; the other 1,947 were from the 1,638 households sampled in the 1991/92 round, which had split off to form new households in the years between the two surveys.

A third survey round was conducted in 2010/11 with the help of the Institute of Microfinance (InM). This third round attempted to revisit all 2,599

Table 4.1 Rate of Household Participation in Microcredit Programs: 1991/92–2010/11

Survey year	Grameen Bank	BRAC	BRDB	ASA	Other programs	Any program	Multiple membership	Non-participant
1991/92	8.7	11.2	6.4	0	0	26.3	0	73.7
(N = 1,509)	(8.6)	(9.0)	(5.8)	(0)	(0)	(23.3)	(0)	
1998/98	15.1	16.2	8.3	4.1	14.9	48.6	8.9	51.4
(N = 1,758)	(13.6)	(10.1)	(4.4)	(3.6)	(11.4)	(38.0)	(4.5)	
2010/11	27.4	20.9	4.7	23.8	32.9	68.5	31.9	31.5
(N = 2,322)	(21.7)	(12.3)	(1.3)	(19.3)	(28.2)	(56.2)	(20.4)	

Sources: World Bank/BIDS survey 1991/92 and 1998/99; World Bank/InM survey 2010/11.
Note: Sample is restricted to 1,509 panel households from the 1991/92 survey common to all three surveys. Sample size is higher for 1998/99 and 2010/11 because of household split-offs. Figures in parentheses are percentages of borrowers. Sum of the figures across columns exceeds 100 percent for 1998/99 and 2010/11 because of household participation in multiple programs. BRAC = Bangladesh Rural Advancement Committee; BRDB = Bangladesh Rural Development Board; ASA = Association for Social Advancement.

households surveyed in the second round (1998/99). Of these, 2,342 households could be traced (with an attrition of about 10 percent). In all, 3,082 households were interviewed in 2010/11, with 740 households splitting off during this period to form new households. The survey began in March 2011 and was completed in September 2011.

This study's analysis is based on the 1,509 households from the first round (1991/92) that are common to all three surveys. Of course, because of household split-off, the number of households is higher for the second (1998/99) and third (2010/11) survey rounds, at 1,758 and 2,322 households, respectively.[5] Table 4.1 indicates that, over the 20-year period, household membership in microcredit programs grew steadily, from 26.3 percent in 1991/92 to 48.6 percent in 1998/99 and to 68.5 percent in 2010/11. The only exception was the Bangladesh Rural Development Board (BRDB) government program, which lost a good share of its members between the second and third survey rounds due to reorganization.[6] Grameen Bank, the largest of all the microcredit programs, increased its membership from 8.7 percent in 1991/92 to 15.1 percent in 1998/99 and to 27.4 percent in 2010/11. In addition to the four major programs—Grameen Bank, Bangladesh Rural Advancement Committee (BRAC), BRDB, and Association for Social Advancement (ASA)—many other programs developed over the past 20 years and are now serving rural communities in a large capacity. In 2010/11, coverage of these programs included nearly 33 percent of rural households, which was higher than that of Grameen Bank.

Recent Growth in Overlapping Membership across Multiple Programs
Today, overlapping membership in multiple programs is an important aspect of microcredit program participation in Bangladesh. This phenomenon hardly existed in the early 1990s. But the third survey round (2010/11) showed that nearly 61 percent of Grameen Bank members were also members of other programs (Khandker and Samad 2014). Overall, about 31.9 percent of rural households were members of multiple microcredit programs in 2010/11, compared to 8.9 percent in 1998/99 and zero in 1991/92 (table 4.1).

Participation in microcredit programs does not necessarily imply borrowing. In many programs, new members must wait for some time before they can borrow, and some programs feature a nonborrowing membership plan that allows individuals to save money with microcredit programs without having to borrow. That said, a great majority of microcredit members are borrowers. In 2010/11, about 69 percent of rural households were microcredit members; borrowers constituted about 56 percent, implying that 13 percent were nonborrowing members (table 4.1).

While microcredit programs have offered various noncredit services in the past, they have become mostly credit-only institutions over time. Through access to credit, not just participation, households can reap the benefits.[7] As such, this chapter's analysis considers the cumulative amount of borrowing as the intervention variable. Cumulative borrowing from the two major microcredit programs, as well as from other microcredit sources, has increased by nearly 100 percent over time.[8] The total amount borrowed per household in 1991/92 was Tk. 9,252, compared to Tk. 17,006 in 2010/11, implying a simple growth rate of more than 4 percent a year over the 20-year period (table 4.2).[9]

The highest growth in borrowing occurred for the smaller programs (reported in the fourth column of table 4.2), which are relatively new compared to Grameen Bank and BRAC. The average borrowing for BRAC grew by 7.8 percent per year, compared to 11.0 percent a year for the smaller programs. More than two-thirds of the loan amounts were received by women, who are particularly targeted by the MFIs (table 4.2). In 2010/11, women's share of microcredit lending was the highest for Grameen Bank (89 percent) and the lowest for BRAC (38 percent). In earlier years, women's share of BRAC loans was much higher (e.g., 95 percent in 1998/99); but over time, many of the BRAC members sampled in our survey received loans for small and medium-size enterprises (SMEs), more of which are operated by men.[10]

Another feature of microfinance operations in Bangladesh is mandatory savings, mostly in the form of weekly savings and deposits, out of a certain

Table 4.2 Household Cumulative Loans and Savings from Microcredit Programs over Time: 1991/92–2010/11

Survey year	Grameen Bank loans	BRAC loans	Other program loans	Aggregate loans from all programs	Aggregate savings for all programs
1991/92	16,289.4	5,276.7	6,453.9	9,252.3	700.3
(N = 769)	(0.73)	(0.71)	(0.38)	(0.67)	(0.08)
1998/98	25,938.4	6,377.1	6,217.2	13,262.1	1,341.5
(N = 1,099)	(0.84)	(0.95)	(0.76)	(0.84)	(0.10)
2010/11	11,597.6	13,452.3	11,346.2	17,005.6	1,689.9
(N = 1,770)	(0.89)	(0.38)	(0.80)	(0.73)	(0.10)

Sources: World Bank/BIDS survey 1991/92 and 1998/99; World Bank/InM survey 2010/11.
Note: Findings are restricted to microcredit participants. Loans and program savings are consumer price index–adjusted (1991/92 = 100). Loans are cumulative for the five years preceding the surveys. Figures in parentheses represent sample size (column 1), share of female loans (columns 2–5), and share of program savings in cumulative loans (column 6). BRAC = Bangladesh Rural Advancement Committee.

percentage of the loans disbursed. In 1991/92, member savings represented about 8 percent of cumulative borrowing, increasing slightly to 10 percent in 1998/99 and 2010/11 (table 4.2), which nonetheless accounted for some 60 percent of MFI loans outstanding in Bangladesh (see chapter 3, figure 3.4).[11]

Before estimating the microcredit effects on the outcomes of particular interest, it is worthwhile to investigate how these outcomes vary by program participation status and across years. Table 4.3 shows that household income grew significantly over time for program participants and nonparticipants alike; in particular, household income more than doubled between 1998/99 and 2010/11.[12] The labor-supply pattern was inconsistent over time for program participants and actually experienced a drop for nonparticipants. The change in household nonland assets and net worth followed a pattern similar to that of income or expenditure, registering substantial monotonic growth.

Like the labor-supply and economic outcomes, the education outcomes also experienced consistent growth over time for both participants and nonparticipants. However, it is worth noting that school enrollment rates for girls have been consistently higher among program participants than nonparticipants.

Although the education outcomes improved over time, the differences between participants and nonparticipants showed no consistent pattern. While per capita household income (in real terms) was slightly higher for participants

Table 4.3 Household-Level Outcome Indicators by Microcredit Participation Status: 1991/92–2010/11

	1991/92		1998/99		2010/11	
Outcome	Participants ($N = 769$, $N_B = 816$, $N_G = 744$)	Non-participants ($N = 483$, $N_B = 425$, $N_G = 397$)	Participants ($N = 1,014$, $N_B = 883$, $N_G = 815$)	Non-participants ($N = 420$, $N_B = 305$, $N_G = 283$)	Participants ($N = 1,554$, $N_B = 180$, $N_G = 179$)	Non-participants ($N = 334$, $N_B = 1,105$, $N_G = 1,200$)
Per capita income (Tk./month)	521.8 (0.74)	495.6	502.7 (−0.86)	523.1	1,066.0 (−0.36)	1,114.3
Male labor supply (hours/month)	195.4 (1.10)	189.5	227.8 (2.31)	206.0	200.9 (8.32)	131.4
Female labor supply (hours/month)	38.8 (0.41)	37.2	30.1 (2.88)	20.1	56.2 (4.34)	39.6
Nonland asset value (Tk.)	18,273.0 (3.73)	12,830.7	20,089.2 (−2.46)	25,415.2	62,595.9 (−0.76)	68,294.3
Net worth (Tk.)	68,400.2 (6.15)	35,953.3	113,613.3 (−1.82)	144,981.7	287,625.0 (0.44)	269,349.1
Boys' school enrollment (ages 5–18)	0.549 (4.69)	0.417	0.562 (−1.75)	0.614	0.696 (−0.12)	0.701
Girls' school enrollment (ages 5–18)	0.510 (3.19)	0.415	0.655 (2.44)	0.581	0.712 (2.02)	0.643

Sources: World Bank/BIDS survey 1991/92 and 1998/99; World Bank/InM survey 2010/11.
Note: Monetary figures are consumer price index–adjusted (1991/92 = 100). The analysis is restricted to microcredit-eligible households of 1991/92 (those who participated and those who were eligible but did not participate in microcredit programs in 1991/92), which constituted 64, 62, and 61 percent of the surveyed households in 1991/92, 1998/99, and 2010/11, respectively. Figures in parentheses are t-statistics of the differences between participants and nonparticipants.

than nonparticipants in 1991/92 (with the difference being statistically nonsignificant), the opposite trend was observed for other years, showing slightly higher income for nonparticipants. A similar trend was observed for nonland assets and net worth, except that, in 2010/11, participants had a slightly higher net worth than nonparticipants.

While the descriptive statistics of the outcome variables can show a trend over time and by participation status, they cannot establish causality linking microfinance participation and changes in outcomes. Appendix B discusses alternative models to estimate program effects using the long panel household survey data. We apply these techniques to derive the benefits of microfinance programs accrued by rural households over time.

Pitfalls of Panel Data Analysis: Household Attrition and Split-Off

Panel data are useful for studying issues of dynamics and resolving the endogeneity of program participation and placement; however, they are not without limitations. Two major issues are sample attrition and split-off.[13] Thus, before applying the panel data to estimate the effects of microfinance, it is important to examine whether these two issues create a problem for long panel estimation.

Attrition is potentially damaging where it is nonrandom; that is, if attrition is selective, it is likely to bias estimates, and may well ruin the advantages that panel data analysis is supposed to have. Therefore, researchers try to minimize attrition and follow a rigorous procedure to locate previously surveyed households. As mentioned above, the survey data were subject to 7.4 percent attrition between the first and second survey rounds and 7.9 percent attrition between the second and third rounds, with an overall attrition rate of 14.7 percent (1991/92–2010/11), averaging less than 1 percent a year. However, the key factor is not the extent of attrition but whether it is nonrandom.

Testing for Nonrandom Attrition

To estimate the determinants of attrition, this study ran a probit regression, using the 1991/92 data with an attrition dummy (1 for households that were lost, 0 otherwise) as the dependent variable, and the outcomes (e.g., household income, expenditure, and school enrollment) and household- and village-level characteristics as explanatory variables.[14] Results of the regressions (not reported here) showed that attrition is positively correlated with households that feature less land or nonland assets and an absence of adult male or female members, as well as those located in villages with poor road conditions (a proxy for infrastructure); that is, attrition is more likely to occur among households with low socioeconomic status and in less developed villages.

These findings are consistent with previous studies on household attrition (Alderman and others 2000; Fitzgerald, Gottschalk, and Moffitt 1998; Thomas, Frankenberg, and Smith 1999; Ziliak and Kniesner 1998). For example, using the Michigan Panel Study of Income Dynamics (PSID), Fitzgerald, Gottschalk, and

Moffitt (1998) found that households with lower earnings, educational levels, and marriage propensities are more prone to attrition. But overall, these variables explain only 7–10 percent of the probability of household attrition, suggesting that up to 93 percent of the portion that cannot be explained by the explanatory variables may be random. We also ran the Wald joint significance test to determine whether the explanatory variables were jointly equal to zero (table 4B.1). The resulting Chi-squared statistics indicate that these variables jointly differ from zero at the highest level of significance (the p-value is 0.000), implying that these variables are significant predictors of attrition; that is, attrition may not be random.

We also performed the Becketti, Gould, Lillard, and Welch test to determine the randomness of attrition. This test involves regressing the outcome variable on household- and community-level exogenous variables, the attrition dummy, and interactions of the attrition dummy and the other explanatory variables (Becketti and others 1988). This is followed by performing a joint significance test of the attrition dummy and interaction variables to determine whether the coefficients of the explanatory variables vary significantly between the households that were lost and those that were resurveyed. If they do, then the null hypothesis that attrition is random can be rejected. The results showed that, at the 5 percent level, randomness of attrition is rejected for all outcomes (table 4B.2).

Correcting for Attrition Bias

If not corrected for, nonrandom attrition will introduce attrition bias in the estimated impacts. Attrition bias can be corrected for in various ways, such as estimating a selection model, which depends on finding suitable instruments (Heckman 1979); using inverse probability weights, which relies on auxiliary variables related to both attrition and the outcome variables (Fitzgerald, Gottschalk, and Moffitt 1998); and using nonparametric techniques (Das, Toepoel, and van Soest 2011). This analysis used the inverse probability weight since it is simple to implement and does not require strong conditions as required by the selection model. The rationale behind the calculation of inverse probability weights is that it gives more weight to the households subsequently lost than to those with similar initial characteristics who were more likely to remain in the panel.[15] We calculated such inverse probability weights for all outcomes and then used them in all of the estimations discussed from this point forward in the chapter.

Treatment of Split-Off Households

Apart from attrition, households were subject to split-offs over time. In most such cases, household members grew up, married, and left their households after the initial survey to form new households. Thus, the households surveyed in the first round may have spawned one or more new households by the time the subsequent surveys were conducted. This analysis treats these households as separate units related by their same initial (first-round) characteristics.[16]

Estimates of Microfinance Impact Using Static Model

Following the general method outlined in appendix B, we consider the following outcome equation with time-varying heterogeneity:

$$Y_{it} = X_{it}\beta_c + C_{ift}\delta_f + C_{imt}\delta_m + \eta_{it} + \mu_i + \varepsilon_{it},\tag{4.1}$$

where (Y_{it}) equals the outcome (e.g., income, labor supply, or nonland asset) of household i in survey year t, conditional on the level of credit demand by males (C_{imt}) and females (C_{ift}); X_{it} is a vector of characteristics at the household level (e.g., sex, age, and education of household head and landholding) and village level (e.g., extent of village electrification and irrigation, availability of infrastructure, and price of consumer goods); β_c is a vector of unknown parameters of X variables to be estimated; δ_m and δ_f measure the effects of borrowing; η_{it} is an unobserved household- or community-level determinant of the outcome that is time-varying; μ_i is an unobserved household- or community-level determinant of the outcome that is time-invariant; and ε_{it} is a nonsystematic error. The household fixed-effects (FE) estimation technique can eliminate the time-invariant parameter (μ_i) by transforming equation (4.1) as follows:

$$Y_{it} - \bar{Y}_i = (X_{it} - \bar{X}_i)\beta_c + (C_{ift} - \bar{C}_{if})\delta_f + (C_{imt} - \bar{C}_{im})\delta_m$$
$$+ (\eta_{it} - \bar{\eta}_i) + (\mu_i - \bar{\mu}) + (\varepsilon_{it} - \bar{\varepsilon}_i),\tag{4.2}$$

where the bar variables (e.g., $\bar{Y}_i$, $\bar{X}_i$, $\bar{C}_{if}$) are average values for each household. Since μ is constant, $\mu_i = \bar{\mu}$ and thus its effect is eliminated. However, since $\eta_{it} \neq \bar{\eta}_i$, the problem of unobserved effects cannot be disregarded completely, and thus the ordinary least squares (OLS) estimation of equation (4.2) will be biased.

The estimation strategy discussed in appendix B suggests that such bias can be eliminated by adopting one of two methods. One estimates FE with propensity-score weight (p-score weighted FE), and the other estimates FE with the instrumental variables (IV) method (FE-IV). The p-score weighted FE works on the assumption that a major source of time-varying heterogeneity is the difference in initial baseline characteristics between participants and nonparticipants, and implementing p-score weighted regression controls for such difference. It is implemented by creating a weight variable from the propensity score (i.e., the predicted probability of participating in microcredit programs, based on a participation equation in terms of X variables observed in the initial year of 1991/92), and using that weight in FE estimation on the panel data.[17] In the FE-IV method, some variables used as instruments enter into the participation equation only and do not directly appear in the outcome equation of (4.2). The instruments proposed are interactions of variables (e.g., whether the village has a microfinance program and whether the household is eligible to participate based on the eligibility condition imposed by the programs in the initial survey year of 1991/92).

Table 4.4 Summary Statistics of Microcredit Intervention Variables

Variable	1991/92	1998/99	2010/11
Cumulative household loans, male (Tk.)	813.8 (3,716.3)	1,833.9 (8,162.3)	5,223.8 (30,073.4)
Cumulative household loans, female (Tk.)	1,615.4 (4,947.2)	6,994.1 (15,901.6)	15,485.6 (27,015.9)
Village average of cumulative household loans, male (Tk.)	1,806.1 (2,767.5)	3,305.2 (5,678.6)	6,456.5 (8,336.0)
Village average of cumulative household loans, female (Tk.)	2,932.4 (3,607.1)	10,128.6 (11,098.4)	20,203.7 (17,383.0)
Household males that borrowed from multiple sources	0	0	0.010 (0.100)
Household females that borrowed from multiple sources	0	0.03 (17.4)	0.184 (0.388)
MFIs operating in village (no.)	0.9 (0.5)	3.9 (1.7)	7.3 (2.6)

Sources: World Bank/BIDS survey 1991/92 and 1998/99; World Bank/InM survey 2010/11.
Note: Monetary figures are consumer price index–adjusted (1991/92 = 100). Figures in parentheses are standard deviations. MFIs = microfinance institutions.

Since we are interested in the impacts of loans accumulated over 20 years (not the current loans reported for each survey year), the loan variable is the aggregate of all loans starting from 1991/92 up to that of the current year (table 4.4). Based on the FE-IV method, the findings show that borrowing by either men or women does not appear to increase per capita income. However, borrowing by women increases women's labor supply, nonland assets, household net worth, and girls' school enrollment. Men's loans lower household income and household nonland assets (table 4.5a).

Table 4.5a also reports statistics from various tests for the suitability of the IV model. While statistics from over-identification and under-identification tests have the correct sign for IV, the endogeneity test suggests that IV is not the appropriate model in most cases. Results using p-score weighted FE are considered appropriate estimates of microfinance borrowing (table 4.5b).

According to p-score weighted FE, men's and women's loans have no impact on household income. However, they both have significant positive impacts on the labor supply of men and women, household nonland assets, and net worth. A 10 percent increase in men's cumulative borrowing raises men's and women's labor supply by 0.5 percent and 0.4 percent, respectively. A similar increase in women's loans increases those outcomes by 0.4 percent and 0.6 percent, respectively. While loans for both genders raise household nonland assets by about the same percentage (0.4), men's loans have a comparatively higher impact on net worth. In terms of children's school enrollment, only women's loans matter. A 10 percent increase in women's loans increases enrollment by about 0.1 percentage point for both boys and girls. These findings confirm many of the earlier findings of the cross-sectional study (Pitt and Khandker 1998), which used only the 1991/92 data, as well as Khandker (2005), which used two-year panel data (1991/92 and 1998/99).

Table 4.5 Impacts of Microcredit Loans on Household and Individual Outcomes

a. Using 2SLS IV with household FE (N = 1,509)

Explanatory variable	Log per capita total income (Tk./month)	Log male labor supply (hours/month)	Log female labor supply (hours/month)	Log household nonland assets (Tk.)	Log household net worth (Tk.)	Boys' school enrollment (ages 5–18)	Girls' school enrollment (ages 5–18)
Log loans of household males (Tk.)	−0.156* (−1.96)	0.029 (0.23)	0.204 (1.40)	−0.201** (−2.07)	0.052 (0.70)	−0.017 (−0.36)	−0.028 (−0.50)
Log loans of household females (Tk.)	0.017 (1.25)	0.011 (0.40)	0.080** (2.92)	0.096** (5.16)	0.028* (1.64)	0.016 (1.47)	0.021** (2.45)
F-statistic for the model	$F_{(27, 85)} = 15.24$, $p > F = 0.000$	$F_{(27, 85)} = 54.72$, $p > F = 0.000$	$F_{(27, 85)} = 26.45$, $p > F = 0.000$	$F_{(27, 85)} = 85.50$, $p > F = 0.000$	$F_{(27, 85)} = 166.65$, $p > F = 0.000$	$F_{(27, 85)} = 11.11$, $p > F = 0.000$	$F_{(27, 85)} = 7.48$, $p > F = 0.000$
Endogeneity test statistic	$\chi^2(2) = 3.87$, $p > \chi^2 = 0.144$	$\chi^2(2) = 1.81$, $p > \chi^2 = 0.405$	$\chi^2(2) = 9.05$, $p > \chi^2 = 0.011$	$\chi^2(2) = 15.72$, $p > \chi^2 = 0.000$	$\chi^2(2) = 6.74$, $p > \chi^2 = 0.034$	$\chi^2(2) = 0.86$, $p > \chi^2 = 0.649$	$\chi^2(2) = 2.09$, $p > \chi^2 = 0.352$
Over-identification test statistic	$\chi^2(3) = 3.53$, $p > \chi^2 = 0.318$	$\chi^2(3) = 4.87$, $p > \chi^2 = 0.181$	$\chi^2(3) = 0.02$, $p > \chi^2 = 0.999$	$\chi^2(3) = 3.24$, $p > \chi^2 = 0.357$	$\chi^2(3) = 0.51$, $p > \chi^2 = 0.916$	$\chi^2(3) = 7.25$, $p > \chi^2 = 0.064$	$\chi^2(3) = 0.15$, $p > \chi^2 = 0.988$
Under-identification test statistic	$\chi^2(4) = 19.05$, $p > \chi^2 = 0.001$	$\chi^2(4) = 18.88$, $p > \chi^2 = 0.001$	$\chi^2(4) = 19.22$, $p > \chi^2 = 0.001$	$\chi^2(4) = 19.07$, $p > \chi^2 = 0.001$	$\chi^2(4) = 18.21$, $p > \chi^2 = 0.001$	$\chi^2(4) = 12.26$, $p > \chi^2 = 0.016$	$\chi^2(4) = 12.97$, $p > \chi^2 = 0.011$

b. Using p-score weighted household FE model (N = 1,509)

Explanatory variable	Log per capita total income (Tk./month)	Log male labor supply (hours/month)	Log female labor supply (hours/month)	Log household nonland assets (Tk.)	Log household net worth (Tk.)	Boys' school enrollment (ages 5–18)	Girls' school enrollment (ages 5–18)
Log loans of household males (Tk.)	−0.002 (−0.11)	0.050** (3.56)	0.038* (1.95)	0.037** (3.69)	0.024** (2.97)	−0.003 (−0.50)	0.005 (0.54)
Log loans of household females (Tk.)	−0.008 (−0.16)	0.039** (4.91)	0.056** (5.54)	0.036** (5.70)	0.011** (2.06)	0.008** (2.35)	0.011** (2.57)
R^2	0.137	0.209	0.238	0.453	0.651	0.073	0.065
Test statistics for equality of male and female loans	$F_{(1, 86)} = 4.61$, $p = 0.035$	$F_{(1, 86)} = 3.89$, $p = 0.051$	$F_{(1, 86)} = 7.18$, $p = 0.009$	$F_{(1, 86)} = 4.79$, $p = 0.031$	$F_{(1, 86)} = 5.76$, $p = 0.019$	$F_{(1, 86)} = 2.91$, $p = 0.091$	$F_{(1, 86)} = 5.31$, $p = 0.024$

Sources: World Bank/BIDS survey 1991/92 and 1998/99; World Bank/InM survey 2010/11.

Note: Figures in parentheses are t-statistics based on robust standard errors clustered at the village level. Loans refer to cumulative amount borrowed from all microcredit sources leading up to the survey year. Regressions include more control variables at the household level (e.g., age, sex, and education of household head and log of land assets) and village level (e.g., price of consumer goods; male and female wages; infrastructure, including schools and electricity availability; and proportion of irrigated land). IV = instrumental variables; FE = fixed effects.

Significance level: * = 10 percent; ** = 5 percent or less.

Estimates of Microfinance Impact Using Dynamic Model

The results presented thus far are based on a static model, which assumes past outcomes have no bearing on current outcomes. But in instances where it is believed that past outcomes affect future outcomes, it may be preferable to include a lagged dependent variable (LDV). Considering that this panel spans more than 20 years with three data points, we cannot rule out the possibility that past outcomes affect current ones (e.g., past nonland assets affect current asset holdings). Also, it is possible that participants whose incomes rose in earlier years invested wisely and in later years benefited even more from lucrative ventures. Even if we are not interested in the effects of the LDV on the outcomes, including it may be important for obtaining consistent estimates of other parameters (see "Dynamic Panel Models," appendix B).

This analysis estimated the dynamic panel model by instrumenting the LDV as described in appendix B. While the LDV captures the dynamics of the panel data and helps in measuring consistent estimates of other parameters, it cannot control for the time-varying heterogeneity (η_{it}), which can bias the estimates of credit effects. To control for such bias, we use p-score weight in the implementation of the dynamic model, just as we did in implementing the static panel model, and refer to this procedure as the p-score weighted LDV method.

Table 4.6 shows the findings based on the dynamic panel model.[18] As shown, female credit has positive impacts on household income, unlike the finding based on the static panel model reported in table 4.5. A 10 percent increase in women's loans increases household per capita income by about 0.2 percent. Like the findings of the static panel model, both men's and women's credit increase men's labor supply. Unlike the static panel findings, however, credit—either by men or women—does not affect women's labor supply. The credit impacts on household nonland assets and net worth are similar for both the static and dynamic panels,

Table 4.6 Impacts of Microcredit Loans on Household Outcomes Using the Dynamic Panel LDV Model
N = 1,509

Explanatory variable	Log per capita total income (Tk./month)	Log male labor supply (hours/month)	Log female labor supply (hours/month)	Log household nonland assets (Tk.)	Log household net worth (Tk.)
Log loans of household males (Tk.)	0.014 (1.62)	0.028** (3.09)	−0.024 (−1.35)	0.038** (3.65)	0.019** (2.82)
Log loans of household females (Tk.)	0.016** (2.76)	0.046** (4.70)	0.011 (0.65)	0.026** (3.32)	0.030** (4.50)
F statistics for the model	F(26, 86) = 6.58, p > 0.000	F(26, 86) = 49.22, p > 0.000	F(26, 86) = 44.37, p > 0.000	F(26, 86) = 33.64, p > 0.000	F(26, 86) = 127.70, p > 0.000

Sources: World Bank/BIDS survey 1991/92 and 1998/99; World Bank/InM survey 2010/11.
Note: Figures in parentheses are t-statistics based on robust standard errors clustered at the village level. Loans refer to cumulative amount borrowed from all microcredit sources leading up to the survey year. Regressions include more control variables at the household level (e.g., age, sex, and education of household head; log of land assets) and village level (e.g., price of consumer goods; male and female wages; infrastructure, including schools and electricity availability; and proportion of irrigated land). LDV = lagged dependent variable.
Significance level: * = 10 percent, ** = 5 percent or less.

while the effects vary in magnitude. A comparison of the model findings suggests that the estimates of credit effects are reasonably robust. For subsequent analysis, we report the findings for both types of estimation.

Short-Term versus Long-Term Impacts of Microfinance

The estimates of credit effects, as previously reported, might differ across years if timing of borrowing matters (i.e., if past credit received affects behavior differently than credit recently received). Unlike the implied assumption in equation (4.1), parameters of the credit demand and other regressors may vary over time, allowing for differential credit impacts over time.[19]

Credit effects may vary by time for a variety of reasons. For example, during the initial years of membership, participants may choose conservative projects (or be influenced to by other members of the group) until they have demonstrated an ability to repay. During this period, they may focus more on accumulating assets and thus cement the new insurance network, a result of group participation. With the passage of time, they may have a larger financial cushion, allowing for some risk-taking behavior with new loans. Second, the unobserved local market conditions that influence a household's demand for credit may change over time so as to exert a favorable impact on credit demand. Third, if the noncredit effects of program participation are important, and if changes in the attitudes they engender are functions of time spent in the group, then the total effect of participation may decline over time. On the other hand, if the knowledge gained through self-employment experience is an important component of the returns to self-employment, credit effects may rise over time. Finally, returns may fall as the rents that accrue to early participants get competed away. It is worth investigating if there are differences in these effects, possibly because of the differences in group dynamics and the types of self-employment activities they undertake over time.

One way to conceptualize the dynamics of credit effect is to assume that past credit has a lingering impact so that it affects both past and future outcomes. This issue is important in assessing the long-term impacts of microcredit, as opposed to its short-term impacts, which are confined to the period of borrowing. To assess its long-term impacts, we rewrite equation (4.1), allowing for the possibility that past credit might affect current outcomes, expressed as follows:

$$Y_{ijt} = X_{ijct}\beta_c + X_{ijpt}\beta_p + C_{ijfct}\delta_{fc} + C_{ijfpt}\delta_{fp} + C_{ijmct}\delta_{mc}$$
$$+ C_{ijmpt}\delta_{mp} + \eta_{ij}^y + \mu_j^y + \varepsilon_{ijt}^y. \tag{4.3}$$

In this equation, subscripts c and p, respectively, refer to current and past credit and current and past sets of control variables (X). The current credit at period t (where t equals 1991/92, 1998/99, or 2010/11) is defined as the cumulative amount of borrowing by household males or females up to that period, and past credit at period t is defined by the cumulative amount of borrowing by household males or females up to period $(t-1)$.[20] Thus, this model assumes that, even if a household stopped borrowing after period 1 (1991/92), it can still benefit in period 2 (1998/99) as past credit may continue to benefit the borrower (provided that $\delta_p > 0$). Thus, we allow the impacts of borrowing to be long term.[21]

Differencing out over time, we obtain the following revised static model:

$$\Delta Y_{ijt} = \Delta X_{ijct}\beta_c + \Delta X_{ijpt}\beta_p + \Delta C_{ijfct}\delta_{fc} + \Delta C_{ijfpt}\delta_{fp} + \Delta C_{ijmct}\delta_{mc}$$

$$+ \Delta C_{ijmpt}\delta_{mp} + \Delta \eta_{ij}^y + \Delta \mu_j^y + \Delta \varepsilon_{ijt}^y. \qquad (4.4)$$

Introducing a dynamic LDV method on the above model, we obtain the first-differenced model, expressed as follows:

$$\Delta Y_{ijt} = \alpha \Delta Y_{(t-1)} + \Delta X_{ijct}\beta_c + \Delta X_{ijpt}\beta_p + \Delta C_{ijfct}\delta_{fc} + \Delta C_{ijfpt}\delta_{fp}$$

$$+ \Delta C_{ijmct}\delta_{mc} + \Delta C_{ijmpt}\delta_{mp} + \Delta \eta_{ij}^y + \Delta \mu_j^y + \Delta \varepsilon_{ijt}^y. \qquad (4.5)$$

Like earlier model estimation, we have applied the p-score weighted FE static model to equation (4.4) and a p-score weighted LDV to estimate equation (4.5). A test for equality of δ_p and δ_c for both sets of models shows that the equality hypothesis cannot be rejected for three out of seven outcomes for the p-score FE model and four out of five outcomes for the LDV model (table 4.7a). This suggests the presence of distinct impacts of past borrowing on current outcomes for the majority of outcomes.[22]

However, the coefficients of the impact estimates for p-score weighted FE for the static model of equation (4.4) and the dynamic LDV model of equation (4.5) do not quite differ (table 4.7). In fact, out of 16 coefficients for 4 outcomes (ignoring boys' and girls' schooling, which are irrelevant for the LDV model), 9 coefficients are statistically significant. Thus, it makes no difference in terms of efficiency gains for the static or dynamic models.

Results of the dynamic LDV estimations, presented in table 4.7b, show that current male borrowing affected current levels for three outcomes, but past borrowing affected none. Current female credit affected current levels for four outcomes, and past credit affected two outcomes. More specifically, current male borrowing affected current male labor supply, nonland assets, and household net worth, but past credit had no impact on current levels of these outcomes. However, both current and past female loans affected the current level of household outcomes. Although current female borrowing had no statistically significant effect on per capita income, past female borrowing had a positive effect on current per capita income. The findings show that a 10 percent increase in past female borrowing increased household per capita income by nearly 3 percent. Past female borrowing had a negative effect on the current period's female labor supply. Thus, for some outcomes, the past credit of female borrowers had lingering effects.

That the response elasticity is positive for female past borrowing on such outcomes as income may indicate increasing, rather than decreasing, returns to borrowing. On the other hand, female past borrowing has a negative effect on current labor supply, indicating decreasing returns to borrowing. These examples

Table 4.7 Impacts of Current and Past Microcredit Loans on Outcomes

a. Household and individual outcomes, using p-score weighted household FE (N = 1,509)

Explanatory variable	Log per capita total income (Tk. month)	Log male labor supply (hours/ month)	Log female labor supply (hours/ month)	Log household nonland assets (Tk.)	Log household net worth (Tk.)	Boys' school enrollment (ages 5–18)	Girls' school enrollment (ages 5–18)
Log loans of household males (Tk.)							
Current loans	−0.008	0.067**	0.043*	0.042**	0.021**	−0.013	−0.006
	(−0.47)	(3.25)	(1.78)	(3.89)	(2.34)	(−1.47)	(−0.71)
Past loans	−0.008	0.031	0.0003	−0.003	0.017	0.005	0.021*
	(−0.37)	(1.15)	(0.01)	(−0.21)	(1.30)	(0.31)	(1.71)
Log loans of household females (Tk.)							
Current loans	−0.001	0.046**	0.057**	0.020**	−0.003	−0.001	0.005
	(−0.09)	(3.44)	(4.22)	(2.76)	(−0.54)	(−0.09)	(1.05)
Past loans	0.010*	0.006	−0.009	−0.012	0.026**	−0.011	0.019**
	(1.83)	(0.43)	(−0.60)	(−1.10)	(3.07)	(−1.43)	(2.93)
R^2	0.138	0.234	0.387	0.491	0.681	0.099	0.103
Test statistics for equality of current and past loans	$F_{(2, 86)} = 0.88$, $p > F = 0.417$	$F_{(2, 86)} = 3.45$, $p > F = 0.036$	$F_{(2, 86)} = 6.10$, $p > F = 0.003$	$F_{(2, 86)} = 7.04$, $p > F = 0.002$	$F_{(2, 86)} = 3.71$, $p > F = 0.028$	$F_{(2, 86)} = 1.05$, $p > F = 0.355$	$F_{(2, 86)} = 5.28$, $p > F = 0.007$

table continues next page

Table 4.7 Impacts of Current and Past Microcredit Loans on Outcomes *(continued)*

b. Household outcomes, using dynamic panel LDV model (N = 1,509)

Explanatory variable	Log per capita total income (Tk. month)	Log male labor supply (hours/month)	Log female labor supply (hours/month)	Log household nonland assets (Tk.)	Log household net worth (Tk.)
Log loans of household males (Tk.)					
Current loans	−0.007	0.031*	−0.002	0.055**	0.034**
	(−0.44)	(1.72)	(−0.08)	(4.98)	(3.24)
Past loans	0.008	−0.005	−0.035	−0.023	−0.019
	(1.01)	(−0.27)	(−0.98)	(−1.37)	(−1.26)
Log loans of household females (Tk.)					
Current loans	0.010	0.067**	0.061**	0.033**	0.034**
	(1.28)	(6.11)	(3.84)	(4.17)	(4.46)
Past loans	0.027*	−0.025	−0.064**	−0.009	−0.005
	(1.73)	(−1.59)	(−2.61)	(−0.99)	(−0.65)
F statistics of the model	$F(28, 86) = 7.00$, $p > F = 0.000$	$F(28, 86) = 45.25$, $p > F = 0.000$	$F(28, 86) = 38.80$, $p > F = 0.000$	$F(28, 86) = 33.16$, $p > F = 0.000$	$F(28, 86) = 132.20$, $p > F = 0.000$
Test statistics for equality of current and past loans	$\chi^2(2) = 1.30$, $p > \chi^2 = 0.523$	$\chi^2(2) = 26.82$, $p > \chi^2 = 0.000$	$\chi^2(2) = 12.12$, $p > \chi^2 = 0.000$	$\chi^2(2) = 14.20$, $p > \chi^2 = 0.001$	$\chi^2(2) = 11.24$, $p > \chi^2 = 0.004$

Sources: World Bank/BIDS survey 1991/92 and 1998/99; World Bank/InM survey 2010/11.

Note: Figures in parentheses are t-statistics based on robust standard errors clustered at the village level. Loans refer to cumulative amount borrowed from all microcredit sources leading up to the survey year. Regressions include more control variables at the household level (e.g., age, sex, and education of household head and log of land assets) and village level (e.g., price of consumer goods; male and female wages; infrastructure, including schools and electricity availability; and proportion of irrigated land). FE = fixed effects; LDV = lagged dependent variable.

Significance level: * = 10 percent, ** = 5 percent or less.

clearly demonstrate that the timing of borrowing matters to the credit effects, especially for female borrowers, for some household outcomes, and that past credit may have impacts independent of current credit. Finally, the effect of past credit may be lingering, increasing, decreasing, or nonexistent, depending on the outcome considered.

Market Saturation and Village Diseconomies of Scale

Market saturation of some type may result in decreasing returns to credit as village participation rates increase. That is, the benefits of being first in the market may compete away the returns of later entrants. For example, early entrants financed by group-based credit can choose from the most profitable self-employment activities, while later entrants will either compete away some of the benefits of being first to enter or will enter into less rewarding activities. Conversely, market saturation yields higher returns to individual borrowing, given that the village attracts investment from more borrowers to enhance village-level externality, producing specialization of certain activities. If, for example, an earlier entrant starts to produce a commodity that attracts investment from other borrowers in such a way that the village becomes the center of certain products or activities, returns may increase, in which case one would expect either positive or negative externality out of the market saturation.

This phenomenon can be captured by modeling the effect of credit that depends on some measure of the village rate of participation, after controlling for village-level FE. In its simplest form, we allow the credit effect (α) to vary by village, expressed as follows:

$$\alpha_j = \alpha_0 + \alpha_\Omega \Omega_j, \tag{4.6}$$

where α_j is the credit effect in village j, and Ω_j is some measure of village-level participation in microcredit programs, such as average number of participants in a village and the village average of household male or female credit participants. The parameter α_j is identified separately from the village FE only with panel data.

Panel data are thus needed to estimate any spillover effects. When there are spillover effects, unobserved village heterogeneity can be correlated with program placement, where the direction of causation is from program placement to unobserved village effects, not from village effects to program placement. This measurement problem implies that placement of a microfinance program may cause a village effect additional to any preexisting (time-invariant) village effects. Assuming that (a) a household's male or female program participation is measured by whether an individual participates in a program instead of the amount of borrowing and (b) the average village-level male or female participation rate is the village program participation intensity, we write the following regression equation:

$$Y_{ijt} = X_{ijt}\beta + C_{ijft}\delta_f + C_{ijmt}\delta_m + \Omega_{jft}\alpha_f + \Omega_{jmt}\alpha_m + \eta_{ijt} + \mu_{jt} + \varepsilon_{ijt}^c, \tag{4.7}$$

where Ω_js represent the external effects of a program in a village and have a value of zero if no program is located in the village. The coefficients δ_m and δ_f capture village-level program effects as well if Ω_j equals zero (i.e., none of the village-specific heterogeneity is caused by programs). If village externalities do exist (i.e., Ω_j does not equal zero), the spillover effects cannot be separately identified from the time-invariant village effects using cross-sectional survey data. With panel data, the extent of market saturation or village economies/diseconomies is captured by the village-level program participation rates. If the Ω_j terms are measured by the average village-level program participation rate, then the spillover effect is measured by the change in behavior of nonparticipants due to change in village-level program participation, captured by α.

As indicated, market saturation or spillover may be good or bad, depending on whether the coefficients of these village-participation variables are positive or negative. To account for the spillover effects, we rewrite the outcome equation, similar to (4.1), as follows:

$$Y_{ijt} = X_{ijt}\beta_y + C_{ijft}\delta_f + C_{ijmt}\delta_m + V_{ijft}\gamma_f + V_{ijmt}\gamma_m + \eta_{ij}^y + \mu_j^y + \varepsilon_{ijt}^y , \quad (4.8)$$

where V equals the village average of male or female loans and a measure of spillover effects.

Table 4.8a presents the results of the static model estimates, while table 4.8b shows the results of the dynamic model estimations, based on equation (4.8). A comparison of the results shows slight qualitative differences. According to the dynamic model, average village-level male borrowing does not appear to have an independent effect on household welfare above and beyond household-level male borrowing. This means there is no externality or spillover effect due to male borrowing. However, this is not the case using the static model (table 4.8a). Like female borrowing, average village-level male borrowing has a significant effect for some outcomes. Average village-level female borrowing increases household net worth but reduces nonland assets and girls' school enrollment. A 10 percent rise in the average village loans of female borrowers increases household net worth by 0.55 percent but reduces household nonland assets by 0.43 percent. By contrast, average village-level male borrowing reduces income and boys' school enrollment.

The negative village-level borrowing effect implies negative externality or village diseconomies, while the positive effect implies positive externality or spillover effect. The results thus suggest that higher average village lending does not necessarily crowd out the benefits of an individual's borrowing. The negative coefficient in the case of women's loans associated with household nonland assets is clear evidence of village diseconomies. But there are positive externalities between household net worth and women's borrowing. Thus, even if there are negative externalities for women's borrowing on nonland asset holdings, women's borrowing appears to have a positive spillover effect on household net worth.

Table 4.8 Impacts and Village Intensity of Microcredit Loans

a. Using p-score weighted household FE, model 1 (N = 1,509)

Explanatory variable	Log per capita total income (Tk./month)	Log male labor supply (hours/month)	Log female labor supply (hours/month)	Log household nonland assets (Tk.)	Log household net worth (Tk.)	Girls' school enrollment (ages 5–18)	Girls' school enrollment (ages 5–18)
Log male loans (Tk.)	0.002	0.049**	0.039*	0.038**	0.025**	−0.001	0.005
	(0.12)	(3.44)	(1.97)	(3.81)	(3.13)	(−0.17)	(0.48)
Log female loans (Tk.)	−0.001	0.043**	0.053**	0.030**	0.004	0.007**	0.013**
	(−0.24)	(4.96)	(5.33)	(4.69)	(0.79)	(2.06)	(2.89)
Log village average, male loans (Tk.)	−0.026**	0.007	−0.009	−0.003	0.002	−0.014**	0.006
	(−2.47)	(0.36)	(−0.30)	(−0.21)	(0.13)	(−2.15)	(0.63)
Log village average, female loans (Tk.)	0.009	−0.027	0.013	−0.043**	0.055**	0.006	−0.013*
	(0.84)	(−1.24)	(0.46)	(2.59)	(3.64)	(1.03)	(−1.76)
R^2	0.140	0.209	0.238	0.458	0.654	0.075	0.066

b. Using dynamic panel LDV model (N = 1,509)

Explanatory variable	Log per capita total income (Tk./month)	Log male labor supply (hours/month)	Log female labor supply (hours/month)	Log household nonland assets (Tk.)	Log household net worth (Tk.)
Log male loans (Tk.)	0.016*	0.032**	−0.028	0.035**	0.020**
	(1.83)	(3.21)	(−1.48)	(3.81)	(3.51)
Log female loans (Tk.)	0.015**	0.044**	0.017	0.018**	0.013*
	(2.20)	(4.84)	(1.01)	(2.31)	(1.83)
Log village average, male loans (Tk.)	−0.008	−0.016	0.009	0.024	0.022
	(−0.64)	(−0.87)	(0.28)	(1.36)	(0.99)
Log village average, female loans (Tk.)	0.041	0.044	−0.168	0.009**	0.008**
	(0.55)	(0.57)	(−1.25)	(2.45)	(4.92)
F statistics for the model	$F_{(28, 87)} = 6.98$, $p = 0.000$	$F_{(28, 86)} = 46.30$, $p = 0.000$	$F_{(28, 87)} = 33.08$, $p = 0.000$	$F_{(28, 87)} = 33.50$, $p = 0.000$	$F_{(28, 87)} = 131.96$, $p = 0.000$

Sources: World Bank/BIDS survey 1991/92 and 1998/99; World Bank/InM survey 2010/11.

Note: Figures in parentheses are t-statistics based on robust standard errors clustered at the village level. Loans refer to cumulative amount borrowed from all microcredit sources leading up to the survey year. Regressions include more control variables at the household level (e.g., age, sex, and education of household head and log of land assets) and village level (e.g., price of consumer goods; male and female wages; infrastructure, including schools and electricity availability; and proportion of irrigated land). FE = fixed effects; LDV = lagged dependent variable.

Significance level: * = 10 percent, ** = 5 percent or less.

Multiple Program Membership and MFI Competition

As previously mentioned, overlapping MFI membership is a relatively recent phenomenon. The 1991/92 survey showed no evidence of multiple program membership; but by 1998/99, some 9 percent of households had become concurrent members of more than one MFI, and this figure reached 32 percent by 2010/11. What accounts for such growth in multiple program membership? Does it reflect a higher demand for credit by borrowers not met by a single source? Is it paying back the loan from one source by borrowing from another? Or is it simply a matter of programs chasing the less credit-risky clients in an area?

The extent of multiple program membership could also be an outcome of market saturation, measured by the average village-level borrowing. Even if market saturation leads to diminishing returns to borrowing (i.e., village diseconomies), this can increase an individual's demand for credit, leading, in turn, to higher incidence of multiple program membership if the extra credit demanded comes from more than one source.[23] In this case, the village-level intensity of program participation would be viewed as a positive phenomenon; that is, the higher the amount of village-level borrowing, the higher the marginal effect of individual borrowing on the incidence of multiple program membership. Conversely, if the additional credit demand is being met by a single source, it would be viewed as having a negative effect on village-level borrowing.

Why is there higher demand for credit when village diseconomies lead to lower returns on borrowing? One possible explanation is that borrowers try to diversify income sources in order to cope with diminishing returns to borrowing and increasing income risks. Thus, higher access to credit helps households to diversify their income-earning activities. But, as village-level borrowing increases with growth in individual-level borrowing, the market becomes saturated; households are likely to specialize in case of positive externalities (village economies yield higher returns) and diversify in case of negative ones (village diseconomies yield lower returns). As already observed, individual-level borrowing has diminishing returns for some outcomes, suggesting a higher demand for extra credit to support income diversification. If this is so, the positive sign of the interactions between village- and individual-level credit must apply to both incidence of multiple income activities and multiple program membership. In either case of village economies and diseconomies, the additional demand for credit may lead to an increase in incidence of multiple program membership, provided that demand is satisfied by more than a single source.[24]

Writing a revised version of equation (4.1) by introducing multiple membership status (M) and village intensity of the MFIs (V) yields the following static model equation:

$$Y_{ijt} = X_{ijt}\beta_y + C_{ijft}\delta_f + C_{ijmt}\delta_m + M_{ijft}\kappa_f + M_{ijmt}\kappa_m + V_{jt}\gamma + \eta_{ij} + \mu_j + \varepsilon_{ijt}. \quad (4.9)$$

Similarly, we can have a dynamic LDV model corresponding to equation (4.9). Table 4.9a presents the p-score FE results according to the static

Table 4.9 Impacts of Borrowing from Multiple Sources and Microcredit Competition

a. Using p-score weighted household FE, model 1 (N = 1,509)

Explanatory variable	Log per capita total income (Tk./month)	Log male labor supply (hours/month)	Log female labor supply (hours/month)	Log household nonland assets (Tk.)	Log household net worth (Tk.)	Boys' school enrollment (ages 5–18)	Girls' school enrollment (ages 5–18)
Log loans (Tk.)							
Household males	−0.0002	0.050**	0.020	0.030**	0.021**	−0.006	0.005
	(−0.01)	(3.35)	(1.03)	(3.24)	(2.41)	(−1.12)	(0.54)
Household females	−0.002	0.034**	0.052**	0.034**	0.011**	0.006*	0.010**
	(−0.33)	(4.63)	(4.81)	(5.38)	(2.11)	(1.87)	(2.24)
Borrowing from multiple sources							
Household males	−0.220	−0.315	0.057**	0.138**	0.191	0.252	0.146
	(−0.79)	(−0.78)	(3.03)	(2.07)	(0.99)	(1.59)	(0.83)
Household females	0.011	0.131	0.051	0.015	−0.089**	0.076*	0.080**
	(0.23)	(1.28)	(0.40)	(0.31)	(−2.01)	(1.94)	(2.26)
MFI in village (no.)	0.032**	0.060**	0.055	0.012	0.025*	0.007	−0.007
	(2.20)	(2.98)	(1.51)	(0.82)	(1.78)	(0.85)	(−0.71)
R^2	0.141	0.212	0.242	0.457	0.652	0.078	0.067

table continues next page

Table 4.9 Impacts of Borrowing from Multiple Sources and Microcredit Competition (continued)

b. Using dynamic panel LDV model (N = 1,509)

Explanatory variable	Log per capita total income (Tk./month)	Log male labor supply (hours/month)	Log female labor supply (hours/month)	Log household nonland assets (Tk.)	Log household net worth (Tk.)
Log male loans (Tk.)	0.014*	0.029**	−0.031	0.033**	0.014**
	(1.66)	(2.98)	(−1.55)	(3.21)	(2.13)
Log female loans (Tk.)	0.014**	0.037**	0.005	0.021**	0.025**
	(2.12)	(3.71)	(0.32)	(2.40)	(3.85)
Household males borrowed from multiple sources (Tk.)	−0.016	−0.321	0.070**	0.304	0.071
	(−1.11)	(−0.65)	(3.51)	(1.57)	(1.62)
Household females borrowed from multiple sources (Tk.)	−0.001	0.091**	0.140	0.031	−0.110*
	(−0.01)	(2.21)	(1.09)	(0.42)	(−1.79)
MFIs in the village (no.)	0.025*	0.024	0.001	0.051**	0.110
	(1.79)	(1.38)	(0.01)	(3.06)	(5.13)
F statistics for the model	$F(29, 86) = 6.64$, $p = 0.000$	$F(29, 86) = 47.01$, $p = 0.000$	$F(29, 86) = 49.40$, $p = 0.000$	$F(29, 86) = 33.67$, $p = 0.000$	$F(29, 86) = 163.65$, $p = 0.000$

Sources: World Bank/BIDS survey 1991/92 and 1998/99; World Bank/InM survey 2010/11.

Note: Figures in parentheses are t-statistics based on robust standard errors clustered at the village level. Loans refer to cumulative amount borrowed from all microcredit sources leading up to the survey year. Regressions include more control variables at the household level (e.g., age, sex, and education of household head and log of land assets) and village level (e.g., price of consumer goods; male and female wages; infrastructure, including schools and electricity availability; and proportion of irrigated land). FE = fixed effect; MFI = microfinance institution; LDV = lagged dependent variable.

Significance level: * = 10 percent, ** = 5 percent or less.

model, while table 4.9b provides the results using the dynamic LDV model. As before, the results of the static and dynamic models do not differ qualitatively. Using the results of the dynamic LDV model (table 4.9b), κ equals zero if multiple membership status does not matter. However, if village density of MFIs does not have a separate and additional effect from what it induced through individual borrowing, the estimated coefficient of MFI village density is insignificant (i.e., γ equals zero).

Multiple sources of borrowing, independent of a household's borrowing from any source, appears to have an independent negative effect on net worth and a positive effect on male labor supply. That is, when higher amounts of individual borrowing are supported by multiple sources, the incidence of borrowing from multiple sources has an "above and beyond" negative effect on household net worth. This is a case of village diseconomies of higher level of borrowing from multiple sources. On the other hand, MFI competition has been a blessing for microcredit borrowers. By providing additional funds to support the income generation and productivity of microenterprises, a higher village density of MFIs is likely to increase (not decrease) household assets and net worth. This shows that village-level MFI density has positive but decreasing returns to household welfare.

Summary

Household-level panel data enable the use of a household-level FE method to treat program endogeneity without complicated estimation techniques and thus offers an alternative to investigate whether the results obtained from the analysis of cross-sectional data hold. Panel data, especially long panel data, also offer a clear substantive advantage over cross-sectional data in estimating microcredit impacts: They help to analyze dynamic issues, such as whether credit effects change (or decline) over time, whether market saturation with village diseconomies is a possibility for microfinance expansion in such countries as Bangladesh where MFIs are heavily concentrated, and whether the phenomenon of multiple program membership is a result of the credit expansion and an indication of income diversification due to village diseconomies. Panel data, however, are not a panacea as they have their own drawbacks in estimation.

Using long panel household survey data carried out at three points (1991/92, 1998/99, and 2010/11) over some 20 years in 87 villages of rural Bangladesh, this chapter investigated various dimensions of microcredit effects on a set of behaviors to validate earlier results obtained with cross-sectional or short panel data. In particular, it provided separate estimates of female and male credit from all sources of microcredit on household per capita income, nonland assets, household net worth, women's and men's labor supply, and schooling of children. It also provided estimates of the time-varying effects of credit on the same set of behaviors, as well as the role of an increasing level of market saturation and MFI competition on household welfare.

The estimates of microfinance effects on household income, assets, and other outcomes of interest thus far discussed indicate that male and female borrowing affect income, labor supply, household assets and net worth, and children's schooling; however, the effects are more pronounced for women's borrowing. The findings also show that past credit has a positive effect on some current outcomes, indicating increasing returns to borrowing—especially women's borrowing—for household outcomes. The static model results are either confirmed or strengthened by the dynamic model, which also controls for the effect of LDVs.

Results of the basic model unequivocally show that group-based credit programs have significant positive effects in raising household welfare, including per capita income, household nonland assets, and net worth. Microfinance increases income, the labor supply of men and women, household nonland assets and net worth, as well as boys' and girls' school enrollment. The results using long-panel data thus confirm most of the earlier findings—that microfinance matters a lot, and more for female than for male borrowers.

The results support the view that microcredit effects change over time, and show that the effects of current borrowing differ from those of past borrowing. For example, past credit has a higher impact on income than current credit. With higher village-level participation in microfinance programs, there is also a sign of village diseconomies due to market saturation. For example, with higher village-level aggregate, current male borrowing, the marginal effect of male borrowing on per capita income is lower.

The results also show certain patterns in participants' inclination to borrow from multiple sources and to diversify income. Multiple program membership, which has grown steadily over the past two decades, appears to have negative effects on some household outcomes. However, microfinance competition—captured by the number of MFIs operating in a village—appears to have beneficial effects, especially on growth in household nonland assets and net worth.

Results of the panel household analysis indicate the presence of market saturation, with possible village diseconomies and diminishing returns. This is due, in part, to credit expansion without much technological breakthrough in local economies. As discussed in chapter 2, our data suggest that more than two-thirds of the activities supported by microcredit programs in rural Bangladesh are in the trade and services sector, and this pattern of loan portfolio even increased over the study period (1991/92–2010/11). Trade is perhaps now saturated with microcredit loans, and households have already started to experience diminishing returns. In such circumstances, households must be assisted through skills training and development of improved marketing networks to expand activities into more rewarding sectors and beyond the local economy; otherwise, microfinance expansion cannot be sustained. In short, the current microfinance policy of credit expansion alone may not be enough for boosting income and productivity and thus sustained poverty reduction.

Annex 4A: Estimated Effects of Microfinance: Literature Review

There are two strands of studies on the beneficial role of microfinance. The first strand is based on nonexerimental research methods, while the second one is based on RCTs. Many of those in the first strand observed that microfinance promotes social, human, and economic development in numerous ways (e.g., Boonperm, Haughton, and Khandker 2009; Chemin 2008; Dunford 2006; Hossain 1988; Imai, Arun, and Annim 2010; Islam and Maitra 2012; Kaboski and Townsend 2005, 2012; Kevane and Wydick 2001; Khandker 1998, 2005; McIntosh 2008; Panjaitan-Drioadisuryo and Cloud 1999; Pitt and Khandker 1996, 1998; Pitt and others. 1999 Shaw 2004). For example, a recent study using panel data from 1997 to 2005 found that medium-term participants benefit more than short-term ones (Islam 2011). Another study using a long-panel survey (1991/92–2010/11) also found that households that remained with microfinance programs without breaks fared better than those who participated irregularly (Khandker and Samad 2014). A macro study using cross-country data also confirmed the positive impacts of microfinance (Imai and others 2012).

Findings from the RCT-based, second strand of studies were mixed. Notable among them are randomized evaluations of microfinance programs in six countries (India, Ethiopia, Mongolia, Morocco, Mexico, and Bosnia and Herzegovina), presented in a special issue of *American Economic Journal*, which we briefly describe here. In a study of 52 randomly selected neighborhoods in Hyderabad, India, Banerjee, Karlan, and Zinman (2015) found that, while expenditure on durable goods increased due to microcredit, overall consumption did not. The same study also found that small business investment and profits in preexisting businesses increased because of microcredit, but no changes were found in health, education, or women's empowerment. In rural areas of two provinces in Ethiopia, Tarozzi, Desai, and Johnson (2015) examined microcredit impacts on various outcomes (e.g., income, labor supply, education, and women's empowerment), using data from an RCT study conducted in 2003–06; they found no impacts for most of the outcomes of interest. A randomized study conducted in Mongolia found that group-based microfinance had positive impacts on female entrepreneurship and food consumption but none on employment hours or income (Attanasio and others 2015). In rural Morocco, a randomized evaluation of a microcredit intervention in 2006 found low uptake in the program areas (13 percent) but a significant increase in investment in self-employment activities among microcredit borrowers, as well as a gain in profit; however, this study also found a reduction in income from casual labor (Crépon and others 2015). Angelucci, Karlan, and Zinman (2015) conducted a randomized study of 16,000 households from the largest microlender in Mexico and Latin America, Compartamos Banco, attempting to assess community-level impacts on a wide range of outcomes (i.e., entrepreneurship, income, labor supply, expenditures, social status, and subjective well-being). The study also examined the distributional effects of microcredit benefits. However, it found no transformative impacts on the outcomes, and observed no heterogeneity in the benefits. Finally,

Augsburg and others (2015) conducted a randomized study of an MFI in Bosnia and Herzegovina, finding evidence of higher self-employment, business assets and profit for microfinance borrowers, with a reported drop in wage employment, consumption, and savings. Various other randomized studies found positive effects of microfinance (Coleman 1999, 2006; de Mel, McKenzie, and Woodruff 2008; Karlan and Zinman 2010; McKenzie and Woodruff 2008), while others did not (e.g., Karlan and Zinman 2011).

Besides the disparity in findings on the impacts of microfinance, there is an ongoing debate on the findings and methodology of Pitt and Khandker (1998), perhaps the most referenced study on microfinance impacts. The study has been questioned on various grounds (e.g., replicability, methodology, and findings) in a sequence of papers and postings by David Roodman (Roodman 2011, 2012; Roodman and Morduch 2009, 2011). Subsequently, Pitt and Khandker (2012) showed that Roodman's claim of nonreplicability of the findings of Pitt and Khandker (1998) was based on flawed techniques, which, upon correction, replicates those findings quite well. Pitt and Khandker (2012) also addressed a question raised by Roodman on the validity of the exclusion restrictions of the instruments used in Pitt and Khandker (1998), showing that the results reported hold up extremely well in the new analysis (Pitt and Khandker 2012). More recently, Pitt (2014) addressed Roodman and Morduch (2014), which sought to refute the findings of Pitt and Khandker (1998), claiming that those findings were not robust to deviations from normality of the second-stage errors, and that this nonnormality is an important source of bias. In response, Pitt (2014) showed that the claim of Roodman and Morduch (2014) is based on a "flawed econometric understanding and a lack of due diligence in formulating and interpreting statistical models." While such debates will continue and perhaps remain inconclusive, they may offer readers a deeper insight into the techniques and methodologies—particularly randomized versus nonrandomized impact methods—adopted in estimating microfinance impacts, or estimating any program effect.

Annex 4B: Joint Significance Test Results

Table 4B.1 Results for Explanatory Variables in the Attrition Equation
N = 1,769

Test statistic	Log per capita total income (Tk. month)	Log male labor supply (hours/ month)	Log female labor supply (hours/ month)	Log household nonland assets (Tk.)	Log household networth (Tk.)	Boys' school enrollment (ages 5–18)	Girls' school enrollment (ages 5–18)
$\chi^2(24)$	108.5	97.95	85.39	88.86	98.92	75.95	101.60
p-value	0.000	0.000	0.000	0.000	0.000	0.000	0.000

Sources: World Bank/BIDS survey 1991/92 and 1998/99; World Bank/InM survey 2010/11.
Note: For each outcome, attrition is estimated with a probit regression using 1991/92 sample where explanatory variables include all household- and community-level exogenous variables and the outcome variable itself. Then a joint significance test is run for all explanatory variables. The null hypothesis is that explanatory variables do not matter to attrition.

Table 4B.2 Results for Attrition and Attrition-Interacted Explanatory Variables in Outcome Equations
N = 1,769

Test statistic	Log per capita total income (Tk. month)	Log male labor supply (hours/ month)	Log female labor supply (hours/ month)	Log household nonland assets (Tk.)	Log household net worth (Tk.)	Boys' school enrollment (ages 5–18)	Girls' school enrollment (ages 5–18)
F(24, 86)	3.17	4.10	4.84	2.43	4.43	4.34	4.94
p-value	0.000	0.000	0.000	0.001	0.000	0.000	0.000

Sources: World Bank/BIDS survey 1991/92 and 1998/99; World Bank/InM survey 2010/11.
Note: The outcome variable is regressed on the attrition dummy, all exogenous variables, and the interactions of attrition and exogenous variables in the 1991/92 sample. Then a joint significance test is run for the attrition variable and the interaction of attrition and exogenous variables.

Notes

1. For example, a study conducted in Guatemala suggests that women entrepreneurs benefit from microcredit programs as they move from self-employment or perhaps from a single hired laborer to two or more hired laborers. As this performance is replicated across a large number of borrowers in a given area, it leads to local economic growth in an economy (Kevane and Wydick 2001).

2. Such studies include the following, among others: Attanasio and others 2011; Augsburg and others 2012; Banerjee and others 2010; Crépon and others 2011; de Mel, McKenzie, and Woodruff 2008; Karlan and Zinman 2010, 2011).

3. The supply-side analysis presented in chapter 3 examines the growth trend in MFI performance indicators (e.g., outreach, savings mobilized, loans outstanding, profitability, loan recovery, and portfolio diversification), using both aggregate-industry and program-level data over the past two decades.

4. The term *upazila* refers to the lowest formal administrative unit in Bangladesh (under division and district units, comparable to a rural subdistrict); in the geographical hierarchy, an upazila is above the village level and consists of about 10–50 villages.

5. Unlike Khandker (2005), the spilt-off households in this study's data analysis are not merged with parent households but are shown having the same parent identification code.

6. After reorganization, BRDB-12 was renamed *Palli Daridra Bimochon Foundation* (PDBF) (Rural Poverty Reduction Foundation). Though this organization is no longer part of BRDB, it is still within the same ministry of local government and rural development. To avoid confusion, the name BRDB is used throughout this book.

7. It should be noted that MFIs in Bangladesh charge interest rates as high as 35 percent, compared to about 13 percent charged by commercial banks; however, commercial banks do not lend to the poor, whose only option is to borrow from the MFIs or, alternatively, from informal lenders, who may charge interest rates as high as 240 percent per year (Faruqee and Khalily 2011).

8. For the purpose of reporting microcredit loan figures, this analysis distinguishes Grameen Bank and BRAC from other microcredit programs because these two programs have been consistently dominant throughout the last 20-year period.

9. These figures are consumer price index—adjusted.

10. It should be noted that women's share of loans (e.g., 38 percent in 2010/11) does not represent the overall distribution of BRAC's membership by gender. BRAC's

microloans, known as "dabi," are available only to women, while its SME loans, called "progoti," are available to both men and women. While it is true that more men than women take out SME loans, the vast majority of BRAC's clients are women. For example, in 2013, BRAC had 4 million microloan clients and 300,000 SME clients; disbursements under the microloans (dabi) totaled US$810 million, compared to US$668 million under the SME loans (progoti). Thus, women's share of BRAC loans was not more than 55 percent if all progoti loans were received by men and was slightly higher if a certain percentage of women received progoti loans.

11. Unlike other MFIs, Grameen Bank also mobilizes voluntary savings from both members and nonmembers; in recent years, its savings accounted for more than 80 percent of loans outstanding.

12. Because of microfinance's critical role in alleviating poverty in rural Bangladesh, we devote a separate chapter to examining the expenditure and poverty aspects of household welfare (chapter 6). We also consider various categories of income (e.g., farm and nonfarm) to determine whether microfinance helps the agriculture sector (chapter 7).

13. The panel data are useful for impact estimation but are not immune to estimation bias, as discussed later in this chapter.

14. This was done separately for the nine outcome variables.

15. Details on implementing this procedure can be found in Baluch and Quisumbing (2011).

16. This procedure differs from that done in Khandker (2005), which analyzed the two-point panel data (consisting of 1991/92 and 1998/99 surveys) by aggregating the split-off households at the second round after testing to ensure such households could be aggregated without incurring bias in the estimation process. Since the spawned households in the current analysis are treated as separate units, it is not necessary to perform such tests.

17. Propensity score weight is defined as follows: $pw = 1/p$ for participants, and $pw = 1/(1 - p)$ for nonparticipants, where p is the propensity score and pw is the propensity score weight. In this way, it is possible to obtain efficient estimates of average treatment effect using weight created from propensity score (Hirano, Imbens, and Ridder 2003).

18. Constructing second LDVs of boys' and girls' school enrollment is not possible since these variables are at the individual level; thus there are no regression results for school enrollment outcomes.

19. Similar time-varying effects of program participation (measured by a dummy variable) can be estimated. Khandker and Samad (2014) differentiated the effects of regular or continuous program participation from the effects of irregular or discontinuous participation.

20. That is, the past credit of a household in 1998/99 is equal to its current credit in 1991/92, and its past credit in 2010/11 is equal to its current credit in 1998/99. The past credit in 1991/92 is defined as zero for all households.

21. The credit demand function is a reduced form equation. However, we could also have allowed the credit demand to depend on past characteristics (lagged model), in addition to current characteristics. But that change in first-stage specification would not have changed the consistency of the second-stage outcome equation. Moreover, if we used the FE method instead of the FE-IV method for the outcome equation in the panel analysis, the first-stage credit equation would become a nonissue.

22. However, for such outcomes as consumption and poverty, the opposite is the case (see chapter 6).

23. In the case of village economies (market saturation with increasing returns), the demand for credit would induce multiple membership if the additional demand for credit were not met by a single source.

24. A single source may not be used to meet demand because (a) the lender has a ceiling per borrower or (b) the lender's perceived credit risk is high.

Bibliography

Alderman, Harold, Jere R. Behrman, Hans-Peter Kohler, John A. Maluccio, and Susan C. Watkins. 2000. "Attrition in Longitudinal Household Survey Data: Some Tests for Three Developing-Country Samples." Policy Research Working Paper 2447, World Bank, Washington, DC.

Angelucci, Manuela, Dean Karlan, and Jonathan Zinman. 2015. "Microcredit Impacts: Evidence from a Randomized Microcredit Program Placement Experiment by Compartamos Banco." *American Economic Journal: Applied Economics* 7 (1): 151–82.

Attanasio, Orazio, Britta Augsburg, Ralph de Haas, Emla Fitzsimons, and Heike Harmgart. 2011. "Group Lending or Individual Lending? Evidence from a Randomised Field Experiment in Mongolia." Working Paper 136, European Bank for Reconstruction and Development, London.

———. 2015. "The Impacts of Microfinance: Evidence from Joint-Liability Lending in Mongolia." *American Economic Journal: Applied Economics* 7 (1): 90–122.

Augsburg, Britta, Ralph de Haas, Heike Harmgart, and Costas Meghir. 2012. "Microfinance at the Margin: Experimental Evidence from Bosnia and Herzegovina." Working Paper 146, European Bank for Reconstruction and Development, London.

———. 2015. "The Impacts of Microfinance: Evidence from Bosnia and Herzegovina." *American Economic Journal: Applied Economics* 7 (1): 183–203.

Baluch, Bob, and Agnes Quisumbing. 2011, "Testing and Adjusting for Attrition in Household Panel Data." Toolkit Note, Chronic Poverty Research Centre, Manchester, UK.

Banerjee, Abhijit, Esther Duflo, Rachel Glennerster, and Cynthia Kinnan. 2010. "The Miracle of Microfinance? Evidence from a Randomized Evaluation." Abdul Latif Jameel Poverty Action Lab, Massachusetts Institute of Technology and Centre for Microfinance, Institute for Financial Management and Research, Cambridge, MA.

Banerjee, Abhijit, Dean Karlan, and Jonathan Zinman. 2015. "Six Randomized Evaluations of Microcredit: Introduction and Further Steps." *American Economic Journal: Applied Economics* 7 (1): 1–21.

Becketti, S., W. Gould, L. Lillard, and F. Welch. 1988. "The Panel Study of Income Dynamics after Fourteen Years: An Evaluation." *Journal of Labor Economics* 6 (4): 472–92.

Boonperm, Jirawan, Jonathan Haughton, and Shahidur R. Khandker. 2009. "Does the Village Fund Matter in Thailand?" World Bank Policy Research Paper 5011, World Bank, Washington, DC.

Chemin, M. 2008. "The Benefits and Costs of Microfinance: Evidence from Bangladesh." *Journal of Development Studies* 44 (4): 463–84.

Coleman, B. E. 1999. "The Impact of Group Lending in Northern Thailand." *Journal of Development Economics* 60 (1): 105–41.

———. 2006. "Microfinance in Northeast Thailand: Who Benefits and How Much?" *World Development* 34 (9): 1612–38.

Crépon, Bruno, Florencia Devoto, Esther Duflo, and William Parienté. 2011. "Impact of Microcredit in Rural Areas of Morocco: Evidence from a Randomized Evaluation." MIT Working Paper, Massachusetts Institute of Technology, Cambridge, MA.

———. 2015. "Estimating the Impact of Microcredit on Those Who Take It Up: Evidence from a Randomized Experiment in Morocco." *American Economic Journal: Applied Economics* 7 (1): 123–50.

Das, Marcel, Vera Toepoel, and Arthur van Soest. 2011. "Nonparametric Tests of Panel Conditioning and Attrition Bias in Panel Surveys." *Sociological Methods and Research* 40: 32–56.

de Mel, Suresh, David McKenzie, and Christopher Woodruff. 2008. "Returns to Capital in Microenterprises: Evidence from a Field Experiment." *Quarterly Journal of Economics* 123 (4): 1329–72.

Dunford, C. 2006. "Evidence of Microfinance's Contribution to Achieving the Millennium Development Goals: Freedom from Hunger." http://microfinancegateway.org /files/35795_file_Evidence_on_MDGS_Dunford.pdf.

Faruqee, Rashid, and M. A. Baqui Khalily. 2011. "Multiple Borrowing by MFI Clients." Policy Paper, Institute of Microfinance, Dhaka.

Fitzgerald, John, Peter Gottschalk, and Robert Moffitt. 1998. "An Analysis of Sample Attrition in Panel Data." *Journal of Human Resources* 33 (2): 251–99.

Heckman, J. 1979. "Sample Selection Bias as a Specification Error." *Econometrica* 47: 153–61.

Hirano, Keisuke, Guido Imbens, and Geert Ridder. 2003. "Efficient Estimation of Average Treatment Effects Using the Estimated Propensity Score." *Econometrica* 71 (4): 1161–89.

Hossain, M. 1988. "Credit for Alleviation of Rural Poverty: The Grameen Bank in Bangladesh." Research Report 65, International Food Policy Research Institute (IFPRI), Washington, DC.

Imai, K. S., T. Arun, and S. K. Annim. 2010. "Microfinance and Household Poverty Reduction: New Evidence from India." *World Development* 38 (12): 1760–74.

Imai, K. S., R. Gaiha, G. Thapa, and S. K. Annim. 2012. "Microfinance and Poverty: A Macro Perspective." *World Development* 40 (8): 1675–89.

Islam, Asadul. 2011. "Medium- and Long-term Participation in Microcredit: An Evaluation Using a New Panel Dataset from Bangladesh." *American Journal of Agricultural Economics* 93 (3): 847–66.

Islam, Asadul, and Pushkar Maitra. 2012. "Health Shocks and Consumption Smoothing in Rural Households: Does Microfinance Have a Role to Play?" *Journal of Development Economics* 97 (2): 232–43.

Kaboski, Joseph P., and Robert M. Townsend. 2005. "Policies and Impact: An Analysis of Village-Level Microfinance Institutions." *Journal of the European Economic Association* 3 (1): 1–50.

———. 2012. "The Impact of Credit on Village Economies." *American Economic Journal* 4 (2): 98–133.

Karlan, Dean, and Jonathan Zinman. 2010. "Expanding Credit Access: Using Randomized Supply Decisions to Estimate the Impacts." *Review of Financial Studies* 23 (1): 433–64.

———. 2011. "Microfinance in Theory and Practice: Using Randomized Credit Scoring for Impact Evaluation." *Science* 332 (6035): 1278–84.

Kevane, Michael, and Bruce Wydick. 2001. "Microenterprise Lending to Female Entrepreneurs: Sacrificing Economic Growth for Poverty Alleviation?" *World Development* 29 (7): 1225–36.

Khandker, Shahidur R. 1998. *Fighting Poverty with Microcredit: Experience in Bangladesh.* New York: Oxford University Press.

———. 2005. "Microfinance and Poverty: Evidence Using Panel Data from Bangladesh." *World Bank Economic Review* 19 (2): 263–86.

Khandker, Shahidur R., and Hussain A. Samad. 2014. "Microfinance Growth and Poverty Reduction in Bangladesh: What Does the Longitudinal Data Say?" *Bangladesh Development Studies* 37 (1 & 2): 127–57.

McIntosh, C. 2008. "Estimating Treatment Effects from Spatial Policy Experiments: An Application to Ugandan Microfinance." *Review of Economics and Statistics* 90 (1): 15–28.

McKenzie, David, and Christopher Woodruff. 2008. "Experimental Evidence on Returns to Capital and Access to Finance in Mexico." *World Bank Economic Review* 22 (3): 457–82.

Morduch, Jonathan. 1998. "Does Microfinance Really Help the Poor? New Evidence from Flagship Programs in Bangladesh." Harvard University, Cambridge, MA.

Panjaitan-Drioadisuryo, R. D. M., and K. Cloud. 1999. "Gender, Self-Employment and Microfinance Programs: An Indonesian Case Study." *The Quarterly Review of Economics and Finance* 39 (5): 769–79.

Pitt, Mark M. 1999. "Reply to Jonathan Morduch's 'Does Microfinance Really Help the Poor? New Evidence from Flagship Programs in Bangladesh.'" Brown University, Providence, RI.

———. 2014. "Re-Re-Reply to 'The Impact of Microcredit on the Poor in Bangladesh: Revisiting the Evidence.'" Policy Research Working Paper 6801, World Bank, Washington, DC.

Pitt, Mark M., and Shahidur R. Khandker. 1996. "Household and Intrahousehold Impact of the Grameen Bank and Similar Targeted Credit Programs in Bangladesh." World Bank Discussion Paper 320, World Bank, Washington, DC.

———. 1998. "The Impact of Group-based Credit Programs on Poor Households in Bangladesh: Does the Gender of Participants Matter?" *Journal of Political Economy* 106: 958–96.

———. 2012. "Replicating Replication Due Diligence in Roodman and Morduch's Replication of Pitt and Khandker (1998)." Policy Research Working Paper 6273, World Bank, Washington, DC.

Pitt, Mark M., Shahidur R. Khandker, and Jennifer Cartwright. 2006. "Empowering Women with Micro Finance: Evidence from Bangladesh." *Economic Development and Cultural Change* 54 (4): 791–831.

Pitt, Mark M., Shahidur R. Khandker, Signe-Mary McKernan, and M. Abdul Latif. 1999. "Credit Programs for the Poor and Reproductive Behavior in Low Income Countries: Are the Reported Causal Relationships the Result of Heterogeneity Bias?" *Demography* 36 (1): 1–21.

Roodman, D. 2011. *Due Diligence: An Impertinent Inquiry into Microfinance.* Washington, DC: CGD Books.

———. 2012. "Latest Impact Research: Inching Towards Generalization." Consultative Group to Assist the Poor microfinance blog. http://microfinance.cgap.org/2012/04/11 /latest-impact-research-inching-towards-generalization/.

Roodman, D., and J. Morduch. 2009. "The Impact of Microcredit on the Poor in Bangladesh: Revisiting the Evidence." CGD Working Paper 174, Center for Global Development, Washington, DC.

———. 2011. "The Impact of Microcredit on the Poor in Bangladesh: Revisiting the Evidence." Revised, CGD Working Paper 174, Center for Global Development, Washington, DC.

———. 2014. "The Impact of Microcredit on the Poor in Bangladesh: Revisiting the Evidence." *Journal of Development Studies* 50 (4): 583–604.

Shaw, J. 2004. "Microenterprise Occupation and Poverty Reduction in Microfinance Programs: Evidence from Sri Lanka." *World Development* 32 (7): 1247–64.

Tarozzi, Alessandro, Jaikishan Desai, and Kristin Johnson. 2015. "The Impacts of Microcredit: Evidence from Ethiopia." *American Economic Journal: Applied Economics* 7 (1): 54–89.

Thomas, Duncan, Elizabeth Frankenberg, and James P. Smith. 1999. "Lost but not Forgotten: Attrition and Follow-up in the Indonesian Family Life Survey." RAND Labor and Population Program Working Paper Series #99-01, RAND Corporation, Santa Monica, CA.

Ziliak, James P., and Thomas J. Kniesner. 1998. "The Importance of Sample Attrition in Life Cycle Labor Supply Estimation." *Journal of Human Resources* 33 (2): 507–30.

CHAPTER 5

Are Borrowers Overindebted?

Introduction

In the past, microfinance providers had a good assessment of borrowers' willingness and ability to repay loans, resulting in high overall repayment rates. But in recent years, the overextension of some microfinance markets has meant that many borrowers have become overindebted, meaning that they took out loans that they eventually found quite difficult to repay. Recently, microfinance programs have come under increasing scrutiny because of the fear that they might have caused some borrowers to fall into a debt trap. As shown in chapter 4, borrowing from multiple sources has been associated with negative growth in nonland assets; nonetheless, a higher density of microfinance institutions (MFIs), by increasing per capita income, has helped to increase household net worth.

Growing indebtedness may not be alarming if a household's net worth (the value of assets net of its liability from all sources, including microfinance) grows along with its loan portfolio, even with membership in multiple programs. For some borrowing households, it is quite likely that net worth has kept pace with or even exceeded rising debt, regardless of whether they borrowed from a single source or multiple sources. But for many others, this may not be the case. Thus, it is important to identify which borrowers are overindebted, understand the reasons for such overindebtedness, and determine corrective measures to overcome it.

To date, no study has focused exclusively on overindebtedness; however, various studies have examined the extent and scope of multiple program membership among microfinance borrowers.[1] For example, a recent study conducted by the Institute of Microfinance (InM) found that, in December 2012, the MFIs reported 35 million microfinance borrowers in Bangladesh, while actual membership was only 25 million unique borrowers, indicating about 40 percent overlapping membership. Khalily and Faridi (2011) found that incidence of multiple program membership in Bangladesh increased by 22 percent over time, rising from only 9 percent in 2000 to 31 percent in 2009; however, they concluded that such households accumulated higher net assets over time despite an increase in

their loans outstanding, suggesting that overlapping membership did not necessarily contribute to overindebtedness.

However, it is possible for overindebtedness to grow if households with overlapping membership fail to increase their level of income used to repay loans,
contribute to net savings, or do both. The findings from studies conducted in
other developing countries suggest that indebtedness and multiple borrowing
may be positively correlated. In Bolivia, for example, Vogelgesang (2003) found
that increasing competition among lenders and easy credit supply are associated
with higher levels of indebtedness. Gonzalez (2008) found a positive correlation
between length of loan maturity and indebtedness; however, those households
who were more experienced with particular lenders were less likely to be
overindebted.

A deeper understanding of the phenomenon of borrower indebtedness and
asset growth among microfinance borrowers is necessary to answer the following
key questions: How serious is the indebtedness of microfinance borrowers? Does
their indebtedness have the potential to nullify all of the welfare benefits of the
microfinance program? Is indebtedness due to low returns on microinvestments
or something else? Are the terms and conditions of microloans too stringent?
Even if microfinance generates benefits over a short period of time, are the
accrued benefits sustainable in the long run?[2]

To answer these questions, this chapter examines the phenomenon of overindebtedness among microfinance borrowers in Bangladesh. The role of overlapping membership, along with a host of other supply-and-demand factors, is
examined, using longitudinal household survey data. The long panel data, covering more than 20 years, are rich enough to measure both short- and long-term
indebtedness. The data are analyzed in terms of the nature and extent of indebtedness among MFI and non-MFI borrowers and the proximate influencing factors over time. The ultimate factors causing indebtedness are assessed, including
the possible effect of multiple program membership. In addition, the long-term
effect of microfinance on indebtedness is estimated after controlling for
household- and community-level explanatory variables, including the extent of
MFI competition as measured by the community-level density of MFIs. Before
turning to these issues, the next section reviews the concept of overindebtedness,
provides examples of its prevalence among developing countries, and discusses
its major drivers.

Definitions and Drivers of Overindebtedness

Overindebtedness is a complex concept that has been variously defined. Haas
(2006), for example, defines it as the inability of borrowers "to repay all debts
fully and on time," while Maurer and Pytkowska (2010) and Wisniwski (2010)
suggest that a household is overindebted if it cannot meet its payment obligations arising from all debt contracts. But the situation of overindebtedness occurs
chronically over time (Wisniwski 2010) and is often beyond the borrowers'
control (Schicks 2010). To count individuals or households as overindebted,

their debt problems need to be at least structural and persistent over a period of time (Canner and Luckett 1991; Faruqee 2013; Fisher 1933).

Researchers differ in assessing the level of repayment problems that are considered overindebted. Some count only legally bankrupt borrowers as overindebted; for others, the category includes cases of defaults or arrears or even all borrowers who struggle with an unhealthy debt balance. Some scholars have proposed several indicators as proxies for indebtedness, including multiple borrowing and asset-debt ratios (Schicks and Rosenberg 2011). An operational definition of overindebtedness can be constructed as a continuous or categorical variable. That is, indebtedness can be a ratio of liability over assets, which is a continuous variable, or overindebtedness can be measured as a categorical variable, showing whether a particular borrower's liability exceeds a certain percentage of his or her asset value. Such a measure of indebtedness is based on stocks of cumulative debt and assets and thus reflects medium- and long-term measures of indebtedness.

Alternatively, a short-term measure of indebtedness may be defined as the ratio of a household's monthly repayments divided by its monthly net income (Maurer and Pytkowska 2010). However, this indebtedness ratio does not indicate the point at which the borrower can be considered overindebted, in which case a threshold is required (e.g., if the borrower household spent more than 50–75 percent of its income on debt servicing).

In some countries, overindebtedness is a serious issue, appearing higher than the conventional wisdom on microfinance would suggest. For example, a survey conducted under a recent study in Ghana found that 26 percent of all respondents considered repayment of their loans easy, while some 33 percent struggled occasionally, 26 percent struggled more frequently, and 17 percent struggled permanently with each installment (Schicks 2010). A study conducted in Bosnia and Herzegovina found that about 28 percent of microfinance clients were seriously indebted or overindebted (Maurer and Pytkowska 2010), concluding that borrowing from multiple sources and overindebtedness go hand in hand. A recent study in Kosovo found that 25 percent of microfinance clients were overindebted to varying degrees (Spannuth and Pytkowska 2011); that study also showed that the level of indebtedness increased with the number of active loan contracts and that women were less frequently insolvent than men (i.e., 3 percent versus 7 percent). These research results suggest that, in some countries, overindebtedness is prevalent among 25–30 percent of MFI borrowers.

Following Schicks (2010), the drivers of overindebtedness may be external, lender related, or borrower related. Among the external factors, adverse shocks to income or expenses can make debt unmanageable. Similarly, a country's institutional and legal environment can influence the behavior of lenders and borrowers and thus exacerbate or reduce the risks of overindebtedness. In the microfinance markets of many developing countries, institutional protection from overindebtedness is weak, and a significant share of the responsibility lies with lenders. The existence of credit bureaus and level of competition can enhance or reduce the risks of overindebtedness. A system that allows for the easy flow of market information, judicial efficiency, and the existence of reasonable credit alternatives is critical to mitigating the problem (Anderloni and Vandone 2008; Vandone 2009).

Sociodemographic and economic characteristics of the borrower also contribute to the tendency to overborrow. For developing countries, typical factors cited by some researchers include natural disasters and changes in government policies (e.g., new taxes that increase input prices) (Stearns 1991), economic or political crises, and fluctuations in foreign currency markets (Bensoussan 2009). Economic characteristics of the borrower that cause indebtedness include low income (Anderloni and Vandone 2008), income instability (Webley and Nyhus 2001), low wealth (Del-Río and Young 2005; Disney, Bridges, and Gathergood 2008), and low returns on the investment for which the loan is used (Gonzalez 2008; Hulme 2007).[3]

MFI policies and operating procedures play a critical role in borrowers' overindebtedness. According to Vogelgesang (2003), MFI policies can determine overindebtedness and default levels. MFIs tend to underestimate their impact on borrowers' debt load, believing that their loans substitute for existing informal loans with poor terms, which may not be the case. In addition, the volume-focused incentive system for their staff members may drive some MFIs to lend clients too much (Brix and McKee 2010; DeVaney 2006; Rahman 1999). MFIs may aggressively market products that overemphasize portfolio growth and that are inappropriate to borrowers' situations. For example, if maturities are short and installment schedules too inflexible, borrowers with volatile incomes may face problems repaying on time. Such difficulties are exacerbated if the MFIs are reluctant to reschedule loans, even when borrowers have liquidity difficulties. Microlender operating procedures can also contribute to overindebtedness (e.g., by being too lax about upfront evaluations of repayment capacity or having nontransparent terms and conditions).

The purpose and manner of loan use also affect repayment capacity. For example, if a loan is used for activities that yield a substantially lower return than the interest rate or no return (e.g., if a loan is used for consumption smoothing), overindebtedness may follow. Also, the timing of loan disbursement can be crucial. For example, the empirical work of Bouquet and others (2007) in Madagascar found that disbursement timing was the product feature most frequently cited by borrowers as the reason for repayment problems. Productive investments, especially those subject to seasonality, require the availability of resources when the investment opportunity exists. If the MFIs fail to disburse on time, borrowers cannot earn the returns required for repayment.

Overindebtedness is also determined by borrower behavior. A borrower's inexperience with the banking system or personal difficulty in resisting temptation or social pressure can lead to irresponsible borrowing decisions. Soman and Cheema (2002), for example, found that borrowers inexperienced with credit that trusted the bank's judgment may have erroneously viewed the high size of their credit limit as the limit of what they could afford.

Evidence on Indebtedness, Multiple Borrowing, and Credit Constraints

In this section, we consider the extent of indebtedness among microfinance program participants over time, using two measures: one asset based and the other flow based. The asset-based measure, defined as the ratio of debts to assets, is a long-term measure of indebtedness, while the flow-based measure, defined as the yearly loan payment over annual household income, is a short-term measure of indebtedness.[4]

Comparison of Indebtedness Types

We define various degrees of indebtedness using some cutoff points. For both measures, households with an indebtedness ratio of 20 percent or less are considered unindebted. The remaining households thus have various levels of indebtedness. Households are considered moderately indebted if their indebtedness ratio is 20–40 percent, overindebted if it is 40–60 percent, and seriously indebted if it exceeds 60 percent. Because it is long-term, the asset-based measure of indebtedness is perhaps better than the short-term, flow-based measure; that is, a household's liability may be better measured against its assets, rather than its income. Moreover, because income generation is a process rather than an end in itself, accumulated debt at a particular point in time is better assessed against accumulated assets. However, from the perspective of debt-servicing obligations, which must be met from income, the flow-based measure may better reflect a household's current situation. Therefore, in this chapter, both measures are used to present the extent of indebtedness.

Table 5.1 presents the distribution of various types of indebtedness among the sampled households over the 20-year study period (1991/92–2010/11). The aggregate measures of indebtedness over the three periods surveyed are remarkably similar for both flow (income-liability) and stock (asset-liability) measures. As indicated, over the 20-year period, an average of 24.3 percent of households were considered indebted using the asset-liability measure, compared to an average of 25.1 percent using the income-liability measure. While 6 percent were overindebted by any measure, more than 10 percent were seriously indebted; that is, liability constituted more than 60 percent of these households' assets or income.

According to the asset-liability measure, 21.6 percent were indebted in 1991/92, compared to 37.2 percent in 2010/11, implying an annual increase of less than one percentage point over the 20-year period. Over the same period, overindebted borrowers increased from 4.8 percent to 6.7 percent, while those considered seriously indebted grew from 9.5 percent to 14.6 percent. Using the income-liability measure, the percentage increase in incidence of indebtedness was higher for all types of indebtedness. For example, the share of seriously indebted households rose from only 1.3 percent in 1991/92 to 19.9 percent in 2010/11. These findings are consistent with those from such developing countries as Bolivia and India.

Beyond Ending Poverty • http://dx.doi.org/10.1596/978-1-4648-0894-4

Table 5.1 Extent of Household Indebtedness in the Three Survey Periods

	Measure of indebtedness	
Extent of household indebtedness	Stocks based[a]	Flow based[b]
1991/92 (N = 1,488)		
Indebtedness index	0.205	0.053
Degree of indebtedness (%)[c]		
Not indebted	78.4	93.0
Moderately indebted	7.3	4.8
Overindebted	4.8	0.9
Seriously indebted	9.5	1.3
1998/99 (N = 1,750)		
Indebtedness index	0.192	0.125
Degree of indebtedness (%)[c]		
Not indebted	77.0	0.791
Moderately indebted	9.4	0.107
Overindebted	4.5	0.057
Seriously indebted	9.1	0.045
2010/11 (N = 2,287)		
Indebtedness index	0.306	0.473
Degree of indebtedness (%)[c]		
Not indebted	62.8	57.3
Moderately indebted	15.9	14.0
Overindebted	6.7	8.8
Seriously indebted	14.6	19.9
Aggregate for the three survey periods (N = 5,525)		
Indebtedness index	0.243	0.251
Degree of indebtedness (%)[c]		
Not indebted	71.5	73.8
Moderately indebted	11.5	10.5
Overindebted	5.5	5.7
Seriously indebted	11.5	10.0

Sources: World Bank/BIDS survey 1991/92, 1998/99; World Bank/InM survey 2010/11.

a. Defined by household debt to nonland ratio.

b. Defined by household annual loan payment to annual income ratio.

c. A household is considered not indebted if the ratio is less than or equal to 0.2, moderately indebted if the ratio is higher than 0.2 but less than or equal to 0.4, overindebted if the ratio is higher than 0.4 but less than or equal to 0.6, and seriously indebted if the ratio is higher than 0.6.

While the findings reported in table 5.1 are based on rural households, table 5.2 shows a similar distribution for MFI and non-MFI borrowers.[5] Interestingly, both of these borrower groups are indebted but at different levels, with the extent of indebtedness generally higher (though not always statistically significant) for MFI borrowers. For example, according to the stocks-based (assets) measure, some 17 percent of MFI borrowers are seriously indebted overall, compared to 13 percent for non-MFI borrowers. Indebtedness is also found to increase for both groups over time. For example, among the

Table 5.2 Extent of Household Indebtedness by Source of Borrowing in the Three Survey Periods

Extent of household indebtedness	Stocks-based measure			Flow-based measure		
	MFI borrowers	Non-MFI borrowers	t-statistic	MFI borrowers	Non-MFI borrowers	t-statistic
1991/92 (N = 763)						
Not indebted (%)	68.0	57.6	2.65	78.0	76.5	0.42
Moderately indebted (%)	10.1	23.8	−4.88	14.0	19.4	−1.79
Overindebted (%)	7.3	6.0	0.64	4.0	0.0	2.88
Seriously indebted (%)	14.6	12.6	0.67	4.0	4.1	−0.08
1998/99 (N = 896)						
Not indebted (%)	53.6	62.8	−1.80	48.6	73.2	−4.80
Moderately indebted (%)	18.2	15.2	0.73	26.6	12.0	3.28
Overindebted (%)	9.4	8.8	0.23	14.4	3.7	3.05
Seriously indebted (%)	18.8	13.2	1.42	10.4	11.1	−0.22
2010/11 (N = 1,461)						
Not indebted (%)	55.6	46.2	1.62	27.2	34.6	−1.41
Moderately indebted (%)	19.0	25.3	−1.36	23.7	26.6	−0.58
Overindebted (%)	8.4	13.3	−1.50	14.9	15.1	−0.05
Seriously indebted (%)	17.0	15.2	0.41	34.2	23.7	1.89
Aggregate for the three survey periods (N = 3,120)						
Not indebted (%)	56.9	56.4	0.17	41.0	64.9	−8.46
Moderately indebted (%)	17.4	21.5	−1.84	23.1	18.8	1.77
Overindebted (%)	8.5	8.7	−0.12	13.1	5.0	4.31
Seriously indebted (%)	17.2	13.4	1.74	22.8	11.3	4.89

Sources: World Bank/BIDS survey 1991/92 and 1998/99; World Bank/InM survey 2010/11.
Note: The sample in this table is restricted to MFI and non-MFI borrowers only; non-MFI borrowing sources are limited to formal sources (e.g., commercial banks, agricultural banks, and cooperatives). MFI = microfinance institution.

MFI borrowers, some 10 percent were moderately indebted in 1991/92, compared to 18 percent and 19 percent in 1998/99 and 2010/11, respectively.

One possible reason for such rising indebtedness is the corresponding incidence of multiple program membership or multiple sources of borrowing. Table 5.3 presents the distribution of program membership (i.e., single- versus multiple-program borrowers) over time by the extent of indebtedness.

As shown, multiple-program membership was nonexistent in 1991/92, increasing to 11.9 percent in 1998/99 and 36.0 percent by 2010/11. Indebtedness was higher for multiple-program members, compared to single-program members. For example, using the stocks-based (assets) measure, overindebtedness in 1998/99 was 9.1 percent for single-source borrowers and 12.3 percent for multiple-source borrowers. The corresponding figures for serious indebtedness over the same period were 17.9 percent and 25.7 percent, respectively. These findings suggest that indebtedness is highly correlated with borrowing from multiple sources. Of course, lenders do not know whether their borrowers have taken out loans from other lenders unless the borrowers reveal this information.

Table 5.3 Extent of Household Indebtedness and Borrowing from Multiple MFI Sources in the Three Survey Periods

Extent of household indebtedness	Stocks-based measure			Flow-based measure		
	Single-source borrowers[a]	Multiple-source borrowers[b]	t-statistic	Single-source borrowers[a]	Multiple-source borrowers[b]	t-statistic
1991/92 (N = 689)[c]						
Not indebted (%)	68.0			77.9		
Moderately indebted (%)	10.1			14.1		
Overindebted (%)	7.3			4.0		
Seriously indebted (%)	14.6			4.0		
Multiple-source borrowers: 0%						
1998/99 (N = 827)						
Not indebted (%)	55.8	36.9	3.56	51.4	27.6	4.48
Moderately indebted (%)	17.2	25.1	−1.90	25.1	37.6	−2.65
Overindebted (%)	9.1	12.3	−1.03	13.7	19.6	−1.55
Seriously indebted (%)	17.9	25.7	−1.86	9.7	15.2	−1.67
Multiple-source borrowers: 11.9%						
2010/11 (N = 1,411)						
Not indebted (%)	63.4	41.8	8.03	35.4	12.7	9.49
Moderately indebted (%)	16.4	23.6	−3.35	26.0	19.6	2.74
Overindebted (%)	6.2	12.3	−4.01	14.2	16.0	−0.93
Seriously indebted (%)	14.0	22.3	−3.98	24.4	51.7	−10.80
Multiple-source borrowers: 36.0%						
Aggregate for the three periods (N = 2,927)						
Not indebted (%)	61.8	41.2	9.74	49.1	15.1	16.63
Moderately indebted (%)	15.4	23.8	−5.13	23.4	22.1	0.63
Overindebted (%)	7.4	12.3	−4.06	12.0	16.5	−3.05
Seriously indebted (%)	15.4	22.7	−4.47	15.5	46.3	−17.75
Multiple-source borrowers: 23.7%						

Sources: World Bank/BIDS survey 1991/92 and 1998/99; World Bank/InM survey 2010/11.
Note: The sample in this table is restricted to MFI borrowers. MFI = microfinance institution.
a. Those who borrowed from one microfinance lender during the preceding five years of a survey period.
b. Those who borrowed from more than one microfinance lender during the preceding five years of a survey period.
c. The blank cells for 1991/92 indicate there were no multiple-source borrowers at that time.

Why Do Households Borrow from Multiple Sources?

One possible reason for households having multiple program membership is credit constraint. A household is considered credit constrained if its desired loan amount is less than the amount it can obtain, given the interest rate and other terms of the loan. In such cases, a household is likely to seek additional credit from other sources to satisfy its unmet demand. A household's decision to borrow from multiple sources may thus depend on the extent of the credit constraint it encounters at the lender of first choice. That is, a single-source borrower may have been less credit constrained than a multiple-source borrower.

A comparison of the distribution of multiple MFI membership with the extent to which households are credit constrained shows that incidence of multiple program membership is much higher among credit-constrained households.[6] Furthermore, this percentage has risen over time.

Table 5.4 shows that, in 1998/99, some 16 percent of credit-constrained households borrowed from multiple programs, compared to 7.5 percent for households that were not credit constrained. In 2010/11, these percentages increased to 55.3 and 33.3 percent, respectively.

Does Extent of Indebtedness Vary by Extent of Credit Constraint?

The research findings show that the extent of indebtedness was higher for credit-constrained households, compared to households without credit constraints, and this difference grew over time (table 5.5). For example, according to the stocks-based (assets) measure of indebtedness, 31 percent of credit-constrained households were indebted in 1991/92; this figure rose to 49 percent in 1998/99 and 57 percent in 2010/11. The corresponding figures for households without credit constraints were 34 percent in 1991/92, 44 percent in 1998/99, and 43 percent in 2010/11.

If borrowing from multiple sources resulted mainly from unmet demand for credit and higher borrowing amounts were mostly for supporting productive uses of loans, we would expect less indebtedness among multiple-source borrowers. But this is not the case. As shown in table 5.4, the extent of indebtedness is higher among multiple-source borrowers, and this finding is consistent for both measures of indebtedness.[7]

Extent of indebtedness may not always be a reliable measure of household welfare. Because it is defined somewhat arbitrarily by cutoff points, we are unsure whether household net worth—a stock measure of total value of assets net of outstanding loans from all sources—accumulated over time follows a similar pattern.

Table 5.6 suggests that, although unindebted households had significantly more net worth than their counterpart indebted households in earlier survey years (1991/92 and 1998/99), the difference in net worth between these two groups was not statistically significant in the more recent survey year (2010/11).

Table 5.4 Extent of Multiple-Source Borrowing by Household Credit Constraint

Survey period	Among households with credit constraints (%)	Among households without credit constraints (%)	t-statistics of the difference
1991/92 (N = 689)	0.0 (N = 508)	0.0 (N = 181)	–
1998/99 (N = 827)	16.0 (N = 423)	7.5 (N = 404)	3.81
2010/11 (N = 1,411)	55.3 (N = 187)	33.3 (N = 1,224)	5.72
Aggregate (N = 2,927)	19.0 (N = 1,118)	26.0 (N = 1,809)	−4.18

Sources: World Bank/BIDS survey 1991/92 and 1998/99; World Bank/InM survey 2010/11.
Note: The sample in this table is restricted to microfinance institution borrowers. There were no multiple-source borrowers in 1991/92. Incidence of multiple borrowing is higher among credit-constrained households for individual years, but aggregate figures show the reverse pattern. In 2010/11, the number of credit-constrained households is much smaller than that of households without credit constraints, which pushes the aggregate average for credit-constrained households to a lower value than that of households without credit constraints.

Table 5.5 Extent of Household Indebtedness by Credit Constraint

Extent of household indebtedness	Stocks-based measure			Flow-based measure		
	Households with credit constraints	Households without credit constraints	t-statistic	Households with credit constraints	Households without credit constraints	t-statistic
1991/92 (N = 689)						
Not indebted (%)	68.8	65.7	0.78	78.4	76.7	0.46
Moderately indebted (%)	9.1	13.1	−1.53	13.7	14.9	−0.41
Overindebted (%)	7.1	7.9	−0.38	4.0	4.0	0.00
Seriously indebted (%)	15.0	13.3	0.56	3.9	4.4	−0.25
1998/99 (N = 827)						
Not indebted (%)	51.0	56.3	−1.54	45.8	51.7	−1.76
Moderately indebted (%)	17.2	19.2	−0.75	28.9	24.0	1.56
Overindebted (%)	10.1	8.8	0.68	15.0	13.8	0.52
Seriously indebted (%)	21.7	15.7	2.20	10.3	10.5	−0.07
2010/11 (N = 1,411)						
Not indebted (%)	43.1	57.3	−3.56	14.9	29.0	−3.92
Moderately indebted (%)	26.9	17.9	2.86	31.1	22.6	2.48
Overindebted (%)	10.1	8.2	0.85	10.9	15.4	−1.55
Seriously indebted (%)	19.9	16.6	1.08	43.1	33.0	2.61
Aggregate for the three periods (N = 2,927)						
Not indebted (%)	55.3	57.6	−1.20	50.2	36.5	7.17
Moderately indebted (%)	16.5	17.9	−0.89	24.3	22.5	1.09
Overindebted (%)	9.1	8.3	0.75	10.5	14.4	−2.95
Seriously indebted (%)	19.1	16.2	1.92	15.0	26.6	−7.13

Sources: World Bank/BIDS survey 1991/92 and 1998/99; World Bank/InM survey 2010/11.
Note: The sample in this table is restricted to microfinance institution borrowers. A household is considered credit constrained if any member of it is credit constrained, which is determined by the member's willingness to borrow more at the same interest rate for a given loan if there were no restrictions on the loan amount.

Similarly, overall net worth is not necessarily higher for a single-source borrower than for a multiple-source borrower (table 5.7).

But the same relationship is not valid for a credit-constrained household, compared to a household without credit constraint. Although household net worth does not vary significantly between households with and without credit constraint in any given year, nonconstrained households have a higher overall net worth, which is statistically significant (table 5.8).

These findings suggest that, even if multiple-program members borrow more and are more credit constrained than single-source borrowers, it does not follow that they are worse off. Thus, incidence of multiple-source borrowing is not necessarily a cause of high indebtedness. Yet, the fact that incidence of multiple-source borrowing has reached up to 40 percent in recent years suggests that rising MFI competition has perhaps contributed to growing multiple-program membership and rising indebtedness in Bangladesh. However, this is not necessarily a major source of concern since the net worth of borrowers is also rising

Table 5.6 Household Net Worth by Extent of Indebtedness in the Three Survey Periods (Tk.)

	Measure of indebtedness			
Extent of household indebtedness	Stocks based		Flow based	
1991/92 (N = 1,472)				
Not indebted	136,988.8	} $t = 2.94$	128,140.1	} $t = 0.63$
Indebted	88,908.4		111,719.2	
1998/99 (N = 1,612)				
Not indebted	289,190.2	} $t = 2.51$	274,076.3	} $t = 1.45$
Indebted	118,791.6		172,129.9	
2010/11 (N = 2,230)				
Not indebted	495,874.4	} $t = 1.34$	529,296.8	} $t = 2.38$
Indebted	406,169.4		374,031.2	
Aggregate for the three periods (N = 5,314)				
Not indebted	320,224.7	} $t = 1.26$	307,351.7	} $t = 0.07$
Indebted	274,653.0		309,853.8	

Sources: World Bank/BIDS survey 1991/92 and 1998/99; World Bank/InM survey 2010/11.

Table 5.7 Household Net Worth by Multiple-Source Borrowing from MFIs (Tk.)

Survey period	Single-source borrowers	Multiple-source borrowers	t-statistics of the difference
1991/92 (N = 678)	67,696.7	—	—
1998/99 (N = 706)	149,118.3	122,956.3	0.76
2010/11 (N = 1,372)	361,718.5	262,934.4	2.41
Overall (N = 2,756)	235,926.4	245,686.9	0.37

Sources: World Bank/BIDS survey 1991/92 and 1998/99; WB/InM survey 2010/11.
Note: The sample in this table is restricted to MFI borrowers. There were no multiple-source borrowers in 1991/92. MFI = microfinance institution; — = not available.

Table 5.8 Household Net Worth by Credit Constraint in the Three Survey Periods

Survey period	Among households with credit constraints (Tk.)	Among households without credit constraints (Tk.)	t-statistics of the difference
1991/92 (N = 678)	70,028.8	60,711.6	1.13
1998/99 (N = 706)	149,060.0	143,347.5	0.27
2010/11 (N = 1,372)	269,760.2	334,045.2	−1.07
Overall (N = 2,756)	147,504.8	281,744.5	−5.68

Sources: World Bank/BIDS survey 1991/92 and 1998/99; World Bank/InM survey 2010/11.
Note: The sample in this table is restricted to microfinance institution borrowers.

over time. In the following sections, we examine whether the village-level density of MFIs in Bangladesh, measured by the number of nongovernmental organizations (NGOs) in a village—a possible source of rising multiple program membership and measure of MFI competition—is causing the extent of overindebtedness in the country.

Determinants of Indebtedness: Does MFI Competition Matter?

As earlier mentioned, both demand- and supply-side variables affect the observed outcomes of indebtedness among microfinance borrowers. Demand-side variables (say a vector X) are measured by household characteristics (e.g., age, education, and gender of the borrower and those of his/her spouse, type of business/enterprise owned, dependency ratio, and land assets), as well as household shocks (e.g., exposure to floods and other natural calamities, death of family members, and loss of income-generating activities). All of these variables are likely to determine the extent of demand for loans, as well as the loan absorption capacity of the borrowers.

Supply-side variables (say vector B) include rates of interest charged for various types of loans or savings products offered by various NGOs, the extent of NGO coverage in each sampled village (which measures the degree of competition among MFIs), and the types of products offered by the NGOs. In addition, we include village and community infrastructure variables (e.g., presence of commercial banks, electricity, roads, schools, and markets). These variables are expected to influence both returns to private investment financed by the NGOs and the portfolios they offer and thus are proxies for both supply- and demand-side indicators of the extent of overindebtedness as observed at the household or enterprise level.

However, the problem in estimating the role of demand, supply, and environmental factors in indebtedness is that program placement by the NGOs in villages is nonrandom, and household participation in microfinance programs is highly self-selected (e.g., Pitt and Khandker 1998). Moreover, environmental factors are contextual and are quite dependent on a village's agroclimate endowments. Therefore, simply regressing indebtedness as a measure of welfare on household-, program-, and community-level variables using cross-sectional data would be biased in estimating what influences the degree of indebtedness. Panel surveys, especially long ones, are useful in estimating the causal effects of these supply- and demand-side factors on the level of indebtedness.[8]

Estimation Strategy

To estimate the net effects of both demand- and supply-side variables on indebtedness, we consider the reduced-form equation of indebtedness outcomes (Y_{ijt}) of i-th household living in j-th village in period t, expressed as follows:

$$Y_{ijt} = \alpha X_{ijt} + \rho B_{jt} + \eta_{ijt} + \mu_{jt} + \varepsilon_{ijt}, \qquad (5.1)$$

where α equals a vector measuring the effects of demand-side variables (X), including household-level program participation in a microfinance program, and ρ vector measures the effects of supply-side variables (B), including the presence of MFIs and commercial banks in the village, and community-level variables, including weather-related shocks; η_{ijt} represents household-level time-varying heterogeneity, μ_{jt} represents community- and NGO-level time-varying heterogeneity, and ε_{ijt} is a nonsystematic error.

Calculating the deviations of all variables from their respective mean values in equation (5.1) can be expressed as follows:

$$\left(Y_{ijt} - \bar{Y}_{ij}\right) = \alpha\left(X_{ijt} - \bar{X}_{ij}\right) + \rho\left(B_{jt} - \bar{B}_j\right) + \left(\eta_{ijt} - \bar{\eta}_{ij}\right) + \left(\mu_{jt} - \bar{\mu}_j\right) + \left(\varepsilon_{ijt} - \bar{\varepsilon}_{ij}\right)$$

$$\Rightarrow \Delta Y_{ijt} = \alpha\Delta X_{ijt} + \rho\Delta B_{jt} + \Delta\eta_{ijt} + \Delta\mu_{jt} + \Delta\varepsilon_{ijt}. \tag{5.2}$$

Since the terms, η, μ, and ε are correlated, consisting of unobserved village and household heterogeneity, and cannot be differenced out over time, the simple ordinary least squares (OLS) estimation of equation (5.2) will be inconsistent. Following the methods adopted in earlier chapters, we estimated the effect of borrowing on the status of household indebtedness using two models: (a) a static model that uses the p-score weighted, household-level FE method and (b) a dynamic model, including the lagged dependent variable (LDV) method to estimate borrowing effect, provided that LDVs appear as additional regressors in estimation.

Regression Results

Table 5.9 provides the descriptive statistics for all relevant explanatory variables used in the regression, including both household- and community-level variables. Overall, some 41 percent of households borrowed from MFI sources, compared to only 5 percent that borrowed from formal sources. Some 13 percent of villages had access to commercial banks, while an average of five MFIs operated in each village, implying a large concentration of MFIs in Bangladesh. Yet 33 percent of MFI borrowers were found to be credit constrained. Interestingly, 32 percent of households borrowed from a single source and about 10 percent from multiple sources. While 48 percent of households experienced natural calamities, some 9 percent lost at least one family member or otherwise incurred losses in their income-generating activities (e.g., loss of a cow), and 4 percent experienced some type of financial loss (e.g., theft) over the three years prior to the survey.

Table 5.10 presents the FE estimates of indebtedness (i.e., whether a household is indebted, meaning its debt liability exceeds 20 percent of income or stock of debt exceeds 20 percent of nonland assets). We have estimates using alternative model specifications (one model uses three years of panel data without shock variables and the other uses two years of panel data with shock variables).[9] The debt-asset measure, a long-term measure of indebtedness, is found to have a declining trend over time.

Among family characteristics, male-headed households are more indebted than female-headed households in the short run, but not over the long term. Similarly, households headed by younger members are more likely to be indebted than those headed by older people in the short run; but age of the household head does not matter for long-term indebtedness. While the education level does

Table 5.9 Descriptive Statistics for Key Variables of Interest in the Three Survey Periods
N = 1,509

Explanatory variable	Mean[a]
Sex of household head (1 = male, 0 = female)	0.892
	(0.311)
Age of household head (years)	44.9
	(13.8)
Education of household head (years)	2.92
	(3.71)
Dependency ratio	0.411
	(0.209)
Household land assets (decimals)	96.5
	(248.1)
Number of relatives household received money from in last 10 years	2.1
	(3.0)
Shocks faced by household in last three years[b]	
Death of family members	0.090
	(0.286)
Loss from income-generating activities	0.093
	(0.291)
Natural calamities	0.482
	(0.500)
Other financial losses/expenditure	0.040
	(0.196)
Household borrowing source	
MFIs	0.411
	(0.492)
Non-MFI commercial sources	0.051
	(0.291)
Single MFI	0.316
	(0.465)
Multiple MFIs	0.098
	(0.297)
Household cumulative borrowing source (Tk.)	
MFIs	7,096.0
	(18,424.7)
MFIs, short term	9,936.3
	(27,646.4)
MFIs, medium term	13,135.0
	(32,428.6)
MFIs, long term	14,176.2
	(34,322.5)
Household is credit constrained	0.330
	(0.470)
Village has commercial banks	0.130
	(0.336)
Number of microfinance programs operating in the village	4.5
	(3.3)

Sources: World Bank/BIDS survey 1991/92 and 1998/99; World Bank/InM survey 2010/11.
Note: MFI = microfinance institution.
a. Figures in parentheses are standard deviations.
b. Summary statistics on shock variables are based on survey years 1998/99 and 2010/11 only since they were not available for the 1991/92 survey.

Table 5.10 Household Fixed-Effects Estimates of Indebtedness

Key explanatory variable	Model 1[a]		Model 2[b]	
	Stocks-based measure	Flow-based measure	Stocks-based measure	Flow-based measure
Period = 1998/99	−0.490	−0.518**		
	(−1.25)	(−1.41)		
Period = 2010/11	−1.406**	−0.498	2.315**	−0.295
	(−2.65)	(−1.04)	(−4.28)	(−0.38)
Sex of household head (1 = male, 0 = female)	−0.011	0.092**	0.043	0.106**
	(−0.41)	(2.93)	(1.48)	(3.10)
Age of household head (years)	−0.001	−0.002**	−0.0001	−0.002**
	(−1.12)	(−2.14)	(−0.16)	(−2.32)
Education of household head (years)	−0.003	−0.004	−0.001	−0.005
	(−0.74)	(−1.10)	(−0.39)	(−1.14)
Dependency ratio	0.106**	0.146**	0.099**	0.146**
	(2.46)	(4.03)	(2.16)	(3.76)
Number of relatives household received money from in last 10 years	−0.003	−0.003	−0.002	−0.003
	(−1.03)	(−1.12)	(−0.59)	(−1.01)
Log household land assets (decimals)	−0.004	0.016**	−0.010	0.025**
	(−0.57)	(2.19)	(−1.08)	(2.65)
Household faced death of family members in last 3 years			−0.021	0.003
			(−0.65)	(0.37)
Household faced losses from income-generating activities in last 3 years			0.037	0.024
			(0.96)	(0.59)
Household faced natural calamities in last 3 years			0.044	0.074**
			(1.46)	(3.06)
Household faced other financial losses in last 3 years			0.020	0.001
			(0.42)	(0.01)
Village has commercial banks	0.052	−0.035	0.133*	0.009
	(1.28)	(−0.97)	(1.84)	(0.19)
Number of microfinance programs operating in the village	0.012**	0.012*	0.001	0.014*
	(2.02)	(1.97)	(0.06)	(1.71)
R^2	0.055	0.188	0.082	0.131
Number of households (groups)	1,509	1,509	1,509	1,509
Number of observations	5,525	5,525	4,037	4,037

Sources: World Bank/BIDS survey 1991/92 and 1998/99; World Bank/InM survey 2010/11.
Note: Estimates control for initial conditions, and the regressions additionally include village-level control variables (e.g., community prices of consumer goods, daily wage rates of men and women, and such infrastructure variables as presence of schools, government and nongovernmental organization food programs, electricity, and paved roads). Figures in parentheses are t-statistics based on robust standard errors clustered at the village level.
a. Model 1 is based on all three survey periods (1991/92, 1998/99, and 2010/11).
b. Model 2 is based on two survey periods (1998/99 and 2010/11).
Significance level: * = 10 percent, ** = 5 percent.

not matter in our sample (perhaps because the average schooling of household heads is only three years), the dependency ratio (proportion of dependents among members) matters a lot, irrespective of model specifications: Higher dependency means higher indebtedness over both the short and long term. Results show that agricultural landholdings increase indebtedness over the short term without affecting long-term indebtedness. This is perhaps because households that are highly dependent on agriculture may find it difficult to smooth income, given the high variability in agricultural income.

Natural calamities increase the probability of short-term indebtedness among rural households without having any significant long-term effects on their overall indebtedness. The greater the number of MFIs serving a rural community, the higher the probability that a borrowing rural household is indebted, and this is equally true for both short- and long-term indebtedness. The presence of commercial banks in a community is also likely to increase the probability of being indebted, at least in the long run. Therefore, like demand-side variables, supply-side variables play an important role in determining the extent of indebtedness.

Thus far, we have considered the impact of both demand- and supply-side variables on the overall measure of indebtedness without distinguishing among the various levels of indebtedness. However, an analysis of the extent or severity of indebtedness is equally important in order to understand the underlying factors that contribute to such severity. Considering that the three indebtedness categories (i.e., moderately indebted, overindebted, and seriously indebted) represent gradually worsening situations, we ran an ordered logit model (OLM) to determine whether the factors contributing to overall indebtedness played similar roles in determining the severity of indebtedness among the indebted households.

Table 5.11 presents the results of this exercise based on the most recent household survey data (2010/11).[10] Restricting the discussion to the flow-based (short-term) measure of indebtedness, we find that both the demand- and supply-side variables that affect the overall measure of indebtedness also affect the degree of indebtedness. For example, the probability of serious indebtedness is higher than the probability of moderate indebtedness when a household is struck with a natural calamity. Similarly, the village density of MFIs increases the probability of being seriously indebted more than the probability of being moderately indebted. Thus, supply-side factors that affect overall indebtedness also affect its severity among indebted households.

Does Participation Density Matter for Indebtedness?

We have explored the role of various factors, including the availability of microfinance programs in a community, in determining the extent and severity of indebtedness, where indebtedness is defined by the extent of debt liability exceeding a certain percentage of a household's income or assets. The findings show that, while MFIs help to expand outreach of institutional finance to households left out by formal financial institutions, the presence and extent of coverage of multiple MFIs (a measure of competition among MFIs) can cause an overflow of credit that may exacerbate a borrower's indebtedness. The village-level density of NGO-MFIs may measure not only supply of, but also demand for, MFI services. Thus, we need to distinguish demand for and supply of community-wide microfinance services by including an additional variable, microfinance program density of a household (C_{ijt}), in equation (5.1), expressed as follows:

$$Y_{ijt} = \alpha X_{ijt} + \rho B_{jt} + \beta C_{ijt} + \eta_{ijt} + \mu_{jt} + \varepsilon_{ijt},\qquad(5.3)$$

where β represents the impact coefficient of microfinance program participation at the household level; that is, equation (5.3) is an indebtedness equation, conditional on the amount of cumulative borrowing from MFIs. One should note that, like the indebtedness outcome, program borrowing is also an outcome endogenously determined by a host of demand- and supply-side variables, as depicted in equation (5.1).

Table 5.11 Determinants of Indebtedness Type, Based on Ordered Logit Estimation
N = 2,287

	Stocks-based measure			Flow-based measure		
Key explanatory variable	Moderately indebted	Over-indebted	Seriously indebted	Moderately indebted	Over-indebted	Seriously indebted
Sex of household head (1 = male, 0 = female)	0.009 (0.68)	0.005 (0.70)	0.012 (0.71)	0.044** (3.94)	0.035** (4.34)	0.083** (4.65)
Age of household head (years)	−0.001** (−3.61)	−0.001** (−3.53)	−0.002** (−3.67)	−0.001** (−4.09)	−0.001** (−4.35)	−0.003** (−4.53)
Education of household head (years)	−0.0004 (−0.29)	−0.0002 (−0.29)	−0.001 (−0.29)	−0.002* (−1.76)	−0.002* (−1.75)	−0.005* (−1.83)
Dependency ratio	0.027 (1.20)	0.016 (1.21)	0.039 (1.20)	0.006 (0.36)	0.005 (0.36)	0.015 (0.36)
Number of relatives household received money from in last 10 years	0.003* (1.81)	0.002* (1.82)	0.004* (1.84)	−0.0002 (−0.16)	−0.0002 (−0.16)	−0.0004 (−0.16)
Log household land assets (decimals)	−0.001 (−0.43)	−0.001 (−0.43)	−0.002 (−0.43)	0.001 (0.49)	0.001 (0.48)	0.003 (0.48)
Household faced death of family members in last 3 years	−0.032 (−0.97)	0.042** (2.47)	0.506** (5.24)	−0.116** (−2.72)	−0.036 (−0.78)	0.707** (5.27)
Household faced loss in income-generating activities in last 3 years	0.044** (3.80)	0.038* (1.94)	0.121 (1.42)	0.014 (0.84)	0.046** (5.91)	0.224** (2.08)
Household faced natural calamities in last 3 years	0.011 (0.91)	0.006 (0.94)	0.015 (0.97)	0.025** (2.98)	0.022** (3.32)	0.053** (3.40)
Household faced other financial losses in last 3 years	0.044** (7.36)	0.039** (3.84)	0.129** (2.87)	−0.014 (−0.12)	0.043 (1.09)	0.357 (0.80)
Village has commercial banks	−0.021 (−1.14)	−0.011 (−1.19)	−0.027 (−1.26)	−0.005 (−0.45)	−0.005 (−0.46)	−0.013 (−0.47)
Number of microfinance programs operating in the village	0.003 (1.24)	0.002 (1.22)	0.004 (1.26)	0.006** (3.50)	0.006** (3.48)	0.015** (3.87)
Pseudo R^2		0.048			0.074	

Source: World Bank/InM survey 2010/11.
Note: Marginal effects are reported. The regression model is based on 2010/11 survey data. Estimates control for initial conditions, and additionally include village-level control variables (e.g., community prices of consumer goods, daily wage rates of men and women, and such infrastructure variables as presence of schools, government and nongovernmental organization food programs, electricity, and paved roads). Figures in parentheses are t-statistics based on robust standard errors clustered at the village level.
Significance level: * = 10 percent, ** = 5 percent.

Thus, following the method previously used, we apply two approaches: (a) p-score weighted FE, where household-level FE is weighted by p-score based on the household-level participation equation and (b) the LDV model, where the current period's indebtedness depends on the past period's indebtedness, as well as other exogenous variables.

Thus far, we have considered Y as a categorical (0/1) variable indicating whether a household is indebted, based on the cutoff point at 20 percent of the debt-income or debt-asset ratio. The issue with estimating impacts on a categorical variable is that the changes are observed only when the underlying continuous variable (e.g., debt-asset ratio) changes across the cutoff point. That is, the categorical variable is insensitive to any changes in the continuous variable as long as they are confined to above or below the cutoff point. For example, the categorical indicator of indebtedness for a household does not change when its debt-asset ratio rises from 0 to 0.19 or falls from 0.70 to 0.21, even though these changes are substantial. Even worse, in certain cases, changes in the categorical variable may be misleading regarding the overall indebtedness situation.[11] Therefore, the categorical indicator of indebtedness may not be the variable of choice when one is interested in changes in indebtedness over the entire spectrum of the debt-asset ratio. That is what we are interested in when we want to assess the impacts of microfinance participation on household indebtedness. The concern for policy-making purposes is whether an increase in debt due to borrowing is accompanied by a relatively higher increase in income or assets induced by the borrowing, rather than whether the debt is less than 20 percent of the income or assets.

Therefore, in equation (5.3), we use the debt-asset ratio or debt service–income ratio rather than the categorical variable of indebtedness as the dependent variable, while the key policy variable on the right-hand side of the equation is the amount of cumulative borrowing from microfinance programs, given the presence and density of MFIs in a village.

Tables 5.12a and 5.12b present the results using the p-score weighted FE and the LDV model, respectively, for three underlying models of program participation. Model 1 presents the estimates of the cumulative borrowing of men and women. Model 2 presents the estimates of cumulative borrowing of men and women from the MFIs, plus the village-level average cumulative borrowing of men and women. Model 3 presents the estimates of male and female household-level borrowing, plus the extent of multiple borrowing by men and women from multiple MFI sources, and the extent of MFI presence in a village. Thus, in model 3, given village-level program density, the coefficient of household-level borrowing from MFIs by men and women measures the net effect of program borrowing on household indebtedness, which is proxied by the ratio of liability to assets or liability to income. Both are continuous rather than categorical variables. This estimation method allows for continuous adjustment due to program participation rather than a quantum jump underlying a categorical indicator of indebtedness.

Table 5.12 Alternate Estimates of Borrowing Impact on Indebtedness

a. Using propensity score–weighted household fixed effects (N = 1,509)

Model	Credit variable	Debt to nonland asset ratio	Debt servicing to income ratio
1	Log loans of household males (Tk.)	−0.004 (−1.14)	−0.007 (−1.48)
	Log loans of household females (Tk.)	−0.016** (−7.04)	−0.031** (−12.33)
	R^2	0.156	0.171
2	Log loans of household males (Tk.)	−0.003 (−0.98)	−0.007 (−1.40)
	Log loans of household females (Tk.)	−0.016** (−6.76)	−0.028** (−12.30)
	Log village average of male loans (Tk.)	−0.004* (−1.64)	−0.004 (−1.51)
	Log village average of female loans (Tk.)	−0.003 (−1.06)	−0.024** (−5.51)
	R^2	0.158	0.186
3	Log loans of household males (Tk.)	−0.006 (−1.48)	−0.009** (−2.13)
	Log loans of household females (Tk.)	−0.017** (−7.30)	−0.033** (−12.97)
	Household males borrowed from multiple sources	0.149** (2.15)	0.230** (3.24)
	Household females borrowed from multiple sources	0.051** (2.66)	0.121** (6.09)
	Number of MFIs in the village	−0.001 (−0.21)	−0.005 (−1.34)
	R^2	0.159	0.186

b. Using dynamic panel LDV model (N = 1,509)

Model	Credit variable	Debt to nonland asset ratio	Debt servicing to income ratio
1	Log loans of household males (Tk.)	−0.009** (−3.25)	−0.014** (−4.89)
	Log loans of household females (Tk.)	−0.014** (−6.36)	−0.023** (−10.84)
	F statistics for the model	$F_{(24, 86)} = 5.89, p > 0.000$	$F_{(26, 86)} = 14.97, p > 0.000$
2	Log loans of household males (Tk.)	−0.011** (−4.54)	−0.014** (−4.66)
	Log loans of household females (Tk.)	−0.013** (−6.26)	−0.022** (−10.18)
	Log village average of male loans (Tk.)	0.005 (1.57)	−0.003 (−0.94)
	Log village average of female loans (Tk.)	−0.012* (−1.95)	−0.010* (−1.65)
	F statistics for the model	$F_{(26, 86)} = 6.51, p > 0.000$	$F_{(26, 86)} = 15.78, p > 0.000$

table continues next page

Table 5.12 Alternate Estimates of Borrowing Impact on Indebtedness *(continued)*

Model	Credit variable	Debt to nonland asset ratio	Debt servicing to income ratio
3	Log loans of household males (Tk.)	−0.009**	−0.014**
		(−3.25)	(−4.79)
	Log loans of household females (Tk.)	−0.014**	−0.023**
		(−6.13)	(−10.46)
	Household males borrowed from multiple sources	−0.214**	−0.199**
		(−8.14)	(−6.00)
	Household females borrowed from multiple sources	0.014	0.051
		(0.40)	(1.23)
	Number of MFIs in the village	−0.005	−0.010
		(−0.88)	(−1.46)
	F statistics for the model	$F(27, 86) = 13.13, p > 0.000$	$F(27, 86) = 17.44, p > 0.000$

Sources: World Bank/BIDS survey 1991/92 and 1998/99; World Bank/InM survey 2010/11.
Note: Figures in parentheses are t–statistics based on robust standard errors clustered at the village level. Loans refer to the cumulative amount borrowed from all microcredit sources leading up to the survey year. Regressions include more control variables at the household level (e.g., age, sex, and education of household head and log of land assets) and village level (e.g., price of consumer goods, daily wage rates of men and women, and such infrastructure variables as presence of schools, electricity availability, and proportion of irrigated land). MFI = microfinance institution; LDV = lagged dependent variable.
Significance level: * = 10 percent, ** = 5 percent.

For brevity, we discuss only the results using the LDV model (table 5.12b). The findings show that estimates of the effect of cumulative borrowing by either men or women on the extent of indebtedness are negative for all three models. According to model 1, the effect of cumulative borrowing by men and women has an unequivocally negative effect on debt liability measured in terms of either flow or stocks (assets). Surprisingly, this finding remains the same with the other two models, which have additional controls for village-level average borrowing or indicators of multiple sources of borrowing. That is, microfinance borrowing by either men or women reduces, rather than increases, debt. For example, according to model 1, a 10 percent increase in the amount of female borrowing reduces the household debt-asset ratio by 0.14 percentage point and the loan servicing-to-income ratio by 0.23 percentage point. That is, the returns to income or assets because of the borrowing appear higher than the increase in liability.

According to model 2, village-level average borrowing, for at least women, an indicator of village externality or spillover, also has a negative effect on the extent of indebtedness. This is a clear sign of village positive externality, meaning that village-level borrowing has a net positive effect on household wealth.

Model 3 presents the effect of borrowing from multiple sources, along with the cumulative amount of borrowing by men and women as additional variables and the village presence of MFIs. The results show that the debt-asset ratio is also negatively related to multiple program membership, but this is true only for men. That is, given the negative effect of borrowing on the debt-asset ratio, the probability of borrowing from multiple sources as opposed to a single source does not necessarily have an adverse effect on the debt-asset ratio.[12] The same pattern also holds for debt servicing relative to income, suggesting that borrowing from multiple sources may be a "blessing in disguise," at least for men.

However, it is possible that the extent of indebtedness varies over time. In the short term, loans can increase assets more than debt, but this trend is reversed for intermediate- and long-term loans. This means there is an inverted U-shape relationship between indebtedness and the amount of borrowing over time. Interestingly, such a relationship may only hold for a long-term measure of indebtedness (e.g., the asset-debt ratio). With increasing amounts of borrowing, the ratio of debt servicing to income is reduced over the short run but increases over the medium and long term. That is, the debt-asset ratio ultimately declines over time, even if continuous borrowing may increase debt payment relative to income in the short run.

Thus far, the findings suggest that MFI borrowing, independent of other factors including village-level program density, has, on average, contributed more to the growth of assets than liabilities. While this pattern may not be obvious in the short or medium term, asset accumulation eventually overtakes debt liability as households continue to borrow and make productive investments.[13] Figure 5.1 clearly depicts this relationship. As shown, three types of indebtedness are first regressed against cumulative borrowing and its squared term (using a logit model). Their predicted probabilities are then plotted against the cumulative borrowing to obtain the long-term trend of indebtedness. Obviously, indebtedness increases at the beginning as borrowing rises; however, it does so at a decreasing rate, and at a certain point its growth theoretically reaches zero.

Figure 5.1 Predicted Probabilities of Three Types of Indebtedness with Change in Microfinance Borrowing Amount over Time

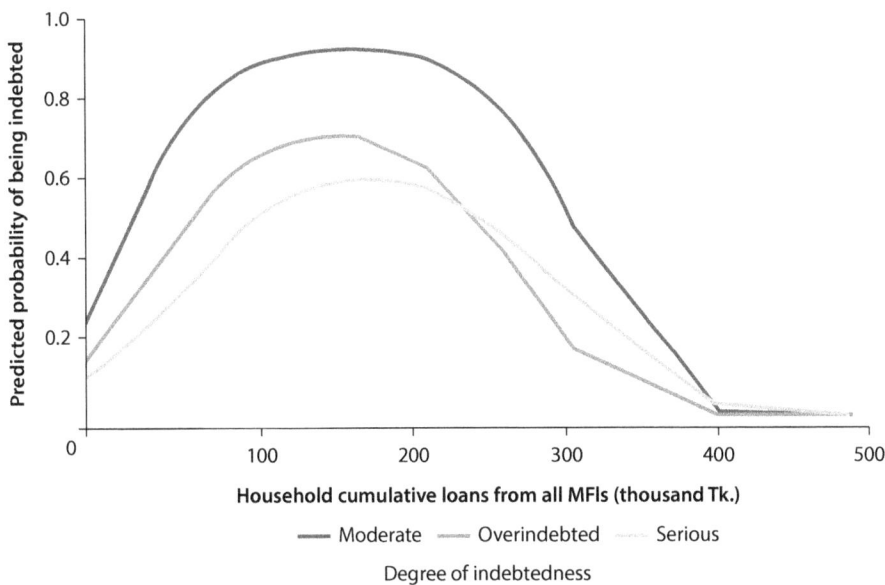

Source: World Bank/InM survey 2010/11.
Note: MFIs = microfinance institutions.

Thus, figure 5.1 shows that the probability of being indebted declines as the amount of borrowing increases. However, the probability of being moderately indebted is higher at each level of borrowing than other measures; perhaps at this earlier stage of indebtedness, borrowers may not be too concerned about the severity of indebtedness. In any case, the declining shape of the indebtedness curve shows that microfinance adds value to assets more than it accumulates debt on average. Thus, there is a declining debt-asset ratio over borrowing.

The message from this analysis is clear: Contrary to what many without any hard evidence have argued, microfinance participants are not necessarily overindebted. This is not to say that all households who borrow from the MFIs will benefit in the same way. Thus, an in-depth analysis is perhaps necessary to determine which households among long-term borrowers or multiple program members are indeed overindebted and what can be done to help them manage the extent of their overindebtedness.

Summary

The available literature describes the potential effects of overindebtedness on both microfinance borrowers and lenders. Overindebtedness affects a lender's financial or institutional sustainability, and the effect on borrowers can be a debt trap that pushes them further into poverty.

When borrowers are indebted, they struggle to make repayments and cut back on basic consumption, as well as other important household expenditures, such as education and health care. In addition, overindebtedness has material costs, such as late fees and, in cases of default, seizure of assets. Furthermore, the resulting loss of creditworthiness can limit access to credit and cause liquidity problems. These consequences may occur despite that microfinance is meant to alleviate poverty through income-generation activities, suggesting that, with regard to the effects of microfinance, the line between the debt trap and poverty alleviation may be thin.

Our long-term panel data analysis confirms that continuous borrowing or borrowing from multiple sources adds more to assets than to liability over time. This perhaps shows that microloans of various types, as developed by the MFIs in Bangladesh, support both investment and consumption, including the creation of a liquidity buffer for meeting emergency-need situations (e.g., health problems or other unanticipated expenses). In fact, barriers to accessing financial services by the poor may cause overindebtedness since lack of access to credit may force many of these consumers to borrow from high-cost informal sources, which can equally increase their risk of falling into overindebtedness. As this analysis finds, borrowing from multiple sources is not necessarily a pathway to overindebtedness. However, in order to achieve the desired effects, it is important for both lenders and borrowers to invest in sectors with sufficient returns.

While long-term borrowing from MFIs, coupled with productive investments, helps households avert the debt trap, many borrowers are not so fortunate.[14]

Risk and vulnerability are everyday realities for the poor, which include microfinance borrowers. Over time, they are expected to develop strategies for managing both their financial challenges and unexpected risks by combining income, savings, credit, informal insurance mechanisms, and accumulated assets.[15]

The risk-management strategies currently being used by many poor people may not adequately protect them against repeated risk events. When economic shocks begin to add up, these strategies often fail because poor households lack enough assets to sustain them. Formal insurance mechanisms in the form of microinsurance can help to fill this gap. Microinsurance not only protects the assets of the poor from economic shocks, but allows poorer consumers to mobilize those assets and increase their income by reducing their need to save so much for a rainy day. Thus, the MFIs may consider introducing an effective microinsurance policy to safeguard both themselves and their borrowers.

Notes

1. *Multiple borrowing* or *overlapping membership* is defined as borrowing by an individual or household from more than one MFI source for the same or similar purpose.

2. For example, a poor assessment of product demand may cause microentrepreneurs to face diminishing returns on their investments; when realized returns fall short of expected ones, they may borrow repeatedly, creating a vicious cycle of microdebt dependency.

3. In this chapter, we implement an empirical model that attempts to identify some of the major drivers of indebtedness from both the demand and supply sides, notwithstanding the limitations of the survey data used.

4. In calculating indebtedness, the stocks-based (assets) measure excludes land assets since the value of land has skyrocketed in the last 8–10 years, making it somewhat unstable. But trends in the asset-debt ratio change little when land is included in assets.

5. Those who borrow from commercial and agricultural development banks are considered non-MFI borrowers.

6. Credit constraint was determined by asking households whether they would have demanded more loans than they obtained if all terms and conditions had remained the same.

7. An alternative explanation is that households with poor credit risk must use multiple lenders to get the credit they want.

8. The empirical model may not capture the role of all factors, including institutional ones, that influence the extent of indebtedness because of lack of information available from the survey data used here. However, because of the panel data fixed-effects (FE) method, the bias due to such omitted variables may be minimal, as these omitted variables may not vary much over time. Hence, their roles are controlled by the FE method.

9. The reason is that 1991/92 data did not include information on household shocks.

10. The results presented here are based on an ordered logit regression (OLR) applied to the 2010/11 data after controlling for initial conditions. Alternately, we tried OLMs using the 1998/99 and 2010/11 panel data; the results did not differ qualitatively from what are reported in table 5.12.

11. This is possible when, for example, the debt-asset ratio worsens by rising from a value slightly below 0.20 to one slightly above 0.20 for a small number of households and, at the same time, improves by dropping from 0.70 to 0.25 for a large number of households. In this case, the categorical indicator would report a rising indebtedness when, in fact, the debt-asset ratio would show a large improvement.

12. Based on p-weighted FE estimates, borrowing from multiple sources has a positive effect on debt-asset ratio. This may be because the endogeneity of multiple-source borrowing is not resolved.

13. Long-term borrowers—those with a borrowing history of 10 years or more—must be making productive investments; otherwise, they would not have stayed with microfinance programs for such a long time.

14. This chapter was unable to analyze who these borrowers were and why they were not as fortunate as others, owing to a lack of sufficient information about their enterprises and other characteristics; thus, a separate in-depth study is recommended on this process of indebtedness.

15. Risks can be anticipated, depending on their likelihood; for example, in more flood-prone regions, the risk of floods can be anticipated and taken into account.

Bibliography

Anderloni, L., and D. Vandone. 2008. "Households Over-Indebtedness in the Economic Literature." Working Paper 2008–46, Department of Economics, Business and Statistics, State University of Milan, Milan.

Bensoussan, P. 2009. "Successes and Limits of Microfinance." Newsletter 4, PlaNet Finance, Saint-Ouen, France.

Bouquet, E., B. Wampfler, E. Ralison, and M. Roesch. 2007. "Trajectoires de crédit et vulnérabilité des ménages ruraux: Le cas des Cecam de Madagascar [Credit Trajectories and Vulnerability of Rural Households: The Case of Cecam in Madagascar]." *Autrepart* 44: 157–72.

Brix, L., and K. McKee. 2010. "Consumer Protection Regulation in Low-Access Environments: Opportunities to Promote Responsible Finance." Focus Note 60, Consultative Group to Assist the Poor (CGAP), Washington, DC.

Canner, G. B., and C. A. Luckett. 1991. "Payment of Household Debts." *Federal Reserve Bulletin* 77 (4): 218.

Del-Río, A., and G. Young. 2005. "The Impact of Unsecured Debt on Financial Distress among British Households." Working Paper 262, Bank of England, London.

DeVaney, P. L. 2006. "Bringing Pro-Consumer Ideals to the Client: A Consumer Protection Guide for Financial Institutions Serving the Poor." ACCION Publications, Washington, DC.

Disney, R., S. Bridges, and J. Gathergood. 2008. "Drivers of Over-Indebtedness: Report to the Department for Business, Enterprise and Regulatory Reform." Centre for Policy Evaluation, University of Nottingham, Nottingham, UK.

Faruqee, Rashid. 2013. "Indebtedness among Microfinance Borrowers" (mimeo). Institute of Microfinance, Dhaka.

Fisher, I. 1933. "The Debt-Deflation Theory of Great Depressions." *Econometrica* 1 (4): 337–57.

Gonzalez, Adrian. 2008. "Microfinance, Incentives to Repay, and Overindebtedness: Evidence from a Household Survey in Bolivia." Paper presented in partial fulfillment of the requirements for the degree Doctor of Philosophy, Ohio State University, Columbus.

Haas, Oliver. 2006. "Overindebtedness in Germany." Working Paper 44, International Labour Organization (ILO), Geneva.

Hulme, D. 2007. "Is Microdebt Good for Poor People? A Note on the Dark Side of Microfinance." In *What's Wrong with Microfinance?*, edited by T. Dichter and M. Harper, 19–22. Warwickshire, UK: Intermediate Technology Publications.

Khalily, M. A. Baqui, and Rushad Faridi. 2011. "Multiple Memberships (Overlapping) in Micro Credit Markets of Bangladesh." Institute of Microfinance (InM) and Palli Karma-Sahayak Foundation (PKSF), Dhaka.

Maurer, K., and J. Pytkowska. 2010. "Indebtedness of Microfinance Clients in Bosnia and Herzegovina, Results from a Comprehensive Field Study." European Fund for Southeast Europe (EFSE), Luxembourg.

Pitt, Mark M., and Shahidur R. Khandker. 1998. "The Impact of Group-based Credit Programs on Poor Households in Bangladesh: Does the Gender of Participants Matter?" *Journal of Political Economy* 106: 958–96.

Rahman, A. 1999. "Micro-Credit Initiatives for Equitable and Sustainable Development: Who Pays?" *World Development* 27 (1): 67–82.

Schicks, Jessica. 2010. "Microfinance Over-Indebtedness: Understanding Its Drivers and Challenging the Common Myths." Centre Emile Bernheim (CEB) Working Paper 10/047, Solvay Brussels School of Business and Management. http://ideas .repc.org/p/sol/wpaper/2013-64675.html.

Schicks, Jessica, and Richard Rosenberg. 2011. "Too Much Microfinance? A Survey of the Evidence on Over-Indebtedness." Occasional Paper 19, Consultative Group to Assist the Poor (CGAP), Washington, DC.

Soman, D., and A. Cheema. 2002. "The Effect of Credit on Spending Decisions: The Role of the Credit Limit and Credibility." *Marketing Science* 21 (1): 32–53.

Spannuth, Sylvia, and Justyna Pytkowska. 2011. "Indebtedness of Microfinance Clients in Kosovo." European Fund for Southeast Europe (EFSE), Luxembourg.

Stearns, K. 1991. "The Hidden Beast: Delinquency in Microenterprise Credit Programs." Discussion Paper Series 5, ACCION International, Washington, DC.

Vandone, Daniela. 2009. *Consumer Credit in Europe: Risks and Opportunities of a Dynamic Industry*. Heidelberg: Physica.

Vogelgesang, U. 2003. "Microfinance in Times of Crisis: The Effects of Competition, Rising Indebtedness, and Economic Crisis on Repayment Behavior." *World Development* 31 (12): 2085–114.

Webley, P., and E. K. Nyhus. 2001. "Life-Cycle and Disproportionate Routes into Problem Debt." *British Journal of Psychology* 92: 423–46.

Wisniwski, Sylvia. 2010. "Overindebtedness: Evidence, Causes and Consequences." Presentation, European Fund for Southeast Europe (EFSE), September 23, Frankfurt, Germany.

CHAPTER 6

Role of Microfinance in Poverty Transition

Introduction

The previous chapters have examined the income effect of microfinance, along with its impact on household assets, labor supply, and net worth, including indebtedness. Because the income and asset effects of microfinance are expected to enhance household consumption and thus reduce poverty, advocates of microfinance have argued that microfinance has a direct effect on poverty reduction through increasing consumption. But opponents argue that, although microfinance has succeeded in reaching the poor, particularly women, and other marginalized groups who lack access to mainstream financial institutions and has helped in consumption smoothing,[1] these are short-term effects that may not be sustainable over time; thus, success in reducing poverty, a stated goal of microcredit programs, is uncertain.

The microfinance system has created such innovations as group liability enforcements and dynamic incentives, claiming that many of the poor, including women and other vulnerable groups, could be lent to profitably, and beneficiaries could accrue both short- and medium-term welfare gains. In our previous chapters, we have shown that microborrowing has both short- and long-term benefits in terms of income, employment, and other welfare gains. However, critics argue that, while microfinance may satisfy the unmet financial demand of the poor and enhance short-term welfare gains, the accrued gains in income and employment may not suffice to affect poverty reduction in a sustainable way.

There are two strands of empirical literature on the poverty-reduction role of microcredit. The first strand of studies, which uses nonexperimental research methods, observes that microcredit helps to reduce consumption and other dimensions of poverty in various ways (e.g., Angelucci, Karlan, and Zinman 2013; Boonperm, Haughton, and Khandker 2009; Chemin 2008; Dunford 2006; Hossain 1988; Imai, Arun, and Annim 2010; Kevane and Wydick 2001;

Khandker 1998, 2005; McIntosh 2008; Panjaitan-Drioadisuryo and Cloud 1999; Pitt and others 1999; Pitt and Khandker 1996, 1998; Shaw 2004).[2] A recent study, using panel data from 1997 to 2005, finds that larger benefits are realized from medium-term, rather short-term, participation (Islam 2011).

The second strand of studies, using randomized control trials (RCTs), finds that microcredit has mixed effects on poverty reduction.[3] Various studies show the positive effects of microfinance (Coleman 1999, 2006; de Mel, McKenzie, and Woodruff 2008; Karlan and Zinman 2009; McKenzie and Woodruff 2008), while others find no evidence for income or consumption gains (Attanasio and others 2012; Augsburg and others 2011; Banerjee and others 2010; Crépon and others 2011; Karlan and Zinman 2011). Summarizing the findings of several RCT studies, a critic states that microfinance does not end poverty despite all the hype (Roodman 2012).[4]

Microfinance has also come under attack for charging "exorbitant" interest rates (e.g., some argue that the nominal on-lending rate of Grameen Bank in Bangladesh is 20 percent, 7 percent higher than the commercial bank rate, which goes against its stated mission of poverty alleviation). Using anecdotal evidence, many critics cite microcredit's high interest rates and inadequate benefits relative to the cost of borrowing as reasons for rising indebtedness among borrowers. Their argument is simple: If microcredit programs were so helpful, indebtedness should not have increased over time relative to asset accumulation; thus, micro-credit is not a "miracle," as its proponents would have us believe. However, while the interest rates of microfinance institutions (MFIs) are higher than those of formal lenders, they are much lower than informal lending rates (Faruqee and Khalily 2011). Thus, as shown in the previous chapter, long-term borrowers are not necessarily trapped in debt by borrowing repeatedly from MFIs because asset accumulation exceeds the debt accrued.

Against the backdrop of these findings, this chapter revisits the controversies surrounding the role of microfinance in poverty reduction.[5] Using a long panel survey of respondents over more than 20 years, it examines whether the earlier findings of Pitt and Khandker (1998) and Khandker (2005) can be substantiated and whether microcredit participants are indeed trapped in poverty as many have argued. The chapter also examines whether the gender of program participants matters, as observed by Pitt and Khandker (1998) and Khandker (2005). The unusually long panel of the complete data set provides a unique opportunity to examine whether households that participated in microcredit programs over a long period remained poor or graduated from poverty.

Using a fixed-effects (FE) method that controls for both time-invariant and time-varying heterogeneity, the net effect of program participation is estimated for an average participant and separately by gender. Contrary to the prevailing view about microfinance dependence, the findings show that microcredit participants are not trapped in poverty,[6] confirming the positive effects of microfinance observed in earlier studies (Khandker 2005; Pitt and Khandker 1998).

Dynamics of Participation Status with Consumption and Poverty: What Is the Correlation?

The outcome of particular interest in this chapter is poverty dynamics over a long period of time. Conceivably, as a result of a higher level of microborrowing and savings mobilized over this period, households enjoyed a higher level of income (assuming it was augmented through activities financed under microcredit programs), a higher level of consumption (since the participating households were poor to begin with), and thus a reduced level of poverty. For purposes of comparison, a set of four key indicators of household welfare was selected: (a) income, (b) expenditure, (c) moderate poverty, and (d) extreme poverty.[7] The expenditure data are expressed in real terms (in 1991/92 Tk.). The cost-of-basic-needs method was used to establish the poverty line, which requires one to establish the cost of a minimum food basket or food poverty line, and then add an allowance for nonfood expenditure to estimate the moderate poverty line. By contrast, extreme poverty was determined by comparing the household's total consumption expenditure on food and nonfood items against the food poverty line.[8] Descriptive statistics of these indicators are presented in table 6.1. The sample for this descriptive analysis was restricted to eligible households from the 1991/92 survey, regardless of their actual participation status.[9] This was done to ensure that comparisons could be made between similar households.

Growth in Food, Nonfood, and Total Consumption

Table 6.1 shows that the average annual growth in per capita expenditure was higher for nonparticipants (4.5 percent) than for participants (3.7 percent) over the 20-year period between the first and third survey rounds (1991/92–2010/11).

Table 6.1 also shows that, over the same period, food as a share of total expenditure declined by about 15–16 percentage points and varied little between participants and nonparticipants. This means that both groups experienced growth in their share of nonfood consumption, indicating a higher level of welfare in rural Bangladesh. Indeed, in 1991/92, nonfood consumption accounted for less than one-fifth of total consumption, compared to about one-third by 2010/11.

Reduction in Moderate and Extreme Poverty

In 2010/11, the incidence of both moderate and extreme poverty was significantly less for participants than for nonparticipants (table 6.1). That survey year saw a 1.7 percentage point gap between participants and nonparticipants for moderate poverty (32.9 percent versus 34.6 percent). The gap for extreme poverty was about four times wider, at 6.9 percentage points (16.2 percent versus 23.1 percent). Thus, it appears that the extent of poverty reduction was higher for program participants than for nonparticipants, despite the scant difference in poverty status between the two groups in earlier years (e.g., 1991/92).

For program participants, extreme poverty was reduced by 2.9 percentage points per year, compared to 2.7 percentage points for nonparticipants. This trend runs counter to the notion that microcredit program participants could be

Table 6.1 Household Expenditure Distribution and Poverty Measures by Microcredit Participation Status in the Three Survey Periods

	1991/92		1998/99		2010/11	
Outcome variable	Participants (N = 769)	Non-participants (N = 483)	Participants (N = 1,014)	Non-participants (N = 420)	Participants (N = 1,554)	Non-participants (N = 334)
Per capita expenditure (Tk./month)	327.3	318.6	440.0	436.9	571.6	604.0
		(1.04)		(0.17)		(−1.71)
Food expenditure as share of total expenditure (%)	81.3	82.1	75.1	76.2	66.2	65.0
		(−1.23)		(−1.15)		(1.59)
Moderate poverty (%)	86.3	87.6	60.6	58.2	32.9	34.6
		(−0.67)		(0.88)		(−0.62)
Extreme poverty (%)	75.1	78.5	43.6	46.5	16.2	23.1
		(−1.38)		(−1.05)		(−3.19)

Sources: World Bank/BIDS survey 1991/92 and 1998/99; World Bank/InM survey 2010/11.
Note: Monetary figures are consumer price index–adjusted Tk. with 1991/92 = 100. The analysis is restricted to 1991/92 microcredit-eligible households (i.e., those who participated in microcredit programs in 1991/92 and those who were eligible to but did not), which constituted 64, 62, and 61 percent of the surveyed households in 1991/92, 1998/99, and 2010/11, respectively. Figures in parentheses are t-statistics of the differences between participants and nonparticipants.

trapped in poverty as critics have claimed.[10] However, this simple comparison between participants and nonparticipants is not compelling enough to suggest that this reduction in poverty is indeed the case since many factors beyond borrowing affect intergroup differences in outcomes. The key question is whether program participation played a causal role in determining income and consumption growth and thus poverty reduction among participants.

Analysis of the Poverty Transition

The range of outcomes discussed thus far provides a picture of the overall welfare of rural households. Among the outcomes of interest to policy makers, researchers, and development practitioners, the poverty measure is most important since poverty alleviation is the focus of all microcredit discussions and debates. Proponents of microcredit most often tout its poverty-alleviation effect as the basis for its success, while critics point to microcredit's inability to lower poverty as the reason for its failure. These opposing views suggest the need for a deeper examination of the poverty trend than what is reported in table 6.1. More specifically, one needs a better understanding of the underlying movements of households between poor and nonpoor status, and whether any distinct pattern emerges in such movements by changes in program participation status over time. To investigate the transition in poverty status over time, a set of households must be followed across the survey years.

This analysis considered four distinct household types, according to their program participation status, as follows: (a) those who were participants in

1991/92 and maintained an unbroken participation status until 2010/11 (denoted by PPP), (b) those who became program participants after 1991/92 (referred to as new participants in the 1998/99 data) and remained participants until 2010/11 (denoted by NPP), (c) those who became program participants for the first time after 1998/99 (referred to as new participants in the 2010/11 data) (denoted by NNP), and (d) those who never participated in microcredit programs (denoted by NNN).[11]

Transition in Moderate Poverty Status

Table 6.2 shows the transition in moderate status over time (1991/92–2010/11) for all possible combinations of poverty status. As shown, three out of the four household types started out on an equal footing in 1991/92, with about 87 percent in moderate poverty; NPP households were the exception, with 91 percent in moderate poverty. The transitions that these household groups experienced over time differed as their participation status varied.

Among the PPP households, nearly 35 percentage points of the 87 percent that were moderately poor in 1991/92 had moved out of poverty by 1998/99. Furthermore, a great majority of these nonpoor households (about 27 percentage points) remained out of poverty at the time of the third survey

Table 6.2 Transition in Moderate Poverty Status by Microcredit Participation

Survey year	Transition in moderate poverty								Aggregate poverty status for the year	
Among continuous participants since 1991/92 (PPP)										
1991/92	87.4				12.6				87.4	12.6
1998/99	52.6		34.8		5.3		7.3		57.9	42.1
2010/11	17.4	35.2	7.7	27.1	2.2	3.1	1.0	6.3	28.3	71.7
Among continuous participants since 1998/99 (NPP)										
1991/92	91.0				9.0				91.0	9.0
1998/99	64.4		26.6		4.2		4.8		68.6	31.4
2010/11	31.1	33.3	4.0	22.6	2.1	2.1	0.2	4.6	37.3	62.7
Among new participants in 2010/11 (NNP)										
1991/92	87.6				12.4				87.6	12.4
1998/99	59.6		28.0		4.7		7.7		64.3	35.7
2010/11	26.5	33.1	6.8	21.2	1.5	3.2	1.1	6.6	35.9	64.1
Among nonparticipants in all three survey years (NNN)										
1991/92	86.7				13.3				86.7	13.3
1998/99	48.6		38.1		1.7		11.6		50.3	49.7
2010/11	23.1	25.5	8.4	29.7	0.0	1.7	2.1	9.5	33.6	66.4

Sources: World Bank/BIDS survey 1991/92 and 1998/99; World Bank/InM survey 2010/11.
Note: Shaded cells indicate the percent of moderately poor households and nonshaded cells show the percent of nonpoor households. These findings are restricted to 1991/92 microcredit-eligible households (i.e., those who participated in microcredit programs in 1991/92 and those who were eligible but did not).

round (2010/11). Among the nearly 53 percentage points of households out of the original 87 percent who remained poor in 1998/99, about 35 percentage points had moved out of poverty by 2010/11. Altogether, about 62 percentage points out of the original 87 percent of PPP households moved out of poverty over the 20-year period, implying a poverty graduation rate of nearly 72 percent.

A similar analysis of the NNN households shows that, out of the nearly 87 percent who were moderately poor in 1991/92, about 55 percentage points had moved out of poverty by 2010/11, with a poverty graduation rate of more than 66 percent. NPP and NNP household types also showed significant reductions in moderate poverty, although less than PPP households. Figure 6.1 also summarizes the trend in moderate poverty reduction for the four household types over time (1991/92–2010/11). Overall, PPP households—those who were regular/continuous microcredit participants over the 20-year period—were found to have the lowest poverty rate in 2010/11, at about 28 percent.

Transition in Extreme Poverty Status

The reduction in extreme poverty showed similar progress for the four household types over time. Table 6.3 shows that, among the some 77 percent of PPP households considered extremely poor in 1991/92, the poverty graduation rate was about 85 percent by 2010/11. The graduation rates among NPP, NNP, and NNN household types were 80 percent, 82 percent, and 77 percent, respectively. Thus, PPP households had the highest poverty graduation rate, as well as the lowest incidence of extreme poverty in 2010/11, at about 13 percent.

Figure 6.2 summarizes the trend in extreme poverty reduction for the four household types over time (1991/92–2010/11). Summing up, the overall

Figure 6.1 Moderate Poverty Reduction over Time by Extent of Microcredit Program Participation

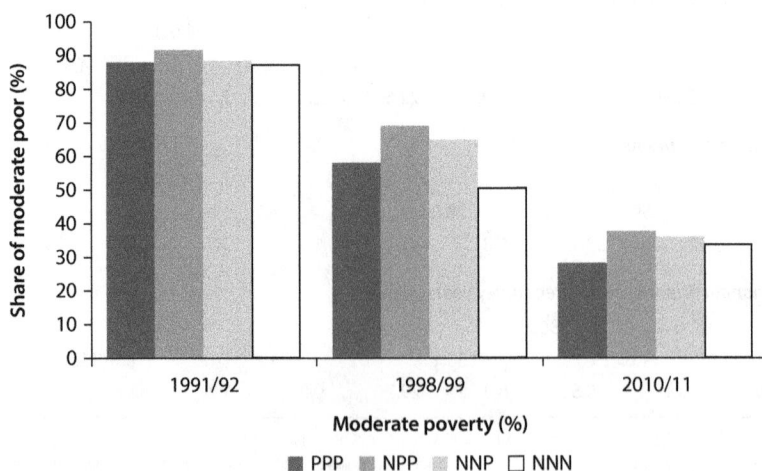

Sources: World Bank/BIDS survey 1991/92 and 1998/99; World Bank/InM survey 2010/11.

Table 6.3 Transition in Extreme Poverty Status by Microcredit Participation

Survey year	Transition in extreme poverty								Aggregate poverty status for the year	
Among continuous participants since 1991/92 (PPP)										
1991/92		76.7				23.3			76.7	23.3
1998/99		34.8		41.9		7.2		16.1	42.0	58.0
2010/11	6.8	28.0	4.7	37.2	1.0	6.2	0.9	15.2	13.4	86.6
Among continuous participants since 1998/99 (NPP)										
1991/92		80.3				19.7			80.3	19.7
1998/99		42.9		37.4		8.0		11.7	50.9	49.1
2010/11	11.4	31.5	4.6	32.8	2.1	5.9	0.6	11.1	18.7	81.3
Among new participants in 2010/11 (NNP)										
1991/92		80.0				20.0			80.0	20.0
1998/99		46.6		33.5		4.5		15.4	51.1	48.9
2010/11	10.8	35.8	3.5	30.0	1.1	3.4	2.5	12.9	17.9	82.1
Among nonparticipants in all three survey years (NNN)										
1991/92		78.4				21.6			78.4	21.6
1998/99		36.9		41.5		4.1		17.5	41.0	59.0
2010/11	7.6	29.3	10.2	31.3	1.6	2.5	2.1	15.4	21.5	78.5

Sources: World Bank/BIDS survey 1991/92 and 1998/99; World Bank/InM survey 2010/11.
Note: Shaded cells indicate the percent of extremely poor households and nonshaded cells show the percent of nonpoor households. These findings are restricted to 1991/92 microcredit-eligible households (i.e., those who participated in microcredit programs in 1991/92 and those who were eligible but did not).

Figure 6.2 Extreme Poverty Reduction over Time by Extent of Microcredit Program Participation

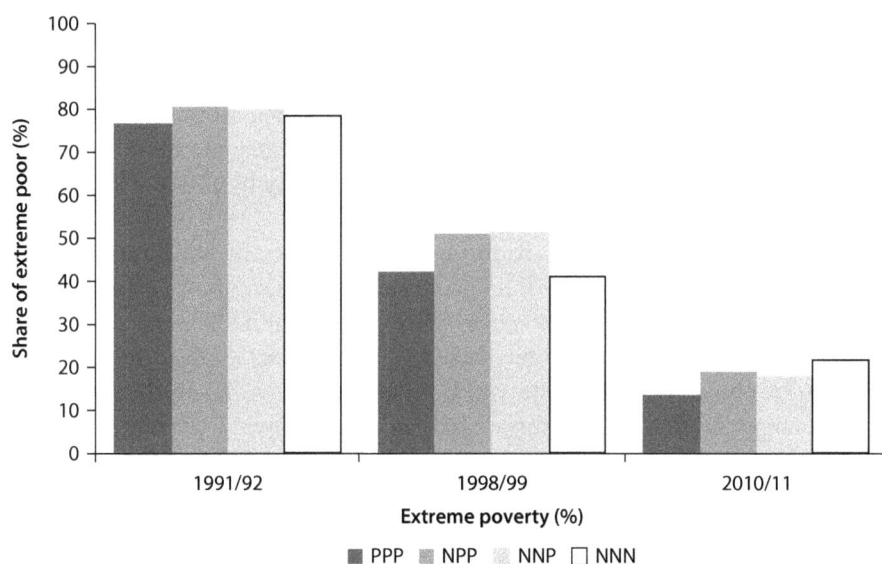

Sources: World Bank/BIDS survey 1991/92 and 1998/99; World Bank/InM survey 2010/11.

findings confirm that the benefits of microcredit programs are higher for house-holds that participated regularly/continuously than for those who participated irregularly (Khandker and Samad 2014).

Estimating Consumption and Poverty Effects of Microcredit Participation

The above analysis shows that participants and nonparticipants in microcredit programs appear to have performed equally well over the years in attaining higher living standards. Participants have done slightly better on average than nonparticipants for such outcomes as extreme-poverty reduction; however, the differences in poverty reduction between the two household groups are not substantially high. If both participants and nonparticipants fared equally well over the 20-year period, then the welfare gains could not necessarily be attributed to microfinance, but perhaps to overall economic growth that affected all groups equally over time. If participants would still have been bet-ter off, then what was the net effect of microcredit participation in this process?

One may counter this argument by saying that participants would probably have been worse off without microcredit because they were less capable than their nonparticipant counterparts. Earlier studies show a negative self-selection bias, suggesting that less capable households are more likely to participate in microcredit programs (Pitt and Khandker 1998). Estimating the causal effect of microcredit program participation requires an econometric analysis, which will show the effect of microcredit net of other changes in the economy that equally affected everyone in the society.

Given the methods employed in chapter 4 (based on appendix B), table 6.4 presents the p-score weighted FE and LDV model estimates of microcredit's impact on three measures of consumption and two measures of poverty. The R square fits well for most of the outcomes, ranging from 0.271 to 0.442. While men's borrowing matters little for the outcomes, women's borrowing matters for most outcomes. For example, a 10 percent increase in women's borrowing reduces both moderate and extreme poverty by about 0.1 percent-age point.

The possibility that past consumption affects current consumption and poverty cannot be ignored in a long panel spanning more than 20 years; thus, the dynamic panel model is also covered, including the LDV as an additional regressor.[12] The reported findings based on the dynamic panel model vary little from those using the static FE model (table 6.4). Both the static and dynamic model results show that men's borrowing plays no role in improving consumption or reducing poverty. For women's borrowing, how-ever, the dynamic model results, unlike those using the static model, show an improvement in per capita food expenditure. For other outcomes, the impacts of women's credit are smaller than those observed using the static FE model.

Table 6.4 Alternate Panel Estimates of Microcredit Borrowing Impacts on Household Outcomes
N = 1,509

Microcredit loan variable	Log per capita total expenditure (Tk./month)	Log per capita food expenditure (Tk./month)	Log per capita nonfood expenditure (Tk./month)	Moderate poverty	Extreme poverty
p-score weighted household FE model					
Log loans of household males (Tk.)	0.002	0.004	0.011	−0.003	−0.002
	(0.73)	(1.13)	(1.24)	(−0.61)	(−0.67)
Log loans of household females (Tk.)	0.007*	0.0003	0.016*	−0.008*	−0.007**
	(1.72)	(1.17)	(1.83)	(−1.74)	(−2.67)
R^2	0.375	0.271	0.442	0.300	0.333
Dynamic panel LDV model					
Log loans of household males (Tk.)	−0.002	−0.002	−0.002	−0.002	−0.004*
	(−0.80)	(−0.95)	(−0.33)	(−0.76)	(−1.79)
Log loans of household females (Tk.)	0.005*	0.004*	0.009*	−0.006*	−0.005**
	(1.87)	(1.80)	(1.78)	(−1.95)	(−2.38)
F statistics of the model	$F(26, 86) = 27.12$, $p > F = 0.00$	$F(26, 86) = 24.80$, $p > F = 0.00$	$F(26, 86) = 25.40$, $p > F = 0.00$	$F(26, 86) = 9.18$, $p > F = 0.00$	$F(26, 86) = 8.00$, $p > F = 0.00$

Sources: World Bank/BIDS survey 1991/92 and 1998/99; World Bank/InM survey 2010/11.
Note: Figures in parentheses are t-statistics based on standard errors clustered at the village level. Regressions include more control variables at the village level (e.g., price of consumer goods, male and female wages, and availability of schools). FE = fixed effect; LDV = lagged dependent variable.
Significance level: * = 10 percent, ** = 5 percent or less.

Marginal Returns to Consumption for Microborrowing?

While the above section presented the response elasticity of consumption with respect to borrowing, this section examines the marginal effects of microcredit borrowing on consumption to determine whether the returns to consumption from microborrowing are declining over time. Of course, the consumption effects of borrowing are only one among an array of welfare dimensions (e.g., income, assets, net worth, and education) that accrue from microfinance participation. By examining the returns to consumption over time, one can at least discover whether consumption gains have been declining from microborrowing when consumption smoothing needs are diminished with higher income accrued to borrowers of microfinance.

Table 6.5 shows the marginal returns to women's borrowing for three categories of per capita expenditure.[13] The estimated returns are presented for both the static FE and dynamic LDV models. The results show that, for each Tk. 100 borrowed, a household's total annual expenditure increases by Tk. 2.3 using the static FE model and by about Tk. 1.9 based on the dynamic panel model. For the same amount of borrowing, the respective increases in nonfood expenditure are Tk. 1.5 and Tk. 1.2. These estimated gains are much less than those reported in Pitt and Khandker (1998) (Tk. 18 for Tk. 100 borrowed) and Khandker (2005) (nearly Tk. 21 for Tk. 100 borrowed), clearly showing that microcredit returns to consumption have diminished substantially over time. Given that the average cost of borrowing runs as high as 14.5 percent

Beyond Ending Poverty • http://dx.doi.org/10.1596/978-1-4648-0894-4

Table 6.5 Marginal Returns to Women's Borrowing for Household Expenditure and Income

Model used	Tk. per year/Tk. 100 borrowed			
	Total expenditure	Food expenditure	Nonfood expenditure	Income
p-score weighted FE estimates[a]	2.30* (1.72)	0.77 (1.17)	1.47* (1.83)	−0.82 (−0.16)
Dynamic panel estimates[a]	1.87* (1.87)	0.89* (1.80)	1.15* (1.78)	8.72** (2.76)

Sources: World Bank/BIDS survey 1991/92 and 1998/99; World Bank/InM survey 2010/11.
Note: Figures in parentheses are t-statistics from the estimates of per capita expenditure reported in table 6.4. FE = fixed effect.
Significance level: * = 10 percent, ** = 5 percent.
a. Based on tables 4.5, 4.6, and 6.4.

(see chapter 3), the consumption gain is not enough to absorb the cost of borrowing. Since microfinance helps borrowers benefit in other ways than consumption gains, as demonstrated in chapter 4, the overall benefits of microcredit borrowing must be higher than its cost. Consider, for example, the marginal returns to income from microborrowing. As per table 6.5, participants get Tk. 8 for each additional Tk. 100 borrowed, gains higher than that of consumption gains.

Predicted versus Estimated Poverty Effects

In our estimation approach using both the static FE and dynamic panel models, we consider poverty as a dichotomous variable that takes a value of 1 if a household is poor and 0 if it is not poor. This means we must run a logistic distribution function with the panel data to obtain a consistent poverty estimate. But such an equation is not viable for panel data analysis; therefore, we used an FE (differenced ordinary least squares) and dynamic panel (LDV estimates). Because they are not the preferred way to estimate a dichotomous outcome equation,[14] we also estimated the poverty effects from consumption effects, which is practiced in the literature. This was done using a three-step process. First, the coefficient of log per capita total expenditure from the regression of consumption was multiplied by the total per capita expenditure to obtain the change in total per capita expenditure due to borrowing. Next, this change was subtracted from the total per capita expenditure to obtain the preborrowing measure of total per capita expenditure. Finally, preborrowing poverty was calculated by comparing preborrowing per capita expenditure with the moderate or extreme poverty line. The poverty effect due to microcredit borrowing is the difference between the average of current poverty and that of preborrowing poverty.

These predicted poverty effects, shown in table 6.6, and the actual estimates of poverty effects, found in table 6.4, are about the same. For example, using the static FE model, both the predicted and estimated effects of women's borrowing on moderate poverty is −0.008; based on the dynamic panel model, the predicted

Table 6.6 Impacts of Microcredit Borrowing on Poverty Calculated from Estimated Effects of Per Capita Expenditure

N = 1,509

Microcredit loan variable	Calculated from p-score weighted FE estimates[a]		Calculated from dynamic panel estimates[a]	
	Moderate poverty	Extreme poverty	Moderate poverty	Extreme poverty
Log male loans (Tk.)	−0.002	−0.003	0.003	0.002
	(−0.73)	(−0.73)	(0.80)	(0.80)
Log female loans (Tk.)	−0.008*	−0.011*	−0.005*	−0.009*
	(−1.72)	(−1.72)	(−1.87)	(−1.87)

Sources: World Bank/BIDS survey 1991/92 and 1998/99; World Bank/InM survey 2010/11.
Note: Figures in parentheses are t-statistics from the estimates of per capita expenditure reported in table 6.4. FE = fixed effect.
Significance level: * = 10 percent.
a. Reported in table 6.4.

effect is −0.005, while the estimated effect is −0.006. Whatever the relative merits and demerits of poverty estimates using alternative techniques, it is clear that microfinance reduces moderate and extreme poverty by about 1 percentage point per 10 percent increase in women's borrowing.

Impacts from Women's Participation

To better understand what the above findings mean for aggregate poverty reduction in rural Bangladesh, this section examines the impacts from microcredit participation (as opposed to borrowing), using both the static FE and dynamic panel models. The reported findings again show that women's participation matters most in estimating microcredit program effects (table 6.7).

As shown, women's participation increased total per capita expenditure by about 5 percentage points based on the static model and 6 percentage points based on the dynamic model. It also lowered moderate poverty by about 3 percentage points according to the static model and 6 percentage points for the dynamic model.

The 3 percentage point reduction in poverty among program participants can be used to estimate microcredit's role in aggregate (moderate) poverty reduction in rural Bangladesh. In 2010, rural Bangladesh had more than 19 million microcredit program borrowers.[15] This means that, over the course of this 20-year study, about 0.57 million households, representing some 2.5 million rural people,[16] were lifted out of poverty due to the microcredit intervention. Over that same period, aggregate poverty reduction in rural Bangladesh was about 25 percentage points for about 105 million rural people,[17] implying that some 25 million rural people were uplifted from poverty. This means that nearly 10 percent of the poverty reduction in rural Bangladesh over that period can be attributed to microfinance.[18]

Table 6.7 Estimates of Microcredit Participation Impacts on Household Outcomes
N = 1,509

Microcredit participation variable	Log per capita expenditure (Tk./month)			Moderate poverty	Extreme poverty
	Total expenditure	Food expenditure	Nonfood expenditure		
p-score weighted household FE					
Men's participation	−0.014	−0.017	0.011	0.0003	−0.051*
	(−0.76)	(−1.38)	(0.31)	(0.01)	(−1.82)
Women's participation	0.049**	0.022	0.078**	−0.029**	−0.034**
	(2.09)	(1.43)	(2.54)	(−2.14)	(−2.11)
R^2	0.376	0.271	0.442	0.300	0.333
Dynamic panel LDV model					
Men's participation	−0.034	−0.016	−0.041	0.003	−0.030
	(−1.25)	(−0.92)	(−0.90)	(0.10)	(−1.18)
Women's participation	0.062*	0.052*	0.083*	−0.060*	−0.041*
	(1.82)	(1.76)	(1.95)	(−1.73)	(−1.70)
F statistics of the model	$F_{(26, 86)} = 29.90$, $p > F = 0.00$	$F_{(26, 86)} = 22.73$, $p > F = 0.00$	$F_{(26, 86)} = 27.08$, $p > F = 0.00$	$F_{(26, 86)} = 9.16$, $p > F = 0.00$	$F_{(26, 86)} = 7.67$, $p > F = 0.00$

Sources: World Bank/BIDS survey 1991/92 and 1998/99; World Bank/InM survey 2010/11.
Note: Figures in parentheses are t-statistics based on standard errors clustered at the village level. Regressions include more control variables at the village level (e.g., price of consumer goods, male and female wages, and availability of schools). FE = fixed effect; LDV = lagged dependent variable.
Significance level: * = 10 percent, ** = 5 percent or less.

Summary

To determine whether microcredit participants are trapped in poverty, as speculated in the public domain in recent years, this chapter examined the trend in welfare gains over the 20-year period covered by the three survey rounds (1991/92, 1998/99, and 2010/11). Our analysis was restricted to panel households of microcredit program participants and nonparticipants. The descriptive analysis found that participants fared better than nonparticipants for certain outcomes, while nonparticipants did better for others. Although simple comparisons do not prove a causal role of microfinance, the simple differences across participants and nonparticipants show the direction of changes in welfare gains over time. Our findings show that poverty rates for both groups fell substantially over time. For participants, extreme poverty fell from 77.8 percent in 1991/92 to only 14.0 percent in 2010/11; the corresponding figures for nonparticipants were 77.7 percent and 22.0 percent.[19]

No doubt, many economic changes occurred in Bangladesh over the 20-year period covered by the three survey rounds beyond the expansion of microcredit, including physical infrastructure and economic policies that may have contributed to the welfare status of both participants and nonparticipants. Also, nonparticipants may have gained from the spillover effects of microcredit expansion over that period. In such a setting, even with the long panel survey data, it is difficult to isolate the net effects of microcredit expansion on the welfare gains of borrowers over time. Thus, this chapter addressed the critical issue: What would have happened to participants over that 20-year period without micro-credit programs?

The study used an econometric estimation technique that took into account the time-varying endogeneity of program borrowers (i.e., certain households borrowed from microcredit and remained borrowers while others did not, even though both groups were eligible to participate and borrow from the outset). Using two robust techniques to control for time-varying, unobserved household- and village-level heterogeneity (i.e., p-score weighted FE and dynamic panel LDV models), we found that program borrowing has indeed mattered for consumption and poverty reduction gains, and more for women than for men. The results show that microcredit has helped to increase consumption and, in the process, reduce both moderate and extreme poverty. Thus, counter to a common perception about a poverty trap among microfinance participants, we find that borrowers on average have gained in terms of improved consumption and reduced poverty and thus are not necessarily trapped in poverty as argued anec-dotally. In fact, our results show that 10 percent of the total reduction in poverty among the rural population over the last 20 years—2.5 million rural people out of 25 million—can be attributed to microfinance.

Notes

1. According to the Consultative Group to Assist the Poor (CGAP), microfinance ben-eficiaries total more than 200 million worldwide. In Bangladesh alone, about one-fifth of the country's 150 million people—including three-fifths of rural households—are members of microfinance institutions.

2. A recent experimental study carried out in Mexico found more positive than negative impacts on average for various dimensions (Angelucci, Karlan, and Zinman 2013).

3. RCT studies have their own methodological weaknesses and thus are not always necessarily better than non-RCT studies (Deaton 2010; Ravallion 2012; Rodrik 2008). Because microcredit operations are small in scale, realizing their impacts may exceed one or two years, which is the typical time frame for minimizing the spillover effects and contamination for most RCT studies (Hermes and Lensink 2007). In fact, the seminal study of Pitt and Khandker (1998), which uses an innovative quasi-experimental design, relies on borrowing data collected over a five-year period from areas where microcredit had been in operation for at least three years.

4. Roodman and Morduch have been critical of the underlying methodology of Pitt and Khandker (1998), the most cited study in the literature on microcredit impacts. Roodman and Morduch (2011) is the most recent in a series of papers and postings that seek to refute the findings of Pitt and Khandker. In 2012, Pitt and Khandker revisited the claims of Roodman and Morduch, observing a lack of due diligence in their replication of the Pitt and Khandker study and confirming that none of their statistical claims invalidate the findings of Pitt and Khandker on the substantial posi-tive effects of microcredit, especially among women borrowers (see also Pitt [2014] for details).

5. In Mexico, Angelucci, Karlan, and Zinman (2013) found that, even at 110 percent interest rate, microfinance had more positive than negative benefits; thus, interest rate

is not a major concern in cases where returns to microinvestment are high enough to support such investments with borrowed funds from the MFIs.

6. Households trapped in poverty are those that participated in microcredit programs but failed to lift themselves out of poverty; in addition, households that continued to borrow but could not raise their assets compared to their debt over time are also trapped in poverty.

7. We considered income along with other indicators of welfare in chapter 4. This chapter considers the effect of microfinance on consumption and poverty.

8. The calculation of moderate poverty is based on the official poverty line, which includes the food poverty line and an allowance for nonfood expenditures. The food poverty line is calculated by estimating the cost of a food basket needed to maintain the per capita daily caloric requirement (2,120 calories) recommended by the Food and Agriculture Organization (FAO) and the World Health Organization (WHO) (FAO/WHO 1973). For Bangladesh, the food basket contains mainly rice, along with such other food items as pulses, milk, meat, fish, fruits, and vegetables in specific quantities. The cost of the food basket is calculated from the local prices for the food items. By contrast, extreme poverty is defined by the household's total consumption expenditure on food and nonfood falling short of the food poverty line.

9. Eligible households are those who participated in microcredit programs and those that could have participated but did not; eligible households constituted 83 percent, 87 percent, and 99 percent of the households surveyed in 1991/92, 1998/99, and 2010/11, respectively.

10. This finding appears counterintuitive since nonparticipants had slightly higher incomes and expenditures, compared to program participants. However, this is possible because the expenditure of participants who were extremely poor grew more than that of extremely poor nonparticipants, while nonparticipants that were moderately poor or nonpoor did better than their participant counterparts.

11. The abbreviations for the four household types—PPP, NPP, NNP, and NNN—denote participation status across years, where P stands for participation and N for non-participation; the leftmost letter refers to the household's participation status in 1991/92, while the middle one refers to its status in 1998/99 and the rightmost in 2010/11. For example, NNP refers to those households who were nonparticipants, according to the 1991/92 and 1998/99 survey data, but who were participants, according to the 2010/11 data.

12. The rationale and derivation of the dynamic panel model are provided in appendix B.

13. Only women's borrowing is considered because the consumption effects of male borrowing are not statistically significant.

14. The problem with the FE logit model is not that it cannot be run but that it drops many observations (i.e., those whose poverty status do not vary over time); such a drop in observations is not necessarily random, casting doubt on the results.

15. This number of borrowers was obtained from "NGO-MFIs in Bangladesh," Vol. 7, June 2010 (cleancookstoves.org/resources/105.html).

16. This number assumes an average household size of 4.3.

17. These figures are based on a national population of 150 million in 2010, 70 percent of whom were living in rural areas.

18. According to the LDV estimates, about 20 percent of the poverty reduction over the last 20 years can be attributed to microfinance. That is, 1 percent poverty reduction

due to microfinance every year. This is similar to 1 percent poverty reduction rate per year observed in an earlier study (Khandker 2005).

19. One should note that the difference in poverty reduction rates is above the attrition rate of 7.4 percent, indicating that the finding is robust.

Bibliography

Angelucci, Manuela, Dean Karlan, and Jonathan Zinman. 2013. "Win Some Lose Some? Evidence from a Randomized Microcredit Program Placement Experiment by Compartamos Banco." NBER Working Paper Series 19119, National Bureau of Economic Research, Cambridge, MA.

Attanasio, O., B. Augsburg, R. D. Haas, E. Fitzsimons, and H. Harmgart. 2012. "Group Lending or Individual Lending? Evidence from a Randomised Field Experiment in Mongolia." Working Paper 136, European Bank for Reconstruction and Development (EBRD), London.

Augsburg, Britta, Ralph De Haas, Heike Hamgart, and Costas Meghir. 2011. "Microfinance at the Margin: Experimental Evidence from Bosnia and Herzegovina." Paper presented at "Mind the Gap: From Evidence to Policy Impact," conference held in Cuernavaca, Mexico, June 16–17.

Banerjee, A., E. Duflo, R. Glennerster, and C. Kinnan. 2010. "The Miracle of Microfinance? Evidence from a Randomized Evaluation." Working Paper, Massachusetts Institute of Technology, Cambridge, MA. http://econ-www.mit.edu/files/4162.

Boonperm, Jirawan, Jonathan Haughton, and Shahidur R. Khandker. 2009. "Does the Village Fund Matter in Thailand?" World Bank Policy Research Working Paper 5011, World Bank, Washington, DC.

Chemin, M. 2008. "The Benefits and Costs of Microfinance: Evidence from Bangladesh." *Journal of Development Studies* 44 (4): 463–84.

Coleman, B. E. 1999. "The Impact of Group Lending in Northeast Thailand." *Journal of Development Economics* 60 (1): 105–41.

———. 2006. "Microfinance in Northeast Thailand: Who Benefits and How Much." *World Development* 34 (9): 1612–38.

Crépon, Bruno, Florencia Devoto, Esther Duflo, and William Parienté. 2011. "Impact of Microcredit in Rural Areas of Morocco: Evidence from a Randomized Evaluation." Massachusetts Institute of Technology, Cambridge, MA.

Deaton, Angus. 2010. "Instruments, Randomization, and Learning about Development." *Journal of Economic Literature* 48 (2): 424–55.

de Mel, Suresh, David McKenzie, and Christopher Woodruff. 2008. "Who Are the Microenterprise Owners? Evidence from Sri Lanka on Tokman v. de Soto." World Bank Policy Research Working Paper 4635, World Bank, Washington, DC.

Dunford, C. 2006. "Evidence of Microfinance's Contribution to Achieving the Millennium Development Goals: Freedom from Hunger." http://microfinancegateway.org/files /35795_file_Evidence_on_ MDGs_Dunford.pdf.

FAO/WHO (Food and Agriculture Organization/World Health Organization). 1973. *Energy and Protein Requirements*. FAO Nutrition Meetings Report Series 52 and WHO Technical Report Series 522; report of a Joint FAO/WHO ad hoc Expert Committee. Geneva: FAO/WHO.

Faruqee, Rashid, and M. A. Baqui Khalily. 2011. "Interest Rates in Bangladesh Microcredit Market." Policy Paper, Institute of Microfinance (InM), Dhaka.

Hermes, N., and R. Lensink. 2007. "The Empirics of Microfinance: What Do We Know?" *Economic Journal* 117 (1): F1–10.

Hossain, M. 1988. *Credit for Alleviation of Rural Poverty: The Grameen Bank in Bangladesh*. Research Report 65. Washington, DC: International Food Policy Research Institute (IFPRI).

Imai, K. S., T. Arun, and S. K. Annim. 2010. "Microfinance and Household Poverty Reduction: New Evidence from India." *World Development* 38 (12): 1760–74.

Islam, Asadul. 2011. "Medium- and Long-term Participation in Microcredit: An Evaluation Using a New Panel Dataset from Bangladesh." *American Journal of Agricultural Economics* 93 (3): 847–66.

Karlan, D., and J. Zinman. 2009. "Expanding Microenterprise Credit Access: Using Randomized Supply Decisions To Estimate the Impacts in Manila." Working Paper, Abdul Latif Jameel Poverty Action Lab, Massachusetts Institute of Technology, Cambridge, MA.

———. 2011. "Microcredit in Theory and Practice: Using Randomized Credit Scoring for Impact Evaluation." *Science* 332 (6035): 1278–84.

Kevane, Michael, and Bruce Wydick. 2001. "Microenterprise Lending to Female Entrepreneurs: Sacrificing Economic Growth for Poverty Alleviation?" *World Development* 29 (7): 1225–36.

Khandker, Shahidur. R. 1998. *Fighting Poverty with Microcredit: Experience in Bangladesh*. New York: Oxford University Press.

———. 2005. "Microfinance and Poverty: Evidence Using Panel Data from Bangladesh." *World Bank Economic Review* 19 (2): 263–86.

Khandker, Shahidur, and Hussain Samad. 2014. "Microfinance Growth and Poverty Reduction in Bangladesh: What Does the Longitudinal Data Say?" *Bangladesh Development Studies* 37 (1&2): 127–57.

McIntosh, C. 2008. "Estimating Treatment Effects from Spatial Policy Experiments: An Application to Ugandan Microfinance." *Review of Economics and Statistics* 90 (1): 15–28.

McKenzie, David, and Christopher Woodruff. 2008. "Experimental Evidence on Returns to Capital and Access to Finance in Mexico." *World Bank Economic Review* 22 (3): 457–82.

Panjaitan-Drioadisuryo, R. D. M., and K. Cloud. 1999. "Gender, Self-Employment and Microcredit Programs: An Indonesian Case Study." *The Quarterly Review of Economics and Finance* 39 (5): 769–79.

Pitt, Mark. 2014. "Response to 'The Impact of Microcredit on the Poor in Bangladesh: Revisiting the Evidence.'" *Journal of Development Studies* 50 (4): 605–10.

Pitt, M., and S. Khandker. 1996. "Household and Intra-household Impact of the Grameen Bank and Similar Targeted Credit Programs in Bangladesh." World Bank Discussion Paper 320, World Bank, Washington, DC.

———. 1998. "The Impact of Group-Based Credit Programmes on Poor Households in Bangladesh: Does Gender of the Participant Matter?" *Journal of Political Economy* 106 (5): 958–96.

————. 2012. "Replicating Replication: Due Diligence in Roodman and Morduch's Replication of Pitt and Khandker (1998)." Policy Research Working Paper 6273, World Bank, Washington, DC.

Pitt, M. M., S. R. Khandker, S.-M. McKernan, and M. A. Latif. 1999. "Credit Programs for the Poor and Reproductive Behavior in Low Income Countries: Are the Reported Causal Relationships the Result of Heterogeneity Bias?" *Demography* 36 (1): 1–21.

Ravallion, M. 2012. "Fighting Poverty One Experiment at a Time: A Review of Abhijit Banerjee and Esther Duflo's *Poor Economics: A Radical Rethinking of the Way to Fight Global Poverty*." *Journal of Economic Literature* 50 (1): 103–14.

Rodrik, Dani. 2008. "The New Development Economics: We Shall Experiment, but How Shall We Learn?" Harvard University, Cambridge, MA.

Roodman, D. 2012. "Latest Impact Research: Inching Towards Generalization." Consultative Group to Assist the Poor microfinance blog. http://microfinance.cgap .org/2012/04/11/latest-impact-research-inching-toward-generalization/.

Roodman, D., and J. Morduch. 2011. "The Impact of Microcredit on the Poor in Bangladesh: Revisiting the Evidence." Revised, Working Paper 174, Center for Global Development, Washington, DC.

Shaw, J. 2004. "Microenterprise Occupation and Poverty Reduction in Microfinance Programs: Evidence from Sri Lanka." *World Development* 32 (7): 1247–64.

CHAPTER 7

Diversification of Income and Employment: How Does Microfinance Affect Agriculture?

Introduction

The previous chapters have considered the effects of microfinance on household consumption, assets, employment, schooling, and poverty, as well as its total income effect. The next key issue is to examine its effect on income and employment diversification among alternative farm and nonfarm sources. As already shown, microfinance in rural Bangladesh mainly supports nonfarm activities in order to promote nonfarm self-employment and income for the rural unemployed. Agriculture still provides the bulk of rural employment and income-earning opportunities, accounting for about 25 percent of the country's gross domestic product (GDP) and 45 percent of its overall employment. But increasing population pressure on the land, along with seasonality of agriculture, means that many poor people who are willing to work in agriculture cannot be fully or even partially absorbed into the sector. At the same time, growth of the population and potential labor force is outpacing industrialization and urbanization.

Thus, one can hypothesize that the surplus labor force willing to work productively will likely borrow from microfinance institutions (MFIs) in order to gain nonagriculture self-employment. This would explain why the MFIs in rural Bangladesh finance mainly nonfarm activities. Even so, microfinance lending may still benefit agriculture directly, given that many marginal farmers are willing to participate in MFI programs to support both farm and nonfarm activities, as well as indirectly since funds are fungible.

How has MFI credit expansion in Bangladesh benefited the country's small farmers and poor rural people engaged in agriculture? At a time when the formal sector, including commercial banks, has been asked increasingly to support agriculture, what role has microfinance played? Over the past decade, the Government of Bangladesh has steadily increased the share of public funds allocated to agricultural lending to help ensure food security in the country.

Between fiscal years 2008/09 and 2009/10 alone, it raised the disbursement target for agricultural credit by 23 percent to Tk. 115 billion (Bangladesh Bank 2010).[1] MFI loan disbursement has also increased steadily in recent years, reaching a total of Tk. 372 billion by 2010, about Tk. 340 billion more than in 1997. Traditionally, commercial and agricultural banks have financed nonagricultural activities for households with sufficient collateral, while MFIs typically have supported nonfarm activities for rural households that are unemployed or engaged as agricultural wage laborers. Unemployment or under-employment in the agricultural wage market is a major concern for the rural poor; thus, providing this segment of the population credit for initiating nonfarm income-generating activities can be a major boost.

From the outset, microfinance has targeted landless or near-landless households in an effort to address the needs of the extreme poor (e.g., Faruqee 2010; Khandker 1998). While large-scale farmers have been more likely to gain access to institutional finance through commercial and agricultural development banks, albeit on a limited scale, small- and medium-scale farmers, whose landholdings rank in the lower end of the distribution, have been left out for the most part. This segment of the population, which constitutes a large share of Bangladesh's farming community, is termed the "missing middle" in the literature (e.g., Khandker 1998). Based on the large number of microfinance borrowers in Bangladesh, currently estimated at about 30 million, it is obvious that the MFIs have been working to meet the credit demand of landless and near-landless households. The past two decades have witnessed the gradual entry of the MFIs into the credit markets and more relaxed enforcement of traditional eligibility conditions (e.g., households having to own less than half an acre of land), making it possible for marginal and small and medium landholding farmers to have received better access to microfinance.[2] If this indeed has occurred, what impact has it had on smallholder farmers' productivity and income growth?

This chapter investigates the impacts of rural credit channels—commercial and agricultural banks and the MFIs—on rural households, taking into account the nature and extent of credit constraints faced by agricultural and nonagricultural households.[3] It examines whether rural credit expansion by Bangladesh's banks and MFIs has helped poor farmers directly by stimulating agricultural productivity and income and/or indirectly by strengthening linkages between farm and nonfarm production and employment. Specifically, the chapter addresses several dynamic policy questions: (a) whether rural credit expansion has been able to handle agricultural loans; (b) how the borrowing needs of agricultural households have changed across landholding distribution; and (c) how easier access to credit has affected agricultural productivity, incomes, and income diversification.

Traditional Role of Institutional Finance in Agriculture

Historically, institutional credit to poor farmers has been limited in most developing countries; when available, it has usually supported nonfarm activities. The presence of credit constraints can significantly impact agricultural outcomes.

For example, using panel data from northern Peru, Guirkinger and Boucher (2008) found that credit constraints lower the value of agricultural output substantially for poor households; however, for those households without credit constraints, productivity is independent of such endowments as land and liquidity. Indeed, several studies across developing countries confirm that credit constraints among agricultural households significantly affect farm output (Feder and others 1990; Sial and Carter 1996), farm profit (Carter 1989; Foltz 2004), and farm investment (Carter and Olinto 2003). Recent efforts by many developing country governments to improve smallholder farmers' access to credit raise an interesting policy question regarding the role of the banks and MFIs as part of this process.[4]

Farmers face many risks to their livelihoods, including unpredictable weather and crop price variation, which may affect how they choose to borrow and invest to improve their businesses. For example, Pitt and Khandker (2002) found that consumption-poor households and those with higher than average seasonal fluctuations in consumption and labor supply are more likely to participate in microfinance programs. Smoothing consumption across seasons is thus an important motivation for participating in these credit programs. The enhanced ability to smooth consumption arising from microfinance may also permit households to choose riskier but higher-yielding contracts from among those offered in the agricultural markets (Pitt 2000), which can potentially increase household consumption across the seasons. Wadud (2013) examined the impact of the recent expansion of microfinance into agricultural loans on farm performance, output, and food security in northern Bangladesh, finding small and marginal farmers used inputs more efficiently as a result.

In terms of the supply-led approach to agricultural credit historically pursued in many developing countries, most studies have found that access to commercial and agricultural banks has created viable alternatives to moneylenders for those households with somewhat greater assets and sources of collateral. For example, Binswanger and Khandker (1995) found that better access to banks spurred fertilizer use and investment in agriculture; however, it was less successful in generating viable institutions to generate agricultural employment.

Credit can also be fungible, and even perfect monitoring does not necessarily mean that credit for nonfarm activities cannot substitute somewhat for consumption credit or prohibited agricultural credit. If a household wishes to devote resources obtained from savings, inter-household transfers, or borrowing from moneylenders or other sources to a production activity in the absence of institutional credit, it may, in the presence of group-based lending programs, substitute group-based credit for those resources, and funds from other sources can be used elsewhere. In this way, simply by relaxing the household's constraints on borrowing and transfers, monitored production credit may help households to alter their mix of income-generating activities, including the mix of agricultural contracts, as well as smooth consumption. Access to group-based microfinance may enhance the household's ability to borrow from other sources or obtain transfers, allowing it to expand self-employment and own-cultivation in field crop agriculture and reduce dependence on the agricultural wage labor market.

Pitt (2000), which examined the effects of group-based credit on the poor in Bangladesh, confirms the hypothesis that nonagricultural self-employment projects financed by microfinance induce households to choose higher-risk agricultural contracts. The study analyzed the effects of group-based credit by gender of participant, participating households' mix of agricultural contracts (quantities of land sharecropped and rented), and supply of agricultural labor (own-cultivation as opposed to agricultural wage labor). As predicted, it found that credit effects were larger for women than for men in increasing sharecropping and reducing male wage labor, as well as increasing agricultural self-employment. These findings are consistent with the presumed effects of diversifying income and smoothing consumption.

The linkages across farm and nonfarm sectors on which agricultural growth depends suggest a major role for finance. In rural Bangladesh, microfinance has traditionally been targeted toward the nonfarm sector. However, as a result of microfinance expansion, greater linkages have developed between the nonfarm and farm sectors over time. Thus, microfinance can indirectly benefit the farm sector.

Recent Credit Initiatives in Agriculture

In recent years, MFIs in developing regions have made some headway in reaching poor farmers with supply credit constraints;[5] however, they have enjoyed little capacity to expand because they typically have lacked required licenses and a wide array of financial products. As a result, they have tended to operate on a small scale, offering local, demand-driven options, such as group-liability lending, to better reach clients and improve lender profitability.

A variety of bilateral and nongovernmental organization–funded programs have recently evolved to provide these options (Kloeppinger-Todd and Sharma 2010). To address limited collateral among smaller farmers, techniques have been developed to tailor lending strategies to the agricultural supply chain. For example, farmers can borrow against output stored in licensed warehouses, or producers and processors can make binding contracts for output after which processors repay the producer's loan to the bank. Other alternatives being used include direct product-distribution channels (e.g., mobile banking), electronic point-of-sale devices (e.g., those run by the Uganda Microfinance Union in rural areas), and partnerships with market-facilitating institutions. Also, agricultural insurance is an emerging policy area for helping farmers to manage production risks (Cai 2012; Giné and Yang 2009; Karlan and others 2013). In the absence of the large-scale government subsidies of the past, policy makers are being challenged to explore new ways of expanding rural financial access effectively and sustainably.

Few randomized studies have evaluated the impacts of rural farmers' improved access to microfinance, particularly on an aggregate or regional scale.[6] Among those that have recently emerged is the Tenant Farmers Development Project (BCUP) Sharecropper Development Programme, introduced by Bangladesh Rural Advancement Committee (BRAC) in 2010. This program is a customized credit service that aims to help sharecroppers without large land holdings to access cultivable land through the tenancy market. Traditionally, this sharecropper group has depended largely on credit borrowed from informal lenders at high interest rates to cover the costs of farming. Currently, the program is being expanded to include new branches introduced in a randomized fashion in order to estimate the effects of borrowing on outcomes for sharecroppers.

In Morocco, Crepón and others (2011) evaluated the expansion of that country's largest MFI into rural areas (by about 60 branches) during 2006/07. The study, which included a survey sample of about 5,500 households (about 4,500 treatment and 1,000 control households) before and after expansion, found no significant effect of program expansion on average consumption among the treatment households. However, the effects depended on activities that households were initially involved in, particularly in self-employed agriculture; a large increase in sales and profits led to substantial increases in expenditure and employment in this sector.

In Bangladesh, agricultural banks and nationalized commercial banks (NCBs) have been lending increasingly in rural areas,[7] but most of this lending has not been targeted to the poor (CDF 2006). Lending to smaller farmers is a relatively recent phenomenon, handled by microfinance agencies through Grameen Bank, Association for Social Advancement (ASA), and BRAC. In cooperation with Palli Karma-Sahayak Foundation (PKSF), Bangladesh's wholesale microfinance lending facility, the World Bank financed the Financial Services for the Poorest Project, a five-year effort initiated in June 2002; this project, which targeted the extreme poor in rural areas, included greater extension of microfinance programs and their linkages with other safety nets. Also, PKSF recently started a Seasonal Loans and Agricultural Lending program, nearly doubling the funds it directs toward crop agriculture during 2007/08 (Faruqee 2010). In addition, the Bangladesh Bank recently expanded its efforts to target marginal farmers, as well as small- and medium-scale landholder farmers, including a new Tk. 5 billion refinancing scheme with BRAC whereby sharecroppers receive collateral-free loans for the first time.[8]

Descriptive Data Analysis

Over the past two decades, microfinance has accounted for more than 90 percent of the improvement in access to institutional finance, increasing from 23 percent in 1991/92 to 38 percent in 1998/99 to 56 percent in 2010/11. Over that 20-year period, access to informal finance also increased (from 15 percent in 1991/92 to 23 percent in 1998/99 to 57 percent in 2010/11). The bulk of informal finance was directed to meeting the needs of non-microfinance participant households (table 7.1).

Interestingly, among microfinance participant households, the demand for informal finance increased, along with the demand for institutional finance (from more than 5 percent in 1991/92 to over 17 percent in 1998/99 to nearly 63 percent in 2010/11). However, microfinance represented a much larger share of lending volume, accounting for 65 percent of total borrowing

Table 7.1 Distribution of Surveyed Households' Borrowing Sources and Share in Total Loans

Borrowing source	Microfinance households	Non-microfinance households	All households
1991/92 (N = 1,509)			
Microfinance	100.0 (97.8)	0 (0)	23.3 (49.8)
Formal finance	1.2 (0.5)	11.2 (69.0)	8.9 (34.1)
Informal source	5.1 (1.7)	17.8 (31.0)	14.8 (16.1)
Any sources	100.0	27.6	44.5
1998/99 (N = 1,758)			
Microfinance	100.0 (91.4)	0 (0)	38.0 (67.2)
Formal finance	5.6 (1.9)	8.3 (26.1)	7.3 (8.3)
Informal source	17.5 (6.7)	27.0 (73.9)	23.3 (24.5)
Any sources	100.0	32.1	57.9
2010/11 (N = 2,322)			
Microfinance	100.0 (65.2)	0 (0)	56.2 (47.6)
Formal finance	7.1 (5.9)	8.8 (26.1)	7.8 (7.8)
Informal source	62.6 (28.9)	50.1 (73.9)	57.1 (44.6)
Any sources	100.0	53.7	79.7

Sources: World Bank/BIDS survey 1991/92 and 1998/99; World Bank/InM survey 2010/11.
Note: Figures in parentheses show loan volume from a borrowing source as a percentage share of total loan volume from all sources.

in 2010/11 (versus 29 percent for informal finance). That said, informal finance has played an increasing role among microfinance participant households; their percentage share of borrowing from informal finance increased from 1.7 percent in 1998/99 to 6.7 percent in 1998/99 to 28.9 percent in 2010/11 (table 7.1).

Several interesting loan-distribution patterns have emerged over the years. First, an increasing percentage of loans has supported consumption—from 18 percent in 1991/92 to 28 percent in 1998/99 and 27 percent in 2010/11. Second, over time, the farm sector has received a higher share of loans from all sources—from less than 22 percent in 1991/92 to more than 28 percent in 1998/99, reaching 33 percent by 2010/11. Formal financial services accounted for the bulk of the higher percentage of farm loans. The percentage of farm-sector loans from commercial and other banks increased from about 60 percent in 1991/92 to nearly 69 percent in 2010/11. Finally, although an overwhelming share of microfinance loans were for nonfarm-sector activities, a higher percentage went to support farm-sector activities over time. That is, in 1991/92, only about 8 percent of microfinance loans went to farming, compared to about 28 percent in 1998/99 and nearly 40 percent in 2010/11 (table 7.2).

Another important observation about the productive role of microfinance is that, although microfinance organizers have managed to enforce a high share of loans going to productive activities, enforcement of this rule has declined over

Table 7.2 Distribution of Loans by Major Purpose for Each Source of Borrowing

Borrowing source	Farm-sector activities	Nonfarm-sector activities	Personal expenditure
1991/92 (N = 1,509)			
Microfinance	8.2	82.7	9.1
Formal finance	59.5	28.9	11.6
Informal source	36.1	20.2	43.7
Any sources	21.5	60.5	18.0
1998/99 (N = 1,758)			
Microfinance	27.5	51.8	20.7
Formal finance	46.7	22.9	30.4
Informal source	26.8	22.8	50.4
Any sources	28.2	43.4	27.8
2010/11 (N = 2,322)			
Microfinance	39.8	56.5	3.7
Formal finance	68.7	26.6	4.7
Informal source	15.6	10.2	74.1
Any sources	33.0	39.9	27.1

Sources: World Bank/BIDS survey 1991/92 and 1998/99; World Bank/InM survey 2010/11.

time. In 1991/92, some 91 percent of microfinance loans went to productive activities (some 83 percent for nonfarm and 8 percent for farm activities), which fell to 79 percent in 1998/99 (52 percent for nonfarm and 28 percent for farm activities). But this share rose to 96 percent in 2010/11 (56 percent for nonfarm and 40 percent for farm activities) (table 7.2).

Institutional finance has increasingly supported farm-sector activities, especially noncrop farming, over time. In 1991/92, about half of microfinance loans for farming activities supported the purchase of equipment, with 28 percent for other agricultural expenditure. By 1998/99, other agricultural expenditure accounted for 47 percent of microfinance farm-sector borrowing and 74 percent by 2010/11. Formal finance has become the dominant source of support for other agricultural expenses. For example, in 1991/92, nearly 30 percent of formal finance for farming went to other agricultural expenditure; this share doubled by 1998/99, reaching nearly 81 percent in 2010/11. Over time, an overwhelming share of loans from all sources has supported noncrop-related farming activities, increasing from just 36 percent in 1991/92 to 48 percent in 1998/99 and nearly 70 percent by 2010/11 (table 7.3).

Marginal farmers, the original target group of microfinance organizations, have agricultural landholdings of less than 0.5 acres (50 decimals); these include landless households involved in agricultural activities outside the home (e.g., sharecropping). Small and medium landholding farmers are defined as having 0.5–2.5 acres (50–250 decimals) of agricultural land; as mentioned earlier, these farmers have often been termed the "missing middle" since they typically have been left out of institutional finance. Finally, large landholding farmers are defined as

Table 7.3 Distribution of Farm-Sector Activities by Borrowing Source

Borrowing source	Purchase of agricultural inputs	Purchase of equipment	Purchase/lease of agricultural land	Other agricultural expenditure[a]
1991/92 (N = 282)				
Microfinance	9.3	50.2	12.4	28.1
Formal finance	53.5	13.9	3.1	29.5
Informal source	31.5	7.5	14.5	46.5
All sources	33.7	20.0	10.1	36.2
1998/99 (N = 1,218)				
Microfinance	35.9	1.3	15.7	47.0
Formal finance	24.5	0.0	15.4	60.1
Informal source	36.0	3.9	13.3	47.8
All sources	35.0	1.8	15.2	48.0
2010/11 (N = 3,253)				
Microfinance	15.4	0.2	10.9	73.5
Formal finance	11.9	0.0	7.6	80.5
Informal source	13.9	3.2	34.1	48.8
All sources	15.0	0.7	14.4	69.9

Sources: World Bank/BIDS survey 1991/92 and 1998/99; World Bank/InM survey 2010/11.
a. Other agricultural expenditure includes expenses for livestock and poultry raising, fisheries, sericulture, nurseries, and forestry.

Table 7.4 Distribution of Borrowing from Alternative Sources by Farm Size
percent

Farm size	Microfinance	Formal finance	Informal source	Any source
1991/92 (N = 703)				
Marginal (< 0.5 acres)	30.4	5.7	11.3	44.7
Small and medium (0.5–2.5 acres)	17.6	10.9	20.5	45.5
Large (> 2.5 acres)	6.2	18.3	17.1	41.3
1998/99 (N = 831)				
Marginal (< 0.5 acres)	44.9	2.9	22.9	61.1
Small and medium (0.5–2.5 acres)	34.4	9.5	25.0	56.1
Large (> 2.5 acres)	12.8	24.2	23.7	47.2
2010/11 (N = 1,439)				
Marginal (< 0.5 acres)	61.2	3.9	55.8	80.0
Small and medium (0.5–2.5 acres)	47.8	15.6	60.2	80.9
Large (> 2.5 acres)	30.5	21.9	62.2	73.2

Sources: World Bank/BIDS survey 1991/92 and 1998/99; World Bank/InM survey 2010/11.

owning more than 2.5 acres (250 decimals) of agricultural land; this group often obtains credit from formal financial institutions, including agricultural development banks (table 7.4).

Table 7.4 shows that, over time, borrowing from any source (microfinance, formal finance, or informal source) increased at a similar pace for all three farm-size categories. Between 1991/92 and 2010/11, it rose from 45 percent to 80 percent for both marginal and small and medium farmers and from 41 percent to 73 percent for large farmers. Over the 20-year period, microfinance borrowing among marginal agricultural households more than doubled (from about 30 to 61 percent), with higher participation rates also realized among small- and medium-scale, as well as large, farmers. Over the same period, borrowing from banks has remained essentially flat for marginal and small- and medium-scale farmers, at 10 percent each, and has even declined for large landholding farmers.

Table 7.5 shows that, for all three survey years, marginal farmers received the highest share of loans, followed by small- and medium-scale farmers and large farmers. In 1991/92, marginal farmers received some 74 percent of loans, with just 23 percent received by small and medium farmers and less than 4 percent by large farmers. By 2010/11, the respective shares were 76 percent for marginal farmers, 21 percent for small and medium farmers, and only 3 percent for large farmers. For the three survey years, the average loan size has remained at similar level for all three farm-size categories.

Table 7.6 shows that, for each of the three farm-size groups, the largest share of loans from any source went to support noncrop farming in all three survey years. In 2010/11, for example, 70 percent of loans to marginal farmers supported noncrop farming, compared to 71 percent for small- and medium-scale farmers and 59 percent for large landholding farmers.

Effects of Borrowing on Agricultural Household Income and Productivity

Since it is already known that microfinance matters for promoting nonfarm income and employment, the issue is whether household-level borrowing from

Table 7.5 Loan Volume for Borrowing Sources by Farm Size

Farm size	Share among borrowers (%)	Cumulative loans by household males (Tk.)	Cumulative loans by household females (Tk.)
1991/92 (N = 703)			
Marginal (< 0.5 acres)	73.8	3,007.2	7,059.6
Small and medium (0.5–2.5 acres)	22.6	4,729.7	6,906.6
Large (> 2.5 acres)	3.6	5,657.2	4,403.9
1998/99 (N = 831)			
Marginal (< 0.5 acres)	69.3	1,765.3	14,271.5
Small and medium (0.5–2.5 acres)	26.8	4,191.2	15,068.5
Large (> 2.5 acres)	3.9	10,076.9	7,052.1
2010/11 (N = 1,439)			
Marginal (< 0.5 acres)	76.2	4,362.7	15,407.0
Small and medium (0.5–2.5 acres)	20.6	8,547.8	13,644.1
Large (> 2.5 acres)	3.2	21,085.8	14,865.6

Sources: World Bank/BIDS survey 1991/92 and 1998/99; World Bank/InM survey 2010/11.

Table 7.6 Distribution of Farm-Sector Activities by Farm Size

Farm size	Purchase of agricultural inputs	Purchase of equipment	Purchase/lease of agricultural land	Other agricultural expenditure
1991/92 (N = 282)				
Marginal (< 0.5 acres)	23.8	28.3	7.1	40.8
Small and medium (0.5–2.5 acres)	39.3	18.5	8.5	33.7
Large (> 2.5 acres)	38.2	9.3	18.8	33.7
1998/99 (N = 1,218)				
Marginal (< 0.5 acres)	30.1	1.9	18.0	50.0
Small and medium (0.5–2.5 acres)	42.3	1.1	14.1	42.5
Large (> 2.5 acres)	30.8	3.4	8.6	57.2
2010/11 (N = 3,253)				
Marginal (< 0.5 acres)	13.2	0.5	16.2	70.3
Small and medium (0.5–2.5 acres)	18.1	1.0	9.6	71.3
Large (> 2.5 acres)	18.3	1.2	21.8	58.7

Sources: World Bank/BIDS survey 1991/92 and 1998/99; World Bank/InM survey 2010/11.

the MFIs matters also for farm income and employment. This subsection considers the microfinance effect on farm income from crops, livestock and poultry raising, and agricultural wages.[9]

Following the general method outlined in appendix B, we consider the following outcome equation for farm income with time-varying heterogeneity:

$$Y_{it} = X_{it}\beta_c + C_{ift}\delta_f + C_{imt}\delta_m + \eta_{it} + \mu_i + \varepsilon_{it}, \tag{7.1}$$

where Y_{it} equals the outcome (e.g., total farm, crop, noncrop, and agricultural wage income) of household i in survey year t, conditional on the level of credit demand by males (C_{imt}) and females (C_{ift}); X_{it} is a vector of characteristics at the household level (e.g., sex, age and education of household head, and landholding assets) and village level (e.g., extent of electrification and irrigation, availability of other infrastructure, and price of consumer goods), β_c is a vector of unknown parameters of X variables to be estimated, δ_m and δ_f measure the effects of borrowing, η_{it} is an unobserved household- or community-level determinant of the outcome that is time-varying, μ_i is an unobserved household- or community-level determinant of the outcome that is time-invariant, and ε_{it} is a nonsystematic error. The household fixed-effects (FE) estimation technique can eliminate the time-invariant parameter (μ_i) by transforming equation (7.1) as follows:

$$Y_{it} - \bar{Y}_i = \left(X_{it} - \bar{X}_i\right)\beta + \left(C_{ift} - \bar{C}_{if}\right)\delta_f + \left(C_{imt} - \bar{C}_{im}\right)\delta_m + \left(\eta_{it} - \bar{\eta}_i\right) + \left(\mu_i - \bar{\mu}\right) + \left(\varepsilon_{it} - \bar{\varepsilon}_i\right)$$

$$\text{or } \Delta Y_{it} = \beta\Delta X_{it} + \delta_f\Delta C_{ift} + \delta_m\Delta C_{imt} + \Delta\eta_{it} + \Delta\varepsilon_{it}, \tag{7.2}$$

where the bar variables (e.g., $\bar{Y}_i, \bar{X}_i, \bar{C}_{if}$) are average values for each household. Since μ is constant, $\bar{\mu}_i = \bar{\mu}$ and thus its effect is eliminated. However, since $\bar{\eta}_i \neq \bar{\eta}$, the problem of unobserved effects cannot be disregarded completely, and thus ordinary least squares (OLS) estimation of equation (7.2) will be biased.

Our empirical strategy uses household-level FE estimation with weights determined by propensity-score (p-score) matching, based on the participation equation to account for unobserved time-varying heterogeneity, as outlined in the methodology (appendix B). This strategy is referred to as the p-score weighted FE method. To account for bias in the lagged dependent variable (LDV), which cannot be resolved using FE, the strategy also follows an alternative LDV method. Two alternative models are also considered: one that assumes the credit effects of men and women do not vary by time of borrowing (i.e., they are time invariant) and the other that assumes they do (i.e., they are time varying).

Table 7.7 presents the estimates of credit effects of male and female borrowers using both p-score weighted FE and LDV methods. The effects are considered for all types of farm income, as well as total farm income. Using both model estimation techniques, there is no significant effect (either positive or negative) of male credit on any type of farm income or total farm income, suggesting that male credit has no role in farm income. However, female credit matters for both crop and noncrop income using both model estimation techniques. Also, female credit has a significant positive effect on total farm income, using the p-score

Table 7.7 Alternate Panel Estimates of the Impacts of Microfinance Borrowing on Household Farm Income
$N = 1,509$

Microfinance loan variables	Income from crop production	Income from livestock, poultry, and fishery	Wage income	Total farm income
p-score weighted household FE model				
Log loans of household males (Tk.)	−0.051	−0.007	−0.042	−0.010
	(−1.45)	(−0.28)	(−1.49)	(−0.54)
Log loans of household females (Tk.)	0.035*	0.028**	0.001	0.007*
	(2.01)	(2.01)	(0.08)	(1.96)
R^2	0.238	0.139	0.087	0.085
Dynamic panel LDV model				
Log loans of household males (Tk.)	−0.007	−0.007	−0.007	−0.003
	(−0.36)	(−0.33)	(−0.36)	(−0.25)
Log loans of household females (Tk.)	0.030*	0.006**	−0.010	0.014
	(1.75)	(2.27)	(−0.66)	(1.28)
F statistics of the model	$F(26, 86) = 13.81,$ $p > F = 0.00$	$F(26, 86) = 5.99,$ $p > F = 0.00$	$F(26, 86) = 27.02,$ $p > F = 0.00$	$F(26, 86) = 10.56,$ $p > F = 0.00$

Sources: World Bank/BIDS survey 1991/92 and 1998/99; World Bank/InM survey 2010/11.

Note: Outcomes are in log per capita Tk. per month. Figures in parentheses are *t*-statistics based on standard errors clustered at the village level. Regressions include more control variables at the household level (e.g., age, sex, and education of household head, and log of land assets) and village level (e.g., price of consumer goods; male and female wages; infrastructure, including schools and electricity availability; and proportion of irrigated land). FE = fixed effect; LDV = lagged dependent variable.

Significance level: * = 10 percent, ** = 5 percent or less.

weighted FE method. Results show that a 10 percent increase in female credit increases crop income by 3.5 percent, noncrop income by 2.8 percent, and total farm income by 0.07 percent.

Table 7.8 presents the alternative estimates of current and past credit effects of male and female borrowers. Using the FE model, the results show that current male credit has a negative effect on wage income, meaning that households with access to microfinance tend to opt out of wage labor in favor of farm self-employment and nonfarm activities. For female borrowers, current borrowing is found to increase noncrop income while past borrowing has a lingering effect on crop, as well as total farm, income.

Table 7.9 presents the credit-effect estimates for men and women by MFI source, using the p-score weighted FE model, having established that the FE model is the appropriate one for estimating farm income and its various components.

Table 7.8 Alternate Panel Estimates of the Impacts of Current and Past Microfinance Borrowing on Household Farm Income

N = 1,509

Microfinance loan variables	Income from crop production	Income from livestock, poultry, and fishery	Wage income	Total farm income
p-score weighted household FE model				
Log male current loans (Tk.)	−0.025	−0.039	−0.089**	−0.019
	(−0.71)	(−1.46)	(−3.13)	(−1.00)
Log male past loans (Tk.)	−0.112	0.031	0.014	−0.001
	(−1.54)	(0.48)	(0.30)	(−0.02)
Log female current loans (Tk.)	0.027	0.033*	0.012	0.013
	(1.45)	(1.81)	(0.59)	(1.27)
Log female past loans (Tk.)	0.056**	0.018	−0.029	0.034**
	(2.00)	(0.81)	(−1.22)	(2.54)
R^2	0.333	0.174	0.064	0.114
Dynamic panel LDV model				
Log male current loans (Tk.)	−0.040	−0.022	−0.097	−0.033
	(−1.22)	(−0.61)	(−0.83)	(−1.45)
Log male past loans (Tk.)	0.044	0.017	0.119**	0.039
	(1.18)	(0.41)	(3.28)	(1.59)
Log female current loans (Tk.)	−0.028	0.044*	0.007	0.024**
	(−1.31)	(1.77)	(0.35)	(2.08)
Log female past loans (Tk.)	−0.001	−0.046	−0.018	−0.011
	(−0.05)	(−1.51)	(−0.82)	(−0.96)
F statistics of the model	$F(26, 86) = 13.02$, $p > F = 0.00$	$F(26, 86) = 5.75$, $p > F = 0.00$	$F(26, 86) = 27.21$, $p > F = 0.00$	$F(26, 86) = 9.95$, $p > F = 0.00$

Sources: World Bank/BIDS survey 1991/92 and 1998/99; World Bank/InM survey 2010/11.

Note: Outcomes are in log per capita Tk. per month. Figures in parentheses are *t*-statistics based on standard errors clustered at the village level. Regressions include more control variables at the household level (e.g., age, sex, and education of household head, and log of land assets) and village level (e.g., price of consumer goods; male and female wages; infrastructure, including schools and electricity availability; and proportion of irrigated land). FE = fixed effects; LDV = lagged dependent variable.

Significance level: * = 10 percent, ** = 5 percent or less.

Table 7.9 Impacts of Microfinance Borrowing on Household Farm Income by Lenders: Propensity-Score Weighted Household FE Estimates

N = 1,509

Microfinance loan variables by source	Income from crop production	Income from livestock, poultry, and fishery	Wage income	Total farm income
Grameen Bank				
Log loans of household males (Tk.)	0.042	−0.069	−0.095*	0.016
	(0.74)	(−1.48)	(−1.66)	(0.58)
Log loans of household females (Tk.)	0.014*	0.039*	−0.017	0.016*
	(1.78)	(1.77)	(−0.97)	(1.96)
BRAC				
Log loans of household males (Tk.)	−0.114	0.023	0.032	−0.040
	(−1.24)	(0.30)	(0.96)	(−0.85)
Log loans of household females (Tk.)	0.094**	−0.040	−0.053**	−0.008
	(4.27)	(−1.26)	(−2.60)	(−0.68)
Other sources[a]				
Log loans of household males (Tk.)	−0.056	0.013	−0.024	−0.002
	(−1.49)	(0.46)	(−0.69)	(−0.12)
Log loans of household females (Tk.)	0.010	0.008	0.018	0.005
	(0.55)	(0.54)	(1.21)	(0.64)
R^2	0.242	0.141	0.089	0.086

Sources: World Bank/BIDS survey 1991/92 and 1998/99; World Bank/InM survey 2010/11.

Note: Outcomes are in log per capita Tk. per month. Figures in parentheses are *t*-statistics based on standard errors clustered at the village level. Regressions include more control variables at the household level (e.g., age, sex, and education of household head, and log of land assets) and village level (e.g., price of consumer goods; infrastructure, including schools and electricity availability; and proportion of irrigated land). FE = fixed effects; BRAC = Bangladesh Rural Advancement Committee.

Significance level: * = 10 percent, ** = 5 percent or less.

a. Other sources include BRDB, ASA, and other smaller MFIs.

While male borrowing from Grameen Bank reduces wage income, female borrowing from Grameen Bank increases crop, noncrop, and total farm income. Borrowing from other MFIs does not have a statistically significant effect on any type of farm income, with the exception of BRAC loans, especially for women borrowers, which increase crop income and reduce wage income. Thus, Grameen Bank appears to increase overall farm income significantly by raising both crop and noncrop income; however, BRAC loans help to increase crop income at a higher pace. For example, a 10 percent increase in female borrowing increases crop income by 9.4 percent for a BRAC loan, compared to 1.4 percent for a Grameen Bank loan. But 10 percent female borrowing from Grameen Bank increases noncrop income by 3.9 percent and total farm income by 1.6 percent. This means that Grameen Bank helps to increase noncrop income more than crop income, which is not surprising since the bulk of Grameen Bank lending supports rural income through diversification from nonfarm sources, as well as from noncrop activities (e.g., livestock and poultry raising and fisheries).

Who benefits the most from male and female microfinance borrowing for farming? Table 7.10 shows that male loans do not matter for any type of farming. But female borrowing increases crop and noncrop income for all three farm-size

Table 7.10 Impacts of Microfinance Borrowing on Household Farm Income by Farm Size: Propensity-Score Weighted Household FE Estimates

N = 1,509

Microfinance loan variables	Income from crop production	Income from livestock, poultry, and fishery	Wage income	Total farm income
Marginal (< 0.5 acres)				
Log loans of household males (Tk.)	−0.032	−0.011	−0.034	−0.004
	(−0.92)	(−0.44)	(−1.17)	(−0.13)
Log loans of household females (Tk.)	0.047**	0.031**	0.001	0.008**
	(2.61)	(2.07)	(0.04)	(2.02)
Small and medium (0.5–2.5 acres)				
Log loans of household males (Tk.)	−0.045	−0.013	−0.041	−0.011
	(−1.30)	(−0.61)	(−1.47)	(−0.61)
Log loans of household females (Tk.)	0.031*	0.025*	0.002	0.005
	(1.80)	(1.80)	(0.09)	(1.39)
Large (> 2.5 acres)				
Log loans of household males (Tk.)	−0.044	−0.002	−0.035	−0.004
	(−1.29)	(−0.06)	(−1.23)	(−0.20)
Log loans of household females (Tk.)	0.045**	0.033**	−0.001	0.010
	(2.43)	(2.19)	(−0.03)	(1.57)
R^2	0.242	0.141	0.087	0.087

Sources: World Bank/BIDS survey 1991/92 and 1998/99; World Bank/InM survey 2010/11.

Note: Outcomes are in log per capita Tk. per month. Figures in parentheses are *t*-statistics based on standard errors clustered at the village level. Regressions include more control variables at the household level (e.g., age, sex, and education of household head, and log of land assets) and village level (e.g., price of consumer goods; infrastructure, including schools and electricity availability; and proportion of irrigated land). FE = fixed effects.

Significance level: * = 10 percent, ** = 5 percent or less.

categories (marginal, small and medium, and large), as well as total farm income for marginal farms. Interestingly, the female credit effects on crop and noncrop income do not differ statistically by farm size. Thus, a 10 percent borrowing by a woman increases crop income by 4.7 percent for marginal farmers, 3.1 percent for small- and medium-scale farmers, and 4.5 percent for large landholding farmers. On the other hand, a 10 percent increase in female borrowing increases noncrop income by 3.1 percent for marginal farmers, 2.5 percent for small and medium farmers, and 3.3 percent for large farmers; it also increases total farm income by 0.08 percent for marginal farmers. These findings suggest that microfinance helps marginal farmers more than the other two farm-size groups.

Do Credit Constraints Affect Microfinance Borrowers' Income and Productivity?

The effects of household-level credit, estimated above, may be affected by the extent of supply-side constraints, determined primarily by the MFIs declining to provide the amount of credit that borrowers request. More specifically, following Boucher, Guirkinger, and Trivelli (2009), borrowers were considered supply-side constrained if they reported not being able to borrow as much as they would have wanted. The possible negative effect of borrowing constraints

Table 7.11 Share of Credit-Constrained Household Borrowers by Farm Size for Selected Finance Sources over Time

percent

Farm size	Microfinance	Formal finance	Both sources
1991/92 (N = 784)			
Marginal (< 0.5 acres)	79.8	71.8	78.4
Small and medium (0.5–2.5 acres)	82.4	64.2	75.3
Large (> 2.5 acres)	70.3	68.2	68.7
All holdings	80.0	68.0	76.5
1998/99 (N = 903)			
Marginal (< 0.5 acres)	48.1	53.7	48.4
Small and medium (0.5–2.5 acres)	57.8	74.9	59.2
Large (> 2.5 acres)	76.2	74.1	72.8
All holdings	51.8	69.7	53.6
2010/11 (N = 1,501)			
Marginal (< 0.5 acres)	7.0	13.8	7.1
Small and medium (0.5–2.5 acres)	10.6	14.9	11.3
Large (> 2.5 acres)	14.7	12.9	10.6
All holdings	8.0	14.2	8.2

Sources: World Bank/BIDS survey 1991/92 and 1998/99; World Bank/InM survey 2010/11.
Note: Households were considered credit constrained if they received less than what they requested.

may prevent farmers from allocating resources efficiently and thus cause them to suffer from efficiency losses. Therefore, it is worth considering how supply-side factors causing demand for microfinance may affect farm-household income and productivity.

Before turning to this issue, we would like to compare the pattern of such constraints among farmers who borrowed from various MFIs and formal finance sources. Table 7.11 shows that supply constraints from both types of finance declined substantially overall, from more than 76 percent in 1991/92 to only about 8 percent in 2010/11. However, microfinance borrowers saw a significantly larger percentage decline over the period. For example, in 1991/92, 80 percent of microfinance borrowers faced supply-side constraints, compared to only 8 percent by 2010/11. Among borrowers of formal finance sources, by contrast, 68 percent were supply constrained in 1991/92, and more than 14 percent remained so in 2010/11.

In examining the role of supply constraints on farm income and productivity among microfinance borrowers beyond the estimated effects of borrowing, we may postulate that the outcome equation (7.2) differs across constrained and nonconstrained households. We can use the reported status of microfinance borrowers in terms of whether they were credit constrained as an additional variable in equation (7.2). We can also interact this constraint status with the amount of borrowing households received from MFI sources to determine whether the borrowing effect varied by the extent of constraint status.

Thus, by interacting credit constraints with the amount of borrowing, the differential impacts of credit constraints have been addressed both directly and indirectly. Table 7.12 shows that the total effect of credit constraint has a particularly strong negative effect on total farm income, but a positive effect on livestock income; that is, microfinance borrowers constrained on the supply side will have a lower income from crop production, which will induce them to seek livestock and poultry activities.

However, by interacting the supply-constraint status with the amount of borrowing alone, the direction of change is unclear. Therefore, we calculate the marginal effect of borrowing on credit-constrained households as opposed to nonconstrained households. We estimate the outcome equation of (7.2) after suppressing gender-specific effects, as well as the effects of other variables, for both types of borrowers, expressed as follows:

$$\Delta Y_{it} = \beta \Delta B_{it} + \gamma \Delta C_{it} + \Delta \eta_{it} + \Delta \varepsilon_{it}, \qquad (7.3)$$

where C indicates the borrowing-constraint status. For those households that are not credit constrained (i.e., $C = 0$), we obtain the estimate of credit effect, β. For those that are constrained, we obtain the marginal credit effect, $(\beta + \gamma)$. Depending on the sign of both coefficients (β and γ), the effect of microfinance will be higher or lower for constrained borrowers.

Table 7.12 Impacts of Microfinance Borrowing and Credit Constraint on Household Farm Income: Propensity-Score Weighted Household FE Estimates

$N = 1,509$

Microfinance loan variable	Income from crop production	Income from livestock, poultry, and fishery	Wage income	Total farm income
Log loans of household males (Tk.)	−0.063	−0.004	−0.039	−0.012
	(−1.44)	(−0.18)	(−1.37)	(−0.67)
Log loans of household females (Tk.)	0.032*	0.033**	0.003	0.010*
	(1.77)	(2.37)	(0.16)	(1.83)
Household is credit constrained	−0.546	0.616**	−0.152	−0.354*
	(−1.59)	(2.03)	(−0.43)	(−1.90)
Log loans of household males x household is credit constrained	0.063*	−0.028	−0.004	0.024
	(1.96)	(−0.89)	(−0.13)	(1.50)
Log loans of household females x household is credit constrained	0.049	−0.063**	0.010	0.023
	(1.56)	(−2.00)	(0.31)	(1.39)
R^2	0.239	0.140	0.087	0.086
Calculated effects of borrowing on credit-constrained households				
Log loans of household males (Tk.)	−0.055	−0.008	−0.040	−0.009
	(−1.53)	(−0.34)	(−1.40)	(−0.50)
Log loans of household females (Tk.)	0.038**	0.025*	0.004	0.012*
	(2.20)	(1.79)	(0.24)	(1.70)

Sources: World Bank/BIDS survey 1991/92 and 1998/99; World Bank/InM survey 2010/11.

Note: Outcomes are in log per capita Tk. per month. Figures in parentheses are *t*-statistics based on standard errors clustered at the village level. Regressions include more control variables at the household level (e.g., age, sex, and education of household head, and log of land assets) and village level (e.g., price of consumer goods; infrastructure, including schools and electricity availability; and proportion of irrigated land). FE = fixed effects. *Significance level:* * = 10 percent, ** = 5 percent or less.

Table 7.12 also shows the calculated marginal credit effect for constrained households by gender of borrowers. Comparing these estimates (in elasticity form) for credit-constrained and nonconstrained households, we find that the marginal credit effect is positive for women only. For example, a 10 percent increase in women's borrowing increases total farm income by 0.10 percent for nonconstrained households, compared to 0.12 percent for those that are constrained. The effects of microfinance appear to matter by the extent of the credit constraint faced by the borrower.

However, being supply constrained may not be exogenous, as assumed in equation (7.3). Therefore, we estimate the outcome equation (7.3) using a switching regression (annex 7A). We allow an endogenous switching of who is likely to be credit constrained and how the effects of borrowing vary by whether a household is constrained. Here we implement the approach of Guirkinger and Boucher (2008), which estimates a dynamic switching model on a two-round panel by differencing the data to remove fixed unobserved heterogeneity and running a switching regression on the differenced model. More specifically, we estimate a switching regression model for equation (7.2) for credit-constrained and nonconstrained households separately with endogenous switching.

Table 7.13 presents the switching regression results of the effect of borrowing on income for credit-constrained and nonconstrained households. As expected, the selection equation reported shows that credit availability (represented by the number of MFIs in a village) lowers the extent of credit constraint for most outcomes (3 out of 4). For example, an additional MFI in a village lowers the credit constraint for microfinance household borrowing by 3.3 percentage points when the outcome is crop-production income. The effect of borrowing on farm income from all sources (except wage income in the case of male borrowing) is insignificant for credit-constrained households, regardless of the borrower's gender, while the credit effects for female borrowing in nonconstrained households are positive and statistically significant for most outcomes. That is, unlike the results reported in table 7.12, where we find positive credit effects for both constrained and nonconstrained borrowers, we find no significant effect of microfinance for credit constrained borrowers after correcting for the endogeneity of being credit constrained. These results suggest that credit constraint is a deterring factor for promoting income and productivity.

Table 7.13 also shows that the correlation coefficient ρ_2 is negative and statistically significant for the regressions for total farm income and wage income, indicating a negative correlation between the error terms of the selection equation and the outcome equations in the nonconstrained zone; that is, nonconstrained households have a higher total farm and wage income than a random household from the sample. But the correlation coefficient ρ_1 is positive and significant for all types of farm income except wage income, suggesting that credit-constrained households have higher crop, livestock, and total farm income, compared to a random household. The likelihood-ratio test for joint independence of the three equations, reported at the bottom of table 7.13, shows that

Table 7.13 Impacts of Microfinance Borrowing on Household Farm Income by Credit Constraint: Switching Regression
N = 1,509

Microfinance loan variable	Income from crop production	Income from livestock, poultry, and fishery	Wage income	Total farm income
Selection equation				
Household is credit constrained (excluded instrument is number of MFIs in the village)	−0.033** (−2.71)	−0.019* (−1.85)	−0.004 (−0.23)	−0.041** (−1.99)
Non-credit-constrained households				
Log loans of household males (Tk.)	−0.045 (−1.27)	0.006 (0.17)	−0.065 (−1.60)	−0.017 (−0.86)
Log loans of household females (Tk.)	0.036* (1.94)	0.040** (2.79)	0.002 (0.11)	0.013* (1.63)
Credit-constrained households				
Log loans of household males (Tk.)	−0.033 (−0.24)	−0.056 (−0.54)	0.118* (1.80)	0.021 (0.40)
Log loans of household females (Tk.)	−0.008 (−0.15)	−0.079 (−0.95)	0.079 (1.37)	0.017 (0.48)
Correlation coefficient between selection equation and nonconstrained regime equation (ρ_1)	0.678** (6.23)	0.719** (5.78)	−0.034 (−0.05)	0.635** (5.16)
Correlation coefficient between selection equation and constrained regime equation (ρ_2)	−0.193 (−0.25)	0.171 (0.29)	−0.862** (−3.11)	−0.685** (−5.14)
Wald test of independence equations	$\chi^2(2) = 3.17$, $p > \chi^2 = 0.205$	$\chi^2(2) = 1.65$, $p > \chi^2 = 0.438$	$\chi^2(2) = 19.15$, $p > \chi^2 = 0.000$	$\chi^2(2) = 4.60$, $p > \chi^2 = 0.1000$

Sources: World Bank/BIDS survey 1991/92 and 1998/99; World Bank/InM survey 2010/11.
Note: Outcomes are in log per capita Tk. per month. Figures in parentheses are *t*-statistics based on standard errors clustered at the village level. Regressions include more control variables at the household level (e.g., age, sex, and education of household head, and log of land assets) and village level (e.g., price of consumer goods; infrastructure, including schools and electricity availability; and proportion of irrigated land). MFI = microfinance institution.
Significance level: * = 10 percent, ** = 5 percent or less.

the equations are not typically independent of one another. Unobserved heterogeneity may still be an unresolved issue with these regressions; however, the results indicate that households with supply-side credit constraints are benefiting little from microfinance.

Effects of Microfinance on Borrowers' Farm Employment

Given that microfinance borrowing increases farm income and productivity, especially crop and noncrop income, the next question is whether it also increases farm employment. Growth in farm income and productivity may be accompanied by higher farm employment unless capital-intensive farm technology is in place that reduces demand for farm labor. However, as shown in chapter 4, microfinance increases nonfarm employment. Therefore, unless a major shift in labor from farm to nonfarm production occurs, it is possible that microfinance can also increase farm employment.

We consider an employment equation where days employed in farm activities by rural households is a function of the amount of borrowing by male and female borrowers, plus a host of household and community characteristics. Following the model specification in equation (7.2), we use the p-score weighted FE method to estimate the employment equation for the farm sector overall, as well as employment in crop activity, noncrop activity, and wage employment.

Table 7.14 reveals two major trends in farm-sector household employment for the three survey years. First, household employment hours declined consistently over time. While average monthly farm-sector employment was 163 hours in 1991/92, it dropped to 109 hours in 1998/99 and 74 hours by 2010/11. Second, it rose with increasing landholding size, and this trend was consistent for all three survey years. The findings also show that small-, medium- and large-scale farmers have devoted most of their labor to crop cultivation, except in 2010/11, when the largest share went to livestock and poultry raising. By contrast, marginal farmers have devoted most of their labor to wage employment, which is not unexpected. However, in 2010/11, like the other farm-size groups, marginal farmers devoted the largest share of their labor to livestock and poultry raising.

Although men's borrowing has no significant effect on any type of farm employment, women's borrowing increases employment for both crop and non-crop activities, as well as total farm employment. Table 7.15 shows that a 10 percent increase in female borrowing increases employment by 0.33 percent for crop production, 0.58 percent for noncrop production, and 0.46 percent for farming overall.

Table 7.14 Farm-Sector Household Employment by Landholding Size

Farm size	Crop production (hours/month)	Livestock, poultry, and fishery (hours/month)	Wage labor (hours/month)	Total farm-sector employment (hours/month)
1991/92 (N = 1,509)				
Marginal (< 0.5 acres)	25.2	24.5	78.4	128.2
Small and medium (0.5–2.5 acres)	112.2	48.7	43.9	204.7
Large (> 2.5 acres)	152.6	55.0	10.2	217.8
All households	68.3	35.9	58.9	163.1
1998/99 (N = 1,509)				
Marginal (< 0.5 acres)	24.3	10.9	65.5	100.7
Small and medium (0.5–2.5 acres)	70.1	10.0	28.9	109.0
Large (> 2.5 acres)	128.3	9.9	8.4	146.6
All households	50.0	10.5	48.0	108.5
2010/11 (N = 1,509)				
Marginal (< 0.5 acres)	7.7	37.3	23.0	68.0
Small and medium (0.5–2.5 acres)	21.9	58.0	7.5	87.5
Large (> 2.5 acres)	21.7	71.9	0.0	93.6
All households	12.0	44.4	14.9	74.3

Sources: World Bank/BIDS survey 1991/92 and 1998/99; World Bank/InM survey 2010/11.

Table 7.15 Impacts of Microfinance Borrowing on Household Farm Employment: Propensity-Score Weighted Household FE Estimates

N = 1,509

Microfinance loan variable	Employment in crop production	Employment in livestock, poultry, and fishery	Employment in wage labor	Total farm-sector employment
Log loans of household males (Tk.)	0.022	0.012	−0.021	0.026
	(1.51)	(0.78)	(−1.18)	(1.34)
Log loans of household females (Tk.)	0.033**	0.058**	0.0001	0.046**
	(3.30)	(5.82)	(0.01)	(4.13)
R^2	0.179	0.351	0.107	0.147

Sources: World Bank/BIDS survey 1991/92 and 1998/99; World Bank/InM survey 2010/11.
Note: Outcomes are in log hours per month. Figures in parentheses are *t*-statistics based on standard errors clustered at the village level. Regressions include more control variables at the household level (e.g., age, sex, and education of household head, and log of land assets) and village level (e.g., price of consumer goods; infrastructure, including schools and electricity availability; and proportion of irrigated land). FE = fixed effects.
Significance level: * = 10 percent, ** = 5 percent or less.

Village-Level Effect of Microfinance on Employment and Wage Rates

Thus far, we have only considered the credit effect on household borrowers' income, employment, and other welfare indicators. An even more important consideration is the aggregate effect of microfinance operations on the rural labor market in terms of farm and nonfarm employment and market wage rates since the spillover effect is likely to affect nonparticipants. For example, even if microfinance borrowers are withdrawing from the wage market, there may be a higher supply of labor from nonparticipating households, in which case, the wage rate determined by both demand and supply of labor may not increase as postulated under an increase in reservation price of own labor. The spillover effects of microfinance—especially when it has been in operation for a long time—can either benefit or harm a local economy. Over a 20-year period, nonparticipants will likely gain or lose from microfinance's induced effects, which means it is important to consider its aggregate effect, including the induced spillover effects.

What then is the expected effect of microfinance on agricultural wage and aggregate farm and nonfarm employment? To answer this question, we examine the aggregate effects of microfinance at the village level on various rural welfare outcomes, including farm and nonfarm employment and agricultural wage rates.

First, we consider the wage effect of microfinance intensity in a village. If there is no discernible microfinance-induced demand for wage labor, we can expect that agricultural wages will not be affected by microfinance interventions in a casual labor market (say, for example, E_0 and W_0 positions in figure 7.1). However, because of microfinance participation, it is possible that households that were previously wage employed may not prefer to demand wage work in an agricultural labor market. In figure 7.1, this shift in labor supply is represented

Figure 7.1 Wage Determination with Microfinance Participation

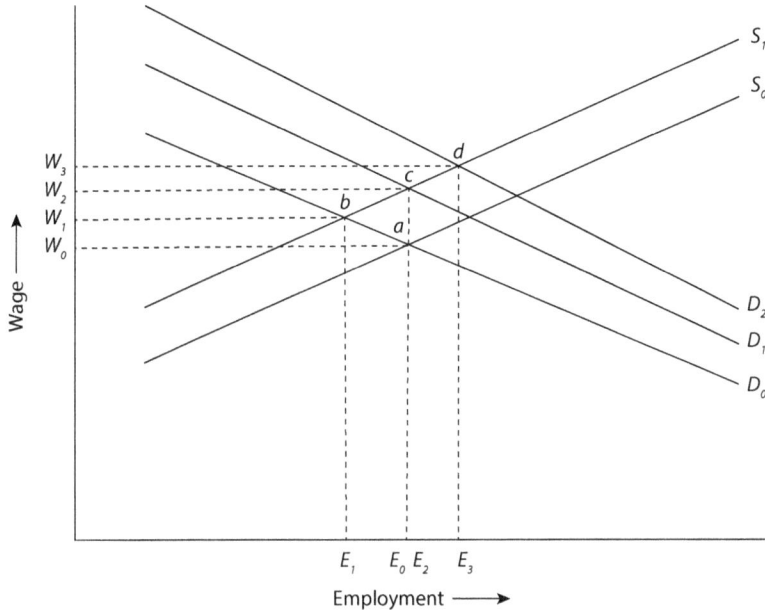

by the leftward shift from S_0 to S_1 (an indication of reservation wage), meaning a higher wage rate (from W_0 to W_1), given the aggregate demand for wage labor in agriculture (D_0). This also means an overall decline in wage employment in agriculture (from S_0 to S_1).

Since microfinance expansion results in higher self-employment in crop and noncrop activities (table 7.15), one can expect that the interactions between farm and nonfarm labor markets will increase agricultural wage rates. Despite the shift in both labor demand and supply curves for the agricultural wage market, an increase in wage rates is only possible if the demand for agricultural labor outweighs the reduction in labor supply. Alternatively, a reduction in labor supply for agricultural wage employment can outweigh the demand for wage employment, which, in turn, may push the wage rate up, given the unchanged demand for wage labor in agriculture. In figure 7.1, the position of c represents an unchanged employment despite a higher wage as a higher demand for wage labor compensates the reduced demand for wage labor by microcredit borrowers. The position of d is likely to occur when an induced demand for hired labor results due to an induced higher income level because of microfinance, characterized by higher levels of employment and wages.

We estimate a real wage function at the village level as a function of microfinance intensity in the village. For this purpose, microfinance intensity is measured in two ways: (a) by the number of MFIs operating in the village and (b) by MFI participation rates by men and women in the village. We thus have two specifications for which we also control for other exogenous factors observed at the village level (e.g., prices of consumer goods and available infrastructure).

Table 7.16 presents the net effect of microfinance intensity on real agricultural wages observed at the village level using the long-panel, village-level data spanning the 20-year period. No matter how the village intensity of microfinance is measured, the results show that microfinance helped to increase agricultural wages.

For example, one additional MFI in the village increased men's wages by 1.5 percent and women's wages by 4.9 percent. A 10 percentage increase in men's participation at the village level increased male wages by 2.0 percent and female wages by 3.1 percent. By contrast, a 10 percentage point increase in women's participation increased male wages by 1.4 percent and female wages by 5.0 percent (table 7.16). Thus, the effect of microfinance—which increases female labor supply more than male labor supply, as shown in chapter 4—is unambiguously a higher demand for female labor in the rural labor market; as a result, we observe a higher effect on women's wages.

Using the same models, we next consider the effects of village-level program intensity on village-level employment, calculated as the village-level average of household employment hours per month. As table 7.17 shows, the placement of MFIs in a village does not affect village-level employment in the farm sector; however, it increases nonfarm and overall employment.

For example, an additional MFI in the village increases village-level employment in the nonfarm sector by 6.3 percent and overall employment by 4.2 percent. Farm-sector employment, however, increases as a result of increased female participation in the village. A 10 percentage point increase in female participation in the village increased village-level employment in the farm sector by 2.4 percent. Both male and female participation in the

Table 7.16 Impacts of Microfinance Program Placement and Participation Intensity on Village-Level Wage: Upazila FE Estimates

N = 87

Microfinance program variable	Model 1		Model 2	
	Village male wage	Village female wage	Village male wage	Village female wage
Number of MFIs in village	0.015** (2.01)	0.049** (2.24)	n.a.	n.a.
Microfinance participation rate by males in village	n.a.	n.a.	0.202** (2.16)	0.312** (2.66)
Microfinance participation rate by females in village	n.a.	n.a.	0.141** (2.00)	0.501** (2.35)
R^2	0.248	0.428	0.155	0.443

Sources: World Bank/BIDS survey 1991/92 and 1998/99; World Bank/InM survey 2010/11.
Note: Outcomes are in log Tk. per day. Figures in parentheses are *t*-statistics based on standard errors clustered at the village level. Regressions include more control variables at the village level (e.g., price of consumer goods; infrastructure, including schools and electricity availability; and proportion of irrigated land). n.a. = not applicable; FE = fixed effects; MFI = microfinance institution.
Significance level: * = 10 percent, ** = 5 percent or less.

Table 7.17 Impacts of Microfinance Program Placement and Participation Intensity on Village-Level Employment: Upazila FE Estimates
$N = 87$

Microfinance program variable	Village household employment (average)		
	Farm	Nonfarm	Total
Model 1			
Number of MFIs in village	−0.002	0.063**	0.042**
	(−0.11)	(2.82)	(4.69)
R^2	0.464	0.210	0.444
Model 2			
Microfinance participation rate by males in village	0.249	0.541*	0.230**
	(0.89)	(1.95)	(1.99)
Microfinance participation rate by females in village	0.237**	0.967**	0.357**
	(2.13)	(4.63)	(4.10)
R^2	0.471	0.257	0.433

Sources: World Bank/BIDS survey 1991/92 and 1998/99; World Bank/InM survey 2010/11.
Note: Outcomes are in log hours per month. Figures in parentheses are *t*-statistics based on standard errors clustered at the village level. Regressions include more control variables at the village level (e.g., price of consumer goods; infrastructure, including schools and electricity availability; and proportion of irrigated land). FE = fixed effects; MFI = microfinance institution. *Significance level:* * = 10 percent, ** = 5 percent or less.

village boosted nonfarm-sector and overall employment, and the effects were higher for women. For example, a 10 percentage point increase in the rate of women's participation increased total village employment by 3.6, compared to 2.3 percent for men.

Summary

Raising agricultural productivity, especially food production, has received greater attention in recent years, particularly amid concerns about rising food insecurity, population pressure, and climate change. Many believe that better institutional access to credit and other financial services from both formal sources of finance (e.g., agricultural and commercial banks) and semiformal sources like microfinance can help rural households to smooth risks and access inputs and other technology to modernize agriculture and improve farm/nonfarm linkages.

Using household panel data from Bangladesh spanning the 1991–2011 period, we find that MFI participation has a significant positive effect for women borrowers in raising crop, noncrop (i.e., livestock/poultry raising and fisheries), and total household farm income. Although men's borrowing is found to reduce wage income in the short term, it has no lingering effect on wage income. Women's borrowing appears to have a long-term effect on both crop and total income. More interestingly, the effects of microfinance differ by program. For example, BRAC has a larger effect on increasing crop income for women borrowers than does Grameen Bank, while Grameen Bank has a larger effect on increasing men's wage income, compared to women's borrowing from BRAC.

That is, while microfinance increases nonfarm income and employment by reducing wage income, it also increases farm income, especially crop and livestock income. Overall, marginal farmers benefit more from microfinance borrowing than any other farm-size group.

The presence of credit constraints matters in raising crop and other sources of farm income. Borrowing from MFIs does not raise incomes if the borrowers are credit constrained, meaning that supply-side constraints act negatively for borrowers. Thus, the effect of borrowing on farm income is higher for credit-constrained, versus nonconstrained, households. Borrowing from agricultural or commercial banks has no significant effect on household outcomes from farm sources. By contrast, microfinance has benefited nonparticipants, as well as participants. Our findings show that microfinance increases aggregate (both farm and nonfarm) employment—nonfarm more than farm—as well as agricultural wages. The evidence confirms that agricultural households are benefiting from improved farm/nonfarm linkages resulting from better access to microfinance. Thus, microfinance programs have potentially direct and indirect effects on agricultural income and productivity as they continue to evolve and expand.

Annex 7A: Switching Regression Method

In the main chapter, we implemented endogenous switching regression to estimate the differential effects of microfinance by credit constraint. In this annex, we implemented the approach of Guirkinger and Boucher (2008), which estimates a dynamic switching model on a two-round panel by differencing the data to remove fixed unobserved heterogeneity and running a switching regression on the differenced model. More specifically, we estimated a switching regression model for equation (B.5a) for credit-constrained and nonconstrained households separately with endogenous switching (appendix B); thus, we could rewrite the outcome equation (B.5b) for credit-constrained and non-constrained households as follows:

$$\Delta Y_{it}^1 = \beta^1 \Delta X_{it} + \delta_{ift}^1 \Delta C_{ift} + \delta_{imt}^1 \Delta C_{imt} + \Delta \eta_{it}^1 + \Delta \varepsilon_t^1 \text{ if } \tilde{b}_{it} = 1 \text{ and} \qquad (7A.1)$$

$$\Delta Y_{it}^0 = \beta^0 \Delta X_{it} + \delta_{ift}^0 \Delta C_{ift} + \delta_{imt}^0 \Delta C_{imt} + \Delta \eta_{it}^0 + \Delta \varepsilon_t^0 \text{ if } \tilde{b}_{it} = 0, \qquad (7A.2)$$

where $\tilde{b}_{it} = 1$ when a household is credit constrained, and $\tilde{b}_{it} = 0$ when it is not; $\tilde{b}_{it}$ is determined by the critical value of a latent variable $\tilde{b}_{it}^*$, expressed as follows:

$$\tilde{b}_{it}^* = \alpha \Delta Z_{it} + \Delta \tilde{\varepsilon}_{it} \text{ and} \qquad (7A.3)$$

$$\tilde{b}_{it} = \begin{cases} 1 \text{ if } \tilde{b}_{it}^* > 0 \\ 0 \text{ if } \tilde{b}_{it}^* \le 0 \end{cases}. \qquad (7A.4)$$

In equation (7A.3), Z_{it} represents a vector of instruments for $\tilde{b}_{it}^*$.

Notes

1. Credit disbursement has been made primarily through formal lending institutions (i.e., state-owned commercial banks and specialized banks simultaneously with private and foreign commercial banks). A portion of targeted agricultural/rural credit disbursement of Bangladesh Krishi Bank (BKB) and Rajshahi Krishi Unnayan Bank (RAKUB), who receive refinancing from the Bangladesh Bank, has been brought under a nongovernmental organization (NGO) linkage program.

2. In Bangladesh, some MFIs have increasingly developed products that cater to the needs of marginal and small- and medium-scale farmers.

3. Because this chapter focuses primarily on the role of institutional finance, the effects resulting from informal borrowing (e.g., through personal contacts or local money-lenders) are not examined.

4. Credit access includes extending agricultural lines of credit directly to local banks, which then provide loans to farmers and rural entrepreneurs. Prior to the 1990s, the World Bank and other multilateral institutions managed the disbursement of agricultural finance directly through project implementation units (World Bank 2003). Examples of recent World Bank–supported credit access programs include the Rural Finance Project in Vietnam, the SAGARPA Program in Mexico, the Financial Services for the Poorest Project in Bangladesh, and programs to provide local financial institutions technology upgrades and training (e.g., Strengthening India's Rural Credit Cooperatives Project and Ghana Rural Financial Services Project).

5. An analysis for Africa is provided in van Empel (2010).

6. For expanding urban households' bank credit and microfinance access, a series of small-scale randomized interventions have been conducted; for example, Karlan and Zinman (2010a) provide an analysis for South Africa (Capetown, Port Elizabeth, and Durban), Karlan and Zinman (2010b) examine the Philippines (Manila), and Banerjee and others (2013) evaluate the slums of India (Hyderabad).

7. Bangladesh's banking sector is dominated by four state-owned NCBs, which control approximately one-half of assets in the banking system.

8. Under this program arrangement, BRAC borrows money at 5 percent interest from the Bangladesh Bank and disburses it at 10 percent interest to sharecropper groups across 150 upazilas in 35 districts throughout the country (Bangladesh Bank 2010).

9. The microfinance effect on farm employment and its various categories are considered later in this chapter. One should note that the authors attempted to estimate the effect of borrowing from commercial banks on farm income and productivity. Commercial finance constituted no more than 10 percent of total household borrowing in any given year, and its effect was not significant; thus, the results are not reported here.

Bibliography

Banerjee, Abhijit, Esther Duflo, Rachel Glennersgter, and Cynthia Kinnan. 2013. "The Miracle of Microfinance? Evidence from a Randomized Evaluation." MIT Department of Economics Working Paper 1309, Massachusetts Institute of Technology, Cambridge, MA.

Bangladesh Bank. 2010. *Annual Agricultural/Rural Credit Policy and Program for Fiscal Year (2009–2010)*. Dhaka: Bangladesh Bank.

Binswanger, Hans, and Shahidur R. Khandker. 1995. "The Impact of Formal Finance on the Rural Economy of India." *Journal of Development Studies* 32: 234–62.

Boucher, Stephen, Catherine Guirkinger, and Carolina Trivelli. 2009. "Direct Elicitation of Credit Constraints: Conceptual and Practical Issues with an Application to Peruvian Agriculture." *Economic Development and Cultural Change* 57 (4): 609–40.

Cai, Jing. 2012. "Social Networks and the Decision to Insure: Evidence from Randomized Experiments in China." Working Paper, University of California-Berkeley, Berkeley, CA.

Carter, M. R. 1989. "The Impact of Credit on Peasant Productivity and Differentiation in Nicaragua." *Journal of Development Economics* 103: 13–36.

Carter, M., and P. Olinto. 2003. "Getting Institutions Right for Whom? Credit Constraints and the Impact of Property Rights on the Quantity and Composition of Investment." *American Journal of Agricultural Economics* 85 (1): 173–86.

CDF (Credit and Development Forum). 2006. *Bangladesh Microfinance Country Profile*. Dhaka: CDF.

Crepón, Bruno, Florencia Devoto, Esther Duflo, and William Pariente. 2011. "Impact of Microfinance in Rural Areas of Morocco: Evidence from a Randomized Evaluation." MIT Working Paper, Massachusetts Institute of Technology, Cambridge, MA.

Faruqee, Rashid. 2010. "Microfinance for Agriculture in Bangladesh: Current Status and Future Potential." InM Working Paper 8, Institute of Microfinance, Dhaka.

Feder, G., L. J. Lau, J. Y. Lin, and X. Luo. 1990. "The Relation between Credit and Productivity in Chinese Agriculture: A Model of Disequilibrium." *American Journal of Agricultural Economics* 72 (5): 1151–57.

Foltz, J. 2004. "Credit Market Access and Profitability in Tunisian Agriculture." *Agricultural Economics* 30: 229–40.

Giné, Xavier, and Dean Yang. 2009. "Insurance, Credit, and Technology Adoption: Field Experimental Evidence from Malawi." *Journal of Development Economics* 89: 1–11.

Guirkinger, Catherine, and Stephen Boucher. 2008. "Credit Constraints and Productivity in Peruvian Agriculture." *Agricultural Economics* 39: 295–308.

Karlan, Dean, Robert Osei, Isaac Osei-Akoto, and Christopher Udry. 2013. "Agricultural Decisions after Relaxing Credit and Risk Constraints." Yale University Economic Growth Center Discussion Paper 1019; Yale Economics Department Working Paper 110, Yale University, New Haven, CT.

Karlan, Dean, and Jonathan Zinman. 2010a. "Expanding Credit Access: Using Randomized Supply Decisions to Estimate the Impacts." *Review of Financial Studies* 23 (1): 433–64.

———. 2010b. "Expanding Microenterprise Credit Access: Using Randomized Supply Decisions to Estimate the Impacts in Manila." Working Paper, Abdul Latif Jameel Poverty Action Lab, Massachusetts Institute of Technology (MIT), Cambridge, MA.

Khandker, Shahidur R. 1998. *Fighting Poverty with Microfinance: Experience in Bangladesh*. New York: Oxford University Press.

Kloeppinger-Todd, Renate, and Manohar Sharma. 2010. *Innovations in Rural and Agricultural Finance*. Washington, DC: International Food Policy Research Institute and World Bank.

Pitt, Mark M. 2000. "The Effect of Nonagricultural Self-Employment Credit on Contractual Relations and Employment in Agriculture: The Case of Microfinance Programs in Bangladesh." Bangladesh Development Studies, June–September, 15–48.

Pitt, M., and S. Khandker. 2002. "Credit Programs for the Poor and Seasonality in Rural Bangladesh." *Journal of Development Studies* 39 (2): 1–24.

Sial, M. H., and M. R. Carter. 1996. "Financial Market Efficiency in an Agrarian Economy: Microeconometric Analysis of the Pakistani Punjab." *Journal of Development Studies* 32 (5): 771–98.

van Empel, Gerard. 2010. "Rural Banking in Africa: The Rabobank Approach." In *Innovations in Rural and Agricultural Finance*, edited by Renate Kloeppinger-Todd and Manohar Sharma. Washington, DC: International Food Policy Research Institute and World Bank.

Wadud, Mohammed Abdul. 2013. "Impact of Microfinance on Agricultural Farm Performance and Food Security in Bangladesh." InM Working Paper 14, Institute of Microfinance, Dhaka.

World Bank. 2003. "Review of the Bank's Rural Finance Experience." Working Paper, Operations Evaluation Department World Bank, Washington, DC.

CHAPTER 8

Distributional Impacts

Introduction

Thus far, our analysis has been limited to the average or marginal effects of microfinance. One can justify a common program effect by assuming that its total induced effects increase a society's overall welfare and that its detrimental effects on certain population segments are minimal or offset by transfer through an overarching social welfare function or from family members or social networks. But assuming a common program effect for microfinance is not quite plausible since the productive use of capital depends on individual borrowers' entrepreneurial skills and abilities, which cannot be equal across all members to ensure equal benefit through borrowing and other program services.

Beyond estimating the average or marginal effect of microfinance programs and policies, researchers and policy makers also find it important to consider how the gains from microfinance programs may vary by individual ability, as well as individual, household, and community characteristics (e.g., age, education, and gender of household head; household income or expenditure; and whether a village is electrified or has access to paved roads). Such considerations are perhaps of paramount importance in considering distributional program gains. Even if the average or marginal program effect is not statistically significant (i.e., does not differ significantly from zero), this does not mean that none of the program participants benefit. Rather, the question is who benefits or loses when the program's average impact is not statistically significant. Indeed, in cases where the average participant does not benefit, the program may have significant beneficial or detrimental effects that are context specific and thus heterogeneous, conditioned by individual, household, and community characteristics. For such reasons, it is quite important to consider the distributional or heterogeneous effects of microfinance.

In recent years, certain critics have argued that microfinance does not reduce poverty, maintaining that poor participants in microfinance institution (MFI) programs are forced to remain members as there is no mechanism for them to repay their loans or leave the programs; they continue to borrow and thus become dependent on the MFIs. Does such an assertion mean that MFI programs benefit no groups and thus their existence cannot be well-justified or does it simply refer to an average of the situation (even if doubted by others)?

A study limited to examining only the average effect of microfinance that finds an average negative effect could well justify negating the role of microfinance in poverty reduction (Banerjee, Karlan, and Zinman 2015). But using such an approach can overlook participant groups that are benefiting if their percentage or combined positive effect cannot outweigh the negative effect of other participant groups. Examining the distributional or heterogeneous effects of microfinance can help to resolve this dilemma by showing who benefits or is harmed by a particular microfinance program and why. By the same token, studies that find microfinance program participants benefit at the margin or on average do not necessarily mean that everyone is gaining from microfinance, reinforcing the need to study microfinance's distributional effects.

One study that analyzed the average effect of microfinance programs found that, among poorer households, better-off ones are more likely to benefit. However, other studies have questioned the development performance of a targeted program that is captured by wealthier or well-educated households in a society (e.g., Araujo and others 2008; Gugerty and Kremer 2008; Mansuri and Rao 2004; Platteau 2004). Also, groups that benefit from a microfinance program in the short run may not benefit over time, and the converse is also true (King and Behrman 2009; van de Walle 2009). For all such compelling reasons, it is important to estimate the distributional gains or heterogeneous effects of microfinance to identify who benefits or loses and why. After all, microfinance is not a charity; the benefits accrued from microfinance depend critically on the productive use of borrowing, which, in turn, relies on the entrepreneurial ability of a borrower, as well as local market conditions or a combination of resource endowments. Therefore, when such skills and resource endowments are not uniformly distributed, the common effect model is not valid. Thus, it behooves policy makers to understand the distributional/heterogeneous effects of microfinance across households and areas over time. This chapter addresses this critical policy issue.

Estimating Benefits Distribution: Do Resource Endowments Matter?

Our analysis uses the long panel survey data spanning more than 20 years (1991/92–2010/11). The first survey round (1991/92) was based on questionnaires asking respondents about microfinance participation over the five years prior to the interview. A similar time frame was used for the second- and third-round surveys in 1998/99 and 2010/11, with the 1991/92 survey taken as the baseline.[1] To examine the role that resource endowments play in distribution of microfinance program benefits, this section presents descriptive statistics on household outcomes for individual, household, and village measures of endowments and then uses nonlinear and quantile regression techniques to estimate whether those households with better resource endowments fare better under microfinance programs.

Descriptive Analysis

Table 8.1 provides descriptive statistics on how the outcomes of interest—household income and expenditure, male and female labor supply, and household assets and net worth—vary by resource endowments observed at the individual level (education, math skills, and occupation) (table 8.1a–c); household level (landholding size) (table 8.1d); and community level (village electrification and accessibility) (table 8.1e and 8.1f).

The findings show that households that are least endowed in terms of years of education and math skills have the lowest values for all outcomes of interest except labor supply (table 8.1a and 8.1b).[2] For example, in 2010/11, households whose heads had completed only primary school had just over one-third the net worth of households whose heads had completed their secondary education. For the same year, households whose heads had not completed primary school had less than half the net worth of those who had (table 8.1a). Furthermore, the per capita total income of households with adult members competent in oral math was 43 percent higher than those without math-competent adult members in 1991/92 and 27 percent higher in 1998/99 (table 8.1b).

Unlike the observations based on household heads' education and oral math competency, we find no distinct patterns in household outcomes based on their main occupation (table 8.1c).[3] That said, households dependent on

Table 8.1 Summary Statistics of Household Outcomes

a. By household head's education (N = 1,509)

Head's education	Per capita total income (Tk./month)	Per capita total expenditure (Tk./month)	Male labor supply (hours/ month)	Female labor supply (hours/ month)	Nonland assets (Tk.)	Net worth (Tk.)
1991/92						
Did not complete primary level	451.7	328.5	184.0	34.3	17,998.7	84,225.7
Completed primary level	712.8	400.4	171.5	23.3	32,795.7	133,818.4
Completed secondary level or above	1,114.2	634.3	164.2	19.0	93,592.0	444,148.9
1998/99						
Did not complete primary level	499.3	418.3	221.2	24.9	21,495.2	149,610.1
Completed primary level	695.6	647.0	165.6	14.0	39,191.0	302,995.8
Completed secondary level or above	1,060.5	865.2	138.6	9.7	80,873.5	992,323.0
2010/11						
Did not complete primary level	1,132.1	581.8	168.9	53.7	46,824.8	269,650.9
Completed primary level	1,205.4	712.8	170.8	48.6	88,825.0	586,662.3
Completed secondary level or above	1,819.2	1,103.5	195.2	52.1	152,414.5	1,561,825.0

table continues next page

Table 8.1 Summary Statistics of Household Outcomes (continued)

b. By adults' oral math competency (N = 1,509)

Adults' oral math competency	Per capita total income (Tk./month)	Per capita total expenditure (Tk./month)	Male labor supply (hours/ month)	Female labor supply (hours/ month)	Nonland assets (Tk.)	Net worth (Tk.)
1991/92						
Household has adults with oral math competency	626.0	402.0	178.8	23.7	35,100.0	157,349.1
Household has no adults with oral math competency	439.2	305.9	181.9	44.4	13,038.9	59,151.9
1998/99						
Household has adults with oral math competency	615.3	522.0	214.1	17.6	32,603.0	292,563.2
Household has no adults with oral math competency	485.6	425.3	187.9	33.1	21,576.8	115,153.7

c. By household head's main occupation (N =1,509)

Household head's main occupation	Per capita total income (Tk./month)	Per capita total expenditure (Tk./month)	Male labor supply (hours/ month)	Female labor supply (hours/ month)	Nonland assets (Tk.)	Net worth (Tk.)
1991/92						
Wage employment	517.1	333.8	190.6	35.7	19,726.9	71,515.3
Self-employment in farm sector	405.9	425.0	143.9	16.8	39,851.5	251,070.5
Self-employment in nonfarm sector	792.4	585.4	195.6	35.8	24,516.1	91,503.6
Mostly from non-earned activities	310.4	368.1	152.9	28.3	127,015.7	250,869.8
1998/99						
Wage employment	398.4	390.4	218.0	26.9	20,904.9	114,675.8
Self-employment in farm sector	443.5	507.1	150.3	13.7	35,389.1	508,997.9
Self-employment in nonfarm sector	447.0	517.1	261.1	22.9	30,015.6	180,753.5
Mostly from non-earned activities	838.9	759.0	83.5	17.1	41,611.2	283,338.5
2010/11						
Wage employment	579.1	553.1	198.7	59.2	44,623.6	287,685.3
Self-employment in farm sector	573.4	647.7	79.3	39.8	97,769.8	1,001,881.0
Self-employment in nonfarm sector	2,204.0	834.1	242.6	53.2	72,751.4	370,296.9
Mostly from non-earned activities	1,073.3	796.8	55.0	42.5	85,425.8	476,672.4

table continues next page

Table 8.1 Summary Statistics of Household Outcomes *(continued)*
d. By land ownership (N = 1,509)

Household landholding size	Per capita total income (Tk./month)	Per capita total expenditure (Tk./month)	Male labor supply (hours/ month)	Female labor supply (hours/ month)	Nonland assets (Tk.)	Net worth (Tk.)
1991/92						
Marginal (<0.5 acres)	501.2	316.1	192.8	38.6	12,312.7	33,909.6
Small and medium (0.5–2.5 acres)	587.5	381.8	178.0	22.3	31,771.8	129,512.0
Large (>2.5 acres)	760.9	565.8	128.3	16.0	81,698.3	499,047.7
1998/99						
Marginal (<0.5 acres)	492.8	423.5	222.4	25.3	19,292.9	68,841.6
Small and medium (0.5–2.5 acres)	610.5	510.7	175.6	19.1	30,804.1	252,663.7
Large (>2.5 acres)	910.0	801.0	190.3	10.8	73,866.7	1,057,525.0
2010/11						
Marginal (<0.5 acres)	1,038.5	567.5	182.2	53.0	44,593.7	172,988.4
Small and medium (0.5–2.5 acres)	1,437.7	807.2	143.9	50.6	100,292.0	728,936.8
Large (>2.5 acres)	2,362.0	1,193.0	162.7	51.2	197,426.5	2,891,637.0

e. By village electrification status (N =1,509)

Village electrification status	Per capita total income (Tk./month)	Per capita total expenditure (Tk./month)	Male labor supply (hours/ month)	Female labor supply (hours/ month)	Nonland assets (Tk.)	Net worth (Tk.)
1991/92						
Village has electricity	644.4	393.4	180.9	28.9	32,444.4	135,168.4
Village does not have electricity	477.1	344.3	178.5	32.6	22,252.7	113,898.3
1998/99						
Village has electricity	607.0	512.8	202.9	20.3	30,207.0	216,180.0
Village does not have electricity	532.2	465.4	207.5	24.0	27,439.3	271,137.4
2010/11						
Village has electricity	1,274.1	667.0	173.7	51.7	69,135.2	490,778.1
Village does not have electricity	433.3	502.4	146.6	60.0	40,501.0	164,558.2

table continues next page

Table 8.1 Summary Statistics of Household Outcomes *(continued)*

f. By village accessibility (N = 1,509)

Village accessibility	Per capita total income (Tk./month)	Per capita total expenditure (Tk./month)	Male labor supply (hours/month)	Female labor supply (hours/month)	Nonland assets (Tk.)	Net worth (Tk.)
1991/92						
Village is accessible year-round	552.7	370.3	179.7	31.7	26,535.4	117,045.6
Village is not accessible year-round	721.2	348.8	181.1	13.9	42,847.8	58,937.2
1998/99						
Village is accessible year-round	579.1	492.3	208.1	22.3	28,688.0	191,007.4
Village is not accessible year-round	559.3	499.7	184.8	18.5	31,418.5	529,693.3
2010/11						
Village is accessible year-round	1,106.7	659.8	171.7	51.1	70,525.1	525,517.3
Village is not accessible year-round	1,612.9	671.5	171.9	56.8	53,948.3	246,493.0

Sources: World Bank/BIDS survey 1991/92 and 1998/99; World Bank/InM survey 2010/11.

self-employed nonfarm activities had the highest income and expenditure, except for 1998/99. For all three survey years, the highest net worth was found among households whose heads were mainly self-employed farmers.

The outcome pattern observed for household landholdings is somewhat similar to those observed for household heads' educational attainment and oral math competency. Table 8.1d shows that, except for employment, outcome variables increase monotonically as household landholdings increase for all survey years. For example, in 2010/11, the household per capita expenditure for small- and medium-sized landholders was 42 percent higher than that of marginal landholders; similarly, large landholders had 47 percent higher per capita expenditure than medium-sized landholders. Marginal landholders accounted for the largest supply of male and female labor supply for all three survey years, which is not surprising, given that they are mostly wage employed.

To investigate how household outcomes varied by community-level endowments, villages were grouped based on whether they (a) had electricity access and (b) were accessible by road year-round. Table 8.1e shows that, barring few exceptions, households in villages with electricity were better off than those in villages without electricity. For village accessibility, however, patterns in outcomes were not uniform (table 8.1f).

Whatever the trends in outcomes, these descriptive analyses clearly show that the outcomes vary by individual-, household-, and village-level endowments.

The key issue is the extent to which such variation can be attributed to microfinance borrowing.

Nonlinear Regression Technique

To test the underlying assumption that the source of heterogeneity in the impact of microfinance borrowing is the differential effect due to the better resource endowments, we estimate the outcome equation with program participation interacted with resource endowments of households and communities. The estimating equation can help us to better understand whether household and community endowments constrain benefits accrued to households. In this way, we can then formally test whether the variation in treatment effects is systematic across households.

Pitt and Khandker (1998), for example, found that land ownership and schooling were important determinants of a household's decision to participate in group-based credit programs and the outcomes they affect (e.g., consumption, nonland assets, and labor supply). It may well be that assets, schooling, and other observed and unobserved individual and household attributes signal the severity of the constraints felt by households in other credit markets, and consequently are associated with less optimal resource allocation. Relaxing these constraints through participation in group-based credit schemes may thus have large impacts for such households. This goes to the heart of the targeting question: Are the least well-off households getting the greatest benefit from microfinance programs?

We can study this issue by allowing for nonlinearities in the credit effect of such behaviors as household consumption, female and male labor supply, and asset holdings. The basic model discussed in appendix B is estimated with interactions of some key policy variables, including household heads' educational attainment, household landholdings, and village access to roads and electricity. That is, credit variables are interacted with household and community endowments (expressed as binary variables) to see whether microfinance effects vary with changes in resource endowments either at the household or village level. With such interactions, the differenced outcome equation can be expressed as follows:

$$Y_{it} = \beta \Delta X_{it} + \gamma_f \Delta P_{ift} + \gamma_m \Delta P_{imt} + \lambda_f \Delta (P_{ift} * R_{it}) + \lambda_m \Delta (P_{imt} * R_{it}) + \Delta \eta_{it} + \Delta \varepsilon_{it}, \tag{8.1}$$

where λ_m and λ_f are parameters for the interaction terms of resource endowments with male and female credit, respectively. Resource endowments (R), such as household head's education, are expressed as dummy variables so that, for example, $R_{it} = 1$ when the head has completed primary education and $R_{it} = 0$ otherwise. When households lack the endowment (e.g., the household head has no primary education and $R_{it} = 0$, equation (8.1)) is reduced to the basic differenced equation:

$$Y_{it} = \beta \Delta X_{it} + \gamma_f \Delta P_{ift} + \gamma_m \Delta P_{imt} + \Delta \eta_{it} + \Delta \varepsilon_{it}, \tag{8.2}$$

and γ_m and γ_f give the estimates of credit effects for households without the resource endowments (those with heads that have no primary education). For households that have the endowment (e.g., the household head has completed primary education and $R_{it} = 1$, equation (8.1)) becomes

$$Y_{it} = \beta\Delta X_{it} + (\gamma_f + \lambda_f)\, \Delta P_{ift} + (\gamma_m + \lambda_m)\, \Delta P_{imt} + \Delta\eta_{it} + \Delta\varepsilon_{it}, \qquad (8.3)$$

and $(\gamma_m + \lambda_m)$ and $(\gamma_f + \lambda_f)$ give the estimates of credit effects for households with resource endowments (those with household heads who have completed primary education).[4]

Table 8.2 presents the distributional impacts of microfinance by landholdings for marginal, small- and medium-scale, and large-scale farmers. As shown, men's credit increases per capita expenditure for marginal farmers, while women's credit increases it for small- and medium-scale farmers. Men's credit increases male labor supply, nonland assets, and net worth for all three categories of farmers. It also increases female labor supply for small- and medium-scale farmers. Women's credit also increases labor supply of male and female family workers,

Table 8.2 Impacts of Microfinance Loans on Household Outcomes by Land Ownership: Propensity-Score Weighted Household FE Estimates

N = 1,509

Microfinance loan variable	Log per capita total income (Tk./month)	Log per capita total expenditure (Tk./month)	Log male labor supply (hours/ month)	Log female labor supply (hours/ month)	Log household nonland assets (Tk.)	Log household net worth (Tk.)
Marginal landholders (< 0.5 acres)						
Log loans of household males (Tk.)	−0.006	0.007*	0.047**	0.031	0.036**	0.024*
	(−0.41)	(1.73)	(2.97)	(1.40)	(2.88)	(1.71)
Log loans of household females (Tk.)	0.013*	0.001	0.045**	0.052**	0.032**	−0.002
	(1.70)	(0.43)	(4.85)	(4.62)	(4.71)	(−0.21)
Small and medium landholders (0.5–2.5 acres)						
Log loans of household males (Tk.)	0.008	0.007	0.052**	0.068**	0.065**	0.072**
	(0.59)	(0.99)	(3.13)	(3.07)	(5.32)	(5.87)
Log loans of household females (Tk.)	0.002	0.003*	0.027**	0.068**	0.063**	0.095**
	(0.38)	(1.80)	(2.18)	(4.29)	(7.22)	(9.34)
Large landholders (> 2.5 acres)						
Log loans of household males (Tk.)	0.015	0.007	0.100**	0.004	0.054**	0.077**
	(0.53)	(1.31)	(3.30)	(0.11)	(2.06)	(2.98)
Log loans of household females (Tk.)	0.042**	0.003	−0.009	0.112**	0.099**	0.151**
	(2.34)	(1.06)	(−0.24)	(4.01)	(5.41)	(6.29)
R^2	0.135	0.372	0.210	0.237	0.376	0.377

Sources: World Bank/BIDS survey 1991/92 and 1998/99; World Bank/InM survey 2010/11.

Note: Figures in parentheses are *t*-statistics based on standard errors clustered at the village level. Regressions include more control variables at the household level (e.g., age, sex, and education of household head) and village level (e.g., price of consumer goods; infrastructure, including schools and electricity availability; and proportion of irrigated land). FE = fixed effects.

Significance level: * = 10 percent, ** = 5 percent or less.

nonland assets, and net worth for marginal and small- and medium-scale farmers. For example, a 10 percent increase in women's borrowing does not increase the net worth of marginal farmers; however, it increases the net worth of small- and medium-scale farmers by 1.0 percent and by 1.5 percent for large farmers.

Table 8.3 presents the heterogeneous impacts of microfinance by the household head's level of education. Among both male and female heads who had completed primary school, credit increased nonland assets and net worth; to a lesser extent, this was also true for household heads who had not completed primary education. However, there was no credit effect among household heads who had completed secondary school. For example, a 10 percent increase in men's credit increased household net worth by 0.17 percent for households headed by individuals with no primary schooling, compared to increases of 0.37 percent and 0.27 for households headed by individuals who had completed primary and secondary school, respectively.

Table 8.4 presents the estimated credit impacts by adult household members' competency in oral math. As shown, competency in oral math increases the

Table 8.3 Impacts of Microfinance Loans on Household Outcomes by Head's Education: Propensity-Score Weighted Household FE Estimates

N = 1,509

Microfinance loan variable	Log per capita total income (Tk./month)	Log per capita total expenditure (Tk./month)	Log male labor supply (hours/ month)	Log female labor supply (hours/ month)	Log household nonland assets (Tk.)	Log household net worth (Tk.)
Did not complete primary level						
Log loans of household males (Tk.)	−0.001	0.002	0.054**	0.014	0.033**	0.017*
	(−0.08)	(0.42)	(3.79)	(0.63)	(3.27)	(1.79)
Log loans of household females (Tk.)	−0.0004	−0.0001	0.041**	0.059**	0.034**	0.009*
	(−0.08)	(-0.04)	(4.63)	(5.40)	(5.18)	(1.63)
Completed primary level						
Log loans of household males (Tk.)	0.002	0.014**	0.052**	0.046**	0.057**	0.037**
	(0.15)	(2.23)	(3.83)	(2.80)	(4.46)	(4.44)
Log loans of household females (Tk.)	0.001	0.005*	0.040**	0.037**	0.036**	0.016*
	(0.19)	(1.68)	(4.70)	(3.35)	(4.23)	(1.98)
Completed secondary level or above						
Log loans of household males (Tk.)	−0.007	0.012	0.052**	0.039	0.010	0.027**
	(−0.38)	(1.22)	(3.69)	(0.80)	(0.68)	(2.10)
Log loans of household females (Tk.)	−0.016	0.017**	0.040**	0.031	0.061**	0.016
	(−1.35)	(3.07)	(4.87)	(0.98)	(3.75)	(1.10)
R^2	0.136	0.375	0.209	0.240	0.454	0.652

Sources: World Bank/BIDS survey 1991/92 and 1998/99; World Bank/InM survey 2010/11.

Note: Figures in parentheses are *t*-statistics based on standard errors clustered at the village level. Regressions include more control variables at the household level (e.g., age and sex of household head; landholdings) and village level (e.g., price of consumer goods; infrastructure, including schools and electricity availability; and proportion of irrigated land). FE = fixed effects.

Significance level: * = 10 percent, ** = 5 percent or less.

Table 8.4 Impacts of Microfinance Loans on Household Outcomes by Adults' Oral Math Competency: Propensity-Score Weighted Household FE Estimates

N = 1,509

Microfinance loan variable	Log per capita total income (Tk./month)	Log per capita total expenditure (Tk./month)	Log male labor supply (hours/month)	Log female labor supply (hours/month)	Log household nonland assets (Tk.)	Log household net worth (Tk.)
Household has adults with oral math competency						
Log loans of household males (Tk.)	0.029 (1.55)	0.003 (0.36)	0.034 (1.16)	0.044 (0.91)	0.008 (0.46)	0.038** (2.15)
Log loans of household females (Tk.)	−0.001 (−0.16)	−0.001 (−0.32)	0.012* (1.83)	0.036* (1.95)	0.041** (4.10)	−0.012 (−1.05)
Household has no adults with oral math competency						
Log loans of household males (Tk.)	0.035 (1.50)	−0.004 (−0.36)	0.019 (0.50)	0.043 (0.75)	−0.014 (−0.65)	0.025* (1.79)
Log loans of household females (Tk.)	−0.006 (−0.81)	−0.002 (−0.36)	−0.005 (−0.27)	0.015** (3.51)	0.039** (5.86)	−0.004 (−0.36)
R^2	0.103	0.196	0.170	0.215	0.239	0.518

Sources: World Bank/BIDS survey 1991/92 and 1998/99; World Bank/InM survey 2010/11.
Note: Figures in parentheses are *t*-statistics based on standard errors clustered at the village level. Regressions include more control variables at the household level (e.g., age and sex of household head; landholdings) and village level (e.g., price of consumer goods; infrastructure, including schools and electricity availability; and proportion of irrigated land). FE = fixed effects.
Significance level: * = 10 percent, ** = 5 percent or less.

impact of women's credit on both male and female labor supply. Also, the effects of credit on nonland assets and net worth are higher for those households whose adult members have competency in oral math.

Table 8.5 shows how the benefits accrued to households from microfinance borrowing vary by occupation. Among employed households, only self-employed ones were able to gain in income and expenditure. Wage-employed households saw gains in employment hours, nonland assets, and net worth. Among households in this category, a 10 percent gain in women's credit increased the labor supply of both males and females by 0.6 percent; however, men's borrowing only increased male labor supply. Self-employed households (both women and men) benefited from microfinance borrowing for most outcomes. Among self-employed farmers, a 10 percent increase in men's credit increased nonland assets and net worth by 0.4 percent and 0.2 percent, respectively. The corresponding figures for women's credit were 0.5 percent and 0.3 percent, respectively. Also, female credit decreased male labor supply.

The benefits of microfinance also vary by village attributes. Table 8.6 shows the heterogeneous effects of credit by whether a village has electricity. Compared to borrowers living in villages without access, the credit effects for men and women in villages with electricity are at least equal to or higher in terms of labor

Table 8.5 Impacts of Microfinance Loans on Household Outcomes by Household's Main Occupation: Propensity-Score Weighted Household FE Estimates

N = 1,509

Microfinance loan variable	Log per capita total income (Tk./month)	Log per capita total expenditure (Tk./month)	Log male labor supply (hours/ month)	Log female labor supply (hours/month)	Log household nonland assets (Tk.)	Log household net worth (Tk.)
Wage employment						
Log loans of household males (Tk.)	−0.015 (−1.35)	0.002 (0.52)	0.062** (3.08)	0.038 (1.41)	0.021* (1.75)	0.018** (1.99)
Log loans of household females (Tk.)	−0.008 (−1.30)	−0.002 (−0.68)	0.055** (5.40)	0.055** (4.32)	0.025** (3.61)	0.007 (1.12)
Self-employment in farm sector						
Log loans of household males (Tk.)	0.044** (2.26)	0.011* (1.68)	0.044** (2.06)	0.052** (2.35)	0.043** (3.97)	0.023** (2.36)
Log loans of household females (Tk.)	0.061** (6.06)	0.003 (0.75)	−0.031** (−2.11)	0.052** (2.85)	0.050** (5.09)	0.029** (3.61)
Self-employment in nonfarm sector						
Log loans of household males (Tk.)	0.031** (3.34)	0.008 (1.44)	0.050** (3.12)	0.029 (1.35)	0.041** (4.03)	0.026** (2.57)
Log loans of household females (Tk.)	0.029** (4.80)	0.004 (1.49)	0.067** (7.13)	0.058** (5.41)	0.042** (5.59)	0.008 (1.31)
Mostly from nonearned activities						
Log loans of household males (Tk.)	0.032 (1.59)	0.003 (0.30)	0.058** (2.34)	0.039 (1.39)	0.030** (2.01)	0.019 (1.46)
Log loans of household females (Tk.)	0.007 (0.77)	0.013** (2.53)	−0.120 (−1.16)	0.046** (2.34)	0.057** (5.50)	0.018** (2.15)
R^2	0.240	0.376	0.269	0.238	0.459	0.652

Sources: World Bank/BIDS survey 1991/92 and 1998/99; World Bank/InM survey 2010/11.

Note: Occupation type is determined by the sector generating highest income when household gets income from multiple sectors. Figures in parentheses are *t*-statistics based on standard errors clustered at the village level. Regressions include more control variables at the household level (e.g., age, education, and sex of household head; landholdings) and village level (e.g., price of consumer goods; infrastructure, including schools and electricity availability; and proportion of irrigated land). FE = fixed effects.

Significance level: * = 10 percent, ** = 5 percent or less.

supply, nonland assets, and net worth. Similarly, returns to household borrowing are higher in villages with year-round access to roads (table 8.7).

The above analysis clearly demonstrates that the impacts of microfinance are not uniform across all types of borrowers; they appear to vary by households' landholdings, education, and occupation, as well as by the status of village electrification and access to all-weather roads.

Table 8.6 Impacts of Microfinance Loans on Household Outcomes by Village Electrification Status: Propensity-Score Weighted Household FE Estimates
N = 1,509

Microfinance loan variable	Log per capita total income (Tk./month)	Log per capita total expenditure (Tk./month)	Log male labor supply (hours/ month)	Log female labor supply (hours/month)	Log household nonland assets (Tk.)	Log household net worth (Tk.)
Village has electricity						
Log loans of household males (Tk.)	−0.002 (−0.13)	0.007* (1.96)	0.050** (3.59)	0.054** (2.24)	0.041** (4.00)	0.026** (3.05)
Log loans of household females (Tk.)	0.004 (0.70)	0.002 (0.56)	0.047** (4.40)	0.056** (5.47)	0.033** (5.42)	0.012** (2.89)
Village does not have electricity						
Log loans of household males (Tk.)	−0.0001 (−0.01)	0.004 (0.63)	0.047** (2.37)	0.035* (1.80)	0.014 (0.85)	0.016 (1.56)
Log loans of household females (Tk.)	−0.012 (−1.47)	0.002 (0.51)	0.027** (3.45)	0.049** (4.32)	0.034** (4.66)	0.006 (1.00)
R^2	0.137	0. 375	0.208	0.238	0.455	0.651

Sources: World Bank/BIDS survey 1991/92 and 1998/99; World Bank/InM survey 2010/11.

Note: Figures in parentheses are *t*-statistics based on standard errors clustered at the village level. Regressions include more control variables at the household level (e.g., age, sex, and household landholdings) and village level (e.g., price of consumer goods; infrastructure, including schools and electricity availability; and proportion of irrigated land). FE = fixed effects.

Significance level: * = 10 percent, ** = 5 percent or less.

Quantile Regression Technique

To determine whether borrowing from a microfinance program works better for households with better existing resource endowments, we reestimate the outcome equation with credit interacted with resource-endowment variables of households and communities. The estimating equation can help us to understand whether household and community endowments constrain benefits accrued to households. Also, we can formally test whether the credit effect of program participation differs at various points in the conditional distribution of the dependent variables, such as per capita consumption, a measure of household welfare. If the findings suggest that returns to borrowing depend on the distribution of income or consumption, this would reflect the view that treatment effects may not be identical for all of those treated; that is, the variation in treatment effects may vary systematically across households.

We apply the quantile regression model introduced by Koenker and Bassett (1978), generalized to the censored quantile regression model by Powell (1984, 1986). For example, we can test whether there are differential returns to credit in terms of household consumption and income per capita at distinct points in the household consumption or income distribution (annex 8A).

Table 8.7 Impacts of Microfinance Loans on Household Outcomes by Village Accessibility: Propensity-Score Weighted Household FE Estimates
N = 1,509

Microfinance loan variable	Log per capita total income (Tk./month)	Log per capita total expenditure (Tk./month)	Log male labor supply (hours/ month)	Log female labor supply (hours/month)	Log household nonland assets (Tk.)	Log household net worth (Tk.)
Village is accessible year-round						
Log loans of household males (Tk.)	0.003	0.007	0.053**	0.040*	0.040**	0.027**
	(0.19)	(1.51)	(3.59)	(1.91)	(4.11)	(3.28)
Log loans of household females (Tk.)	−0.004	0.001	0.040**	0.056**	0.036**	0.011*
	(−0.77)	(0.23)	(4.90)	(5.41)	(5.63)	(1.96)
Village is not accessible year-round						
Log loans of household males (Tk.)	−0.015	0.004	0.041*	0.031	0.030*	0.015
	(−0.99)	(0.44)	(1.63)	(1.32)	(1.80)	(1.18)
Log loans of household females (Tk.)	0.022**	0.002	0.038**	0.051**	0.038**	0.013
	(2.70)	(0.84)	(2.37)	(3.05)	(4.30)	(1.54)
R^2	0.139	0.376	0.209	0.237	0.453	0.651

Sources: World Bank/BIDS survey 1991/92 and 1998/99; World Bank/InM survey 2010/11.
Note: Figures in parentheses are *t*-statistics based on standard errors clustered at the village level. Regressions include more control variables at the household level (e.g., age, sex, and household landholdings) and village level (e.g., price of consumer goods; infrastructure, including schools and electricity availability; and proportion of irrigated land). FE = fixed effects.
Significance level: * = 10 percent, ** = 5 percent or less.

Results of the quantile regression, reported in table 8.8, show that household borrowers (both men and women) in the lower expenditure brackets benefit more from microfinance than those in the higher brackets. For example, in the lower quantiles, a 10 percent increase in men's participation increases per capita expenditure by 0.03 percent but has no effect on expenditure in the higher quantiles. Similarly, women's participation increases per capita income more for the lower income groups than the higher ones. For example, a 10 percent increase in women's participation in microfinance programs increases per capita income by 0.11 percent for both the 15th and 25th quantiles, 0.07 percent for the 50th quantile, and nothing for the 75th and 85th quantiles. Conversely, for men's participation, the higher income groups benefit more from microfinance than the lower ones. For example, a 10 percent increase in men's participation increases per capita income by 0.18 percent for the 85th quantile, 0.14 percent for the 75th quantile, 0.11 percent for the 50th quantile, 0.09 percent for the 25th quantile, and only 0.07 percent for the 15th quantile.

These results demonstrate that the benefits of microfinance borrowing are not equally distributed. They also show that women's borrowing is more pro-poor than men's borrowing in terms of raising household income and expenditure.

Table 8.8 Impacts of Microfinance Loans on Household Income and Expenditure: Quantile Regression Results

N = 1,509

Microfinance loan variable (log loans, Tk.)	Log per capita total income (Tk./month)	Log per capita total expenditure (Tk./month)
15th quantile		
Household males	0.007*	0.003**
	(1.64)	(2.25)
Household females	0.011**	0.004**
	(2.62)	(2.44)
25th quantile		
Household males	0.009**	0.003**
	(3.65)	(3.42)
Household females	0.011**	0.004*
	(3.99)	(1.89)
50th quantile		
Household males	0.011**	0.003**
	(3.18)	(2.20)
Household females	0.007**	0.002*
	(2.34)	(1.64)
75th quantile		
Household males	0.014**	0.0002
	(3.38)	(0.10)
Household females	0.003	0.0002
	(1.04)	(0.10)
85th quantile		
Household males	0.018**	0.002
	(3.13)	(0.83)
Household females	−0.0002	−0.005*
	(−0.04)	(−1.70)
Pseudo R^2	0.057 at 15th,	0.220 at 15th,
	0.070 at 25th,	0.226 at 25th,
	0.089 at 50th,	0.227 at 50th,
	0.109 at 75th,	0.215 at 75th,
	0.120 at 85th	0.213 at 85th

Sources: World Bank/BIDS survey 1991/92 and 1998/99; World Bank/InM survey 2010/11.

Note: Figures in parentheses are *t*-statistics based on standard errors clustered at the village level. Regressions include more control variables at the household level (e.g., age, sex, and education of household head) and village level (e.g., price of consumer goods; infrastructure, including schools and electricity availability; and proportion of irrigated land). Significance level: * = 10 percent, ** = 5 percent or less.

Who Are the Losers?

To reiterate, microfinance does not benefit all participants equally, and some MFI members will inevitably lose out. One way to assess the extent of microfinance losses is to examine the degree of indebtedness among borrowers (chapter 5). Another way is to discover which participants dropped out and why. For example, some MFI members may have left the program as they graduated, while others may have decided to drop out because they were not benefiting. It is an empirical issue to determine which is the case. In this section, we use our long panel survey data of 1,530 households to identify the characteristics of those who dropped out over the 20-year period to better understand why they left.

Indebtedness Features of MFI Member Households

Using our long panel survey data, we find that the annual dropout rate was 13.8 percent on average, with 11.8 percent in 1998/99 and 13.8 percent in 2010/11. Table 8.9 reports the statistical significance of the differences in characteristics between the two groups of MFI participant households.

As shown, one key difference between dropout and continuing participant households is the higher average loans observed for dropout members for both men and women borrowers. For example, the average loan amount for women members who dropped out was Tk. 6,130, compared to Tk. 3,645 for those women who continued. One also observes that dropout members were older, less well-educated, and less wealthy in terms of landholdings, compared to those members who continued. More importantly, households who dropped out had lower-level reading and oral math skills, compared to those who continued with microfinance programs.[5]

What Factors Explain the Dropout Rate?

Table 8.10 presents the factors determining who dropped out. Characteristics of the first survey round in 1991/92 were used to explain who dropped out in 1998/99 and 2010/11. Two models were used: one without the loan amount and the other with it. The model including the loan amount is considered an additional explanatory variable. The findings show that the higher the loan amount borrowed from a microfinance program, regardless of a borrower's gender, the higher the probability of a member dropping out from the program; that is, the higher the amount of borrowing, the higher the risk of loan default and thus the greater probability of dropout. By contrast, those members with higher competency in either reading or oral math skills were less likely to drop out from a microfinance program. Thus, program dropout is not random, and both individual and household characteristics matter.

The next question is whether members dropped out because they were net losers of microfinance. To examine this question, we look at the welfare outcomes of those who dropped out and those who continued during the initial year (when the dropouts were participants) and the dropout year (when the dropouts ceased to participate). Table 8.11 shows that, in the initial year, those who later dropped out were better off than non-dropouts in terms of most outcomes (i.e., the t-statistics of the difference in outcomes between the two groups is statistically significant). But over time, the situation was reversed (i.e., the t-statistics of the difference in outcomes either lost its statistical significance or changed sign). For example, by the time they dropped out, the

---

Table 8.9 Salient Features of Households by Dropout Status

Characteristic	Households that dropped out (N = 292)	Households that did not drop out (N = 2,022)	t-statistics of the difference
Sex of head (1 = male, 0 = female)	0.90	0.916	−0.92
Age of head (years)	48.0	44.97	3.18**
Education of head (years)	1.99	2.56	−2.27**
Number of adult males in household	1.97	1.70	3.67**
Number of adult females in household	1.53	1.52	0.16
Land assets (decimals)	101.3	136.6	−1.73*
Share of adult male members with reading competency	0.279	0.335	−1.86*
Share of adult female members with reading competency	0.169	0.177	−0.35
Share of adult male members with writing competency	0.188	0.215	−0.99
Share of adult female members with writing competency	0.116	0.095	1.11
Share of adult male members with oral math competency	0.514	0.581	−2.09**
Share of adult female members with oral math competency	0.233	0.322	−3.18**
Share of adult male members with written math competency	0.212	0.235	−0.84
Share of adult female members with written math competency	0.098	0.087	0.60
Average microfinance loan amount by males (Tk.)	2,337.5	885.3	4.24**
Average microfinance loan amount by females (Tk.)	6,129.5	3,644.8	3.42**

Sources: World Bank/BIDS survey 1991/92 and 1998/99; World Bank/InM survey 2010/11.

Note: For a given year, a household is considered dropout if it is nonparticipant in that year but was participant in the preceding year; thus, dropout is missing for the first survey year (1991/92). Figures show past characteristics (from preceding survey).

Significance level: * = 10 percent, ** = 5 percent or less.

dropout members had less nonland assets than nondropouts. This trend suggests that dropouts did not do as well under microfinance as the other borrowers. It is possible that the factors that contributed to member dropout (e.g., age, education, and oral math competency) also contributed to their diminished outcomes.

Table 8.10 Determinants of Household Dropout from Microfinance
N = 1,711

Characteristic	Model 1	Model 2
Sex of head (1 =male, 0 = female)	0.015 (0.28)	0.008 (0.15)
Age of head (years)	0.004** (3.66)	0.003** (3.41)
Education of head (years)	−0.005 (−1.54)	−0.004 (−1.30)
Number of adult males in household	0.024** (2.29)	0.022** (2.28)
Number of adult females in household	−0.010 (−0.82)	−0.010 (−0.86)
Land assets (decimals)	0.005 (0.80)	0.007 (1.10)
Share of adult male members with reading competency	0.005 (0.19)	0.001 (0.05)
Share of adult female members with reading competency	−0.033 (−1.42)	−0.035 (−1.50)
Share of adult male members with writing competency	0.009 (0.28)	0.009 (0.32)
Share of adult female members with writing competency	0.045 (1.14)	0.048 (1.33)
Share of adult male members with oral math competency	−0.020* (−1.83)	−0.015* (−1.88)
Share of adult female members with oral math competency	−0.034* (−1.77)	−0.038* (−2.04)
Share of adult male members with written math competency	−0.001 (−0.05)	−0.007 (−0.29)
Share of adult female members with written math competency	−0.045 (−1.07)	−0.047 (−1.15)
Average microfinance loan amount by males (Tk.)		0.014** (4.24)
Average microfinance loan amount by females (Tk.)		0.019** (8.26)
R^2	0.038	0.094
Mean of dependent variable (dropout rate)	0.054	

Sources: World Bank/BIDS survey 1991/92 and 1998/99; World Bank/InM survey 2010/11.
Note: Regressors are past characteristics (from preceding survey). Figures in parentheses are *t*-statistics based on standard errors clustered at the village level. Regressions include more control variables at the household level (e.g., age, sex, and education of household head) and village level (e.g., price of consumer goods; infrastructure, including schools and electricity availability; and proportion of irrigated land).
Significance level: * = 10 percent, ** = 5 percent or less.

Triple Difference Estimation

Since dropout is not random—it is determined by human endowments—and outcomes vary over time by dropout phenomenon, it is possible that microfinance impacts also vary by that phenomenon. Thus, the challenge is to determine the differential impacts for dropouts and non-dropouts. We capture such impacts

Table 8.11 Selected Household Welfare Outcomes by Dropout Status

	In participation year			In dropout year		
Outcome	Households that dropped out (N = 292)	Households that did not drop out (N = 3,682)	t- statistics of the difference	Households that dropped out (N = 292)	Households that did not drop out (N = 3,682)	t-statistics of the difference
Per capita income (Tk./month)	571.3	574.8	−0.08	888.9	947.5	−0.40
Per capita expenditure (Tk./month)	499.3	435.8	2.59**	556.8	594.4	−1.18
Moderate poverty (%)	59.8	64.0	−1.25	36.3	38.3	−0.58
Extreme poverty (%)	41.7	50.0	−2.28**	23.9	24.3	−0.11
Nonland assets (Tk.)	52,600.3	30,985.6	4.22**	35,769.2	51,966.2	−2.37**
Net worth (Tk.)	206,067.4	208,987.7	−0.04	254,126.5	380,923.8	−1.34

Sources: World Bank/BIDS survey 1991/92 and 1998/99; World Bank/InM survey 2010/11.

using a difference-in-difference-in-difference (DDD) or triple difference estimation technique.

If DD_r is the impact for regular or continuous members and DD_d is the impact for dropout members, we would like to find out whether $DD_r = DD_d$. In a DDD framework, this can be expressed as follows:

$$Y_{it} = \beta T_t + \lambda_r M_{it}^r + \lambda_d M_{it}^d + \gamma_1 T_t M_{it}^r + \gamma_2 T_t M_{it}^d + \gamma_3 M_{it}^r M_{it}^d + \gamma_4 T_t M_{it}^r M_{it}^d + \varepsilon_{it}, \quad (8.4)$$

where T_t equals time control, M_{it}^r is the intervention variable for continuous participants, M_{it}^d is the intervention variable for dropout members, ε_{it} is the random error, and β, λ, and γ are parameters to be estimated. The parameter of interest here is γ_4, which captures the incremental effects for regular participants over dropout members. In practice, we capture the effects of regular and dropout members by adding dummy variables for each type.

Table 8.12 shows the participation effects on household outcomes for two scenarios: when member dropout is controlled for and when it is not.[6] As reported, controlling for member dropout does not change the microfinance impacts by much. For household income and expenditure, there is no difference (i.e., the t-statistics are not significant). Not controlling for member dropout underestimates the credit effects for male labor supply and overestimates them for female labor supply and nonland assets. There is no difference in the effects in terms of household net worth and children's schooling.[7] Summing up, when member dropout is controlled for, the change in credit impacts is quite small.

Table 8.12 Impacts of Microfinance Borrowing on Household Outcomes with Controlling for Program Dropout: Propensity-Score Weighted Household FE Estimates
N = 1,758

Microfinance input variable	Not controlling for program dropout	Controlling for program dropout
Log per capita total income (Tk./month)		
Household male borrowed	0.020	0.059
	(0.22)	(0.63)
Household female borrowed	0.009	0.002
	(0.23)	(0.05)
R^2	0.120	0.122
Log per capita total expenditure (Tk./month)		
Household male borrowed	0.030	0.042
	(0.87)	(1.17)
Household female borrowed	−0.030	−0.017
	(−1.44)	(−0.74)
R^2	0.274	0.275
Log male labor supply (hours/month)		
Household male borrowed	0.347**	0.402**
	(2.21)	(2.45)
Household female borrowed	0.221**	0.250**
	(2.72)	(2.84)
R^2	0.199	0.200
Log female labor supply (hours/month)		
Household male borrowed	0.174	0.171
	(1.19)	(1.07)
Household female borrowed	0.330**	0.282**
	(3.48)	(2.59)
R^2	0.334	0.335
Log household nonland assets (Tk.)		
Household male borrowed	0.260**	0.236**
	(4.01)	(3.44)
Household female borrowed	0.148**	0.126*
	(2.66)	(1.90)
R^2	0.466	0.467
Log household net worth (Tk.)		
Household male borrowed	0.053	0.040
	(0.96)	(0.65)
Household female borrowed	−0.121	−0.121
	(−0.90)	(−0.69)
R^2	0.669	0.669
Boys' school enrollment rate (ages 5–18)		
Household male borrowed	−0.026	−0.047
	(−0.45)	(−0.79)
Household female borrowed	0.042	0.010
	(0.84)	(0.20)
R^2	0.076	0.078

table continues next page

Table 8.12 Impacts of Microfinance Borrowing on Household Outcomes with Controlling for Program Dropout: Propensity-Score Weighted Household FE Estimates *(continued)*

Microfinance input variable	Not controlling for program dropout	Controlling for program dropout
Girls' school enrollment rate (ages 5–18)		
Household male borrowed	−0.004	−0.025
	(−0.07)	(−0.41)
Household female borrowed	0.055	0.040
	(1.39)	(0.94)
R^2	0.060	0.062

Sources: World Bank/BIDS survey 1991/92 and 1998/99; World Bank/InM survey 2010/11.
Note: Figures in parentheses are *t*-statistics based on standard errors clustered at the village level. Regressions include more control variables at the household level (e.g., age, sex, and education of household head) and village level (e.g., price of consumer goods; infrastructure, including schools and electricity availability; and proportion of irrigated land). FE = fixed effects. *Significance level:* * = 10 percent, ** = 5 percent or less.

Summary

This chapter has examined the heterogeneous impacts of microfinance intervention in rural Bangladesh. Heterogeneity in program effects may arise due to household and community endowments. For household resource endowments, we considered household landholdings, household head's education, competency in oral math (a proxy for entrepreneurial ability), and employment types. For village endowments, we considered village electrification and accessibility by road.

We find that, while large landholding farmers have experienced income gains from microfinance, marginal and small- and medium-scale landholders have witnessed no effects on their income. For other outcomes—labor supply of males and females, nonland assets, and net worth—all households have benefited, but large and medium landholding farmers appear to have benefited more than marginal farmers. For level of education completed by the household head, the findings are mixed. In terms of labor supply (of both males and females), there is little variation in impacts by education of household head; however, in terms of nonland assets and net worth, households whose heads have completed primary or secondary school appear to have fared better under microfinance than those whose heads have not completed primary school. Since education in rural Bangladesh may not reflect the true ability to utilize loans, we also examined microfinance impacts by competency of adult household members in oral math, which is perhaps a better proxy for entrepreneurial ability. As expected, having adult members with competency in oral math is found to help households reap more benefits from microfinance. For the effects of employment on microfinance returns, only self-employed households were found to gain in income and expenditure from microfinance borrowing. Also, self-employed households gained more than wage-employed ones in nonland assets and net worth. In terms of community endowments, the findings show that households living in villages with access to electricity and paved roads benefit more from microfinance, compared to those living in villages without electricity and poor accessibility.

Quantile regression estimates that measure average gains from participation of different groups show that, except for the effects of male participation, households in the lower welfare brackets in terms of income and expenditure benefit more than those in the higher ones. This means that microfinance programs are well targeted. This is quite critical as alleviating poverty is a stated objective of microfinance interventions.

This chapter has also tried to identify the MFI program dropouts and whether they can be considered losers of microfinance. The findings show that households with older heads or more adult male members are more likely to drop out. Most importantly, those households with adult members that are less competent in oral math are more likely to drop out, which may be indicative of less ability to make productive use of microloans. Such households borrowed more than their counterpart members who continued on with the MFI programs. Perhaps the dropout members, having borrowed more than they could handle, along with their lower entrepreneurial ability, did not fare well. In fact, the trend in their outcomes over time clearly suggests that. In terms of welfare measures, the dropout members were either better off or at least similar to their counterpart continuing members during their initial participation years, but they failed to maintain their prosperity over time. That said, the findings also suggest that the differential impacts of microfinance by program dropouts are not large enough to affect the overall impacts of microfinance.

Annex 8A: Quantile Regression to Estimate the Distributional Impacts of Microfinance

We used quantile regression to estimate returns to borrowing based on the distribution of outcomes such as income and expenditure. We apply the quantile regression model introduced by Koenker and Bassett (1978), generalized to the censored quantile regression model by Powell (1984, 1986). For example, we can test whether there are differential returns to credit in terms of household consumption and income per capita at distinct points in the household consumption or income distribution.

It is potentially important to investigate changes in the outcomes observed at various points in the distribution since simply investigating changes in the mean may not suffice when the entire shape of the distribution changes significantly (Buchinsky 1998). While the objective of ordinary regression is to estimate the mean of the dependent variable, the objective of quantile regression is to estimate a quantile value (median or other quantile values, such as 0.25, 0.60) of the dependent variable.

Technically, a quantile regression minimizes the sum of absolute residuals corresponding to the quantile value in question as opposed to minimizing the sum of squares of the residuals achieved by ordinary regression. By design, microfinance programs try to reach the poorest groups, especially women, and so it is expected that the poorer households may benefit more from these programs than better-off ones. A quantile regression enables us to investigate this issue.

Following the model proposed by Koenker and Bassett (1978), we assume that $Y_i = 1, 2, \dots n$ is a sample of observations on the outcome and X_i is a $K \times 1$ vector comprising the household- and village-level characteristics controlled on the right-hand side of the outcome equation. The quantile regression model can be expressed as follows:

$$Y_i = X_i' \beta_\theta + \varepsilon_{\theta i}, \ Quant_\theta(Y_i | X_i) = X_i' \beta_\theta, \ \theta \in (0,1), \qquad (8A.1)$$

where $Quant_\theta (Y_i | X_i)$ denotes the quantile θ of log per capita expenditure or income conditional on the vector of covariates. In general, the θ-th sample quantile of Y solves the following:

$$\min_\beta \frac{1}{n} \left[\sum_{i:Y_i \geq X_i' \beta} \theta \left| Y_i - X_i' \beta_\theta \right| + \sum_{i:Y_i < X_i' \beta} (1-\theta) \left| Y_i - X_i' \beta_\theta \right| \right] = \min_\beta \frac{1}{n} \sum_{i=1}^n \rho_\theta(\varepsilon_{\theta i}), \quad (8A.2)$$

where, $\rho_\theta(\varepsilon_{\theta i})$ denoted as the check function, is defined as follows:

$$\rho_\theta(\varepsilon_{\theta i}) = \begin{cases} \theta \varepsilon_{\theta i} \ if \ \varepsilon_{\theta i} \geq 0 \\ (\theta-1)\varepsilon_{\theta i} \ if \ \varepsilon_{\theta i} < 0 \end{cases}. \qquad (8A.3)$$

Parameters are estimated semi-parametrically by minimizing the sum of weighted absolute deviations, which fits medians to a linear function of covariates, and can be performed using linear programming methods (Buchinsky 1998). To account for possible heteroskedasticity in the error term, the variance-covariance matrix of coefficients is estimated using bootstrap resampling. Specifically, the quantile's coefficients can be interpreted as the partial derivative of the conditional quantile of Y_i with respect to one of the regressors X_i, namely $\partial Quant (Y_i | X_i) / \partial X_i$.

To estimate quantile regression for panel data, we use a semi-parametric approach to examine the distributional effects of nonrandom treatment.[8] This method involves a panel quantile regression model that estimates the treatment impact on outcomes Y by distributional quantile. More specifically, we use the quantile regression equations for the two data periods to estimate the distributional effects of microfinance participation (P) on household/individual outcomes Y, as follows:

$$Q_\tau(Y_{ijt} | Z_{ijt}, E_{ijt}, \eta_{ijt}) = \psi_\tau Z_{ijt} + \delta_\tau P_{ijt} + \eta_{ijt}, \ \tau \in (0,1), \qquad (8A.4)$$

where $Q_t(Y_{ijt}|Z_{ijt}, P_{ijt}, \eta_{ijt})$ denotes quantile τ of Y in period t, conditional on the fixed effect and household and community covariates in period t. Vector Z measures both household (X) and village (V) exogenous attributes, while η subsumes unobserved community and household heterogeneity.

One problem in applying the quantile regression model to panel data is that differencing variables are not generally equal to the difference in the conditional quantiles because quantiles are not linear operators. To overcome this obstacle, we follow Gamper-Rabindran, Khan, and Timmins (2010), who specify the unobserved effect η nonparametrically as an unknown function $\phi(\cdot)$ of the covariates X, as follows:[9]

$$\eta = \varphi(Z_{ij1}, Z_{ij2}, ..., Z_{ijt}). \tag{8A.5}$$

Substituting equation (8A.5) in each conditional quantile in equation (8A.4) allows us to estimate the distributional impact of income on outcomes Y.[10] In practice, we transform equation (8A.4) and take the quantile over the difference of the outcome and its mean, expressed as follows:

$$Q_\tau(\Delta Y_{ijt}) = \psi_\tau \Delta Z_{ijt} + \delta_\tau \Delta P_{ijt} + \theta_{1\tau} Z_{ij1} + \theta_{2\tau} Z_{ij2} + \theta_{3\tau} Z_{ij3} + \Delta \varepsilon_{ijt}. \tag{8A.6}$$

Notes

1. For microfinance participant households in 1991/92, there is no baseline information before program participation.

2. While education (years of schooling) is a good measure of human endowment, it does not necessarily imply competency or skills needed for entrepreneurial or material success, especially when the quality of education is questionable as it is in most developing countries. Thus, we use adult oral math skills as an alternate, and perhaps more practical, measure of competency. The household members surveyed in 1991/92 and 1998/99 were subjected to skills tests specifically developed to obtain a measure of their basic literacy in reading, writing, and oral and written math. Based on these test scores, members were evaluated as either competent or incompetent. In this descriptive analysis, we grouped households based on whether they had adult members with oral math competency. Among the four basic skills, we considered competency in oral math as the most important for entrepreneurship, even though the findings for the other skills did not vary by much.

3. A household head's main occupation is determined by the activity or source that brings in the highest income.

4. In practice, we measure the credit effects of households with endowments by computing point estimates of the terms $(P_{ift} + P_{ift} * E_{it})$ and $(P_{imt} + P_{imt} * E_{it})$ after running the regression for equation (8.1).

5. Test batteries for oral and written math skills were developed and applied for all members ages 10-65 years from the same households surveyed in 1991/92. Assuming that these skills are time invarying, we included them as exogenous regressors in the dropout regression. Details of the test are provided in Greaney, Khandker and Alam (1998).

6. This estimation is done for 1998/99 and 2010/11 observations only since dropout information is indeterminate in the first survey year (1991/92).

7. We also estimated the credit effects using the cumulative borrowing amount and found no difference in its impacts using participation variables.

8. Gamper-Rabindran, Khan, and Timmins (2010) apply this method in the context of providing piped water in Brazil.

9. Abrevaya and Dahl (2008) apply a similar approach based on the correlated fixed-effects (FE) model of Chamberlain (1982), where the FE are specified as a parametric (linear) function of the covariates X.

10. Gamper-Rabindran, Khan, and Timmins (2010) show how the quantile regression (QTE) can be estimated using a two-step procedure. First, $\hat{Q}_\tau(Y_{ijt}|Z_{ijt},P_{ijt},\eta_{ijt})$ should be nonparametrically estimated for each period t, with Z and E entering linearly into the equation. Second, the differenced fitted values

$$\hat{Q}_\tau(Y_{ijt}|Z_{ijt},P_{ijt},\eta_{ijt}) - \hat{Q}_\tau(Y_{ijt-1}|Z_{ijt-1},P_{ijt-1},\eta_{ijt-1})$$ from the estimations can be regressed on the differenced regressors since the proxies for the FE fall out of the estimation.

Bibliography

Abrevaya, Jason, and Christian M. Dahl. 2008. "The Effects of Birth Inputs on Birthweight: Evidence from Quantile Estimation on Panel Data." *Journal of Business and Economic Statistics* 26: 379–97.

Araujo, M. Caridad, Francisco H. G. Ferreira, Peter Lanjouw, and Berk Özler. 2008. "Local Inequality and Project Choice: Theory and Evidence from Ecuador." *Journal of Public Economics* 92 (5–6): 1022–46.

Banerjee, Abhijit, Dean Karlan, and Jonathan Zinman. 2015. "Six Randomized Evaluations of Microcredit: Introduction and Further Steps." *American Economic Journal: Applied Economics* 7 (1): 1–21.

Buchinsky, Moshe. 1998. "Recent Advances in Quantile Regression Models: A Practical Guide for Empirical Research." *Journal of Human Resources* 33: 88–126.

Chamberlain, Gray. 1982. "Multivariate Regression Models for Panel Data." *Journal of Econometrics* 18: 5–46.

Gamper-Rabindran, Shanti, Shakeeb Khan, and Christopher Timmins. 2010. "The Impact of Piped Water Provision on Infant Mortality in Brazil: A Quantile Panel Data Approach." *Journal of Development Economics* 92 (2): 188–200.

Greaney, Vincent, Shahidur Khandker, and Mahmudul Alam. 1998. *Bangladesh: Assessing Basic Learning Skills*. Dhaka: University Press Limited for the World Bank.

Gugerty, Mary Kay, and Michael Kremer. 2008. "Outside Funding and the Dynamics of Participation in Community Associations." *American Journal of Political Science* 52 (3): 585–602.

King, Elizabeth M., and Jere R. Behrman. 2009. "Timing and Duration of Exposure in Evaluations of Social Programs." *World Bank Research Observer* 24 (1): 55–82.

Koenker, Roger, and Gilbert Bassett. 1978. "Regression Quantiles." *Econometrica* 46 (1): 33–50.

Mansuri, Ghazala, and Vijayendra Rao. 2004. "Community-Based and -Driven Development: A Critical Review." *World Bank Research Observer* 19 (1): 1–39.

Pitt, Mark M., and Shahidur R. Khandker. 1998. "The Impact of Group-Based Credit Programs on Poor Households in Bangladesh: Does the Gender of Participants Matter?" *Journal of Political Economy* 106 (June): 958–96.

Platteau, Jean-Philippe. 2004. "Monitoring Elite Capture in Community-Driven Development." *Development and Change* 35 (2): 223–46.

Powell, J. L. 1984. "Least Absolute Deviations Estimation for the Censored Regression Model." *Journal of Econometrics* 25: 303–25.

———. 1986. "Censored Regression Quantiles." *Journal of Econometrics* 32: 143–55.

van de Walle, Dominique. 2009. "Impact Evaluation of Rural Road Projects." *Journal of Development Effectiveness* 1 (1): 15–36.

CHAPTER 9

Effects of Noncredit Participation

Introduction

Although most of the microfinance literature centers on the credit effects of programs, microfinance also provides a variety of nonfinancial services, ranging from awareness building among the poor (especially women) and skills-based training to product marketing support, extension services for inputs, and small savings mobilization. While credit extension and savings mobilization account for the majority of service categories, nonfinancial services (i.e., training and extension) also constitute high-visibility products of microfinance institutions (MFIs) in many countries.

In Bangladesh, MFIs require that borrowers make regular (e.g., weekly) deposits into savings accounts, even if in small amounts. Such savings behavior is an especially good practice for the poor. Because their livelihood depends on a vulnerable agroclimate, small savings funds can ultimately be used to mitigate those effects by smoothing income and consumption. Similarly, for illiterate people without easy access to market information, awareness building, skills-based training, and extension services can help to raise productivity for labor and enterprises.

Identifying the separate effects of MFI programs' financial and nonfinancial services becomes an important exercise for two major reasons. First, many MFIs depend on subsidized funds to develop and market microfinance products. Second, because of the high transaction costs associated with MFI product development and delivery, lending rates are often high (above 40 percent in some cases). Therefore, estimating the effects of microfinance beyond credit is a relevant exercise for determining whether subsidized funds or high microlending rates are justified. To date, Alam (2013), Karlan and Valdivia (2015), and McKernan (2002) are among the few studies that have attempted to document the noncredit effects of MFI programs.

If noncredit MFI services matter separately from microcredit services, then the noncredit effects will vary according to how MFI programs are designed in terms of the nonfinancial services provided. For example, among Bangladesh's leading MFI programs, Grameen Bank provides mainly financial services (savings mobilization and lending), while the Bangladesh Rural Advancement Committee (BRAC), the country's largest nongovernmental organization, provides both financial and nonfinancial services; the latter services include both awareness building and a variety of skills-based training programs.[1] The newer generation of MFIs, supported by Palli Karma-Sahayak Foundation (PKSF), the country's leading microfinance facility, follows a model that incorporates features of both Grameen Bank and BRAC. We distinguish three types of MFI programs in Bangladesh: Grameen Bank, BRAC, and other MFIs. Because these MFI categories differ by program design and product services, they may have an independent effect beyond the financial and nonfinancial services they deliver to their members. Using the long panel survey data spanning more than 20 years, this chapter aims to differentiate the impacts of these three types of MFI programs in Bangladesh, exploring the potential benefits from credit and noncredit inputs and program design.

Evidence on the Role of Noncredit Services

As mentioned above, MFI programs provide their members a variety of noncredit services both explicitly and implicitly separate from credit. These include vocational training and organizational and social development inputs to improve literacy, health, and social balance. It is only natural that these services have separate impacts on members' behavior and welfare. However, many people believe that the poor have their own rational view that helps them to maximize profit subject to their financial constraints (e.g., Yunus 1999). Even so, de Mel, McKenzie, and Woodruff (2008a, 2008b) found considerable heterogeneity among microentrepreneurs in Sri Lanka, suggesting that higher cognitive abilities yield higher returns. Interestingly, the existing studies failed to establish any highly significant impact of financial training on borrowers' performance.

Karlan and Valdivia (2015) attempted to identify the impact of business training on MFI clients in Peru, using a randomized control trial (RCT). They found little or no evidence of changes in key outcomes (e.g., business revenue or profits and employment) due to a training session conducted over a 1–2 year period. Comparing the outcome variables of present and baseline values, basic business training for preexisting microcredit clients appears to have not generated higher profits or revenue. They divided their analysis into four categories: (a) business outcomes; (b) business processes and knowledge; (c) household outcomes, including empowerment in decision making and child labor; and (d) microfinance institutional outcomes. The difference estimators, however, showed improvements in business knowledge and increased MFI client retention rates. Similarly, Epstein and Yuthas (2014) reported a better understanding of revenue, expenses, and profits among microcredit members who received cash-flow training.

Given the paucity of impact from financial training on borrowers' performance in the microfinance sector, one might wonder whether there is any MFI impact beyond the credit received by program participants. Collins (2013), for example, observed that mandatory financial education improves self-reported behaviors, but found no measurable effects on credit or savings. Studying the impact of a comprehensive business and financial literacy program on the firm outcomes of young entrepreneurs in Bosnia and Herzegovina, Bruhn and Zia (2013) found that the training program did not influence business survival; but it did significantly improve business practices, investments, and terms for surviving businesses. Bruhn, Ibarra, and McKenzie (2014), who conducted randomized experiments around a large-scale financial literacy course in Mexico, found that attendance in financial education training increased financial knowledge and self-reported measures of savings, but had no impact on borrowing behavior.

Admitting the difficulty in measuring the impact of the noncredit aspects of microfinance programs, McKernan (2002) used the productivity of all capital as an indicator. She examined the impact of microcredit borrowing on business profits, finding that both the total effect of borrowing and the noncredit effect of business capital have a positive impact on borrowers' profits. The former result was derived by estimating a profit equation, while the latter resulted from estimating the profit equation conditional on productive capital. The study utilized data on participant and nonparticipant households in the microcredit programs of Grameen Bank, BRAC, and the Bangladesh Rural Development Board (BRDB) RD-12 to measure the total and noncredit effect. Treating productive capital and program participation as endogenous in the conditional profit equation, McKernan (2002) found large positive effects for participation and its noncredit aspects on self-employment profits. That study's results also suggested that microcredit programs have the greatest impact on households with the least capital.

Alam (2013) examined the impacts of the credit and noncredit aspects of microcredit programs on self-employment profits, replicating McKernan (2002) in a simpler way. For example, McKernan (2002) takes profit and productive capital as a limited dependent variable with a threshold level, breaks error terms up into five components in order to capture unobservable household- and village-level characteristics, and takes all productive capital (credit or savings) into account. By contrast, Alam (2013) includes both the magnitude and dummy variables for commercial credit, along with the three microcredit programs in McKernan's study. As a result, Alam shows that the noncredit social aspects of microcredit programs affect profit and increase self-employment. For commercial loans, they generate a larger credit effect but a smaller noncredit effect compared to microcredit.

Noncredit Services of MFIs in Bangladesh

Early microcredit programs in Bangladesh (e.g., BRAC) started out with an integrated credit and noncredit approach; but over time, as commercialization has grown, the share of noncredit services has declined. However, PKSF, which has training embedded in its designated credit program, is an exception. Thirteen percent of borrowers from this apex MFI receive training from more than 200 of its MFI partner organizations (POs), whose coverage represents 30 percent of the country's microfinance-sector membership (about 10 million). By comparison,

Grameen Bank, BRAC, and the Association for Social Advancement cover 22, 21, and 15 percent of their respective memberships (Faruqee and Badruddoza 2011).[2]

To better understand the effect of PKSF's noncredit services, we divide its training programs into the following broad categories: (a) agriculture (e.g., crops, fruits, vegetables, and spices); (b) livestock (e.g., goat rearing, cattle fattening, poultry raising, and dairy production) and fisheries; (c) off-farm (e.g., motorized and non-motorized transport, small business and trade, and handicrafts); (d) vocational (e.g., electric gadgetry repair, sewing machines, metalworking, and welding); and (e) social development (e.g., education, health, social awareness, and credit management). Figure 9.1 shows that in FY2009, livestock and fisheries accounted for the highest percentage of MFI PO borrower training, at 34 percent. By FY2013, agriculture had taken the lead, at 28 percent. The four-year period also saw an increasing share of vocational and social development training and a decreasing share of off-farm training.

In most cases, PKSF has tied these training programs to particular microcredit products. The results reported are a promising signal that the dominance of livestock training, particularly in goat rearing, is decreasing, while training in agricultural production is becoming more diverse. The declining share of off-farm training activities reported in FY2013 may be attributed to the country's political disorder. The findings also reveal a positive trend in social development training, particularly in social awareness, health, and education. Vocational training is crucial for a country like Bangladesh, which has an enormous unskilled labor force. Although vocational training doubled over the four-year period, it represented just 6 percent of borrower training in FY2013, suggesting the need for suitable infrastructure.

Figure 9.1 Borrower Training Provided by PKSF MFI Partner Organizations
percent

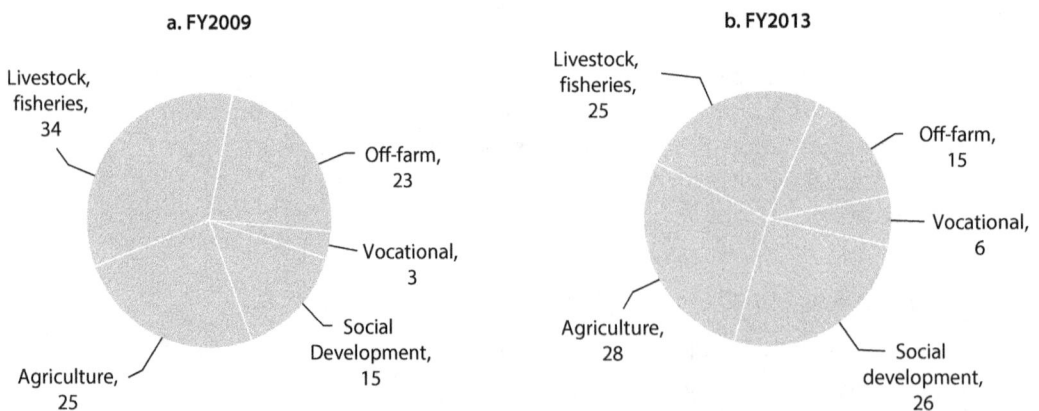

a. FY2009

Livestock, fisheries, 34
Off-farm, 23
Vocational, 3
Social Development, 15
Agriculture, 25

b. FY2013

Livestock, fisheries, 25
Off-farm, 15
Vocational, 6
Agriculture, 28
Social development, 26

Source: Calculations based on PKSF annual reports (2007–12).
Note: Figures show sector-wise percentage of borrowers who received training under various projects of PRIME (Programme Initiative for Monga Eradication), MFTS (Microfinance and Technical Support), MFMSF (Microfinance for Marginal and Small Farmers), ASM (Agriculture Sector Microcredit), and ME (Microenterprise). PKSF = Palli Karma-Sahayak Foundation; MFI = microfinance institution.

Do Noncredit Inputs Matter in Enhancing Household Welfare?

As mentioned above, noncredit provision was an integral part of the services provided by the first generation of MFI programs developed in the 1980s. Using results of the 1991/92 survey round, table 9.1 shows the various types of training provided at that time and the share of MFI members that were trained. Among the types of training received, health and hygiene ranked first, including about 67 percent of all members (58 percent of male members and 68 percent of female members). Literacy ranked second, with more than 63 percent of members receiving such training (55 percent of male members and 62 percent of female members). About 32 percent of members received training in occupational skills development, while 18 percent received marketing training.[3] Overall, virtually all members received some form of training.

In contrast to the first generation of MFIs, later programs in the mid-1990s began disbursing loans without providing any major training. They still provided noncredit services in the form of information sharing on various types of skills to help members develop human and social capital and better utilize their current loans. For example, group members waiting for their turn to get a loan would learn lessons from other program members in a group setting on such topics as entrepreneurship, business development, discipline, and accountability. In addition, in order to qualify for borrowing, all MFI program members were required to save a certain amount on a regular (often weekly) basis. To improve credit discipline and savings behavior among the poor, members that were eligible to borrow also deposited a certain percentage toward savings.

Capturing the Noncredit Dimension of MFI Membership

Given that specific measures of training activities were unavailable, we captured the noncredit dimension of microfinance program membership by distinguishing between borrowing and simple participation. Table 9.2 shows that not all MFI program participants were borrowers at any given time. For example, in 2010/11, 60 percent of male members and 82 percent of female members were borrowers, confirming that program participation captures both the credit and noncredit dimensions of membership. Noncredit inputs can affect

Table 9.1 Share of Microfinance Members Receiving Various Types of Training in 1991/92
N = 769

Training type	Male members (%)	Female members (%)	All members
Health	58.1	67.9	66.6
Literacy	55.3	62.5	63.4
Occupational skills development	41.7	28.6	32.2
Marketing	14.2	17.4	18.0
Other training	31.9	31.6	32.2
All training	94.4	97.8	99.4

Source: World Bank/BIDS survey 1991/92.

Table 9.2 Incidence of Microfinance Participation and Borrowing
N = 1,509

	Participation		Borrowing incidence	
Survey year	Men (%)	Women (%)	Men (%)	Women (%)
1991/92	10.5	19.5	8.7	17.1
1998/99	14.3	40.9	6.9	33.2
2010/11	13.4	62.9	8.0	51.5

Sources: World Bank/BIDS survey 1991/92 and 1998/99; World Bank/InM survey 2010/11.

household outcomes independent of credit impacts. As a result, the aggregate effect of program participation captures the effects of both credit and noncredit inputs.[4]

We first attempt to estimate the aggregate effects of MFI program participation. Following the general method outlined in appendix B, we can write the outcome equation that captures the effects of participation as follows:

$$Y_{it} = X_{it}\beta_c + P_{ift}\gamma_f + P_{imt}\gamma_m + \eta_{it} + \mu_i + \varepsilon_{it}, \tag{9.1}$$

where Y_{it} equals the outcome (e.g, income, labor supply, and net worth) of household i in survey year t, conditional on microfinance participation of men (P_{imt}) and women (P_{ift}); X_{it} is a vector of characteristics at the household level (e.g., sex, age, and education of household head; landholdings) and village level (e.g., extent of electrification and irrigation, availability of other infrastructure, and price of consumer goods), β_c is a vector of unknown parameters of X variables to be estimated, γ_m and γ_f measure the effects of noncredit inputs, η_{it} is an unobserved household- or community-level determinant of the outcome that is time varying, μ_i is an unobserved household- or community-level determinant of the outcome that is time invariant, and ε_{it} is a nonsystematic error.

The household fixed-effects (FE) estimation technique can eliminate the time-invariant parameter (μ_i) through transformation of equation (9.1) as follows:

$$Y_{it} - \bar{Y}_i = (X_{it} - \bar{X}_i)\beta + (P_{ift} - \bar{P}_{if})\gamma_f + (P_{imt} - \bar{P}_{im})\gamma_m$$
$$+ (\eta_{it} - \bar{\eta}_i) + (\mu_i - \bar{\mu}) + (\varepsilon_{it} - \bar{\varepsilon}_i) \tag{9.2}$$
$$\text{or} \quad \Delta Y_{it} = \beta \Delta X_{it} + \gamma_f \Delta P_{ift} + \gamma_m \Delta P_{imt} + \Delta \eta_{it} + \Delta \varepsilon_{it},$$

where the bar variables $\left(\text{e.g.}, \bar{Y}_i, \bar{X}_i, \bar{P}_{if}\right)$ are average values for each household across years. Since μ is constant, $\mu_i = \bar{\mu}$ and thus its effect is eliminated. However, since $\eta_{it} \neq \bar{\eta}_i$, the problem of unobserved effects cannot be disregarded completely, and thus the ordinary least squares (OLS) estimation of equation (9.2) will be biased. As in the previous chapters, the propensity-score (p-score) weighted FE method was used to control for time-varying unobserved effects.

Table 9.3 reports the findings on total participation effects of microfinance programs. As shown, program participation improves household male and female labor supply, nonland assets, household net worth, and school enrollment. Results by gender show that men's program participation increases female labor supply by nearly 21 percent without affecting male labor supply. Women's participation increases male and female labor supply by 19 and 46 percentage points, respectively. Men's program participation increases household nonland assets by 23 percent and net worth by 15 percent, while women's participation improves nonland assets but not net worth. Women's program participation increases boys' and girls' school enrollment by about 9 percentage points and 10 percentage points, respectively.

To estimate how program participation impacts vary by individual programs, we use the following equation:

$$\Delta Y_{it} = \beta \Delta X_{it} + \sum_{k=1}^{n} \gamma_{fk} \Delta P_{ifkt} + \sum_{k=1}^{n} \gamma_{mk} \Delta P_{imkt} + \Delta \eta_{it} + \Delta \varepsilon_{it}, \tag{9.3}$$

where $k = 1, 2, \ldots n$ indicates a specific program (e.g., Grameen Bank). The findings show that household income is improved only by men's participation in Grameen Bank, and household expenditure is unaffected by any program participation by men or women. Households' male labor supply is improved by male and female membership in Grameen Bank (by 54 percentage points and 30 percentage points, respectively), and women's membership in other MFIs (by 18 percentage points). Households' female labor supply is increased by women's membership in all programs. For example, women's participation in Grameen Bank, BRAC, and other MFIs increases female labor supply by 37 percentage points, 25 percentage points, and 45 percentage points, respectively. Households'

Table 9.3 Impacts of Microfinance Participation on Household Outcomes: Propensity-Score Weighted Household FE Estimates

N = 1,509

Microfinance input variable	Log per capita total income (Tk./month)	Log per capita total expenditure (Tk./month)	Log male labor supply (hours/ month)	Log female labor supply (hours/ month)	Log household nonland assets (Tk.)	Log household net worth (Tk.)	Boys' enrollment rate (ages 5–18)	Girls' enrollment rate (ages 5–18)
Men's participation	−0.059 (−1.03)	0.025 (1.14)	0.102 (0.99)	0.206* (1.80)	0.232** (4.70)	0.146* (3.34)	−0.023 (−0.74)	0.031 (0.73)
Women's participation	−0.046 (−1.10)	−0.012 (−0.59)	0.185** (2.54)	0.456** (6.84)	0.194** (4.17)	0.035 (0.92)	0.091** (3.10)	0.098** (2.88)
R^2	0.137	0.374	0.206	0.240	0.452	0.651	0.076	0.066

Sources: World Bank/BIDS survey 1991/92 and 1998/99; World Bank/InM survey 2010/11.
Note: Figures in parentheses are *t*-statistics based on standard errors clustered at the village level. Regressions include more control variables at the household level (e.g., age, sex, and education of household head) and village level (e.g., price of consumer goods; infrastructure, including schools and electricity availability; and proportion of irrigated land). FE = fixed effects.
Significance level: * = 10 percent, ** = 5 percent or less.

nonland assets and net worth are improved by both male and female membership in Grameen Bank, with higher effects for male participation. For both nonland assets and net worth, beneficial effects are found from men's participation
in other MFIs, while women's participation in other MFIs does not impact those
outcomes. In terms of school enrollment, girls benefited more than boys from
program participation. BRAC membership by men and women increased girls'
enrollment rate by 12.5 percentage points and 6.5 percentage points, respectively (table 9.4).

The next step is to disaggregate program effect into credit and noncredit
effects by rewriting equations (9.2) and (9.3) as follows:

$$\Delta Y_{it} = \beta \Delta X_{it} + \delta_f \Delta B_{ift} + \delta_m \Delta B_{imt} + \gamma_f \Delta P_{ift} + \gamma_m \Delta P_{imt} + \Delta \eta_{it} + \Delta \varepsilon_{it} \tag{9.4}$$

$$\text{and } \Delta Y_{it} = \beta \Delta X_{it} + \sum_{k=1}^{n} \delta_{fk} \Delta B_{ifkt} + \sum_{k=1}^{n} \delta_{mk} \Delta B_{imkt} + \sum_{k=1}^{n} \gamma_{fk} \Delta P_{ifkt}$$

$$+ \sum_{k=1}^{n} \gamma_{mk} \Delta P_{imkt} + \Delta \eta_{it} + \Delta \varepsilon_{it}, \tag{9.5}$$

where B_{imt} and B_{ift} refer to male and female borrowing, respectively. Since we
control for borrowing effects in equations (9.4) and (9.5), participation dum-
mies (P_{imt} and P_{ift}) capture the effects of noncredit effects (parameters γ_m and γ_f).
Table 9.5 shows the overall effects of borrowing and participation, while
table 9.6 does so by credit program.

Table 9.5 shows that household per capita income and expenditure improve
as a result of women's borrowing but not from their program participation (i.e.,
noncredit inputs). However, households' female labor supply improves as a result
of women's borrowing and nonborrowing program participation. Interestingly,
women's borrowing increases household female labor supply by 3.3 percentage
points, while women's program participation increases it by nearly 43 percentage
points, demonstrating that the noncredit effects of women's program participation matter more for labor supply than borrowing.

Male borrowing and noncredit participation have distinct effects on nonland
assets, improving it by 15 percent (men's borrowing) and 14 percent (men's
participation). Children's school enrollment is improved mainly by women's
participation. Women's noncredit inputs increase boys' and girls' enrollment by
11 percentage points and 16 percentage points, respectively. Thus, it follows
that, apart from credit, noncredit inputs also matter, especially for women
members.

Table 9.6 compares the household outcomes for the selected MFI by borrower and participation (nonborrower) status. For example, women's borrowing
from Grameen Bank and BRAC increases household income, while men's borrowing from BRAC and other MFIs improves household expenditure. Among
the nonborrower status variables, only men's participation in Grameen Bank
improves household expenditure. Also, men's borrowing and participation

Table 9.4 Impacts of Microfinance Participation on Household Outcomes by Program: Propensity-Score Weighted Household FE Estimates

N = 1,509

Microfinance input variable, participation	Log per capita total income (Tk./month)	Log per capita total expenditure (Tk./month)	Log male labor supply (hours/month)	Log female labor supply (hours/month)	Log household nonland assets (Tk.)	Log household net worth (Tk.)	Boys' enrollment rate (ages 5–18)	Girls' enrollment rate (ages 5–18)
Men, Grameen Bank	0.218** (2.54)	−0.004 (−0.07)	0.544** (2.60)	0.273 (1.12)	0.204* (1.83)	0.148* (1.65)	−0.052 (−0.54)	0.066 (0.97)
Men, BRAC	−0.290 (−1.37)	0.003 (0.08)	−0.097 (−0.43)	0.262 (1.43)	0.120 (1.16)	0.123 (1.57)	−0.007 (−0.14)	0.125** (2.33)
Men, other MFIs	0.070 (0.77)	0.049 (1.20)	0.232* (1.95)	0.065 (0.33)	0.225** (2.72)	0.179** (2.57)	−0.025 (−0.42)	0.034 (0.38)
Women, Grameen Bank	0.035 (0.68)	0.022 (0.91)	0.295** (3.50)	0.369** (3.35)	0.177** (3.10)	0.097* (1.84)	0.068* (1.70)	−0.018 (−0.49)
Women, BRAC	−0.029 (−0.67)	−0.011 (−0.47)	0.099 (1.14)	0.249** (2.14)	0.188** (4.04)	0.079 (1.56)	0.030 (0.81)	0.065* (1.74)
Women, other MFIs	0.008 (0.19)	−0.021 (−1.01)	0.182* (1.85)	0.446** (3.49)	0.042 (0.89)	−0.024 (−0.50)	0.039 (1.05)	0.125** (3.51)
R^2	0.141	0.374	0.210	0.243	0.452	0.652	0.074	0.071

Sources: World Bank/BIDS survey 1991/92 and 1998/99; World Bank/InM survey 2010/11.

Note: Figures in parentheses are *t*-statistics based on standard errors clustered at the village level. Regressions include more control variables at the household level (e.g., age, sex, and education of household head) and village level (e.g., price of consumer goods; infrastructure, including schools and electricity availability; and proportion of irrigated land). FE = fixed effects; BRAC = Bangladesh Rural Advancement Committee; MFI = microfinance institution.

Significance level: * = 10 percent, ** = 5 percent or less.

Table 9.5 Impacts of Microfinance Borrowing and Participation on Household Outcomes: Propensity-Score Weighted Household FE Estimates

N = 1,509

Microfinance input variable	Log per capita total income (Tk./month)	Log per capita total expenditure (Tk./month)	Log male labor supply (hours/month)	Log female labor supply (hours/month)	Log household nonland assets (Tk.)	Log household net worth (Tk.)	Boys' enrollment rate (ages 5–18)	Girls' enrollment rate (ages 5–18)
Borrowers								
Men	−0.027	−0.015	0.098	−0.328	0.148**	0.067	−0.100	0.032
	(−0.39)	(−0.58)	(0.77)	(−1.13)	(2.08)	(0.85)	(−1.11)	(0.59)
Women	0.072*	0.054*	0.304**	0.033*	0.113*	−0.053	−0.014	0.040
	(1.77)	(1.92)	(3.70)	(1.73)	(1.88)	(−1.04)	(−0.31)	(0.64)
Participants								
Men	−0.043	−0.007	0.040	0.402**	0.143**	0.107*	0.040	0.011
	(−0.70)	(−0.28)	(0.30)	(2.60)	(2.13)	(1.67)	(0.83)	(0.20)
Women	−0.108	0.001	−0.074	0.429**	0.097	0.079	0.106**	0.064*
	(−1.10)	(0.02)	(−0.74)	(3.02)	(1.46)	(1.40)	(2.17)	(1.76)
R^2	0.138	0.375	0.208	0.242	0.454	0.651	0.076	0.067

Sources: World Bank/BIDS survey 1991/92 and 1998/99; World Bank/InM survey 2010/11.

Note: Figures in parentheses are *t*-statistics based on standard errors clustered at the village level. Regressions include more control variables at the household level (e.g., age, sex, and education of household head) and village level (e.g., price of consumer goods; infrastructure, including schools and electricity availability; and proportion of irrigated land). FE = fixed effects.

Significance level: * = 10 percent, ** = 5 percent or less.

improve households' male and female labor supply. For all MFI programs, women's participation increases households' female labor supply—by 23 percent for Grameen Bank, 28 percent for BRAC, and 53 percent for other MFIs. For Grameen Bank and BRAC, women's participation increases household nonland assets and net worth. Also, women's participation, more so than that of men, improves children's school enrollment.

Does Duration of Program Membership Matter?

The prior sections have considered the separate and joint household welfare effects of two variables—whether MFI members are borrowing or nonborrowing participants. But since we are using a long panel, we must determine whether duration of program membership matters. At any given time, some members are not borrowers; thus, in most cases, the duration of program membership is longer than a member's borrowing period. As mentioned previously, during their nonborrowing participation phases, members can learn valuable lessons about savings behavior, which can have separate beneficial effects on household welfare outcomes. Therefore, program savings as a distinct product of MFI programs can be considered a major noncredit input. Program savings can earn interest, which can be invested in income-generating activities funded by microcredit loans. Members can also withdraw their voluntary savings (either partially or completely) and invest it in activities or asset acquisition.[5] The effect of such savings is distinct from that of credit.

Table 9.6 Impacts of Microfinance Borrowing and Participation on Household Outcomes by Program: Propensity-Score Weighted Household FE Estimates
N = 1,509

Microfinance input variable	Log per capita total income (Tk./month)	Log per capita total expenditure (Tk./month)	Log male labor supply (hours/month)	Log female labor supply (hours/month)	Log household nonland assets (Tk.)	Log household net worth (Tk.)	Boys' enrollment rate (ages 5–18)	Girls' enrollment rate (ages 5–18)
Borrowers, MFI								
Men, Grameen Bank	0.106	−0.058	0.065	0.502**	0.197*	0.124	0.223	0.058
	(0.82)	(−0.88)	(0.31)	(2.01)	(1.72)	(0.99)	(1.29)	(0.70)
Men, BRAC	−0.325	0.061*	0.197	−0.185	0.434	0.171	−0.223	0.032
	(−1.52)	(1.70)	(0.71)	(−1.18)	(1.57)	(0.96)	(−1.17)	(0.35)
Men, other MFIs	−0.073	0.069**	−0.075	−0.112	0.165**	0.051	−0.085	−0.010
	(−0.90)	(2.36)	(−0.54)	(−0.59)	(2.56)	(0.66)	(−1.39)	(−0.15)
Women, Grameen Bank	0.038*	−0.022	0.225*	0.385**	0.045	−0.126	0.092	0.187*
	(1.80)	(−0.55)	(1.64)	(2.19)	(0.49)	(−1.56)	(1.25)	(1.84)
Women, BRAC	0.105*	−0.003	0.092*	−0.030	0.016	−0.130	−0.069	0.025
	(1.68)	(−0.12)	(1.69)	(−0.20)	(0.25)	(−1.06)	(−1.38)	(0.35)
Women, other MFIs	−0.015	−0.020	0.120	−0.140	0.084	−0.031	0.052	0.013
	(−0.29)	(−0.76)	(1.50)	(−1.11)	(1.14)	(−0.58)	(1.52)	(0.28)
Participation, MFI								
Men, Grameen Bank	0.144*	0.039	0.499**	−0.105	0.060	0.051	−0.212	0.023
	(1.77)	(0.94)	(3.32)	(−0.43)	(0.48)	(0.35)	(−1.14)	(0.27)
Men, BRAC	−0.135	−0.032	−0.182	0.527**	−0.090	0.041	0.134	0.115
	(−1.26)	(−0.62)	(−0.60)	(2.51)	(−0.44)	(0.31)	(1.46)	(1.37)
Men, other MFIs	0.114	0.001	0.296*	0.130	0.121	0.139*	0.039	0.037
	(1.03)	(0.03)	(1.88)	(0.57)	(1.39)	(1.73)	(0.55)	(0.46)
Women, Grameen Bank	0.067	0.043	0.102	0.227**	0.142*	0.202**	−0.027	−0.187
	(0.89)	(0.95)	(0.76)	(2.14)	(1.63)	(2.13)	(−0.33)	(−0.73)
Women, BRAC	−0.092	−0.010	0.030	0.283*	0.154**	0.169**	0.097*	0.043*
	(−1.33)	(−0.30)	(0.20)	(1.87)	(2.26)	(2.26)	(1.98)	(1.69)
Women, other MFIs	0.013	−0.004	0.100	0.533**	−0.004	−0.001	−0.002	0.115**
	(0.27)	(−0.18)	(0.93)	(3.25)	(−0.07)	(−0.02)	(−0.06)	(2.91)
R^2	0.144	0.376	0.211	0.246	0.454	0.653	0.076	0.075

Sources: World Bank/BIDS survey 1991/92 and 1998/99; World Bank/InM survey 2010/11.

Note: Figures in parentheses are *t*-statistics based on standard errors clustered at the village level. Regressions include more control variables at the household level (e.g., age, sex, and education of household head) and village level (e.g., price of consumer goods; infrastructure, including schools and electricity availability; and proportion of irrigated land). FE = fixed effects; MFI = microfinance institution; BRAC = Bangladesh Rural Advancement Committee.

Significance level: * = 10 percent, ** = 5 percent or less.

By incorporating the effects of program duration and savings into equation (9.4), we derive the following equation:

$$\Delta Y_{it} = \beta \Delta X_{it} + \delta_f \Delta C_{ift} + \delta_m \Delta C_{imt} + \gamma_f \Delta D_{ift} + \gamma_m \Delta D_{imt}$$
$$+ \lambda_f \Delta S_{ift} + \lambda_m \Delta S_{imt} + \Delta \eta_{it} + \Delta \varepsilon_{it},$$

(9.6)

where the parameters γ and λ capture the effects of program duration and savings, respectively.

Like the effects of program participation, those of program duration and savings can also vary by MFI program. Given that Bangladesh's MFI programs follow similar strategies in providing credit and other services (e.g., group-based credit schemes), one might expect that their program impacts may not vary. Since this may not always be the case for all behavioral outcomes, we need to investigate whether program specificity matters.[6] To account for the program-specific effects of credit, savings, and length of membership, we use an outcome equation similar to (9.3).

Table 9.7 shows that the average duration of the men's MFI program participation was 4.4 years in 1991/92, increasing to 9.6 years by 2010/11. The corresponding figures for women participants were 4.2 years and 10.4 years, respectively. Participants' savings can be both voluntary and mandatory. Microcredit borrowers must deposit a fixed weekly amount as savings, on which the MFIs are to pay at least 6 percent annual interest. The findings show that, while program participants' savings grew over time, the annual growth rate was slow, at just 1 percent for men and 2 percent for women.[7] As expected, women borrowers, who had been with microcredit programs for a longer period than men and in much greater numbers, had larger savings than men borrowers. Over time, savings as a percentage of borrowing declined, and the decrease was higher for male members.

Table 9.8 shows program duration by credit source.[8] Statistics for the two major programs—Grameen Bank and BRAC—are reported separately, while those for the other MFIs are combined. As shown, program duration for both male and female participants is higher among Grameen Bank members than BRAC members; however, it is highest for the other MFIs. This finding is not unexpected since it captures the sum of duration for all MFIs

Table 9.7 Descriptive Statistics of Program Duration and Savings

Survey year	Program duration (years)		Program savings (Tk.)[a]	
	Men	Women	Men	Women
1991/92, N = 769	4.4	4.2	557.7 (0.07)	594.4 (0.07)
1998/99, N = 1,099	6.4	5.9	607.5 (0.08)	870.1 (0.07)
2010/11, N = 1,770	9.6	10.4	665.7 (0.03)	845.8 (0.06)

Sources: World Bank/BIDS survey 1991/92 and 1998/99; World Bank/InM survey 2010/11.
Note: This analysis is restricted to program participants. Figures in parentheses are share of program savings in cumulative loans over the 5 years preceding the survey year.
a. It was not possible to separate voluntary and mandatory savings from the data; thus, their aggregate is reported here.

Table 9.8 Descriptive Statistics of Program Duration (Years) by MFI
N = 1,612

	Grameen Bank		BRAC		Other MFIs[a]	
Survey year	Household males	Household females	Household males	Household females	Household males	Household females
1991/92	1.2	1.5	1.9	2.1	1.4	0.5
1998/99	1.8	2.4	1.5	2.3	3.2	1.5
2010/11	3.4	4.2	1.7	3.7	5.0	4.8

Sources: World Bank/BIDS survey 1991/92 and 1998/99; World Bank/InM survey 2010/11.
Note: This analysis is restricted to program participants. MFI = microfinance institution; BRAC = Bangladesh Rural Advancement Committee; BRDB = Bangladesh Rural Development Board.
a. For 1991/92, other MFIs refers to BRDB only (i.e., multiple program membership did not yet exist).

(except Grameen Bank and BRAC) in which individuals participate.[9] It should be noted that participation in multiple MFI programs has been a common phenomenon in Bangladesh since the late-1990s. In 2010, the average duration of program participation was 5.0 years for men and 4.8 years for women.

The noncredit inputs of microfinance do not affect household income, but they do affect the other welfare outcomes. Table 9.9 reports that microcredit savings by women participants have a significant positive impact on households' male and female labor supply, after controlling for credit and duration; a 10 percent increase in women's savings raises male labor supply by 0.2 percent and female labor supply by 0.4 percent. Interestingly, men's program duration increases female labor supply, but women's program duration has no effect on male or female labor supply. The largest impact of noncredit inputs is on household nonland assets, resulting from program savings by both men and women, with men's savings having the stronger effect. Household nonland assets are also affected by men's program duration; a one-year increase in duration raises household nonland assets by 1 percent. Household net worth is affected only by men's program savings. Women's program duration improves girls' school enrollment, while women's savings improve boys' school enrollment. For most outcomes, one observes that, in the presence of noncredit inputs, the credit effects of microfinance programs change little from the findings reported in chapter 4.

Table 9.10 presents the impacts of noncredit inputs by microfinance lender. As earlier observed in this chapter, participation itself does not impact household income at the aggregate level (table 9.3). However, after disaggregating noncredit inputs by individual MFI lending programs, we find that the duration of men's participation in Grameen Bank positively affects household income, with a one-year increase raising household per capita income by 1.3 percent. The household expenditure outcome is affected only by the duration of women's participation in BRAC. Like household income, male labor supply is positively affected by the duration of men's participation in Grameen Bank, with each additional year raising it by 3.3 percent. Households' male labor supply is also affected by the duration of women's participation in BRAC. Duration in other MFI programs also increases household labor supply, with men's duration affecting both male and

Table 9.9 **Impacts of Microfinance Credit and Noncredit Inputs on Household Outcomes: Propensity-Score Weighted Household FE Estimates**
N = 1,509

Microfinance input variable	Log per capita total income (Tk./month)	Log per capita total expenditure (Tk./month)	Log male labor supply (hours/month)	Log female labor supply (hours/month)	Log household nonland asset (Tk.)	Log household net worth (Tk.)	Boys' enrollment rate (ages 5–18)	Girls' enrollment rate (ages 5–18)
Log loans of household males (Tk.)	0.003 (0.22)	0.007 (1.16)	0.048** (2.93)	0.036* (1.66)	0.020* (1.74)	0.015* (1.72)	−0.117 (−1.19)	−0.165 (−1.62)
Log loans of household females (Tk.)	−0.006 (−0.93)	0.004* (1.76)	0.023** (2.03)	0.027** (2.09)	0.025** (3.37)	0.017** (2.40)	0.062 (1.13)	−0.010 (−0.15)
Program duration of household males (years)	−0.003 (−0.50)	−0.004 (−1.08)	0.014 (1.40)	0.018* (1.90)	0.010** (2.04)	0.001 (0.20)	0.012 (0.56)	−0.028 (−1.16)
Program duration of household females (years)	0.002 (0.62)	0.0001 (0.07)	0.006 (1.03)	0.010 (1.20)	0.004 (1.15)	0.001 (0.28)	−0.026 (−1.28)	0.065** (2.94)
Log program savings of household males (Tk.)	−0.008 (−0.74)	0.004 (0.94)	−0.008 (−0.56)	−0.011 (−0.54)	0.030** (3.21)	0.020** (2.48)	0.010 (0.44)	−0.004 (−0.15)
Log program savings of household females (Tk.)	0.007 (0.92)	−0.003 (−1.05)	0.023* (1.79)	0.040** (2.70)	0.017** (2.37)	−0.010 (−1.31)	0.015* (1.72)	0.022 (0.45)
R^2	0.138	0.376	0.211	0.242	0.457	0.652	0.324	0.229

Sources: World Bank/BIDS survey 1991/92 and 1998/99; World Bank/InM survey 2010/11.

Note: Figures in parentheses are *t*-statistics based on standard errors clustered at the village level. Regressions include more control variables at the household level (e.g., age, sex, and education of household head) and village level (e.g., price of consumer goods; infrastructure, including schools and electricity availability; and proportion of irrigated land). FE = fixed effects.

Significance level: * = 10 percent, ** = 5 percent or less.

Table 9.10 Impacts of Microfinance Credit and Noncredit Inputs on Household Outcomes by MFI Lender: Propensity-Score Weighted Household FE Estimates

N = 1,509

Microfinance input variable	Log per capita total income (Tk./month)	Log per capita total expenditure (Tk./month)	Log male labor supply (hours/month)	Log female labor supply (hours/month)	Log household nonland assets (Tk.)	Log household net worth (Tk.)	Boys' enrollment rate (ages 5–18)	Girls' enrollment rate (ages 5–18)
Household loans								
Log Grameen Bank, males (Tk.)	0.032	0.004	0.057	0.055	0.013	0.023	−0.017	−0.012
	(1.28)	(0.45)	(1.14)	(1.34)	(0.62)	(1.41)	(−0.79)	(−0.86)
Log Grameen Bank, females (Tk.)	0.003	0.005*	0.030**	0.017*	0.010	0.010*	0.006	−0.005
	(0.29)	(1.90)	(2.17)	(1.72)	(1.40)	(1.65)	(1.22)	(−0.060)
Log BRAC, males (Tk.)	−0.053	−0.007	0.042**	0.062	0.056**	0.008	−0.002	0.031**
	(−1.47)	(−0.76)	(2.18)	(1.56)	(2.52)	(0.53)	(−0.19)	(2.84)
Log BRAC, females (Tk.)	0.007	0.001	0.003	−0.001	0.018**	0.002	0.001	0.003
	(0.80)	(0.21)	(0.23)	(−0.08)	(2.21)	(0.22)	(0.01)	(0.53)
Log other MFIs, males (Tk.)	0.016	0.009	0.035**	0.029	0.013	0.013	0.001	0.003
	(1.35)	(1.41)	(2.05)	(1.22)	(1.22)	(1.27)	(0.20)	(0.27)
Log other MFIs, females (Tk.)	0.001	−0.002	0.016*	0.001	−0.002	−0.003	0.001	0.008*
	(0.13)	(−0.92)	(1.73)	(0.10)	(−0.03)	(−0.51)	(0.17)	(1.83)
Household duration (years)								
Grameen Bank, males	0.013**	0.001	0.033**	−0.006	0.010	0.005	−0.009	0.002
	(2.05)	(0.49)	(3.12)	(−0.44)	(1.39)	(0.08)	(−0.87)	(0.54)
Grameen Bank, females	0.002	0.002	−0.003	−0.005	0.001	−0.007	−0.002	0.001
	(0.54)	(0.89)	(−0.36)	(−0.52)	(0.24)	(−1.15)	(−0.52)	(0.15)
BRAC, males	−0.026	−0.002	−0.031	0.003	−0.001	0.005	0.010	0.012
	(−1.62)	(−0.62)	(−1.08)	(0.15)	(−0.04)	(0.59)	(1.24)	(1.52)

table continues next page

Table 9.10 Impacts of Microfinance Credit and Noncredit Inputs on Household Outcomes by MFI Lender: Propensity-Score Weighted Household FE Estimates
(continued)
N = 1,509

Microfinance input variable	Log per capita total income (Tk./month)	Log per capita total expenditure (Tk./month)	Log male labor supply (hours/month)	Log female labor supply (hours/month)	Log household nonland assets (Tk.)	Log household net worth (Tk.)	Boys' enrollment rate (ages 5–18)	Girls' enrollment rate (ages 5–18)
BRAC, females	−0.003	0.002*	0.015*	0.018	0.009	0.016**	0.005	−0.003
	(−0.61)	(1.88)	(1.80)	(1.54)	(1.44)	(2.80)	(1.36)	(−0.58)
Other MFIs, males	−0.005	−0.007	0.017*	0.032**	0.012*	−0.001	0.002	−0.002
	(−0.63)	(−1.22)	(1.63)	(2.42)	(1.84)	(−0.08)	(0.41)	(−0.04)
Other MFIs, females	0.002	−0.003	0.004	0.040**	0.004	0.005	−0.005	0.013**
	(0.46)	(−1.21)	(0.42)	(2.89)	(0.73)	(0.90)	(−0.09)	(3.24)
Household savings[a]								
Log program savings, males (Tk.)	−0.009	0.004	−0.004	−0.009	0.030**	0.021**	−0.002	0.003
	(−0.99)	(1.00)	(−0.30)	(−0.47)	(3.44)	(2.61)	(−0.34)	(0.36)
Log program savings, females (Tk.)	0.001	−0.002	0.022*	0.045**	0.024**	−0.003	0.008*	0.004
	(0.21)	(−0.56)	(1.80)	(3.19)	(3.86)	(−0.53)	(1.77)	(0.62)
R²	0.145	0.378	0.215	0.247	0.458	0.654	0.078	0.075

Sources: World Bank/BIDS survey 1991/92 and 1998/99; World Bank/InM survey 2010/11.
Note: Figures in parentheses are *t*-statistics based on standard errors clustered at the village level. Regressions include more control variables at the household level (e.g., age, sex, and education of household head) and village level (e.g., price of consumer goods; infrastructure, including schools and electricity availability; and proportion of irrigated land). MFI = microfinance institution; FE = fixed effects; BRAC = Bangladesh Rural Advancement Committee.
Significance level: * = 10 percent; ** = 5 percent or less.
a. Since savings data were not collected for individual lending programs, they are used in aggregate form in the regression.

female labor supply and women's affecting female labor supply only. Household nonland assets and net worth are also affected by the duration of participation in other MFI lending programs; each additional year of men's participation increases nonland assets by 1.2 percent, while each additional year of women's participation increases net worth by 1.6 percent.

The effects of program savings on household outcomes are similar to what were reported in table 9.9, with women's program savings having a bit stronger impact on households' female labor supply and nonland assets. As reported in table 9.10, a 10 percent increase in women's program savings increases female labor supply by 0.45 percent and household nonland assets by 0.24 percent. Women's savings also improves male labor supply and boys' school enrollment. Overall, these findings suggest that, in addition to the credit effects of microfinance programs, their noncredit inputs have distinct, substantial impacts on household welfare outcomes.

Summary

Microfinance programs in Bangladesh are not limited to financial services. They also provide an array of noncredit services (e.g., skills-based and extension training and marketing) that may equally promote individual and household welfare. Past research results on identifying the impact of noncredit inputs on welfare outcomes have been mixed. Some studies conducted in other developing countries have found that noncredit services play a substantial role, but most are not as encouraging as those conducted in the Bangladesh context.

The central problem in identifying the effects of noncredit microfinance services involves defining noncredit inputs. For example, it is difficult to identify the effects of noncredit training services if training types are not specified in the survey data. Also, Bangladesh's MFI programs offer a variety of noncredit services beyond training, making it difficult to disentangle the effects of borrowing and nonborrowing services. Using the long panel survey data, this chapter has attempted to document the role of noncredit inputs, distinct from borrowing inputs, on household welfare.

MFI program participation is defined by membership status. Nonborrowing program members can also benefit from savings and nonsavings inputs (e.g., training, awareness building, and social discipline activities). At any given time, a certain number of nonborrowing members are awaiting their turn at securing a loan; thus, program membership comprises changing proportions of simple nonborrowers and borrowers. But observing these changes within a single cross-sectional survey is not enough to understand the dynamics of program membership. Using the long panel survey data (three rounds spanning more than 20 years), we were able to capture these dynamics. Not only could we distinguish borrowing from nonborrowing status; we were also able to identify the duration of program membership as a category distinct from the cumulative amount of borrowing. The purpose was to discover whether length of membership matters, given that borrowing and nonborrowing members may be changing groups of households over any given period. Because improving savings behavior is a part of credit discipline that programs want to promote, we included the cumulative amount of savings as a separate category of noncredit inputs in a regression. We also identified the roles of credit versus noncredit inputs by microfinance program lender (e.g., Grameen Bank, BRAC, and other MFIs).

Interestingly, we found that both credit and noncredit inputs (nonborrowing status, membership length, and savings) matter. For augmenting household income and expenditure, credit services matter more for women members, while noncredit inputs matter more for men. This means that women are more credit constrained than men in terms of income-generating activities, and men need noncredit inputs more than women to improve welfare. For improving children's schooling, noncredit inputs matter more than credit for women, demonstrating the high added value of noncredit inputs for social and human capital investment.

Also, program specificity affects the role of credit and noncredit inputs. In terms of the impact of women's participation on overall household welfare, BRAC outperforms Grameen Bank and other MFIs in exerting noncredit effects, while Grameen Bank outperforms BRAC and other MFIs in exerting credit effects. For example, women's participation in BRAC increases female labor supply, household nonland assets and net worth, and school enrollment for both boys and girls. By comparison, women's participation in Grameen Bank raises female labor supply, as well as household nonland assets and net worth; while, for other MFIs, women's participation increases only female labor supply and girls' school enrollment.

In addition, length of program membership has an identifiable effect on welfare, independent of the positive effects of borrowing. For example, a 10 percent increase in the duration of men's membership raises household nonland assets by 0.1 percentage point, while a similar percent increase in the duration of women's membership raises girls' schooling by 0.7 percentage point.

Furthermore, savings play a critical role in raising household welfare, independent of credit and noncredit (measured by membership length) inputs. Men's savings helps to increase households' nonland assets and net worth, while women's savings increases male and female labor supply for a higher level of productive activity, household nonland assets, and boys' schooling. These effects are independent of certain positive effects of credit and length of program membership. In fact, in some cases, savings contributes more than borrowing to household welfare. For example, a 10 percent increase in men's borrowing raises household nonland assets by 0.20 percent and net worth by 0.15 percent. In contrast, a 10 percent increase in men's savings raises nonland assets by 0.30 percent and net worth by 0.20 percent.

Summing up, noncredit inputs matter for microfinance program members, sometimes more so than borrowing. Beyond credit, the array of noncredit services provided by the MFIs, including skills training and information networking, are critical to helping poor rural people to gain access to publicly provided services and thus realize benefits for themselves, their families, and society at large.

Notes

1. Though Grameen Bank also provides awareness-building training, it does not offer skills-based training to the extent covered by BRAC.

2. The percentage of borrowers that received noncredit training becomes negligible if Grameen Bank and the Association for Social Advancement (ASA), two large MFIs without explicit training programs, are included.

3. Occupational development skills and marketing training are quite important to MFIs, given that they can contribute directly to the productivity of the activities supported by microcredit loans.

4. This does not suggest that the participation effects will be higher than the credit or noncredit effects.

5. Members can also withdraw their mandatory savings once their loans are paid off.

6. In a cross-sectional analysis of 1991/92 data, Pitt and Khandker (1998) observed that some of the effects of borrowing were higher for Grameen Bank than for BRAC and BRDB's RD-12; however, this was not the case using two-period data analysis for the consumption and poverty effects of credit, as shown in Khandker (2005).

7. This shows that members withdrew money from the voluntary portion of their savings during the course of their loan term.

8. Savings information by credit program was not collected and thus is not available.

9. The aggregate duration from all programs is about the same as what is reported in table 9.7.

Bibliography

Alam, Saad. 2013. "The Impact of Credit and Non-Credit Aspects on Self-Employment Profit: A Comparison of Microcredit Programs and Commercial Lenders in Rural Bangladesh." Journal of Developing Areas 47: 123–45.

Bruhn, Miriam, Gabriel Lara Ibarra, and David McKenzie. 2014. "The Minimal Impact of a Large-Scale Financial Education Program in Mexico City." *Journal of Development Economics* 108: 184–89.

Bruhn, Miriam, and Bilal Zia. 2013. "Stimulating Managerial Capital in Emerging Markets: The Impact of Business Training for Young Entrepreneurs." *Journal of Development Effectiveness* 5 (2): 232–66.

Collins, J. Michael. 2013. "The Impacts of Mandatory Financial Education: Evidence from a Randomized Field Study." *Journal of Economic Behavior and Organization* 95: 146–58.

de Mel, Suresh, David McKenzie, and Christopher Woodruff. 2008a. "Returns to Capital in Microenterprises: Evidence from a Field Experiment." *Quarterly Journal of Economics* 123 (4): 1329–72.

———. 2008b. "Who Are the Microenterprise Owners? Evidence from Sri Lanka on Tokman v. de Soto." Policy Research Working Paper 4635, World Bank, Washington, DC.

Epstein, Marc J., and Kristi Yuthas. 2014. *Measuring and Improving Social Impacts: A Guide for Nonprofits, Companies, and Impact Investors.* Oakland, CA: Berrett-Koehler Publishers.

Faruqee, Rashid, and Syed Badruddoza. 2011. "Microfinance in Bangladesh: Past, Present, and Future." InM Occasional Paper, Institute of Microfinance, Dhaka.

Karlan, Dean, and Martin Valdivia. 2015. "Business Training Plus for Female Entrepreneurship? Short and Medium-Term Experimental Evidence from Peru." *Journal of Development Economics* 113 (C): 33–51.

Khandker, Shahidur R. 2005. "Microfinance and Poverty: Evidence Using Panel Data from Bangladesh." *World Bank Economic Review* 19 (2): 263–86.

McKernan, Signe-Mary. 2002. "The Impact of Microcredit Programs on Self-Employment Profits: Do Non-Credit Program Aspects Matter?" *Review of Economics and Statistics* 84 (1): 93–115.

Pitt, Mark M., and Shahidur R. Khandker. 1998. "The Impact of Group-Based Credit Programs on Poor Households in Bangladesh: Does the Gender of Participants Matter?" *Journal of Political Economy* 106 (June): 958–96.

PKSF (Palli Karma-Sahayak Foundation). 2007–12. *Annual Report*. Dhaka: Palli Karma-Sahayak Foundation.

Yunus, Muhammad. 1999. *Banker to the Poor: Micro-Lending and the Battle against World Poverty*. New York: Public Affairs.

CHAPTER 10

Does Microfinance Pay Off?

Introduction

Rural nonfarm (RNF) enterprise growth is pivotal to poverty reduction in many developing countries, given that the sector has backward and forward linkages to the farm and modern sectors, which can lead to broad-based rural growth (e.g., Deininger and Jin 2007; Khandker, Samad, and Ali 2013). In the 1990s, RNF enterprises surpassed agricultural activities as a source of Bangladesh's income and employment growth, at 4.2 percent and 2.7 percent versus 0.3 percent and 1 percent, respectively (World Bank 2004). The main driver of higher RNF employment was not productivity growth in agriculture but the RNF enterprise sector itself. Employment in manufacturing and other nonagricultural occupations had a substantial premium over daily wage work in agriculture, even after controlling for differences in individual and regional characteristics (World Bank 2004). Businesses with fewer than 10 employees dominate the sector. Survey data from the 2001 and 2003 rounds of the Economic Census and the 2005 National Report of the Bangladesh Bureau of Statistics (BBS) suggest that 64 percent of enterprises and half of employment in manufacturing, trade, and service enterprises are in rural areas (Islam and others 2011). Furthermore, microenterprises comprise 99 percent of the country's RNF enterprises and account for nearly 90 percent of workers in RNF enterprises. These statistics suggest that RNF productivity growth, especially in enterprise activities, is necessary for addressing Bangladesh's rural income growth and poverty reduction for the foreseeable future.

Because microfinance institutions (MFIs) have played a critical role in initiating and sustaining RNF enterprise growth in Bangladesh (chapter 2), any evaluation of the sector must consider whether microfinance pays off over time. That is, the sector's growth and sizable effect on income, employment, and poverty depend on whether MFI borrowers make enough money from their investments to not only pay off their debt but also contribute to promoting growth of their businesses. Thus, further financing of RNF enterprises through microfinance depends critically on the rate of return to capital investment.

Diversification of the RNF enterprise sector is important for supporting higher incomes for a variety of reasons. In cases where large numbers of microfinance borrowers are engaged in traditional activities owing to limited markets and skills, the rates of return to investment supported by the MFIs may decline. Thus, an investigation of this dynamic sector, particularly the rates of return to investment, is critical to fostering the sector's growth and understanding whether MFI-financed investment is worth supporting on an ongoing basis. It is also hypothesized that substantial complementary investments in public infrastructure (e.g., roads, electricity, and markets) are necessary to facilitate higher returns and growth of RNF enterprises.

This chapter thus seeks to understand the growth and rates of return on MFI-supported RNF enterprises in rural Bangladesh over the past decade. To identify future sources of growth in the RNF enterprise sector, alternate estimation techniques are used to derive the relative returns for various sector components. The chapter examines the demand- and supply-side dimensions of major constraints encountered by the sector, as well as opportunities for growth, assessing the roles of public infrastructure investment and other factors that influence the productivity of RNF enterprises. The sector's forward and backward linkages with agriculture and the diversification of income-earning activities within the sector are also addressed.

Calculating the Costs of RNF Enterprise Operations

Before analyzing the RNF enterprise sector's profitability and return in detail, we must first examine the various types of costs related to enterprise operations. Table 10.1 presents basic statistics on cost, revenue, and profit for major microenterprise sectors over time, using data from consecutive rounds of the Household Income and Expenditure Survey (HIES) (table 10.1a), and the long panel survey (table 10.1b).

Definitions of Inputs and Productivity Indicators

Cost comprises operating and family labor costs. Operating cost, defined as the costs incurred by the enterprise, includes all expenses for conducting enterprise activities (e.g., rent, raw materials, power sources [e.g., electricity or kerosene], finished goods purchased for reselling, hired labor, transport, interest payment, and taxes). Family labor, which is unpaid, is included in operating cost because of the opportunity cost involved. The cost of family labor is imputed (calculated) by multiplying the total man days of labor provided by family members by the prevailing daily nonfarm wage in the village.[1] Total enterprise asset, consisting of working capital and the value of the enterprise, is used to calculate the enterprise's rate of return.[2] Profit is defined as the revenue generated in 12 months, minus all costs (including family labor cost). Profit margin is defined by the profit as a percentage of the revenue, while rate of return is calculated by dividing the profit by the total enterprise asset.

Opinions vary on how to measure rates of return from microenterprises since many RNF enterprises are informal and the cost of their inputs and outputs can be difficult to assess. The most common productivity measure used is the rate of

Table 10.1 Microenterprise Inputs and Productivity by Sector

a. Using HIES data

Input/productivity indicators	Manufacturing and processing	Transport	Trade	Services	Miscellaneous activities	All activities
2000 (N = 1,427)						
Operating cost (Tk./year)[a]	125,850.8	43,580.4	105,655.5	158,918.9	119,173.0	138,497.0
Family labor cost (imputed) (Tk./year)[b]	5,262.4	4,243.2	6,148.4	5,950.2	5,097.6	5,619.0
Value of the enterprise asset (Tk.)	82,046.1	134,102.0	450,225.8	121,976.2	78,898.2	121,537.8
Revenue (Tk./year)	161,406.8	76,204.2	202,254.1	206,668.1	156,504.5	183,408.2
Profit (Tk./year)[c]	30,337.4	30,230.3	118,330.9	42,862.6	32,823.0	40,903.5
Profit margin (%)[d]	35.5	61.6	44.3	26.6	38.5	32.7
Rate of return (%)[e]	66.6	75.8	59.9	61.3	66.2	63.8
2005 (N = 1,426)						
Operating cost (Tk./year)[a]	179,708.3	17,683.9	214,706.8	215,058.3	10,718.8	193,208.7
Family labor cost (imputed) (Tk./year)[b]	10,423.7	5,113.1	10,110.5	7,795.9	7,562.6	7,942.6
Value of the enterprise asset (Tk.)	65,783.5	36,464.2	123,537.4	79,658.5	56,944.0	75,458.1
Revenue (Tk./year)	220,174.2	39,119.9	246,975.2	254,255.0	132,028.1	230,789.4
Profit (Tk./year)[c]	32,399.8	16,651.8	24,461.2	32,078.7	23,247.2	30,497.9
Profit margin (%)[d]	39.0	61.6	20.0	20.9	28.8	25.7
Rate of return (%)[e]	64.1	75.7	54.2	62.5	54.0	62.8
2010 (N = 1,909)						
Operating cost (Tk./year)[a]	115,637.7	23,861.8	57,037.3	180,705.6	95,778.3	140,388.7
Family labor cost (imputed) (Tk./year)[b]	8,410.7	6,134.3	8,665.5	9,610.7	19,220.5	9,847.2
Value of the enterprise asset (Tk.)	73,327.8	86,196.9	67,478.4	120,897.9	107,755.1	107,303.9
Revenue (Tk./year)	149,489.2	54,570.3	88,782.1	223,631.1	134,237.4	178,780.4
Profit (Tk./year)[c]	32,399.8	16,651.8	24,461.2	32,078.7	23,247.2	31,263.9
Profit margin (%)[d]	31.8	62.3	37.9	31.5	42.4	36.7
Rate of return (%)[e]	47.7	68.3	52.6	50.0	46.6	51.9

b. Using long panel survey data

Input/productivity indicators	Manufacturing and processing	Transport	Agricultural trade	Non-agricultural trade	Services	All activities
1991/92 (N = 790)						
Operating cost (Tk./year)[a]	80,923.0	4,857.0	154,758.5	135,787.0	51,884.1	100,700.3
Family labor cost (imputed) (Tk./year)[b]	4,745.9	6,614.5	7,278.1	7,240.9	7,166.1	6,494.6
Value of the enterprise asset (Tk.)	19,555.4	36,973.8	75,716.7	36,619.7	44,823.4	41,392.2
Revenue (Tk./year)	81,078.1	18,798.0	200,677.2	164,593.9	82,820.2	124,592.4
Profit (Tk./year)[c]	8,099.8	8,395.5	48,066.4	31,501.2	25,425.5	25,636.0
Profit margin (%)[d]	22.3	34.4	24.3	19.0	38.1	24.4
Rate of return (%)[e]	38.0	25.8	43.3	45.7	54.8	41.7

table continues next page

Table 10.1 **Microenterprise Inputs and Productivity by Sector** *(continued)*

Input/productivity indicators	Manufacturing and processing	Transport	Agricultural trade	Non-agricultural trade	Services	All activities
1998/99 (N = 987)						
Operating cost (Tk./year)[a]	118,213.8	3,287.2	254,757.0	165,170.7	40,546.6	123,177.6
Family labor cost (imputed) (Tk./year)[b]	11,756.9	12,076.6	10,616.1	13,827.2	7,727.5	12,350.3
Value of the enterprise asset (Tk.)	41,971.4	8,502.8	29,423.0	25,955.2	19,541.7	23,485.4
Revenue (Tk./year)	143,831.0	15,383.3	281,452.9	194,309.6	57,760.8	146,391.4
Profit (Tk./year)[c]	15,467.8	2,151.8	16,487.6	16,625.9	10,196.8	12,274.5
Profit margin (%)[d]	13.5	13.4	7.2	9.2	29.5	11.5
Rate of return (%)[e]	26.1	21.5	50.4	53.6	38.4	40.3
2010/11 (N = 1,081)						
Operating cost (Tk./year)[a]	349,240.5	6,648.8	158,378.2	114,839.6	58,616.4	103,201.8
Family labor cost (imputed) (Tk./year)[b]	7,832.7	17,761.8	3,317.5	3,065.8	4,260.4	8,295.5
Value of the enterprise asset (Tk.)	122,617.8	7,132.2	239,236.7	89,822.5	109,240.9	91,620.4
Revenue (Tk./year)	299,532.6	21,392.7	308,305.3	209,761.3	119,526.9	168,387.4
Profit (Tk./year)[c]	40,416.4	2,098.9	161,360.1	105,822.1	60,732.7	74,345.1
Profit margin (%)[d]	50.5	5.6	68.0	56.7	65.6	41.9
Rate of return (%)[e]	64.2	10.9	59.4	81.3	68.0	56.7

Sources: HIES 2000, 2005, and 2010; World Bank/BIDS survey 1991/92 and 1998/99; World Bank/InM survey 2010/11.
Note: Figures are consumer price index–adjusted: 2000 = 100 (table 10.1a); 1991/92 = 100 (table 10.1b).
a. Operating cost includes all business expenses (e.g., raw materials, rent, fuel, hired labor, and other incurred costs).
b. Family labor cost is calculated by multiplying man-days spent by family members by the prevailing wage rate.
c. Profit equals revenue minus operating cost, including family labor cost.
d. Profit margin is defined by the profit as a percentage of the revenue.
e. Rate of return is calculated by dividing profit by the value of enterprise assets.

return on assets (ROA), which is the enterprise profit as a percentage of enterprise assets. The ROA measures how well the enterprise utilizes assets to generate profits. Creditors and investors making lending or investment decisions often use this productivity measure as proxy for repayment and comparison with the opportunity cost of capital.

The definition of capital assets varies by study. For example, the Living Standards Measurement Study (LSMS) generally collects information on fixed assets (e.g., land, buildings, equipment and machinery, furniture, small or large tools, vehicles, and other durable goods), raw materials, and finished-goods inventory but not financial working capital, such as cash (Grosh and Glewwe 2000). In their study on return to capital in Sri Lanka, de Mel, McKenzie, and Woodruff (2009) include both fixed and working capital. In their comprehensive analysis of rate of return using the Thai Monthly Survey, Samphantharak and Townsend (2012) present 10 measures of household enterprise income or assets and their associated ROA; this strategy allows for studying the sensitivity of ROA when one component of either profit or assets is changed.

Following Samphantharak and Townsend (2012), we began by calculating the profit (accounting for the cost of family labor). We then took a measure of capital assets by combining the working capital and the imputed value of the enterprise. Finally, we divided the profit by this imputed value of assets to generate the rate of return. We also identified profit margin as a second measure of productivity. Profit margin is an indicator of the cost-effectiveness of an enterprise's performance (i.e., its pricing strategies and how well it controls costs) across sectors. Thus, a higher profit margin indicates a higher margin of safety.

Results by Microenterprise Sector

According to the HIES, the transport sector had the highest profit margin, at about 62 percent for all three survey years (2000, 2005, and 2010), indicating that the sector has performed well (table 10.1a). Relative to other major sectors, transport also earned a higher overall ROA, probably because of previously improved road infrastructure, which subsequently led to better returns from investment in transport vehicles and transport-related businesses. By contrast, services and trade sectors had the lowest overall profit margins, indicating room for improvement. For the services sector, the ROAs for the three survey years (2000, 2005, 2010) were 61 percent, 62 percent, and 50 percent, respectively; corresponding figures for the trade sector were 60 percent, 54 percent, and 53 percent. Based on its relatively low profit margin, the manufacturing sector appears exposed to high risk; the ROA for this sector tends toward the average for all enterprises in all activities.

According to the long panel survey data, nonagricultural trade had the highest ROA, nearly doubling over the 20-year period (from 46 percent in 1991/92 to 54 percent in 1998/99 to 81 percent in 2010/11 [table 10.1b]). The services sector had the highest overall profit margin, increasing from 38 percent in 1991/92 to 66 percent in 2010/11. The manufacturing and processing sector also fared well; its ROA was 38 percent in 1991/92, falling to 26 percent in 1998/99, and rising to 64 percent in 2010/11. Over the period, the overall average ROA across sectors rose by about 15 percentage points (from 42 percent in 1991/92 to 57 percent in 2010/11). Interestingly, the average ROA across all sectors was similar for both surveys, at 52 percent (HIES 2010) and 57 percent (long panel survey, 2010/11). Over time, however, the average return increased based on the long panel survey data (from 42 percent in 1991/92 to 57 percent in 2010/11) but declined according to the HIES data (from 64 percent in 2000 to 52 percent in 2010).

Results by Household Borrowing Status

For all three survey years, input and output variables were higher for microcredit nonborrowers, possibly because nonborrower households were wealthier to begin with (table 10.2).

Our estimates of average ROAs for microfinance participants are as high as those for nonborrowers. Also these return estimates are consistent with the findings of other studies in developing countries. For example, Kremer and others (2013)

Table 10.2 Microenterprise Inputs and Productivity by Microcredit Borrowing

Input/productivity indicator	1991/92 (N = 790)		1998/99 (N = 987)		2010/11 (N = 1,081)	
	Microcredit borrowers	Non-borrowers	Microcredit borrowers	Non-borrowers	Microcredit borrowers	Non-borrowers
Operating cost (Tk./year)[a]	79,503.1	112,365.0	92,173.4	153,411.9	92,173.4	183,914.7
Family labor cost (imputed) (Tk./year)[b]	5,824.0	6,863.6	11,595.5	13,086.3	11,595.5	7,442.4
Value of the enterprise asset (Tk.)	27,250.2	49,244.7	16,567.5	30,231.6	56,567.5	149,499.4
Revenue (Tk./year)	96,773.6	139,900.9	111,319.9	180,591.9	111,319.9	273,664.3
Profit (Tk./year)[c]	17,699.1	30,003.6	8,920.6	15,545.1	8,920.6	109,965.4
Profit margin (%)[d]	22.6	25.4	10.9	12.1	10.9	47.1
Rate of return (%)[e]	44.6	40.1	38.6	42.1	38.6	56.2

Sources: World Bank/BIDS survey 1991/92 and 1998/99; World Bank/InM survey 2010/11.
Note: Figures are consumer price index–adjusted (1991/92 = 100).
a. Operating cost includes all business expenses (e.g., raw materials, rent, fuel, hired labor, and other incurred costs).
b. Family labor cost is calculated by multiplying man-days spent by family members by the prevailing wage rate.
c. Profit equals revenue minus operating cost, including family labor cost.
d. Profit margin is defined by the profit as a percentage of the revenue.
e. Rate of return is calculated by dividing profit by the value of enterprise assets.

take advantage of the characteristics of the retail industry in rural Kenya to create estimates and bounds on the rate of return to inventory capital in a set of retail firms. Using administrative data on whether firms purchased enough to take advantage of quantity discounts from wholesalers, they estimate a lower bound on rates of return for the median shop of greater than 100 percent per year. McKenzie and Woodruff (2006) similarly find large returns to small entrepreneurs. Exploiting county-level variation in credit supply due to the Community Reinvestment Act, Zinman (2002) estimates gross rates of return to capital in the United States in the range of 20–58 percent per year. Anagol and Udry (2006) take the elegant approach of using data on prices of used car parts of varying expected lifetimes to estimate a lower bound to the opportunity cost of capital of 60 percent for taxi drivers in Ghana. Banerjee and Duflo (2005) compute the rate of return to capital in the economy at about 22 percent in India, while Caselli and Feyrer (2007) calculate the marginal product of capital at 19 percent at most for Sri Lanka.

Analyzing Rates of Return: Production or Profit Function Approaches?

Alternative approaches and estimation techniques may be used to derive the relative ROA for various components of the RNF enterprise sector. Several studies have measured marginal returns, as opposed to average returns, through experimental design (e.g., by increasing capital stocks through cash or capital grants). When natural experiments were not possible, other studies have estimated returns to capital using a production function (typically translog and Cobb-Douglas) with ordinary least squares (OLS) regression or instrumenting capital with price. Using this method, Bigsten and others (2000) estimated returns to physical and human capital in five African countries, finding rates of return in a range of 10–32 percent. McKenzie and Woodruff (2003), estimating both para-metric and nonparametric relationships between firm earnings and capital, found enormous returns to capital for small firms with less than US$200 invested; the monthly rate of return of 15 percent was well above the informal interest rates of pawn shops or those of microcredit programs (at about 3 percent). With investment, their estimated monthly rates of return declined but still remained high, at 7–10 percent for firms in the US$200–500 investment range and 5 per-cent for those in the US$500–1,000 range.

However, the production-function approaches suffer from methodological weaknesses. First, the investment levels are likely to be correlated with omitted variables, such as unobserved entrepreneurial ability. For example, in a world without credit constraints, investment will be positively correlated with the expected returns to investment, generating a positive ability bias (Olley and Pakes 1996). McKenzie and Woodruff (2003, 2006) attempted to control for managerial ability by including the firm owner's wage in previous employment. But this may only partly resolve the issue if individuals choose to enter self-employment with a higher expected return than their productivity in a salaried job. Conversely, there could be a negative ability bias if capital is allocated to firms in order to avoid failure. Taking advantage of a redefinition of the so-called priority sector in India,[3] Banerjee and Duflo (2004) used a variation in the eligi-bility rule over time to construct an instrumental variable for access to capital and estimate the impact of working capital on sales and profits. They found estimated returns to capital of at least 74 percent for these firms. A study con-ducted in the Philippines found that the net return to the fixed assets rate was 10 percent for farm machinery products and more than 30 percent for ready-made garment products (Onchan 2001). The same study found the rate of return on total capital ranging from 10 percent (for farm carts) to 44 percent (for ready-made garment products).

To compare and contrast the findings, we utilized both production- and profit-function approaches to estimate the rate of return to capital. Unlike the cross-sectional approach, which suffers from an omitted variable or simultaneity bias, the panel data–based approach has a number of advantages. It follows a standard production framework model, where we derive profit as revenue less all variable costs, which is a function of fixed assets and other attributes (at the household, enterprise, and community level) that can influence the production technology and environment in which the enterprise operates. Thus, the estimated marginal returns, unlike the average returns calculated in the earlier section using produc-tivity measures, are net of the effects of factors influencing the production and profitability of an enterprise other than capital.[4] We consider the following profit equation in semilogarithmic form:

$$\ln \Pi_{kjt} = \alpha \tau_t + \beta \sum_k K_{kjt} + \gamma H_{kjt} + \mu_{kj} + \eta_{jk} + \eta_{jt} + \varepsilon_{jkt}, \qquad (10.1)$$

where Π_{kjt} is the profit of k-th type of enterprise located in j-th upazila in year t; τ is the year variable; K_{kjt} is the fixed assets utilized in the enterprise; and H_{kjt} is the vector of household-, enterprise-, and village-level characteristics. Profit is also influenced by unobserved enterprise or household-level heterogeneity (μ_{kj}), upazila-level enterprise-specific heterogeneity (η_{jk}), and upazila-level heterogeneity (η_{jt}) common to all households living in an upazila but varying over time. Upazila-level initial conditions are applied to control for time-varying unobserved heterogeneity. Yet the unobserved household-level heterogeneity, such as entrepreneurial ability, may not be controlled for using the HIES data analysis.

But this is not the case using the long panel data analysis. Since we have three observations for each household and its enterprise characteristics, we have a unique data set that can help to control for the unobserved sources of household-level heterogeneity, such as entrepreneurial ability. Thus, a profit or production function is estimated similar to equation (10.1) using household-level panel data. We also use initial household- and village-level characteristics as an additional control for time-varying heterogeneity for a long panel survey.

Production Function Estimates

Table 10.3 presents the Cobb-Douglas type of production-function estimates, using both the HIES and long panel survey data. For the HIES, we used the upazila-level fixed effects (FE) to reduce the role of upazila-level unobserved characteristics influencing the production estimates, which is subject to bias due to omitted household-level entrepreneurial ability. This problem does not arise in the case of the long panel survey, as we used the household-level FE method to estimate the role of capital and other factors in RNF enterprise production. The HIES data fit slightly better than the long panel survey data: the R^2 is 0.82 for the HIES and 0.73 for the long panel survey.

Estimates of the response elasticity of output with respect to such factors as capital and labor are similar for both sets of results. For example, the output response elasticity of capital is 0.35 for the HIES and 0.28 for the long panel survey; that is, a 10 percent increase in the capital stock can increase revenue (a measure of output) by as much as 3.5 percent using the HIES data and 2.8 percent using long panel data. Also, a 10 percent increase in nonlabor input (operating cost) increases output by about 3 percent for both the HIES and long panel survey. Household participation in microcredit participation has no impact on enterprise revenue.[5]

The RNF enterprise sector's output is more sensitive to nonlabor than labor inputs; thus, we observe a much lower response elasticity for labor.[6] Using the long panel survey, a 10 percent increase in nonlabor input increases output by 3.0 percent, while a similar increase in hired labor input increases output by about 0.4 percent.

Profit Function Estimates

Table 10.4 presents the profit-function estimates, showing the net effects of enterprise, enterprise-owning households, and village characteristics on enterprise profit. Like estimating the production function, we take the log of the profit variable to interpret the coefficients as elasticity. Enterprise characteristics

Table 10.3 Fixed-Effects Estimates of RNF Enterprise Production Function

Log revenue in Tk./year

Explanatory variable	HIES data (N = 2,732)	Long panel survey data (N = 2,842)
Year is 2005 (1 = yes, 0 = no)	−0.783 (−0.93)	n.a.
Year is 2010 (1 = yes, 0 = no)	−1.097 (−1.34)	n.a.
Year is 1998/99 (1 = yes, 0 = no)	n.a.	−0.646 (−0.75)
Year is 2010/11 (1 = yes, 0 = no)	n.a.	−0.655 (−0.64)
Activity type[a]		
Manufacturing and processing	−0.020 (−0.25)	0.428** (4.16)
Trade	−0.072 (−0.68)	n.a.
Agricultural trade	n.a.	1.060** (8.99)
Nonagricultural trade	n.a.	0.743** (7.72)
Services	0.016 (0.23)	0.565** (4.80)
Transport	−0.013 (−0.14)	n.a.
Log value of enterprise capital asset (Tk.)	0.347** (15.32)	0.281** (15.66)
Log of cost of hired labor (Tk./year)	0.035** (9.62)	0.030** (4.89)
Log of imputed cost of family labor (Tk./year)	0.019 (1.55)	0.018** (2.62)
Log of operating cost (excluding labor cost) (Tk./year)	0.326** (20.01)	0.285** (13.42)
Household is microcredit borrower	n.a.	−0.017 (−0.43)
R^2	0.823	0.729

Sources: HIES 2000, 2005, and 2010; World Bank/BIDS survey 1991/92 and 1998/99; World Bank/InM survey 2010/11.

Note: Fixed-effects are estimated at the upazila level for the HIES data and at the household level for the long panel survey data. Figures in parentheses are *t*-statistics. Regression also controls for enterprise characteristics (e.g., enterprise age, months of operation per year, whether it is home based, and household and community characteristics), as well as exogenous characteristics of the initial year and household occupation dummies based on major income source. n.a. = not applicable; RNF = rural nonfarm; HIES = Household Income and Expenditure Survey.

Significance level: * = 10 percent, ** = 5 percent.

a. Excluded categories are miscellaneous (HIES data) and transport (long panel survey data).

included in the regression are years of operation and its squared term, whether the enterprise is registered, and whether it is home based. We also control for the number of months of operation per year, share of hired labor among workers, type of enterprise activity (dummy variables are used for manufacturing and processing, transport, trade, services, and other miscellaneous activity), and

Table 10.4 Fixed-Effects Estimates of RNF Enterprise Profit Function
Log profit in Tk./year

Explanatory variable	HIES data (N = 2,732)	Long panel survey data (N = 2,842)
Year is 2005 (1 = yes, 0 = no)	5.621* (1.79)	n.a.
Year is 2010 (1 = yes, 0 = no)	4.870 (1.61)	n.a.
Year is 1998/99 (1 = yes, 0 = no)	n.a.	6.526 (1.56)
Year is 2010/11 (1 = yes, 0 = no)	n.a.	7.176 (1.58)
Activity type[a]		
Manufacturing and processing	0.640** (2.69)	1.442** (4.25)
Trade	0.570 (1.57)	n.a.
Agricultural trade	n.a.	1.506** (6.01)
Nonagricultural trade	n.a.	1.794** (7.21)
Services	0.361* (1.77)	1.639** (4.07)
Transport	0.822** (3.89)	n.a.
Log value of enterprise capital asset (Tk.)	0.997** (19.23)	1.853** (34.34)
Household is microcredit borrower	n.a.	0.103* (1.66)
R^2	0.402	0.611

Sources: HIES 2000, 2005, and 2010; World Bank/BIDS survey 1991/92 and 1998/99; World Bank/InM survey 2010/11.
Note: Fixed-effects are estimated at the upazila level for the HIES data and at the household level for the long panel survey data. Figures in parentheses are *t*-statistics. Regression also controls for enterprise characteristics (e.g., enterprise age, months of operation per year, whether it is home based, and household and community characteristics), as well as exogenous characteristics of the initial year and household occupation dummies based on major income source. n.a. = not applicable; RNF = rural nonfarm; HIES = Household Income and Expenditure Survey.
Significance level: * = 10 percent, ** = 5 percent.
a. Excluded categories are miscellaneous (HIES data) and transport (long panel survey data).

sources of start-up capital (e.g., own resources, loan from microcredit, loan from commercial bank, and loan from relatives and friends).

Enterprise assets are found to have a significant impact on enterprise profit. The estimated capital sensitivity of profit in the RNF sector is quite high for both survey types and higher using the long panel estimates. For example, a 10 percent increase in enterprise capital increases profit by at least the same amount (10.0 percent in the case of HIES and 18.5 percent in the case of the long panel survey). Unlike the production function, the profit function plays a statistically significant role in microcredit participation. More specifically, microcredit borrowing raises enterprise profit by 10 percent. The profit function fits well for both data sets; but unlike the production-function estimates, the long panel data estimates (R^2 equals 0.61) fit slightly better than the HIES data estimates (R^2 equals 0.40).

Marginal Returns to Capital and Other Inputs

The returns to enterprise capital reported in tables 10.3 and 10.4 are in elasticity form (log-log); that is, they do not report marginal return on enterprise capital or labor.[7] Marginal return is defined as the increase in profit or output level for an increase of additional unit of capital or other inputs. Table 10.5 reports the marginal returns to enterprise capital and labor inputs based on the findings reported in tables 10.3 and 10.4. Marginal return is reported for each activity, as well as for all activities combined.

Using the profit estimates, the marginal return to capital for all activities combined is Tk. 11.9 for the HIES data (table 10.5a); that is, for a Tk. 100 increase in enterprise capital, the annual profit rises by as much as Tk. 11.9. In contrast, the marginal return on revenue using the production-function estimates is Tk. 16.6 for capital and Tk. 50.6 for labor,[8] meaning that the revenue increases by up to Tk. 16.6 for a Tk. 100 increase in capital and by nearly Tk. 51 for a Tk. 100 increase in labor. From the profit-function estimates, service activities have the highest marginal return, at about 24 percent, followed by manufacturing and

Table 10.5 Marginal Returns of Microenterprises by Activity Type

a. Using HIES data

Activity type	Tk. revenue/Tk. 100 capital	Tk. revenue/Tk. 100 labor cost	Tk. profit/Tk. 100 capital
Manufacturing and processing	6.9	88.6	4.3
Trade	0.9	16.6	0.7
Services	32.5	97.6	23.5
Transport	13.2	24.5	3.9
Miscellaneous small activities	7.2	43.9	2.8
All activities	16.6	50.6	11.9

b. Using long panel survey data

Activity type	Tk. revenue/Tk. 100 Capital			Tk. revenue/Tk. 100 labor cost			Tk. profit/Tk. 100 capital		
	Borrowers	Non-borrowers	All	Borrowers	Non-borrowers	All	Borrowers	Non-borrowers	All
Manufacturing and processing	7.4	12.2	9.7	8.4	10.7	9.5	17.4	17.3	17.3
Agricultural trade	7.2	12.3	9.6	13.6	18.1	15.8	23.0	23.6	23.2
Nonagricultural trade	12.8	16.5	15.7	33.5	37.6	35.6	60.5	53.3	55.8
Services	2.6	4.8	3.6	3.6	5.2	4.3	7.1	8.4	7.6
Transport	25.3	21.5	24.8	17.3	11.4	14.7	45.4	23.3	33.3
All activities	14.8	16.2	15.6	21.3	23.0	21.9	42.9	33.9	37.1

Sources: HIES 2000, 2005, and 2010; World Bank/BIDS survey 1991/92 and 1998/99; World Bank/InM survey 2010/11.

Note: HIES = Household Income and Expenditure Survey.

processing activities, at about 4 percent. The marginal return to labor is the highest in the services sector (Tk. 98), followed by manufacturing and processing (Tk. 89), transport (Tk. 24), and trade (Tk. 17).

For the panel data, we look at marginal returns by microcredit borrowing (table 10.5b). Activity-wise, we find differences in return by microcredit borrowing. For example, regardless of input and output type, returns to transport-sector activities are higher for microcredit borrowers than for nonborrowers, and such difference is the widest for return to profit: Microcredit borrowers make nearly twice as much profit for a Tk. 100 capital investment as nonborrowers do for the same investment. For other activities, the returns vary by borrowing status, but the differences are not as much as for the transport activity.

For all activities combined, the difference in returns is highest for profit in favor of the borrowers. For borrowers and nonborrowers combined, nonagricultural trade has the highest returns (profit) to capital (Tk. 56), followed by transport (Tk. 33), agricultural trade (Tk. 23), manufacturing and processing (Tk. 17), and services (Tk. 8). The returns-to-capital estimates are consistent with the findings in the literature. For example, McKenzie and Woodruff (2008) estimated a significantly higher marginal rate of return (20–33 percent per month) for the retail sector in Mexico; Anagol and Udry (2006) estimated a marginal rate of return of 60 percent per year for the informal auto parts sector in Ghana, and Bigsten and others (2000) estimated a marginal effect of 10 percent per year for the manufacturing sector in Zambia (compared to 4.9 percent in this study's estimate).[9] Nonagricultural trade has the highest marginal return to labor (Tk. 36), followed by agricultural trade (Tk. 16), transport (Tk. 15), manufacturing and processing (Tk. 10), and services (Tk. 4).

Comparing the findings for the two data sets, the estimated returns for revenue to capital are about the same; returns for revenue to labor are higher for the HIES, while returns for profit are higher for the long panel survey data. If we believe that the household panel data are better for estimating the returns and that the profit-function framework is better than the production-function framework, owing to the simultaneous bias inherent in the production function, then our estimates suggest that the marginal returns to capital in the RNF enterprise sector could be as low as 15.6 percent and as high as 37.1 percent.

Constraints to Sector Expansion and Productivity Growth

Having observed that RNF enterprises can have substantial rates of return, to what extent do alternative factors limit the sector's growth? More specifically, is enterprise growth in rural Bangladesh limited by a lack of access to finance, as well as nonfinancial constraints? Constraints limit the ability of enterprises to operate at their optimal level, thereby lowering their productivity and ability to repay loans meant for carrying out enterprise operations. Nonconstrained firms are likely to have higher marginal returns to capital and labor, suggesting that constrained firms would do better if the constraints were removed.

Sobering Statistics on Rural Microenterprises

An overwhelming percentage of microentrepreneurs in rural Bangladesh establish their businesses using their own savings rather than borrowing from the MFIs or commercial banks. According to both the HIES and long panel survey, enterprises are largely self-financed (table 10.6). This means that lack of capital (for fixed capital) is a major constraint to expanding enterprise growth among the poor, who most deserve assistance in setting up microenterprises to be productively employed.

Table 10.7 shows that the extent of constraints for rural enterprises is pervasive. According to the HIES data, more than two-thirds of enterprises were constrained in 2000, while about one-half were constrained a decade later.[10] Among the various types of constraints in 2010, inadequate capital or credit was the most common one (accounting for more than 22 percent of the sample), followed by inadequate demand for products and services (7 percent), transport problems (5 percent), and high operating cost (4 percent).

Enterprise Distribution by Self-Reported Credit versus Noncredit Constraint

Table 10.8a shows the extent of credit and noncredit constraints by enterprise activity using the HIES data. In 2010, the services sector was constrained the most, at 57 percent, followed by miscellaneous activities (49 percent), manufacturing and processing (44 percent), trade (31 percent), and transport

Table 10.6 Distribution of Major Sources of Start-Up Capital for RNF Enterprises

Source of start-up capital	Share of sources, by survey round (%)		
HIES data	2000 (N = 1,427)	2005 (N = 1,426)	2010 (N = 1,909)
Own resources (e.g., assets, inheritance, savings)	78.3	78.7	79.9
Microcredit loans	3.3	5.8	8.2
Commercial bank loans	0.8	0.6	1.0
Informal moneylenders	2.4	0.7	1.1
Loans from relatives/friends	5.5	4.0	5.6
Other	9.7	10.2	4.2
Long panel survey data	1991/92 (N = 775)	1998/99 (N = 1,031)	2010/11 (N = 1,089)
Own resources (e.g., assets, inheritance, savings)	64.0	50.6	55.7
Microcredit loans	8.5	21.6	26.1
Commercial bank loans	1.3	0.3	0.4
Informal moneylenders	13.6	8.6	5.0
Loans from relatives/friends	6.1	8.0	8.0
Other	6.5	10.9	4.8

Sources: HIES 2000, 2005, and 2010; World Bank/BIDS survey 1991/92 and 1998/99; World Bank/InM survey 2010/11.

Note: RNF = rural nonfarm; HIES = Household Income and Expenditure Survey.

Table 10.7 Enterprise Distribution by Self-Reported Constraints Faced in Operation

Major constraint	2000 (N = 1,427)	2005 (N = 1,426)	2010 (N = 1,909)
None	33.0	23.8	49.8
Inadequate capital or credit	27.1	25.5	22.1
Inadequate know-how	3.8	3.9	2.2
High operating cost	0.1	0.0	3.6
Unreliable/inadequate power/water supply	1.2	1.4	3.7
Problems with equipment/spare parts	1.7	0.6	0.4
Government regulations	2.5	4.0	1.1
Lack of raw materials	10.5	18.1	2.8
Inadequate product demand	8.3	6.2	7.1
Transport problems	2.5	7.1	5.0
Other	9.3	9.4	2.2

Sources: HIES 2000, 2005, and 2010.
Note: The constraints reported here are limited to the most severe ones faced by the surveyed enterprises; in reality, the microentrepreneurs may face multiple constraints.

Table 10.8 Extent of Self-Reported Credit and Noncredit Constraints by Enterprise Activity

a. Using HIES data

Enterprise type	Major constraint (% of enterprises)		
	Credit	Noncredit	Any
2000 (N = 1,427)			
Manufacturing and processing	26.6	42.6	69.2
Transport	6.1	50.7	56.8
Trade	35.4	20.2	55.6
Services	32.1	38.5	70.6
Miscellaneous activities	14.1	40.2	54.3
All activities	27.1	39.8	66.9
2005 (N = 1,426)			
Manufacturing and processing	15.0	54.5	69.5
Transport	8.8	55.5	64.3
Trade	19.5	35.8	55.3
Services	27.8	50.0	77.8
Miscellaneous activities	33.1	49.0	82.1
All activities	25.4	50.4	75.8
2010 (N = 1,910)			
Manufacturing and processing	15.7	25.9	44.4
Transport	7.0	23.0	30.0
Trade	11.9	19.0	30.9
Services	26.7	29.9	56.6
Miscellaneous activities	20.9	28.4	49.3
All activities	22.1	28.0	50.1

table continues next page

Table 10.8 Extent of Self-Reported Credit and Noncredit Constraints by Enterprise Activity *(continued)*

b. Using long panel survey data

Enterprise type	Credit-constrained enterprises (%)
1998/99 (N = 1,031)	
Manufacturing and processing	11.8
Transport	11.7
Agricultural trade	8.5
Nonagricultural trade	10.4
Services	6.5
All activities	7.8
2010/11 (N = 1,089)	
Manufacturing and processing	1.2
Transport	1.0
Agricultural trade	1.6
Nonagricultural trade	0.3
Services	0.3
All activities	0.6

Sources: HIES 2000, 2005, and 2010; World Bank/BIDS survey 1998/99; World Bank/InM survey 2010/11.
Note: Unlike the HIES constraints, which were self-reported, constraints for the long panel survey were determined from borrowing information, whereby households were considered credit constrained if the amount they received was less than the amount they requested. HIES = Household Income and Expenditure Survey.

(30 percent). Among enterprises that were constrained in 2010, some 22 percent faced credit as a major constraint, while 28 percent had major noncredit constraints. In terms of credit-constrained sectors in 2010, services was the most constrained, at 27 percent, followed by miscellaneous activities (21 percent), manufacturing and processing (16 percent), trade (12 percent), and transport (7 percent).

As table 10.8b suggests, the long panel survey lacks sufficient detailed data on the types of constraints that enterprises face. Indeed, the 1991/92 survey round provided no information on constraints. However, information in the second and third survey rounds (1998/99 and 2010/11) did provide information that helps us to determine the extent of credit constraint among households with enterprises. The results show that the extent of credit constraints fell substantially over the 11-year period, from about 8 percent to less than 1 percent (table 10.8b). In terms of credit-constrained sectors in 1998/99, manufacturing and processing and transport were the most credit constrained, at nearly 12 percent each, followed by nonagricultural trade (10 percent), agricultural trade (8 percent), and service activities (6 percent).

Distribution of Rates of Return for Constrained and Nonconstrained Enterprises

The next step was to examine whether the constraints matter for an enterprise's productivity.[11] In theory, a constrained enterprise is more likely to have inefficient resource allocation and be less productive; thus, it is more likely that constrained enterprises will have higher marginal rates of return to assets than those without constraints, given that capital, labor, and other resources are not operating at the production frontier. That is, if the market is distorted and the factors are not getting market-cleared prices, it is possible that returns to investment are higher in constrained activities. Indeed, using the HIES data, we find that in 2000–10, rates of return were marginally higher for constrained enterprises, similar to the findings in the Sri Lanka case (McKenzie and Woodruff 2008). In 2000, the average rate of return was about 66 percent for constrained enterprises, compared to about 60 percent for nonconstrained enterprises. Among the constrained ones, rates of return were highest in the transport sector (79 percent), followed by miscellaneous activities (71 percent), trade (70 percent), manufacturing and processing (68 percent), and service activities (64 percent) (table 10.9a).

Using the long panel survey data, we find that constrained enterprises had lower rates of return compared to nonconstrained enterprises in 1998/99 (39 percent versus 54 percent) but higher rates of return in 2010/11 (58 percent versus 54 percent) (table 10.9b). However, even then, some activities experienced higher returns to capital when they were not constrained, while the opposite was true for other activities.

Estimation Techniques to Determine the Causal Effects of Constraints on Productivity

In this section, we attempt to examine the causal effects of credit and noncredit constraints on enterprise productivity. We consider the following profitability equation, which is a function of both types of constraints, plus a host of other factors:

$$Y_{ikjt} = \alpha^y T_t + \beta^y X_{ikjt} + \gamma^y V_{jt} + \delta^y C_{ikjt} + \rho^y N_{ikjt} + \mu_{ikj}^y + \eta_{kj}^y + v_j^y + \varepsilon_{ikjt}^y, \quad (10.2)$$

where Y_{ikjt} is the profitability (denoted by profit or profit margin) of i-th enterprise in k-th sector operating in j-th upazila during year t, X_{ikjt} refers to enterprise-specific exogenous characteristics, V_{jt} refers to community-specific exogenous characteristics, C_{ikjt} is a dummy variable on whether the enterprise faced credit constraint (1 = yes, 0 = no), N_{ikjt} is whether the enterprise faced noncredit constraint, μ_{ikj}^y is the entrepreneur-specific unobserved heterogeneity, η_{kj}^y is the sector-specific unobserved heterogeneity, v_j^y is upazila-specific unobserved heterogeneity, ε_{ikjt}^y is a nonsystematic error, and T is the year. An equation similar to (10.2) can be written that uses household- instead of upazila-level panel data.

Our interest is to estimate the vector parameters, δ^y and ρ^y, measuring the respective effects of credit and noncredit constraints on an enterprise's performance. If the measures of the constraints, C_{ikjt} and N_{ikjt}, were exogenous, given exogenous enterprise and community characteristics, we could use an upazila-specific, fixed-effects model to estimate the parameters of interest.

Table 10.9 Distribution of Rate of Return for Enterprises by Constraint and Activity Type

a. Using HIES data

Activity type	Constrained enterprises (%)	Nonconstrained enterprises (%)	t-statistics of the difference
2000 (N = 1,427)			
Manufacturing and processing	68.1	63.1	0.60
Transport	78.9	71.6	0.96
Trade	69.6	47.9	1.10
Services	63.7	55.6	2.35
Miscellaneous activities	70.6	60.8	1.17
All activities	66.2	59.8	2.65
2005 (N = 1,426)			
Manufacturing and processing	63.4	57.2	−0.28
Transport	77.6	72.2	0.55
Trade	51.7	57.2	−0.29
Services	63.1	60.3	0.76
Miscellaneous activities	53.6	55.7	−0.16
All activities	63.2	61.8	0.45
2010 (N = 1,909)			
Manufacturing and processing	48.3	47.2	−0.19
Transport	65.7	69.4	−0.66
Trade	57.8	50.3	0.69
Services	51.4	48.3	1.17
Miscellaneous activities	45.9	47.2	−0.20
All activities	51.7	52.0	−0.14

b. Using long panel survey data

Activity type	Constrained enterprises (%)	Nonconstrained enterprises (%)	t-statistics of the difference
1998/99 (N = 1,031)			
Manufacturing and processing	13.4	29.0	−2.62
Transport	23.3	23.6	−0.08
Agricultural trade	36.1	55.7	−3.82
Nonagricultural trade	57.8	51.8	1.35
Services	21.0	42.3	−2.47
All activities	38.6	54.3	−0.67
2010/11 (N = 1,089)			
Manufacturing and processing	49.3	58.6	−0.35
Transport	12.8	8.0	1.21
Agricultural trade	55.8	59.8	−0.44
Nonagricultural trade	84.6	90.8	−0.70
Services	89.7	60.8	1.47
All activities	57.9	54.3	0.59

Sources: HIES 2000, 2005, and 2010; World Bank/BIDS survey 1998/99; World Bank/InM survey 2010/11.
Note: HIES = Household Income and Expenditure Survey.

However, the constraints may not be exogenously distributed across enterprises; instead, they may be determined by the same unobserved factors that affect Y_{ikjt}. We further explain with the following equations of the constraints:

$$C_{ikjt} = \alpha^c T_t + \beta^c X_{ikjt} + \gamma^c V_{jt} + \mu_{ikj}^c + \eta_{kj}^c + v_j^c + \varepsilon_{ikjt}^c , \qquad (10.3)$$

$$\text{and } N_{ikjt} = \alpha^n T_t + \beta^n X_{ikjt} + \gamma^n V_{jt} + \mu_{ikj}^n + \eta_{kj}^n + v_j^n + \varepsilon_{ikjt}^n . \qquad (10.4)$$

Because of the possibility of systematic relation between the errors in equations (10.2), (10.3), and (10.4) (i.e., between ε_{ikjt}^y and ε_{ikjt}^c and between ε_{ikjt}^y and ε_{ikjt}^n) the entrepreneur-level unobserved heterogeneity (μ_{ikj}^y) and sector-specific heterogeneity (η_{kj}^y) cannot be cancelled out through an upazila-level FE method, which can only take care of upazila-specific unobserved heterogeneity (v_j^y).

One way to account for the endogeneity in estimating equation (10.2) is to use an instrumental variables (IV) technique in the FE model. For that we must find instruments that enter into equations (10.3) and (10.4) only; that is, they will affect the constraints directly and the profitability of the enterprises indirectly through the constraints. Aterido, Hallward-Driemeier, and Pagés (2011) used as instruments a set of business-climate or environmental factors that affect enterprises of a certain size in a specific sector within a given location. Following that, we construct a measure of each type of constraint (credit or noncredit) faced by enterprise by averaging the responses (whether the enterprises faced a certain constraint) of all firms of a certain size operating in a given sector (e.g., manufacturing and processing) within a given upazila (excluding the value of i-th enterprise from the computation of the average).[12] The idea was to develop a broader measure of exogenous business environment in which an enterprise operates. We then used these measures in equations (10.3) and (10.4) as additional regressors, which could be treated as instruments. Because not all entrepreneurs will respond to such business environment in the same manner, we interacted entrepreneur characteristics (e.g., age, education, and sex) with the average upazila-specific, business-environment factors and included them in equations (10.3.) and (10.4) as additional instruments to identify the performance equation (10.2).

Estimates of Causal Impact of Credit and Noncredit Constraints on Enterprise Productivity

Before turning to the findings on the impacts of constraints on enterprise profitability, we first discuss the determinants of the constraints themselves. An upazila-level FE logit is applied to estimate equations (10.3) and (10.4) to discover which factors affect the probability of the enterprises being credit constrained.

Table 10.10 provides the results for variables of particular interest. As shown, the higher the educational level of the entrepreneur, the lower the probability of his or her being credit constrained. While nonland assets reduce the probability of being credit constrained, they increase the probability of having

Table 10.10 Determinants of Constraints Faced by Enterprises
FE logit (N = 4,762)

Explanatory variable	Credit constraints	Noncredit constraints
Year is 2005 (1 = yes, 0 = no)	0.196	−0.084
	(0.88)	(−0.29)
Year is 2010 (1 = yes, 0 = no)	0.522**	0.036
	(2.20)	(0.11)
Sex of owner (1 = male, 0 = female)	−0.031	−0.018
	(−0.86)	(−0.56)
Age of owner (years)	−0.001	−0.0002
	(−0.95)	(−0.29)
Education of owner (years)	−0.004**	0.003
	(−2.27)	(1.56)
Log household land (decimals)	0.001	−0.005
	(0.27)	(−0.97)
Log household nonland asset (Tk.)	−0.022**	0.023**
	(−2.74)	(2.57)
Years enterprise has been in business	0.001**	−0.003**
	(2.12)	(−3.25)
Enterprise is formally registered	−0.046**	0.005
(1 = yes, 0 = no)	(−2.41)	(0.20)
Enterprise is household based	−0.059**	0.026
(1 = yes, 0 = no)	(−3.37)	(1.16)
Total number of employees	−0.004**	0.012**
	(−2.22)	(3.12)
Share of hired labor in total workforce	−0.031	0.109**
	(−1.02)	(2.70)
Enterprise sector[a]		
Manufacturing and processing	0.070**	−0.056
(1 = yes, 0 = no)	(2.28)	(−1.53)
Transport (1 = yes, 0 = no)	−0.115**	0.001
	(−3.97)	(0.04)
Trade (1 = yes, 0 = no)	−0.005	−0.069
	(−0.10)	(−1.23)
Services (1 = yes, 0 = no)	0.115**	−0.035
	(4.45)	(−1.17)
Village characteristic		
Electricity (1 = yes, 0 = no)	−0.048*	0.027
	(−1.85)	(0.75)
Paved roads (1 = yes, 0 = no)	0.010	−0.015
	(0.41)	(0.48)
Share of irrigated land	0.079*	0.030
	(1.64)	(0.46)
Commercial banks (1 = yes, 0 = no)	−0.006	0.022
	(−0.19)	(0.54)
Presence of microcredit organizations	0.051	0.031
(1 = yes, 0 = no)	(1.08)	(0.49)
R^2	0.093	0.104

Sources: HIES 2000, 2005, and 2010.
Note: Figures in parentheses are *t*-statistics. Regression also controls for enterprise characteristics (e.g., enterprise age, months of operation per year, and whether it is home based) and household and community characteristics (as reported in table 10.3), as well as exogenous characteristics of the initial year and household occupation dummies based on major income source. FE = fixed effects.
Significance level: * = 10 percent, ** = 5 percent.
a. Miscellaneous activities sector is excluded.

noncredit constraints. The longer an enterprise is in operation, the higher the probability of credit constraint and lower the probability of noncredit constraint. Home-based enterprises and registered enterprises are less likely to be credit-constrained. The higher the number of employees, the lower the probability of credit constraints but the higher the probability of noncredit constraints. Manufacturing and processing, as well as service, enterprises are more likely to be credit-constrained, and transport activities are less credit-constrained than miscellaneous ones. There is less probability of being credit-constrained in a developed village (e.g., one with greater access to electricity). The converse is true for villages with higher percentages of irrigated land.

Table 10.11 presents the estimated effects of both types of constraints on the profitability of an enterprise using the HIES and the long panel survey. We use enterprise profit (log form) and profit margin as the outcomes and report the findings of both the FE and FE-IV models. Table 10.11a presents the estimates

Table 10.11 Estimates of the Impacts of Credit and Noncredit Constraints on Microenterprise Productivity
a. Using HIES data (N = 4,762)

Explanatory variable	Upazila FE		Upazila FE with IV	
	Log profit (Tk./year)	Profit margin (%)	Log profit (Tk./year)	Profit margin (%)
Year is 2005 (1 = yes, 0 = no)	5.593* (1.78)	72.6* (1.82)	−51.2 (−1.53)	−6.1 (−1.35)
Year is 2010 (1 = yes, 0 = no)	4.837 (1.59)	90.1** (2.34)	−65.2 (−1.04)	13.1 (1.30)
Enterprise has credit constraints	0.017 (0.14)	−7.2** (−5.36)	22.6 (1.18)	−8.8** (−3.61)
Enterprise has noncredit constraints	−0.011 (−0.08)	−4.4** (−3.15)	−4.3 (−0.22)	−8.7** (−3.85)
Activity type[a]				
Manufacturing and processing	0.637** (2.66)	1.3 (0.41)	0.625** (2.41)	−0.1 (−0.03)
Transport	0.824** (3.86)	23.3** (7.36)	0.956** (4.07)	23.4** (7.07)
Trade	0.572 (1.56)	0.8 (0.17)	0.358 (1.00)	−1.5 (−0.30)
Services	0.357* (1.74)	−6.3** (−2.40)	0.387* (1.71)	−6.9** (−2.48)
Log value of enterprise capital asset (Tk.)	0.997** (19.13)	0.042** (7.89)	1.165** (20.07)	0.044** (8.98)
R^2	0.402	0.280	0.343	0.253
Endogeneity test for endogenous regressors			$\chi^2(2) = 2.108, p = 0.349$	$\chi^2(2) = 7.298, p = 0.026$
Over-identification test for instruments (Hansen J statistics)			$\chi^2(8) = 8.731, p = 0.366$	$\chi^2(8) = 11.333, p = 0.184$

table continues next page

Table 10.11 Estimates of the Impacts of Credit and Noncredit Constraints on Microenterprise Productivity (continued)

Explanatory variable	Upazila FE		Upazila FE with IV	
	Log profit (Tk./year)	Profit margin (%)	Log profit (Tk./year)	Profit margin (%)
Under-identification test for instruments (KP statistics)			$\chi^2(9) = 114.52$, $p = 0.000$	$\chi^2(9) = 114.52$, $p = 0.000$
Weak identification for instruments (CD statistics)			$F = 172.99$	$F = 172.99$
Stock-Yogo weak identification test critical value for 5% bias			18.76	18.76

b. Using long panel survey data (N = 1,758)

Explanatory variable	Household FE		Household FE with IV	
	Log profit (Tk./year)	Profit margin (%)	Log profit (Tk./year)	Profit margin (%)
Year is 2010/11 (1 = yes, 0 = no)	−0.190 (−0.04)	−54.9 (−1.45)	−0.336 (−0.17)	−34.3* (−1.86)
Enterprise is credit constrained	−0.729** (−2.44)	−2.7 (−0.58)	−0.829 (−0.94)	−28.0* (−1.66)
Activity type[a]				
Manufacturing and processing	1.363** (3.06)	−16.8** (−3.07)	1.533** (3.51)	−15.0** (−2.77)
Agricultural trade	1.505** (4.18)	−16.3** (−4.37)	1.416** (4.10)	−16.1** (−4.59)
Nonagricultural trade	2.139** (6.42)	−8.6** (−2.90)	2.086** (6.30)	−8.2** (−2.77)
Services	1.661** (2.73)	−5.9 (−1.21)	1.725** (2.75)	−4.6 (−0.97)
Log value of enterprise capital asset (Tk.)	1.680** (23.94)	0.101** (20.41)	1.687** (25.64)	0.098** (21.74)
R^2	0.608	0.644	0.593	0.602
Endogeneity test for endogenous regressors			$\chi^2(1) = 0.130$, $p = 0.718$	$\chi^2(1) = 4.393$, $p = 0.036$
Over-identification test for instruments (Hansen J statistics)			$\chi^2(7) = 11.178$, $p = 0.083$	$\chi^2(7) = 5.308$, $p = 0.505$
Under-identification test for instruments (KP statistics)			$\chi^2(7) = 10.01$, $p = 0.188$	$\chi^2(7) = 9.325$, $p = 0.230$
Weak identification for instruments (CD statistics)			$F = 6.560$	$F = 6.505$
Stock-Yogo weak identification test critical value for 5% bias			19.86	19.86

Sources: HIES 2000, 2005, and 2010; World Bank/BIDS survey 1991/92 and 1998/99; World Bank/InM survey 2010/11.
Note: Figures in parentheses are *t*-statistics. Regression also controls for such enterprise characteristics as enterprise age, months of operation per year, whether it is home based, and household and community characteristics (as reported in table 10.3), as well as exogenous characteristics of the initial year and household occupation dummies based on major income source. KP = Kleibergen-Paap statistics; CD = Cragg-Donald statistics; HIES = Household Income and Expenditure Survey; FE = fixed effects; IV = instrumental variables.
Significance level: * = 10 percent, ** = 5 percent.
a. Excluded categories are miscellaneous (table 10.11a) and transport (table 10.11b).

using HIES data, while table 10.11b presents the same results using the long panel survey data.

The findings reported in table 10.11a show that the constraints (both credit and noncredit) have no significant effects on the level of profit; however, they have significant negative effects on profit margin. As shown, credit constraint lowers profit margin by 7.2 percentage points in the FE model and by 8.8 percentage points in FE-IV model. This means that, as their revenue grows, the profit of credit-constrained enterprises does not grow as much, which may be due to inefficient or suboptimal operations. Apparently, activity type matters to both profit and profit margin. The FE-IV results show that manufacturing and processing enterprises have a profit 60 percent higher than miscellaneous activities, the excluded category. Transport enterprises are highly profitable and also have a higher profit margin. While service enterprises have a higher profit than miscellaneous activities, they have a lower profit margin.

Table 10.11a also reports various test statistics on the appropriateness of the IV model using the HIES data. While we reject the exogeneity of the constraint variables in the equation for profit margin, we cannot do so in the equation for profit. The instruments pass the validity of the over-identification test as we cannot reject the null hypothesis of valid over-identifying restrictions at 5 percent level. They also pass the tests for under-identification as we reject the null hypothesis of under-identifying instruments in both equations. Finally, they pass the test for weak instruments as shown by the Cragg-Donald Wald F statistics and Stock-Yogo weak ID test critical values for 5 percent relative bias.

Next, using the long panel survey data, we estimate an equation similar to equation (10.2) by adding a dummy variable for whether an enterprise is credit constrained. Table 10.11b shows the results. The exclusion restrictions used for the FE-IV model suggest that FE-IV is more appropriate than simple FE to estimate the causal effect of credit constraint on profitability of an enterprise. While credit has no significant effects on profit level, it has a significant negative effect on profit margin. As shown, the profit margin for credit-constrained enterprises is 28 percentage points lower than that for nonconstrained enterprises.

Using both the HIES and long panel survey data, the results show that the constraints enterprises face matter little for their level of profit; however, they do negatively impact their profit margin. At least from the HIES data analysis, we find that credit and noncredit constraints equally affect an enterprise's profitability; the profit margin of constrained enterprises (both credit and noncredit) is about 9 percentage points lower than that of nonconstrained ones.

Can Better Access to Finance Promote Rural Enterprise Growth?

Since credit is a constraint to microenterprise profitability, as observed above, does better access to finance through MFIs or other semiformal institutions offer a viable solution? In rural Bangladesh, microentrepreneurs generally lack access to loans from formal financial institutions and instead rely on their own savings and perhaps informal loans from family members and friends. They may also borrow from informal moneylenders, but the exorbitant interest rates charged (in a range of 180–240 percent a year) make it difficult to sustain borrowing from such sources. The large network of MFIs in rural Bangladesh can potentially alleviate these credit constraints. But there is a concern among policy makers in Bangladesh and throughout the world that the interest rates charged by the MFIs are also too high, imposing a burden on poor households (e.g., Faruqee and Khalily 2011).

Although the interest rates charged by the MFIs are higher than those charged by commercial banks (25–36 percent versus 12 percent, respectively), they are much less than the informal interest rates of the moneylenders (table 10.12). But rural microentrepreneurs in Bangladesh typically lack access to commercial bank loans due to their lack of collateral, connections, and financial literacy. Thus, until the formal banking sector is reformed or the commercial banks become more accessible to rural microenterprises, it is more pragmatic to compare the interest rates charged by the MFIs with the microenterprises' rate of return. Whether microentrepreneurs can borrow sustainably from the MFIs to support microenterprise growth and profitability depends on whether their rate of return is higher than their total cost of borrowing from the MFIs, including interest rates and other borrowing fees.

The effective interest rate for MFI loans is determined not only by the stated interest rate but also the method used to calculate it and other loan fees charged. The interest rate can be either simple or compound. Two techniques are widely used among the MFIs for charging interest on principal: (a) the declining balance method and (b) the flat rate method.[13] The declining balance method imposes lower costs on the borrower than does the flat rate method. Thus, the calculation of the effective interest rate is based on the details of the repayment schedule for the client. The higher the number of installments, the higher the effective interest rate since the calculation must take into account any variables in the timing of repayments and all fees, compensating balances, and additional charges paid by the client. To compare the cost of borrowing from the MFIs with the microenterprises' ROA, we must control for the fact that MFIs calculate the interest rate using either the declining balance or flat rate method. It is estimated that the average effective interest rate charged to microenterprises is 26.65 percent if they repay monthly and 31.59 percent if they repay on a weekly basis. The average effective interest rate charged for rural microcredit programs is about 32.05 percent (Faruqee and Khalily 2011) (table 10.12).

Table 10.12 Effective Annual Interest Rate of PKSF Partner Organizations

Loan type	Highest rate (%)	Lowest rate (%)	Average rate (%)
Rural microcredit (regular)	35.75	28.11	32.05
Microenterprise (weekly payment)	34.67	28.39	31.59
Microenterprise (monthly payment)	30.39	25.30	26.65

Source: Faruqee and Khalily 2011.
Note: The effective rate calculation takes into account all fees and additional charges paid by the borrowers and thus correctly reflects the cost of borrowing. PKSF = Palli Karma-Sahayak Foundation.

The average rate of return earned by Bangladeshi microenterprises falls in a range of 40–64 percent (as opposed to marginal returns of 16–37 percent), according to the findings from our sample, using the two data sets. Thus, expanded MFI lending could serve to eradicate the credit constraints of microentrepreneurs. One must also bear in mind that the effective interest rates of the MFIs vary significantly by their size and funding sources. For example, those that borrow from PKSF and obtain donations from foreign organizations can afford to charge low effective interest rates. Thus, to ensure that the MFIs remain a sustainable source of borrowing for microenterprises, efforts must be made to keep the average effective interest rates lower than the average rate of return for these enterprises.[14]

In terms of comparisons with bank savings, Grameen Bank pays its depositors an interest rate of 8 percent (Faruqee and Khalily 2011), while the interest rate on savings at commercial banks averages 7.5–8.0 percent. Many other organizations pay below-market interest rates that are much lower than the average rate of return earned by microenterprises (Hossain and Ahmed 2000). However, because needed start-up capital may be much higher than a microentrepreneur's own savings, many households are constrained in initiating their enterprises. Therefore, expanding credit access for start-up capital is critical for expanding RNF growth.

Summary

This chapter has estimated the rates of return to investment in the RNF enterprise sector using alternative techniques and investigated whether borrowing from microfinance to support RNF enterprises pays off for borrowers, not only in terms of debt but also family labor. Like the analyses of previous chapters, the three most recent rounds of the nationally representative HIES (2000, 2005, and 2010) and the long panel household survey (1991/92, 1998/99, and 2010/11) were used to address these issues. Our analysis confirms that better access to credit is an important factor in promoting both coverage and level of household participation in the RNF enterprise sector.

The findings show that the average rate of return to RNF enterprise investment is high, at about 40–64 percent per year. This means that an entrepreneur with an incremental investment of Tk. 1,000 in an activity can obtain at least Tk. 400 in profit per year. Because the rate of return does not decline over time, it is not a major constraint to enterprise growth using microfinance borrowing. In fact, microfinance borrowers enjoy a higher marginal return to their capital in terms of profit than do their nonborrower counterparts. Unfortunately, lack of access to affordable finance restricts enterprise growth more than noncredit constraints (e.g., lack of market demand or access to transport and electricity). Analysis of the household survey data shows that microentrepreneurs' own savings account for more than 80 percent of their start-up capital, along with an additional 5 percent borrowed from friends and relatives. Thus, the opportunity cost of start-up capital is high in rural Bangladesh, suggesting that households must either save or borrow from wealthy friends and relatives in order to set up an enterprise.

As previously mentioned, informal lenders can also provide funds to operate enterprise activities, but their exorbitant interest rates make this option infeasible for financing microenterprise investments. Commercial banks, which charge interest rates of 10–12 percent, could potentially be the most cost-effective way to finance rural enterprises; but formal financial institutions rarely finance rural microenterprise activities because of the high transaction costs involved in dispensing small loans without adequate collateral. This study's data analysis shows that barely 1 percent of microentrepreneurs borrow from commercial banks to fund their start-up capital.

In such circumstances, MFIs can serve as a major source of capital for microenterprise expansion and growth for several major reasons. First, they have a large network of outreach. Second, they do not require physical collateral to lend. Finally, their effective interest rate, while higher than what the commercial banks charge, is much less than that of informal lenders. Despite these comparative advantages, our findings show that only about 8 percent of microentrepreneurs acquired loans from the MFIs to start up microenterprise activities in 2010. Thus, lack of access to affordable finance for start-up capital is a major barrier to microenterprise growth.[15]

Our findings also suggest that improved access to affordable loans through microfinance or other sources would help further enterprise growth and promote poverty reduction in Bangladesh. As the returns to enterprise investment are high and meet the cost of borrowing from the MFIs, there is clearly a large potential for microfinance to support rural enterprise growth in Bangladesh.

Notes

1. The cost of family labor is quite low, constituting not more than 10 percent of the operating cost (table 10.1).

2. In cases where the survey data underestimated the value of the enterprise, it was imputed by regressing it on a set of variables explaining its value for a subsample of households without outliers; the covariates included such factors as duration of the enterprise, number of months it had operated in the past year, whether it was registered with the local government, whether it was household based, dummy variables for its activity type, and sources of start-up capital. Next, an out-of-sample prediction was made. Finally, the outliers were replaced with the predicted value of the enterprise.

3. The redefinition of India's priority sector changed the eligibility of firms applying for low-interest loans, thus allowing them access to capital to circumvent these difficulties.

4. Moreover, household and community characteristics are used to control for the endogeneity of assets utilized in an enterprise.

5. Endogeneity is still an issue unresolved within the production function framework.

6. Response elasticity for family labor is slightly less than that for hired labor.

Beyond Ending Poverty • http://dx.doi.org/10.1596/978-1-4648-0894-4

7. Marginal return from the log-log equation $\log Y = \beta \log X$ can be calculated from the formula $\dfrac{dY}{dX} = \beta \dfrac{\bar{Y}}{\bar{X}}$, where $\bar{X}$ and $\bar{Y}$ are the respective sample means of X and Y. This formula is used to calculate the overall return. However, activity-specific returns are calculated from the interaction of activity dummy and the input variable. For example, considering the formula $\log P = A \log C$, where P = profit or revenue, A = activity dummy (e.g., manufacturing and processing or trading), and C = capital or labor cost, then the marginal return can be calculated using this formula: $MR = \beta \bar{A} \bar{P} * 100 / \bar{C}$ where $\bar{A}, \bar{P},$ and $\bar{C}$ are sample means of A, P, and C, respectively.

8. In the calculation, family labor and hired labor are combined.

9. The marginal returns are lower than average returns for all activity types, meaning that the returns to investment are diminishing; for manufacturing and processing, for example, the marginal return to investment is 4.3 percent based on the profit-function estimates (table 10.5a), while the average return is 47.7 percent based on the HIES data for 2010 (table 10.1a).

10. Providing similar information on category-wise constraints was not possible using the long panel survey data.

11. In the case of Sri Lanka, McKenzie and Woodruff (2008) find high rates of return (70–79 percent) for credit-constrained enterprises and much lower returns for those without credit constraints; they also report that the possibility of zero return cannot be rejected for firms without credit constraints.

12. To capture the size, enterprises are grouped into five groups of equal size, based on their revenue. Alternately, they can be grouped by number of workers; however, revenue-based groups provide more variation.

13. Details are provided in Faruqee and Khalily (2011).

14. In 2011, Bangladesh's Microcredit Regulatory Authority (MRA) set a 27 percent ceiling on MFI interest rates, which has forced some of the MFIs to lower their interest rates. A recent study by the Institute of Microfinance (InM) identified the cost of MFI funds at 7 percent, with an average break-even rate of 23–24 percent, suggesting further room for lowering the interest rate ceiling (Faruqee and Khalily 2011). Also, for certain activities, the discrepancy between the average cost of borrowing and the average rate of return may be wider (meaning a lower return against a higher cost of capital), although we found that average returns are higher than the average interest rates charged by financial institutions, including the MFIs.

15. It is possible that the MFIs offer working capital to support RNF enterprises; however, the HIES does not provide such information. It should be noted that the MFIs also support livestock and poultry raising, as well as gardening and other farm-related activities, which are not defined as part of the RNF enterprise sector.

Bibliography

Anagol, S., and C. Udry. 2006. "The Return to Capital in Ghana." *American Economic Review Papers and Proceedings* 96 (2): 388.

Aterido, Reyes, Mary Hallward-Driemeier, and Carmen Pagés. 2011. "Big Constraints to Small Firms' Growth? Business Environment and Employment Growth across Firms." *Economic Development and Cultural Change* 59 (3): 609–47.

Banerjee, Abhijit, and Esther Duflo. 2004. "Do Firms Want to Borrow More? Testing C.redit Constraints Using a Directed Lending Program." BREAD Working Paper 005, Bureau for Research in Economic Analysis of Development, Duke University, Durham, NC.

———. 2005. "Growth Theory through the Lens of Development Economics." In *Handbook of Economic Growth*, edited by Philippe Aghion and Steven Durlauf. Amsterdam: Elsevier Press.

Bigsten, Arne, Anders Isaksson, Mans Soderbom, Paul Collier, Albert Zeufack, Stephan Dercon, Marcel Fafchamps, Jan Willem Gunning, Francis Teal, Simon Appleton, Bernard Gauthier, Abena Oduro, Remco Oostendrop, and Cathy Pattillo. 2000. "Rates of Return on Physical and Human Capital in Africa's Manufacturing Sector." *Economic Development and Cultural Change* 48 (4): 801–27.

Caselli, F., and J. Feyrer. 2007. "The Marginal Product of Capital." *Quarterly Journal of Economics* 122 (2): 535–68.

Deininger, Klaus, and Songqing Jin. 2007. "Sri Lanka's Non-Farm Economy: Removing Constraints to Pro-Poor Growth." *World Development* 35 (12): 2056–78.

de Mel, Suresh, David J. McKenzie, and Christopher Woodruff. 2009. "Measuring Microenterprise Profits: Don't Ask How the Sausage Is Made." *Journal of Development Economics* 88: 19–31.

Faruqee, Rashid, and Baqui Khalily. 2011. "Interest Rates in Bangladesh Microcredit Market." InM Policy Paper, Institute of Microfinance, Dhaka.

Grosh, Margaret, and Paul Glewwe, eds. 2000. *Designing Household Questionnaires for Developing Countries: Lessons from Fifteen Years of the Living Standard Measurement Study.* Vols. 1–3. Washington, DC: World Bank.

HIES (Household Income and Expenditure Survey). 2000, 2005, and 2010. Bangladesh Bureau of Statistics, Dhaka.

Hossain, Khandker Zakir, and Faruque Ahmed. 2000. "Growth and Dimension of Microfinance Sector in Bangladesh." Paper 23 presented at the Asia Regional Conference.

Islam, Aminul, M. Khan, A. Obaidullah, and M. Alam. 2011. "Effect of Entrepreneur and Firm Characteristics on the Business Success of Small and Medium Enterprises in Bangladesh." *International Journal of Business and Management* 6 (3): 289–99.

Khandker, Shahidur R., Hussain A.Samad, and Rubaba Ali. 2013. "Does Access to Finance Matter in Microenterprise Growth? Evidence from Bangaldesh." Policy Research Working Paper No. 6333, World Bank, Washington, DC.

Kremer, Michael, Jean N. Lee, Jonathan M. Robinson, and Olga Rostapshova. 2013. "Behavioral Biases and Firm Behavior: Evidence from Kenyan Retail Shops." *American Economic Review: Papers and Proceedings* 103 (3): 362–68.

McKenzie, David, and Christopher Woodruff. 2003. "Do Entry Costs Provide an Empirical Basis for Poverty Traps? Evidence from Mexican Microenterprises." BREAD Working Paper 2003–20, Bureau for Research in Economic Analysis of Development, Duke University, Durham, NC.

———. 2006. "Do Entry Costs Provide an Empirical Basis for Poverty Traps? Evidence from Mexican Microenterprises." *Economic Development and Cultural Change* 55 (1): 3–42.

———. 2008. "Experimental Evidence on Returns to Capital and Access to Finance in Mexico." *World Bank Economic Review* 22 (3): 457–82.

Olley, G. Steven, and Ariel Pakes. 1996. "The Dynamics of Productivity in the Telecommunications Equipment Industry." *Econometrica* 64 (6): 1263–97.

Onchan, Tongroj. 2001. *Non-Farm Employment Opportunities in Rural Areas in Asia. Report of the APO Seminar on Nonfarm Employment Opportunities in Rural Areas, Philippines*. Tokyo: Asian Productivity Organization.

Samphantharak, Krislert, and Robert M. Townsend. 2012. "Measuring the Return on Household Enterprise: What Matters Most for Whom?" *Journal of Development Economics* 98 (1): 58–70.

World Bank. 2004. *Bangladesh: Promoting the Rural Nonfarm Sector in Bangladesh*. Vol. 1, Summary Report 29719-BD, Rural Development Unit. Washington, DC: World Bank.

Zinman, J. 2002. "Do Credit Market Interventions Work? Evidence from the Community Reinvestment Act." Federal Reserve Bank of New York, New York.

CHAPTER 11

Beyond Ending Poverty

Introduction

Bangladesh has witnessed phenomenal growth in microfinance over the past 25 years. Today, the country has more than 750 registered microfinance institutions (MFIs) with a network of over 17,000 branches. As previously mentioned, by 2013, some 32 million MFI members had received more than US$7.2 billion in annual disbursements, with an outstanding balance of US$4.5 billion (CDF 2013), equivalent to 3 percent of gross domestic product (GDP). That 65 percent of the country's 110 million rural people can now be linked with institutional financial services is a milestone in the movement to reduce poverty through the inclusive finance provided by microfinance.

Evolution of the Microfinance Sector

Bangladesh's microfinance sector has undergone a major transformation since the 1970s, when its primary outreach goal was poverty alleviation of the rural poor through microcredit loans, extended mainly to poor women borrowers. The early MFI programs, pioneered by Grameen Bank, along with the Bangladesh Rural Advancement Committee (BRAC) and a few other institutions, focused on rural nonfarm (RNF) income-generating activities and employment via mobilization of group-based savings and lending, with funding provided mainly by the Government of Bangladesh and bilateral donors. As the sector has matured, major changes have occurred in the nature of outreach, loan size and portfolio focus, sources of financing, and the regulatory framework. In the 1990s, Palli Karma-Sahayak Foundation (PKSF) emerged as the wholesale funding agency, and many small nongovernmental organizations (NGOs) entered the market. Instead of relying on the savings of borrowers, as the traditional MFIs did, the newer MFIs had access to institutional funds, including commercial banks, for their own lending. The importance of requiring large donor funds to support operations has gradually diminished, and MFIs are no longer limited to providing microcredit and other services to the poor as defined by landholdings. Many MFI members have attained complete self-sufficiency and have graduated from subsidy dependence.

Microfinance in modern Bangladesh is a highly competitive, thriving industry, comprising a variety of financial and nonfinancial services. Its original, purely microcredit focus to support home-based, income-generating activities and self-employment has expanded to encompass savings and insurance, growth-oriented microenterprises, and productive employment. Currently, microenterprise loans constitute nearly 28 percent of MFI loan portfolios. More than 72 percent of MFIs provide social development interventions, including training, health services, education, and microinsurance. By late 2013, loans of up to Tk. 1 million were provided, with an average MFI loan size of Tk. 25,000, five times larger than in the mid-1990s. Member savings now finance nearly 55 percent of loans outstanding, and donor dependency of the MFIs is almost negligible. As its roles have diversified over time, microfinance has become more appealing to policy makers as an instrument for promoting universal access to finance rather than simply microcredit for employment generation and poverty reduction.

Does Microfinance Ultimately Matter?

Since its inception in Bangladesh, microfinance growth has attracted worldwide attention. In many developing countries, microfinance services have expanded by many times to reach the poor, especially women and small producers. Results of earlier research pioneered by the World Bank, documented in *Fighting Poverty with Microcredit: Experience in Bangladesh* (Khandker 1998), found that microcredit helped to promote household welfare and that its impacts benefited women more than men. That evaluation's findings resulted from examining three well-known credit programs in Bangladesh using cross-sectional household survey data jointly collected in 1991/92 by the Bangladesh Institute of Development Studies (BIDS) and the World Bank. Critics have since debated the study's findings. Using randomized control trial (RCT) methods, which have less restrictive assumptions, they found limited or no benefits resulting from microfinance. Such studies have often been based on assessments of short-term program effects (e.g., limited to 18 months of intervention). However, measuring the effects of microfinance requires a certain minimum length of program membership, and the benefits from self-employed activities take time to be realized. Furthermore, context matters.

The past decade has witnessed fierce competition among the MFIs, multiple-source borrowing, and something close to market saturation in lending. Critics argue that too much credit or too many MFIs are not good for participant borrowers or the economy. They allege that the MFIs have drifted off course, charging interest rates that are too high, and question whether participants are becoming overindebted or trapped in poverty. Thus, it is an empirical challenge to demonstrate that microfinance ultimately matters for the poor. Critics have often failed to realize that improved access to financial services from institutions has provided many poor people an opportunity to borrow at much lower interest rates than those charged by informal moneylenders, the only alternative borrowing source for many. The recent phenomena of borrowers' indebtedness and multiple program membership are dynamic issues that have evolved over time. Thus, evaluating today's microfinance is a more complex task than it was 25 years ago.

Obviously, assessing the dynamics of program benefits accrued to households amid increasing levels of indebtedness and multiple program membership requires long household panel data. By the same token, only an in-depth analysis of long panel data can reveal the dynamics of MFI outreach and cost efficiency in the context of what has become a highly competitive industry. Thus, the long panel survey data used in this study provided a unique opportunity to revisit the policy quagmires currently facing MFIs around the world. This study's results verified the 1998 research findings that used cross-sectional and a 2005 study of short-term panel surveys, reconfirming the earlier witnessed positive effects of microfinance on the household welfare of borrowers and nonborrower participants.

Institutional Cost Effectiveness

This study found that multiple program membership has increased over time; it was nonexistent in 1991/92, increasing to 8.9 percent of borrowers in 1998/99 and 31.9 percent by 2010/11. Yet such growth has not caused a decline in MFI loan recoveries. Since the outreach and financial viability of the MFIs are interlinked with the performance of program borrowers, evaluating members' benefit structures also means evaluating the MFI cost structures to determine whether the services they provide are cost-effective for both the MFIs and borrowers. This study examined the most recent (2004–12) operational efficiency data and critical performance indicators for Bangladesh's leading MFIs, relative to those of India, Indonesia, Mexico, Thailand, and Vietnam. It found that Grameen Bank and BRAC are among the top few of the world's most operationally efficient MFIs, as defined by the Consultative Group to Assist the Poor (CGAP). For example, in 2010, Grameen Bank's break-even interest rate was only 10.3 percent against its lending rate of 18.94 percent. All of Bangladesh's larger MFIs were financially more efficient than its smaller NGO-MFIs.

This study's analysis also confirms that the MFIs in Bangladesh are relying increasingly on resources mobilized by the MFIs and less on donor or concessionary funds. Despite the rapid growth of existing MFIs, the surge in new ones, and increased borrowing across multiple MFIs by poor clients, we find evidence somewhat counter to policy claims that the newer MFIs are less risk averse in their targeting or that increased borrowing among households due to MFI competition has led to lower recovery rates. For the newest MFIs, loan recovery rates are highest among women in rural areas, suggesting that MFIs operating in such areas could offer distinct products to attract better-risk clients.

Accomplishments for Members

Growth in RNF enterprises and the dynamics of that sector have influenced overall income growth and poverty reduction. Using two data sets, each comprising survey rounds conducted at three points—Household Income and Expenditure Study (HIES) (2000, 2005, and 2010) and the long panel survey data (1991/92, 1998/99, and 2010/11)—our findings show that household income grew over the period, as did household share of nonfarm income. Income from self-employed enterprises comprises 30 percent of total nonfarm income in 2010, and this share is increasing over time. For households that adopted RNF enterprise activities, income growth over the 20-year period was nearly 29 percent higher than that of their nonadopter counterparts, and reduction in moderate and extreme poverty was nearly 8 percent higher. The direction of change in RNF growth was driven mainly by farm income growth: A 10 percent increase in farm income growth increases nonfarm growth by 6 percent. RNF income growth matters significantly to growth in overall income. Within the RNF sector, enterprise income matters most in promoting both income growth and poverty reduction.

This study's econometric analysis confirms that, while household assets, education, and other factors matter in helping microenterprise activities to grow over time, placement of microcredit programs, such as Grameen Bank, also helped rural households to adopt enterprise activities. And village population density in terms of program participation influenced household participation in rural enterprise activities. The research showed that a 10 percent increase in a village population's microcredit participation increased household participation in RNF enterprise activities by 2.4 percentage points, showing a demonstration effect.

The study also finds significant positive effects resulting from women's participation in MFI borrowing, as well as benefits to marginal farmers. Results show that a 10 percent increase in women's credit increases crop income by 3.5 percent, noncrop income by 2.8 percent, and total farm income by 0.7 percent. Microfinance increases nonfarm income and employment by reducing wage income. It also increases farm income, especially crop and livestock income. Overall, marginal farmers benefit the most, compared to other farm-size groups. The evidence confirms that agricultural households are benefiting from improved farm/nonfarm linkages, resulting from better access to microfinance.

Validation of Earlier Research Results

Using the long panel survey data, the study investigated various dimensions of microcredit effects on a set of behaviors to validate the earlier results obtained with cross-sectional (e.g., Khandker 1998; Pitt and Khandker 1998) and short panel data (Khandker 2005). The findings confirm that microfinance matters a lot, and more for women than for men. Specifically, male and female borrowing affects income, labor supply, household assets and net worth, and children's schooling. And the effects are more pronounced for women's borrowing. Furthermore, past credit has a positive effect on some current outcomes, indicating increasing returns to borrowing—especially women's borrowing—for household outcomes. Unequivocally, the results show that group-based credit programs have significant positive effects on raising household welfare. Microfinance increases income, expenditure, labor supply of men and women, household nonland assets and net worth, and children's school enrollment.

The results also support the view that the effects change over time, and show that the effects of current borrowing differ from those of past borrowing. Past credit has a greater impact on income than current credit. For example, a 10 percent increase in past women's borrowing increased household per capita income by nearly 3 percent. With higher village-level participation, there is also a sign of village diseconomies due to market saturation. Multiple program membership, which has grown steadily over the past two decades, appears to have negative effects on some household outcomes. But microfinance competition in a village appears to have beneficial effects, especially on growth in household nonland assets and net worth.

Dynamics of Microfinance Benefits
Our long-term panel data analysis confirms that borrowing from multiple sources adds more to assets than liability over time; thus, borrowing from multiple sources is not necessarily a pathway to overindebtedness. Opponents of microcredit have argued that the short-term successes in reaching the poor, particularly women and other marginalized groups, may not be sustainable over time. However, our findings show that microcredit accounted for a 10 percent reduction in rural poverty over the 20-year period examined. Without the presence of the MFIs over that period, 2.5 million rural people would not have been uplifted from poverty. Had our study been able to capture the effects of microfinance programs offering financial and nonfinancial services over the same period, rather than simply the poverty-reduction effects of pure microcredit, the impacts would have been much greater.[1]

Household Benefits of Noncredit Services
Nonetheless, the study was able to evaluate the impact of noncredit inputs, distinct from those of credit, on household-level outcomes. The findings showed that noncredit inputs (e.g., nonborrowing status, membership length, and savings) matter and sometimes more so than credit. For augmenting household income and expenditure, credit services matter more for women members, while noncredit inputs matter more for men. For improving children's schooling, noncredit inputs matter more than credit for women, demonstrating the high added value of noncredit inputs for social and human capital investment. Length of program membership has an identifiable effect on welfare, independent of the positive effects of borrowing. For example, a 10 percent increase in the duration of membership raises household nonland assets by 0.1 percentage point for

men's borrowing and girls' schooling by 0.7 percentage point for women's borrowing. Furthermore, savings—sometimes more than borrowing—play a critical role in raising household welfare, independent of credit and noncredit (measured by membership length) inputs. For example, a 10 percent increase in men's savings raises household nonland assets and net worth by 0.30 percent and 0.20 percent, respectively, compared to 0.20 percent and 0.15 percent for the same percent increase in men's borrowing.

Winners and Losers

Household borrowers whose heads had completed primary or secondary school appear to have fared better under microfinance than those whose heads had not completed their primary education. More important, having adult members with competency in oral math (a proxy for entrepreneurial ability) helped households to reap more benefits from microfinance. Households with adult members less competent in oral math were more likely to drop out, which may be indicative of their lower ability to make productive use of microloans. Such households borrowed more than their counterpart members who continued on with the MFI programs. Perhaps the dropout members, having borrowed more than they could handle, along with less entrepreneurial ability, did not fare well.

Only self-employed households were found to gain from microfinance borrowing in terms of income and expenditure. In addition, self-employed households gained more than wage-employed households in terms of nonland assets and net worth. In terms of community endowments, households living in villages with access to electricity and paved roads benefited more from microfinance, compared to those in villages without electricity or poor accessibility. Quantile regression estimates show that, except for the effects of male borrowing, households in the lower welfare brackets in terms of income and expenditure benefited more than those in the higher ones, suggesting that microfinance programs are well targeted.

Has Microfinance Paid Off for Borrowers?

Our analysis confirms that better access to credit is an important factor in promoting both coverage and level of household participation in the RNF sector. The average rate of return to RNF enterprise investment is high, at 40–64 percent per year, meaning that a microentrepreneur with an incremental investment of Tk. 1,000 can obtain at least Tk. 400 in annual profits. Microfinance borrowers enjoy a higher marginal return to their capital in terms of profit than do their nonborrower counterparts. These findings are supported by evidence in other recent studies (e.g., Khalily and Khaleque 2013; Muneer and Khalily 2015; Osmani and others 2015). However, lack of access to affordable and sizable finance, more than noncredit constraints, restricts enterprise growth. Analysis of the household survey data shows that microentrepreneurs' own savings account for more than four-fifths of their start-up capital, highlighting the high opportunity cost.

Emerging Policy Concerns

The demand-side findings show that both the financial and nonfinancial services provided by the MFIs have diversified over the past two decades. Demand for microenterprise loans has been increasing over time; in 2013, microenterprises accounted for nearly one-third of the loans disbursed. With increasing intensity of training, higher loan size, growing share of microenterprises, and provision for microinsurance, microfinance has been creating positive impacts that are reflected at the macroeconomic level. Raihan, Osmani, and Khalily (2015), for example, show that, in 2012, microfinance services contributed 9 percent to aggregate GDP and 12 percent to rural GDP. Muneer and Khalily (2015) find that microenterprises with access to finance have created an average of 1.90 full-time jobs per enterprise; they show that some 10 million jobs, including full-time self-employment and wage employment, have been created through the enterprise financing of the MFIs. Over time, demand for financial and nonfinancial services will increase. As in the past, high-magnitude idiosyncratic and covariate shocks will inevitably cause some failures in the future, and these challenges will need to be addressed.

Overcoming Barriers to Sustained Poverty Reduction

The study results indicate the presence of market saturation with possible village diseconomies and diminishing returns due, in part, to credit expansion without much technological breakthrough in local economies. More than two-thirds of the activities supported by microcredit programs are in the trade and services sector. As previously mentioned, trade is perhaps now saturated, and households have begun to experience diminishing returns. The current microfinance policy of extending small-size credit may have been a constraint to induce both higher labor and capital productivity. But credit alone may not be enough to boost income and productivity and thus sustained poverty reduction. Additional inputs, such as skills training and development of improved marketing networks, are needed to expand activities in more rewarding sectors.

As part of their risk-minimizing strategies, the MFIs generally diversify their loan portfolios through providing small loans for various economic activities. To achieve the desired effects, however, it is important for both lenders and borrowers to invest in sectors with sufficient returns. With the exception of female-headed households and those with day labor as the sole source of income, this study reveals that multiple borrowing has, in fact, contributed to short- and long-term positive returns. Khalily, Faridi, and Saeed (2015) report similar findings. Despite the positive effects of multiple borrowing and risk-minimizing strategies of both lenders and borrowers, the microfinance sector remains funds constrained. Also, borrowers may not adequately protect themselves against repeated risk events. To safeguard themselves and their borrowers (both multiple- and single-source) against various types of shocks, the MFIs might consider introducing an effective microinsurance policy. PKSF has been implementing a livestock insurance product on an experimental basis, and numerous

MFIs have been informally providing microinsurance, with encouraging results. The critical concern is how to deliver microinsurance services to poor households, given the high transaction costs involved. An alternate institutional arrangement for microinsurance needs to be tested and structured.

Even though their rates are much lower than those charged by the moneylenders, the MFIs have room to reduce their rates and still realize sufficient returns. This argument is consistent with the evidence of Quayes and Khalily (2014) and Khalily, Khaleque, and Badruddoza (2014), which show that the MFIs are increasingly becoming cost-efficient. In 2011, the Microcredit Regulatory Authority (MRA) capped the interest rates that the MFIs can charge at 27 percent, which, in fact, has encouraged the licensed MFIs to become more cost-efficient. Even so, many poorer households still cannot afford to borrow. Our findings show that in 2010, only about 8 percent of microentrepreneurs started up their businesses by acquiring loans from the MFIs. Similar findings are reported in other recent studies (e.g., Khalily and Khaleque 2013; Muneer and Khalily 2015). But average rates of financial and economic return are positive. The MFIs' limited role in providing microentrepreneurs with start-up capital can be attributed to their shifting focus toward financing graduating members, as well as funding constraints. Thus, for many poor households, lack of access to affordable financial services for start-up capital remains a major barrier to microenterprise growth. Depending on the extent of their credit demand, poorer households may become overindebted, leading them to borrow from multiple MFIs and, in some cases, high-cost informal lenders. This situation calls for developing alternate technology and an appropriate regulatory mechanism for providing microfinance services at an affordable cost.

Although annual loan disbursement has been increasing over time, there is increasing demand for microenterprise loans among graduating MFI members and lateral entrants. The MRA allows the licensed MFIs to lend a maximum of 50 percent of their loanable funds, but their existing available funds are not sufficient to finance the growing demand. During the 2011–13 period, member savings and retained earnings, as well as equity, contributed to about 70 percent of the loans outstanding. This ratio may decline over time because of the growing demand for higher levels of credit. Annual demand for loans is expected to reach more than Tk. 1 trillion within the next five years, but existing institutional mechanisms are not sufficient to finance such an enormous amount. Thus, alternate funding sources need to be explored. In recent years, the MFIs have started to become an important source of commercial bank lending, accounting for some 16 percent. Nonetheless, policy options, which need to be carefully considered, might include allowing the MFIs to accept public deposits, establishing more wholesale lending agencies, or developing the MFIs into microfinance banks.

The Changing Role of Microfinance

What direction are the MFIs taking with respect to their original socially motivated outlook? Recent regulation of the microfinance sector has imposed cost on the previously self-regulated MFIs, which influences their portfolio decisions.

Khalily, Khaleque, and Badruddoza (2014) show that, since 2006, regulation by the MRA has contributed to the MFIs' cost efficiency but also higher loan size. This raises questions of whether the MFIs have drifted from their social mission of alleviating poverty through providing financial and nonfinancial services and whether the extreme poor may be deprived of required services. Over time, the MFIs have expanded from a poverty-centered approach to one of inclusive growth, which requires that all financially constrained individuals and firms be brought under financial inclusion. But banks are functionally unable to achieve this because of the high transaction costs involved. Khalily and others (2015) show that the MFIs provide financial services to about 48 percent of households and an even higher percentage in the rural financial market. These institutions need to be strengthened and made competitively efficient so that they may induce inclusive growth at a higher level. This may even call for setting up rural microfinance banks. This policy issue needs to be carefully examined and debated to establish a policy consensus.

This study reveals the impact of microfinance; however, it does not fully capture the effects of nonfinancial services, which have increased enormously over the past decade. With the increasing share of microenterprise loans and provision for microinsurance, the real impacts of microfinance will be much higher. Field-level observations suggest that most microenterprise borrowers are graduating members of microfinance institutions. Therefore, a higher level of impact of microfinance services will be evident in future. However, challenges, as highlighted above, will require some restructuring of the microfinance market in order to ensure the sustainability of institutions and the ability to meet growing demand for credit and other financial services. In addition, the MFIs have been grappling with the issue of climate change. Bangladesh is expected to be one of the hardest-hit countries, with poor households—the majority of whom are microfinance beneficiaries—disproportionately affected. The adverse effects of climate change may outweigh the societal gains accrued from microfinance expansion. This is an area where the MFIs need to innovate through introducing alternate technologies and diversifying members' economic portfolios.

The MFIs currently operating in Bangladesh are of various sizes in terms of outreach. The top 20 control more than three-quarters of the market, and many of the remaining 730 are operating with a single branch. Given the expansion strategy of the large MFIs, the smaller ones may find it difficult to operate at an optimum level with a positive rate of profit. Unless they are supported with concessionary funds or an appropriate branching policy, many may be forced to withdraw from the market or merge with other MFIs. The MRA needs to consider appropriate policies to protect the smaller MFIs and mergers of MFIs if such a situation becomes inevitable. The regulated MFIs now play a critical role in promoting inclusive growth through the rural financial markets and inclusive finance. Microfinance services have contributed to reducing poverty, promoting microenterprises, and creating employment opportunities. Their future growth needs to be orchestrated in a way that meets the country's dual challenges of transitioning to middle-income status and ending poverty.

Note

1. Since the baseline survey year (1991/92) contained no data on nonfinancial services—they were virtually nonexistent at that time—our follow-up surveys (1998/99 and 2010/11) likewise did not contain such information.

Bibliography

CDF (Credit Development Forum). 2013. *Bangladesh Micro Finance Statistics.* Dhaka: CDF.

Khalily, M. A. Baqui, Rushad Faridi, and Farzana Saeed. 2015. "Does Overlapping Lead to Over-indebtedness? Evidence from Bangladesh." Institute of Microfinance, Dhaka.

Khalily, M. A. Baqui, and M. Abdul Khaleque. 2013. "Access to Credit and Productivity of Enterprises in Bangladesh: Is There Causality?" Working Paper 20, Institute of Microfinance, Dhaka.

Khalily, M. A. Baqui, M. A. Khaleque, and S. Badruddoza. 2014. "Impact of Regulation on the Cost Efficiency of Microfinance Institutions in Bangladesh." In *Microfinance Institutions: Financial and Social Performance,* edited by Roy Mersland and R. Øystein Strøm. Basingstoke, U.K.: Palgrave Macmillan.

Khalily, M. A. Baqui, Pablo Mia, Nahid Akhter, and Mehadi Hasan. 2015. "Access to Financial Services in Bangladesh." Institute of Microfinance, Dhaka.

Khandker, Shahidur R. 1998. *Fighting Poverty with Microcredit: Experience in Bangladesh.* New York: Oxford University Press.

———. 2005. "Microfinance and Poverty: Evidence Using Panel Data from Bangladesh." *World Bank Economic Review* 19 (2): 263–86.

Muneer, Farah, and M. A. Baqui Khalily. 2015. "Access to Credit and Economic Returns and Productivity of Micro Enterprises in Bangladesh." Institute of Microfinance, Dhaka.

Osmani, S. R., Meherun Ahmed, M. A. Latif, and Binayak Sen. 2015. *Poverty and Vulnerability in Rural Bangladesh.* Dhaka: Institute of Microfinance and University Press Limited.

Pitt, Mark, and Shahidur Khandker. 1998. "The Impact of Group-Based Credit Programs on Poor Households in Bangladesh: Does Gender of the Participant Matter?" *Journal of Political Economy* 106: 958–96.

Quayes, M. Shakil, and Baqui Khalily. 2014. "Efficiency of Microfinance Institutions in Bangladesh." *Economics Bulletin* 34 (3): 2014.

Raihan, Salim, S. R. Osmani, and Baqui Khalily. 2015. "Contribution of Micro Finance to GDP in Bangladesh." Institute of Microfinance, Dhaka.

Data Description

This appendix describes the several types of data—household survey, program-level, and institutional—on which the findings of this study are based.

Household Survey Data

This study uses two rich household data sets: (a) the World Bank–sponsored microcredit long panel data spanning more than 20 years with three data points (1991/92, 1998/99, and 2010/11) and (b) the Household Income and Expenditure Survey (HIES), which comprises repeated cross-sectional data with three survey points (2000, 2005, and 2010). These two data sets are briefly described below.

Microcredit Long Panel Survey Data

This survey covers a time frame of 20 years with three data points. The first survey, jointly conducted by the World Bank and the Bangladesh Institute of Development Studies (BIDS) in 1991/92, studied the role of microfinance as provided by the three major credit programs (i.e., Grameen Bank, Bangladesh Rural Advancement Committee [BRAC], and the Rural Development-12 program of the Bangladesh Rural Development Board) in the socioeconomic advancement of the poor. The survey covered both target and nontarget households in areas where microfinance programs were operating (program villages) and areas where no microfinance programs were operating (control villages). Target households were defined as those who met the eligibility criteria to participate in microfinance programs (i.e., owning less than half an acre of land), while nontarget households were defined as those who did not.

The surveyed households, totaling 1,769, were randomly drawn from 87 villages (72 program villages and 15 control villages) in 29 *upazilas* (rural subdistricts) of rural Bangladesh.[1] A detailed household questionnaire was designed to collect a broad range of information on households and individuals (e.g., income, employment, education, consumption, borrowing, assets ownership, savings, fertility behavior, and contraceptive use). In addition to the household survey, a village survey questionnaire was administered to collect information on the prices of food items; crops and fertilizers; wages for men, women, and children; interest rates in the informal credit markets; infrastructure (roads, electricity, and schools); and distance from upazila headquarters. The survey was administered three times to the same households, corresponding to the three crop seasons: *aman* (November–February), *boro* (March–June), and *aus* (July–October).

The households surveyed in 1991/92 were revisited in 1998/99, again with the help of BIDS. However, 131 households from the 1991/92 survey could not be traced, leaving 1,638 households available for resurvey, implying an attrition rate of 7.4 percent. The resurvey included some new households from the originally surveyed villages, along with some newly included villages. Altogether, 2,599 households were surveyed in 1998/99, of which 2,226 were from the originally surveyed villages (allowing for household split-off) and 373 from new ones. Among the 2,226 households from the original villages, 279 were newly selected and 1,947 were from the 1,638 households of 1991/92, which had split to form new households in the years between the two surveys.

The households were resurveyed again in 2010/11, this time jointly with the Institute of Microfinance (InM). The resurvey tried to revisit all of the 2,599 households surveyed in 1998/99. However, due to attrition, 2,342 households were located, which spawned 3,082 households due to split-off. The analysis of this study is based on 1,509 households from the 1991/92 survey common to all three surveys. Because of household split-off, the number of households were higher for 1998/99 (1,758) and 2010/11 (2,322).

HIES Data from Repeated Cross-Sectional Surveys

These data come from three rounds (2000, 2005, and 2010) of the HIES, carried out by the Bangladesh Bureau of Statistics (BBS) to determine the poverty profile of Bangladesh with urban and rural breakdown and provide information on the standard of living and nutritional status of the population. The surveys were geographically representative of Bangladesh overall; they adopted a two-stage stratified sampling technique, selecting primary sampling units (PSUs) (roughly comparable to villages in rural areas or street blocks in urban areas) in the first stage and households in the second stage. The number of PSUs selected was 442 in 2000, 504 in 2005, and 612 in 2010. Some 20 households were randomly selected from each of the PSUs, resulting in 7,440 households in 2000, 10,080 in 2005, and 12,240 households in 2010.[2] While the PSUs across the surveys were not comparable, there was significant overlap of upazilas across the surveys. The number of upazilas covered was 295 in 2000, 366 in 2005, and 386 in 2010. Since individual households could not be tracked across the surveys, panel analysis across years was possible only at the upazila level. The final, cleaned data set contained 5,030 rural households from 2000, 6,031 from 2005, and 7,840 from 2010. Like the microcredit long panel surveys, the HIES collected information on a wide range of characteristics at the household level (e.g., income, employment, education, consumption, and assets ownership) and community level (e.g., prices of food items and availability of various types of infrastructure).

Both data sets have comparative advantages and disadvantages. The HIES is a large data set well represented by Bangladesh's population and regions. But the long panel survey covers primarily low-income areas, which were targeted by the microfinance institutions (MFIs) in the early 1990s; thus, the panel data have sample bias toward the country's poorer areas. Also, the HIES data are not panel at either the household or village level. The data can be made panel only at the upazila level, which has limitations (e.g., biases due to unobserved household- or village-level abilities may not be controlled for). However, the long panel surveys covered the same households over a 20-year period; thus, this is true panel at the household level, allowing for the unobserved household and community characteristics to be controlled for in estimation.

Table A.1 compares the important outcome variables from the two data sets. Since the HIES is nationally representative, whereas the long panel survey covers mostly poorer areas, lower-income households from the HIES are compared with households from the long panel survey. More specifically, the lower 60 percent of the HIES sample (based on income) are compared with the full sample of the long panel data, after excluding the nontarget (i.e., nonpoor) population from the latter (based on the first-round survey of 1991/92). Also, comparisons are made between the 2000 HIES and 1998/99 long panel data and the 2010 HIES and 2010/11 long panel data; only these two pairs of survey years are close enough for comparability between the two data sets. As table A.1 shows, among the six income and expenditure variables reported for the two sets of survey years, the differences between the outcomes are not statistically significant in most cases. For the HIES 2010 and 2010/11 long panel data comparisons, only total income and nonfarm income were found to differ (i.e., t-statistics of the differences were statistically significant).

Figure A.1 presents the breakdown of the original 1,509 households of the long panel survey from 1991/92 to 2010/11 by status of program participation. In 1991/92, only 26.3 percent of the 1,509 households were microcredit program participants. By 1998/99, the share of participants dropped by 2.8 percentage points, while there was a 26.4 percentage point increase in participation among the original nonparticipants. The continuation of similar

Table A.1 Comparison of Household Outcomes between HIES and Long Panel Data

Outcome variable[a]	HIES, 2000	Long panel survey, 1998/99	t-statistics of the difference	HIES, 2010	Long panel survey, 2010/11	t-statistics of the difference
Total income	509.0	510.4	−0.01	487.1	1,097.0	−3.13
Farm income	245.4	131.4	0.39	230.5	123.3	0.47
Nonfarm income	263.6	378.9	−0.36	256.6	973.7	−2.84
Total expenditure	530.3	438.9	0.35	905.5	578.2	0.72
Food expenditure	337.7	296.2	0.26	555.0	354.8	0.77
Nonfood expenditure	192.5	142.7	0.34	350.5	223.3	0.43

Sources: HIES 2000, 2010; World Bank/BIDS survey 1998/99; World Bank/InM survey 2010/11.
Note: Comparison is made between the lower 60% of the HIES sample data, based on income, and the full sample of the long panel data.
HIES = Household Income and Expenditure Survey.
a. per capita Tk./month.

Figure A.1 Transition of Microcredit Participation Status over Time

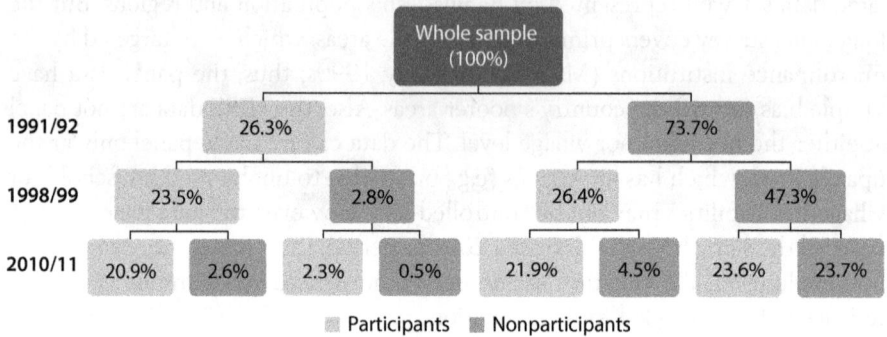

Sources: World Bank/BIDS survey 1998/99; World Bank/InM survey 2010/11.

transitions over time, as observed from the 2010/11 survey data, show a clear trend; that is, at each stage over time, a high proportion of participants remained with the microfinance programs and a significant proportion of nonparticipating households eventually joined, resulting in substantial membership growth. Importantly, more than 80 percent of the participants from earlier years remained in the programs for at least 10 years.

Program-Level Aggregate Time-Series Data

Credit and Development Forum (CDF) Statistics (2006) and various issues of Bangladesh Microfinance Statistics (2007–11), jointly published by CDF and InM, were the sources for program-level, aggregate time-series data. The sample is not balanced and includes some 500 NGO-MFIs. We combined all such information to obtain a time-series from 1996 to 2011. The microfinance statistics mainly report MFI outreach and product information; however, they do not provide any financial information.

Institutional-Level Panel Data

We collected institutional-level data from the annual reports of 300 semi-randomly selected MFIs that were identified by Bangladesh Microfinance Statistics (2007–11) or recognized as Palli Karma-Sahayak Foundation partner organizations. The largest number of annual reports received were for FY2009–10. Our definition of MFI size is similar to that of the Microcredit Regulatory Authority (MRA): small (up to 25,000 members), medium (25,000–100,000 members), large (100,000–500,000 members), and very large (more than 500,000 members). Although we randomly selected small MFIs, we endeavored to maximize the inclusion of large and very large ones. The MRA uses the same cut-off points using borrowers. Four MFIs are very large: BRAC, Association for Social Advancement (ASA), BURO Bangladesh (Basic Unit for Resources and Opportunities of

Table A.2 Distribution of Microfinance Institutions by Year and Size

Fiscal year[a]	Small	Medium	Large	Very large	Grameen Bank	Total
2006	108	29	10	4	1	152
2007	108	35	11	4	1	159
2008	189	49	15	4	1	258
2009	198	46	16	4	1	265
2010	211	54	22	4	1	292
2011	203	55	16	4	1	279

Sources: CDF 1996–2007; Grameen Bank 2010; InM and CDF 2008–10.
a. Ending June 30.

Bangladesh), and Thengamara Mohila Sabuj Sangha (TMSS). Since Grameen Bank is the only non-NGO MFI, we report it separately (table A.2).

Under the aforementioned project, we collected outreach data (e.g., number of borrowers and members) from the annual reports and cross-checked the information with Bangladesh Microfinance Statistics (2007–11). Financial information came from balance sheet and income statements for the respective fiscal years.

Notes

1. The term upazila is defined in chapter 2 (endnote 8).
2. Except for 140 urban PSUs in the 2000 survey, where 10 households were selected per PSU, 20 households were selected per PSU for all PSUs across all surveys.

Alternative Models to Estimate the Impact of Microfinance

This appendix discusses the alternate quasi-experimental methods applied to the data study of this book.

Quasi-Experimental Methods

Let us consider the following reduced-form demand equation for the amount of credit by women (C_{if}) and men (C_{im}) of i-th household in a cross-sectional data, as follows:

$$C_{if} = X_i\beta_f + \eta_{if} + \varepsilon_{if} \text{ and} \tag{B.1}$$

$$C_{im} = X_i\beta_m + \eta_{im} + \varepsilon_{im}, \tag{B.2}$$

where X is a vector of characteristics at the household level (e.g., sex, age, and education of household head and landholdings) and village level (e.g., extent of village electrification and irrigation, availability of infrastructure, and price of consumer goods); β is a vector of unknown parameters to be estimated; η is an unmeasured determinant of the credit demand; and ε is a nonsystematic error.

The demand for outcomes (Y_i) (e.g., consumption, children's schooling, or women's labor supply), conditional on the level of credit demand (C_i), is expressed as follows:

$$Y_i = X_i\beta_y + C_{if}\delta_f + C_{im}\delta_m + \eta_i + \varepsilon_i, \tag{B.3}$$

where δ_f and δ_m are the effects for female and male credit, respectively, and η_i is the unmeasured determinant of the outcome.

With cross-sectional data, endogeneity arises as a result of the possible correlation among η_{if}, η_{im}, and η_i and among ε_{if}, ε_{im}, and ε_i. Sources of endogeneity can come from nonrandom program placement in villages, as well as household self-selection into programs. Pitt and Khandker (1998), while analyzing the first-round data

(1991/92), used a village-level fixed-effect (FE) method to resolve program place-ment endogeneity, and adopted a two-stage instrumental variable (IV) technique to resolve the endogeneity of a household's participation (self-selection).[1]

The analysis of this book has the advantage of using the panel data of three data points (1991/92, 1998/99, and 2010/11). With the availability of panel data, equation (B.3) can be rewritten as follows:

$$Y_{it} = X_{it}\beta_y + C_{ift}\delta_f + C_{imt}\delta_m + \eta_{it} + \mu_i + \varepsilon_{it}, \tag{B.4}$$

where t is the survey rounds, η_{it} is an unobserved household- or community-level determinant of the outcome that is time varying, μ_i is an unobserved household- or community-level determinant of the outcome that is time invariant, and ε_{it} is a nonsystematic error as previously defined. Since the households are repeated in the panel data, the most common technique applied to panel data is the household FE method. The household FE estimation technique can eliminate the time-invariant parameter (μ_i) by transforming equation (B.4) as follows:

$$Y_{it} - \bar{Y}_i = (X_{it} - \bar{X}_i)\beta_y + (C_{ift} - \bar{C}_{if})\delta_f + (C_{imt} - \bar{C}_{im})\delta_m$$
$$+ (\eta_{it} - \bar{\eta}_i) + (\mu_i - \bar{\mu}) + (\varepsilon_{it} - \bar{\varepsilon}_i), \tag{B.5a}$$

where the bar variables (e.g., $\bar{Y}_i$, $\bar{X}_i$, and $\bar{C}_{if}$) are average values for each household. Since μ is constant, $\mu_i = \bar{\mu}$ and thus its effect is eliminated. Therefore, equation B.5a can be written as follows:

$$\Delta Y_{it} = \beta_y \Delta X_{it} + \delta_f \Delta C_{ift} + \delta_m \Delta C_{imt} + \Delta \eta_{it} + \Delta \varepsilon_{it}. \tag{B.5b}$$

Since $\eta_{it} \neq \bar{\eta}_i$, the problem of unobserved effects cannot be disregarded completely; thus, the ordinary least squares (OLS) estimation of equation (B.5b) will be biased.

Static Methods

The bias of the OLS estimation of equation (B.5b) can be eliminated in various ways. One can expand the FE by incorporating propensity-score weight (p-score weighted FE) (Hirano, Imbens, and Ridder 2003). Alternately, the IV method can be implemented with FE (FE-IV) using suitable instruments. The p-score weighted FE works on the assumption that a major source of time-varying heterogeneity is the difference in initial (baseline) characteristics between par-ticipants and nonparticipants, and implementing p-score weighted regression controls for such difference. It is implemented by creating a weight variable from the propensity score (i.e., the predicted probability of participating in micro-credit programs, based on a participation equation in terms of X variables observed in the initial year of 1991/92), and using that weight in FE estimation on the panel data. In the FE-IV method, variables used as instruments enter into the participation equation only and do not directly appear in the outcome equation of (B.5b).[2,3]

Dynamic Panel Models

Dynamic panel models, also called auto-regressive (AR) models, assume that past outcomes affect future ones and thus include a lagged dependent variable (LDV) as an additional regressor. In the estimation of microcredit impacts, we cannot rule out the possibility that past outcomes affect current ones (e.g., past nonland assets affect current asset holdings). Also, it is possible that participants whose incomes rose in earlier years invested wisely and in later years benefited even more from lucrative ventures. Even if we are not interested in the effects of the LDV on the outcomes, including it may be important for obtaining consistent estimates of other parameters.

To explore the dynamic panel model incorporating the LDV as a regressor, we revise equation (B.4) as follows:

$$Y_{it} = Y_{i(t-1)}\gamma + X_{it}\beta_y + C_{ift}\delta_f + C_{imt}\delta_m + \eta_{it} + \mu_i + \varepsilon_{it}. \tag{B.6}$$

The first difference transformation removes the FE from this equation, expressed as follows:

$$\Delta Y_{it} = \Delta Y_{i(t-1)}\gamma + \Delta X_{it}\beta_y + \Delta C_{ift}\delta_f + \Delta C_{imt}\delta_m + \Delta \eta_{it_i} + \Delta \varepsilon_{it}. \tag{B.7}$$

However, for panel data with only a small number of time periods, as in this analysis, the transformed equation (B.7) suffers from endogeneity because the transformed LDV ($\Delta Y_{i(t-1)}$) is correlated with the transformed error term ($\Delta \varepsilon_{it}$). To resolve the endogeneity of the LDV, Anderson and Hsiao (1982) proposed using a second LDV ($Y_{i(t-2)}$) as an instrument for the first LDV ($\Delta Y_{i(t-1)}$). If the error term (ε_{it}) is iid (independent and identically distributed), $Y_{i(t-2)}$ will be correlated with $\Delta Y_{i(t-1)}$ but not with $\Delta \varepsilon_{it}$, thereby making the resulting estimate of γ consistent. With the availability of more time periods (T > 3), an even deeper lag of dependent variables can be used as instruments. In fact, Arellano and Bond (1991) proposed a method that exploits all possible instruments. Using the generalized method of moments (GMM) developed by Hansen (1982), they obtained estimators using the moment conditions generated by various lags of the dependent variables with the error term. Using simulations, Arellano and Bond (1991) showed that GMM estimates have the smallest bias.

In this analysis, however, we did not attempt to obtain GMM estimates owing to the difficulty of its implementation with the small panel, which has only three time periods. Arellano and Bond (1991) proposed tests to check the validity of the model, particularly to detect serial correlation among the error terms. But the panel requires four or more time periods in order for these tests to be done properly. Thus, this study used the dynamic panel model (equation B.7) by instrumenting the LDV as described. Even then, we did not use the LDV model for all estimation scenarios because, given the small T, the LDV model did not always yield consistent estimates. Thus, in most cases, we used p-weighted FE or its variants to estimate microfinance impacts.

Notes

1. In implementing the IV framework, Pitt and Khandker (1998) used exogenous gender- and landholding-based exclusion restrictions for program participation to create discontinuous household program choice variables for females and males. The program choice variables were further interacted with households' observable exogenous characteristics to create instruments.

2. The instruments proposed are similar to what were used in the estimation of Pitt and Khandker (1998); that is, whether the village has a microfinance program and whether the household is eligible to participate based on the eligibility condition imposed by the programs in the initial survey year (1991/92) and then interacting this variable with household exogenous variables.

3. A good example of FE with IV is the evaluation of the Thai Million Baht Village Fund program (Kaboski and Townsend 2011). The intervention was exogenous in that it was open to all villages, and the total disbursement to each village was the same (1 million baht) regardless of village size (number of households in the village). Since village size varied considerably within the sample, exogenous variation in credit was obtained by dividing the village-level disbursement (1 million baht) by the number of households in the village, which was used as the instrument in the first-stage regression using seven years of data (1997–2003). The credit effects were estimated in the second stage after controlling for household and time FE.

Bibliography

Anderson, T. W., and C. Hsiao. 1982. "Formulation and Estimation of Dynamic Models Using Panel Data." *Journal of Econometrics* 18 (1): 47–82.

Arellano, Manuel, and Stephen Bond. 1991. "Some Tests of Specification for Panel Data: Monte Carlo Evidence and an Application to Employment Equations." *Review of Economic Studies* 58: 277–97.

Hansen, Lars Peter. 1982. "Large Sample Properties of Generalized Method of Moments Estimators." *Econometrica* 50 (4): 1029–54.

Hirano, Keisuke, Guido Imbens, and Geert Ridder. 2003. "Efficient Estimation of Average Treatment Effects Using the Estimated Propensity Score." *Econometrica* 71 (4): 1161–89.

Kaboski, Joseph P., and Robert M. Townsend. 2011. "A Structural Evaluation of a Large-Scale Quasi-Experimental Microfinance Initiative." *Econometrica* 79 (5): 1357–406.

Pitt, Mark M., and Shahidur R. Khandker. 1998. "The Impact of Group-Based Credit Programs on Poor Households in Bangladesh: Does the Gender of Participants Matter?" *Journal of Political Economy* 106: 958–96.

Environmental Benefits Statement

The World Bank Group is committed to reducing its environmental footprint. In support of this commitment, the Publishing and Knowledge Division leverages electronic publishing options and print-on-demand technology, which is located in regional hubs worldwide. Together, these initiatives enable print runs to be lowered and shipping distances decreased, resulting in reduced paper consumption, chemical use, greenhouse gas emissions, and waste.

The Publishing and Knowledge Division follows the recommended standards for paper use set by the Green Press Initiative. The majority of our books are printed on Forest Stewardship Council (FSC)–certified paper, with nearly all containing 50–100 percent recycled content. The recycled fiber in our book paper is either unbleached or bleached using totally chlorine-free (TCF), processed chlorine-free (PCF), or enhanced elemental chlorine-free (EECF) processes.

More information about the Bank's environmental philosophy can be found at http://www.worldbank.org/corporateresponsibility.

green press INITIATIVE

www.ingramcontent.com/pod-product-compliance
Lightning Source LLC
Chambersburg PA
CBHW080415270326
41929CB00018B/3037